EXCEL MODELING AND ESTIMATION
IN THE FUNDAMENTALS OF INVESTMENTS
Third Edition

CRAIG W. HOLDEN
Max Barney Faculty Fellow and Associate Professor
Kelley School of Business
Indiana University

PEARSON
Prentice Hall

Upper Saddle River, NJ 07458

To Kathryn, Diana and Jimmy

CIP date on file with the Library of Congress.

Executive Editor: Mark Pfaltzgraff
VP/Editorial Director: Sally Yagan
Product Development Manager: Ashley Santora
Project Manager: Susie Abraham
Editorial Assistant: Vanessa Bain
Marketing Manager: Jodi Bassett
Marketing Assistant: Ian Gold
Senior Managing Editor: Judy Leale
Project Manager: Ana Jankowski
Operations Specialist: Michelle Klein
Cover Design: Jayne Conte
Printer/Binder: Bind-rite Graphic / Robbinsville

Credits and acknowledgments borrowed from other sources and reproduced, with permission, in this textbook appear on appropriate page within text.

Microsoft® and Windows® are registered trademarks of the Microsoft Corporation in the U.S.A. and other countries. Screen shots and icons reprinted with permission from the Microsoft Corporation. This book is not sponsored or endorsed by or affiliated with the Microsoft Corporation.

Pearson Education LTD.
Pearson Education Singapore, Pte. Ltd
Pearson Education, Canada, Ltd
Pearson Education–Japan

Pearson Education Australia PTY, Limited
Pearson Education North Asia Ltd
Pearson Educación de Mexico, S.A. de C.V.
Pearson Education Malaysia, Pte. Ltd.

10 9 8 7 6 5 4 3 2 1
ISBN-13: 978-0-13-207991-4
ISBN-10: 0-13-207991-7

CONTENTS

CONTENTS ON CD

Readme.txt

Excel Mod Est in Fun Inv 3e.pdf

Ch 01 Bond Pricing.xlsx

Ch 02 Bond Duration.xlsx

Ch 03 Bond Convexity.xlsx

Ch 04 US Yield Curve Dynam.xlsx

Ch 05-06 Port Optimization.xlsm

Ch 07 Asset Pricing.xlsm

Ch 08 Dealer Simulation.xlsm

Ch 08 Trader Simulation.xlsm

Ch 09 Portfolio Diversific.xlsx

Ch 10 Life-Cycle Fin Plan.xlsx

Ch 11 Div Discount Models.xlsx

Ch 12 Option Payoff-Profit.xlsx

Ch 13 Option Trading Strat.xlsx

Ch 14 Put-Call Parity.xlsx

Ch 15 Binomial Option Pric.xlsx

Ch 16 Black Scholes Opt Pr.xlsx

Ch 17 Spot-Futures Parity.xlsx

Files in Excel 97-2003 Format

Preface

For more than 20 years, since the emergence of PCs, Lotus 1-2-3, and Microsoft Excel in the 1980's, spreadsheet models have been the dominant vehicles for finance professionals in the business world to implement their financial knowledge. Yet even today, most Fundamentals of Investments textbooks rely on calculators as the primary tool and have little coverage of how to build and estimate Excel models. This book fills that gap. It teaches students how to build and estimate financial models in Excel. It provides step-by-step instructions so that students can build and estimate models themselves (active learning), rather than being handed already completed spreadsheets (passive learning). It progresses from simple examples to practical, real-world applications. It spans nearly all quantitative models in the fundamentals of investments.

My goal is simply to *change finance education from being calculator based to being Excel based*. This change will better prepare students for the 21st century business world. This change will increase student evaluations of teacher performance by enabling more practical, real-world content and by allowing a more hands-on, active learning pedagogy.

Third Edition Changes

New to this edition, the biggest innovation is **Ready-To-Build Spreadsheets on the CD.** The CD provides ready-to-build spreadsheets for every chapter with:

The model setup, such as input values, labels, and graphs

Step-by-step instructions for building and estimating the model on the spreadsheet itself

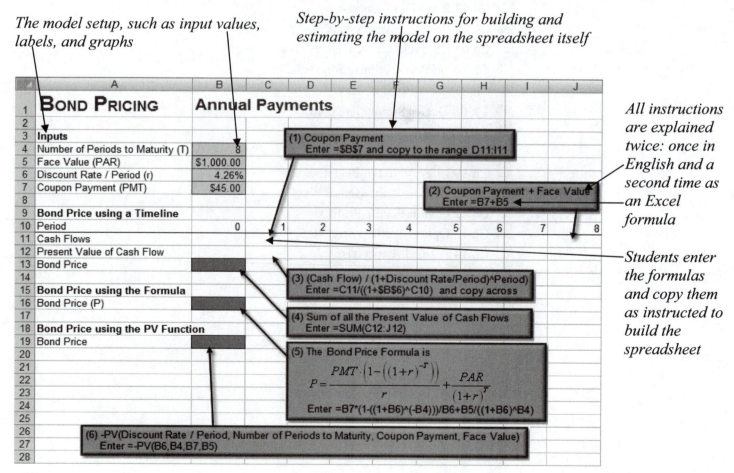

All instructions are explained twice: once in English and a second time as an Excel formula

Students enter the formulas and copy them as instructed to build the spreadsheet

Many spreadsheets use real-world data

ASSET PRICING — Static CAPM Using Fama-MacBeth Method

Inputs

Market Portfolio Benchmark: ○ SPDR ETF ● CRSP VWMR ○ DJ World Stock | 2

Asset Type: ○ Stock ● US Port ○ Country Port | 2

> (1) Monthly Return(Asset i, Month t) - Riskfree Rate(Month t)
> Enter =B10-$AC10 and copy to B133:V252

Monthly Excess Returns

	Stock Barrick	Stock Hanson	Stock IBM	Stock Nokia	Stock Telefonos	Stock YPF	US Portfolio Small-Growth
Dec 2006	-3.90%	-0.64%	1.66%	8.36%	8.23%	0.10%	-0.99%
Nov 2006	-2.79%	4.46%	5.27%	0.09%	8.59%	-1.37%	2.16%
Oct 2006	1.38%	3.37%	-0.53%	1.29%	-1.49%	3.08%	5.46%
Sep 2006	0.51%	-3.90%	12.28%	0.52%	2.73%	6.61%	0.68%
Aug 2006	-8.65%	13.94%	0.78%	-6.10%	6.34%	-4.25%	2.80%
Jul 2006	8.28%	3.32%	4.60%	4.80%	2.62%	1.60%	-6.16%
Jun 2006	3.66%	0.48%	0.38%	-2.42%	12.11%	9.58%	-1.05%

Spin buttons, option buttons, and graphs facilitate visual, interactive learning

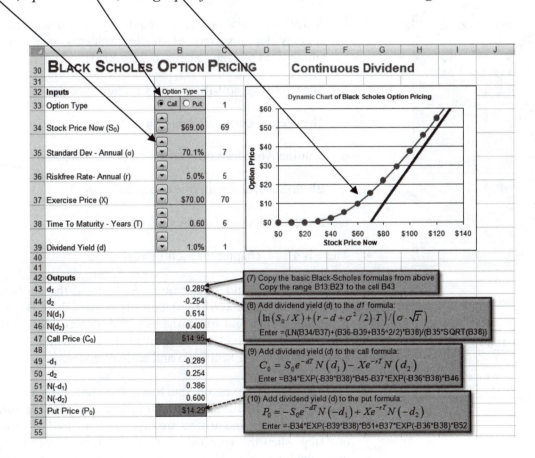

The Third Edition advances in many ways:

- The new **Ready-To-Build spreadsheets on the CD** are very popular with students. They can open a spreadsheet that is set up and ready to be constructed. Then they can follow the on-spreadsheet instructions to complete the Excel model and don't have to refer back to the book for each step. Once they are done, they can double-check their work against the completed spreadsheet shown in the book. This approach concentrates student time on *implementing financial formulas and estimation.*

- There is great new fundamentals of investments content, including:

  o Estimating the Static CAPM using the Fama-MacBeth method,

  o Estimating the APT or Intertemporal CAPM using the Fama-MacBeth method, including the Fama-French three factor model,

  o Estimating portfolio optimization with constraints (i.e. no short-sales, no borrowing, etc.),

  o A trader simulation, which requires you to determine the optimal trading strategy for a variety of trading problems in a limit order book market,

  o A dealer simulation, which requires you to determine the optimal dealer strategy for a variety of dealer problems in a dealer market – both simulations use the Excel add-in @RISK,

  o The Cox-Ingersoll-Ross term structure model,

  o The Merton corporate bond model,

  o Valuing American options with discrete dividends,

  o Black-Scholes sensitivities (Greeks), and

  o Eleven varieties of exotic options.

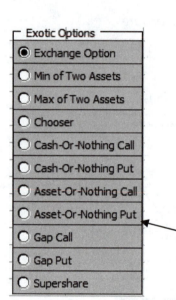

- There is a new chapter on useful Excel tricks.

- The Ready-To-Build spreadsheets on CD and the explanations in the book are based on **Excel 2007** by default. However, the CD also contains a folder with Ready-To-Build spreadsheets based on **Excel 97-2003** format. Also, the book contains "Excel 2003 Equivalent" boxes that explain how to do the equivalent step in Excel 2003 and earlier versions.

Excel 2003 Equivalent

To call up a Data Table in Excel 2003. click on **Data | Table**

- The instruction boxes on the Ready-To-Build spreadsheets are *bitmapped images* so that the formulas cannot just be copied to the spreadsheet. Both the instruction boxes and arrows are *objects*, so that all of them can be deleted in one step when the spreadsheet is complete and everything else will be left untouched. Click on **Home | Editing | Find & Select down-arrow | Select Objects**, then select all of the instruction boxes and arrows, and press the delete key. Furthermore, any blank rows can be deleted, leaving a clean spreadsheet for future use.

- The book contains a significant number of comparative statics exercises (lower risk aversion, higher short-rate, etc.) and explores a variety of optional choices (alternative models to forecast expected return, alternative spreads and combinations, etc.). In each case, a picture is show of how things change and there is a discussion of what this means in economic terms. For example, below is Figure 6.16 which explores what happens to the optimal portfolio when risk aversion is lowered?

FIGURE 6.16 Risk Aversion of 1.8 and 0.2

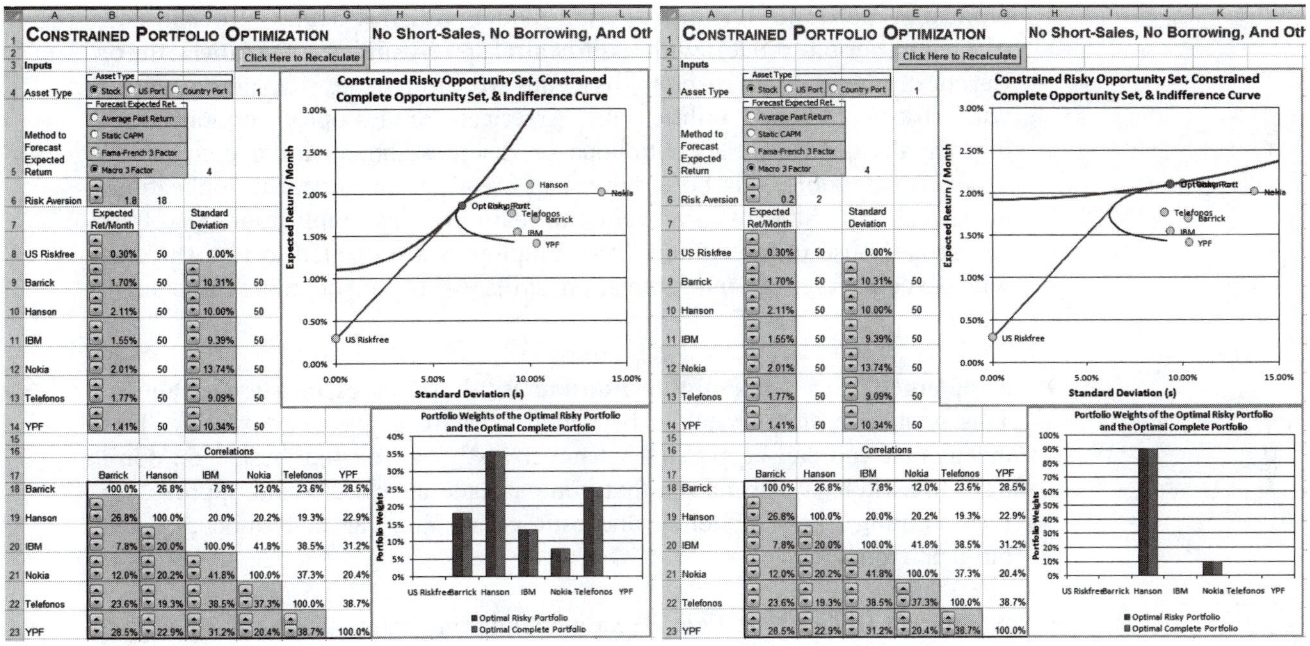

What Is Unique About This Book

There are many features which distinguish this book from any other:

- **Plain Vanilla Excel.** Other books on the market emphasize teaching students programming using Visual Basic for Applications (VBA) or using macros. By contrast, this book does nearly everything in plain vanilla Excel.[1] Although programming is liked by a minority of students, it is seriously disliked by the majority. Plain vanilla Excel has the advantage of being a very intuitive, user-friendly environment that is accessible to all. It is fully

---

[1] I have made two exceptions. The Constrained Portfolio Optimization spreadsheet uses a macro to repeatedly call Solver to map out the Constrained Risky Opportunity Set and the Constrained Complete Opportunity Set. The Trader and Dealer Simulations use macros to automate analyzing many trading problems and many trading strategies.

capable of handling a wide range of applications, including quite sophisticated ones. Further, your students already know the basics of Excel and nothing more is assumed. Students are assumed to be able to enter formulas in a cell and to copy formulas from one cell to another. All other features of Excel (such as built-in functions, Data Tables, Solver, etc.) are explained as they are used.

- **Build From Simple Examples To Practical, Real-World Applications.** The general approach is to start with a simple example and build up to a practical, real-world application. In many chapters, the previous Excel model is carried forward to the next more complex model. For example, the chapter on binomial option pricing carries forward Excel models as follows: (a.) single-period model with replicating portfolio, (b.) eight-period model with replicating portfolio, (c.) eight-period model with risk-neutral probabilities, (d.) eight-period model with risk-neutral probabilities for American or European options with discrete dividends, (e.) full-scale, fifty-period model with risk-neutral probabilities for American or European options with discrete dividends using continuous or discrete annualization convention. Whenever possible, this book builds up to full-scale, practical applications using real data. Students are excited to learn practical applications that they can actually use in their future jobs. Employers are excited to hire students with Excel modeling and estimation skills, who can be more productive faster.

- **Supplement For All Popular Fundamentals of Investments Textbooks.** This book is a supplement to be combined with a primary textbook. This means that you can keep using whatever textbook you like best. You don't have to switch. It also means that you can take an incremental approach to incorporating Excel modeling and estimation. You can start modestly and build up from there.

- **A Change In Content Too.** Excel modeling and estimation is not merely a new medium, but an opportunity to cover some unique content items which require computer support to be feasible. For example, using 10 years of monthly returns for individual stocks, U.S. portfolios, and country portfolios to estimate the (unconstrained) Risky Opportunity Set and the (unconstrained) Complete Opportunity Set. The same data is used by Solver to numerically solver for the Constrained Risky Opportunity Set and the Constrained Complete Opportunity Set. The same data is used to estimate the Static CAPM using the Fama-MacBeth method and to estimate the APT or Intertemporal CAPM using the Fama-MacBeth method. A Trader Simulation in a limit order market and a Dealer Simulation in a dealer market make sophisticated use @RISK (an Excel Add-in) to simulate the arrival of orders and information. The Excel model in US Yield Curve Dynamics shows 37 years of monthly US yield curve history in just a few minutes. Real call and put prices are fed into the Black Scholes Option Pricing model and Excel's Solver is used to back-solve for the implied volatilities. Then the "smile" pattern (or more like a "scowl" pattern) of implied volatilities is graphed. As a practical matter, all of these sophisticated applications require Excel.

Conventions Used In This Book

This book uses a number of conventions.

- **Time Goes Across The Columns And Variables Go Down The Rows.** When something happens over time, I let each column represent a period of time. For example in life-cycle financial planning, date 0 is in column B, date 1 is in column C, date 2 is in column D, etc. Each row represents a different variable, which is usually a labeled in column A. This manner of organizing Excel models is so common because it is how financial statements are organized.

- **Color Coding.** A standard color scheme is used to clarify the structure of the Excel models. The Ready-To-Build spreadsheets on CD uses: (1) yellow shading for input values, (2) no shading (i.e. white) for throughput formulas, and (3) green shading for final results ("the bottom line"). A few Excel models include choice variables. Choice variables use blue shading. The Constrained Portfolio Optimization spreadsheet includes constraints. Constaints use pink-purple shading.

- **The Time Line Technique.** The most natural technique for discounting cash flows in an Excel model is the time line technique, where each column corresponds to a period of time. As an example, see the section labeled Calculate Bond Price using a Timeline in the figure below.

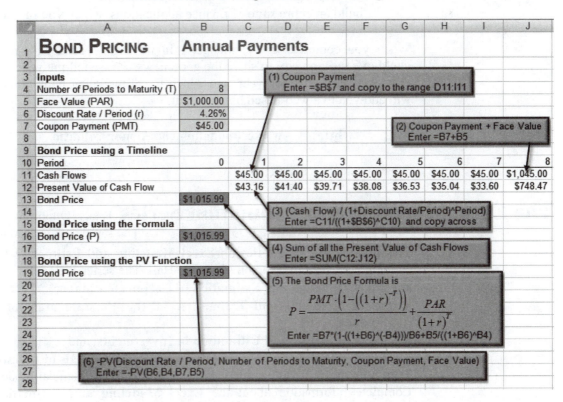

- **Using As Many Different Techniques As Possible.** In the figure above, the bond price is calculated using as many different techniques as possible.

Specifically, it is calculated three ways: (1) discounting each cash flow on a time line, (2) using the closed-form formula, and (3) using Excel's PV function. This approach makes the point that all three techniques are equivalent. This approach also develops skill at double-checking these calculations, which is a very important method for avoiding errors in practice.

- **Symbolic Notation is Self-Contained.** Every spreadsheet that contains symbolic notation in the instruction boxes is self-contained (i.e., all symbolic notation is defined on the spreadsheet). Further, I have stopped using symbolic notation for named ranges that was used in prior editions. Therefore, there is no need for alternative notation versions that were provided on the CD in the prior edition and they have been eliminated.

Craig's Challenge

I challenge the readers of this book to dramatically improve your finance education by personally constructing all of the Excel models in this book. This will take you about 7 – 15 hours hours depending on your current Excel modeling skills. Let me assure you that it will be an excellent investment. You will:

- gain a practical understanding of the core concepts of Investments,
- develop hands-on, Excel modeling skills, and
- build an entire suite of finance applications, which you fully understand.

When you complete this challenge, I invite you to send an e-mail to me at **cholden@indiana.edu** to share the good news. Please tell me your name, school, (prospective) graduation year, and which Excel modeling book you completed. I will add you to a web-based honor roll at:

http://www.excelmodeling.com/honor-roll.htm

We can celebrate together!

The Excel Modeling and Estimation Series

This book is part of a series on **Excel Modeling and Estimation** by Craig W. Holden, published by Pearson / Prentice Hall. The series includes:
- **Excel Modeling and Estimation in Corporate Finance,**
- **Excel Modeling and Estimation in the Fundamentals of Corporate Finance,**
- **Excel Modeling and Estimation in Investments,** and
- **Excel Modeling and Estimation in the Fundamentals of Investments.**

Each book teaches value-added skills in constructing financial models in Excel. Complete information about the **Excel Modeling and Estimation** series is available at my web site:

http://www.excelmodeling.com

All of the **Excel Modeling and Estimation** books can be purchased any time at:
http://www.amazon.com

If you have any suggestions or corrections, please e-mail them to me at **cholden@indiana.edu**. I will consider your suggestions and will implement any corrections in the next edition.

This book provides educational examples of how to estimate financial models from real data. In doing so, this book uses a tiny amount of data that is copyrighted by others. I rely upon the fair use provision of law (Section 107 of the Copyright Act of 1976) as the legal and legitimate basis for doing so.[2]

Suggestions for Faculty Members

There is no single best way to use **Excel Modeling and Estimation in the Fundamentals of Investments**. There are as many different techniques as there are different styles and philosophies of teaching. You need to discover what works best for you. Let me highlight several possibilities:

1. **Out-of-class individual projects with help.** This is a technique that I have used and it works well. I require completion of several short Excel modeling projects of every individual student in the class. To provide help, I schedule special "help lab" sessions in a computer lab during which time myself and my graduate assistant are available to answer questions while students do each assignment in about an hour. Typically about half the questions are Excel questions and half are finance questions. I have always graded such projects, but an alternative approach would be to treat them as ungraded homework.

2. **Out-of-class individual projects without help.** Another technique is to assign Excel modeling projects for individual students to do on their own out of class. One instructor assigns seven Excel modeling projects at the beginning of the semester and has individual students turn in all seven completed Excel models for grading at the end of the semester. At the end of each chapter are problems that can be assigned with or without help. Faculty members can download the completed Excel models at **http://www.prenhall.com/holden**. See your local Pearson / Prentice Hall (or Pearson Education) representative to gain access.

3. **Out-of-class group projects.** A technique that I have used for the last fifteen years is to require students to do big Excel modeling projects in groups. I have students write a report to a hypothetical boss, which intuitively explains their method of analysis, key assumptions, and key results.

---

[2] Consistent with the fair use statute, I make transformative use of the data for teaching purposes, the nature of the data is factual data that is important to the educational purpose, the amount of data used is a tiny, and its use has no significant impact on the potential market for the data.

4. **In-class reinforcement of key concepts.** The class session is scheduled in a computer lab or equivalently students are required to bring their (required) laptop computers to a technology classroom, which has a data jack and a power outlet at every student station. I explain a key concept in words and equations. Then I turn to a 10-15 minute segment in which students open a Ready-To-Build spreadsheet and build the Excel model in real-time in the class. This provides real-time, hands-on reinforcement of a key concept. This technique can be done often throughout the semester.

5. **In-class demonstration of Excel modeling.** The instructor can perform an in-class demonstration of how to build Excel models. Typically, only a small portion of the total Excel model would be demonstrated.

6. **In-class demonstration of key relationships using Spin Buttons, Option Buttons, and Charts.** The instructor can dynamically illustrate comparative statics or dynamic properties over time using visual, interactive elements. For example, one spreadsheet provides a "movie" of 37 years of U.S. term structure dynamics. Another spreadsheet provides an interactive graph of the sensitivity of bond prices to changes in the coupon rate, yield-to-maturity, number of payments / year, and face value.

I'm sure I haven't exhausted the list of potential teaching techniques. Feel free to send an e-mail to **cholden@indiana.edu** to let me know novel ways in which you use this book.

Acknowledgements

I thank Mark Pfaltzgraff, David Alexander, Jackie Aaron, P.J. Boardman, Mickey Cox, Maureen Riopelle, and Paul Donnelly of Pearson / Prentice Hall for their vision, innovativeness, and encouragement of **Excel Modeling and Estimation in the Fundamentals of Investments**. I thank Susan Abraham, Kate Murray, Lori Braumberger, Holly Brown, Debbie Clare, Cheryl Clayton, Kevin Hancock, Josh McClary, Bill Minic, Melanie Olsen, Beth Ann Romph, Erika Rusnak, Gladys Soto, and Lauren Tarino of Pearson / Prentice Hall for many useful contributions. I thank Professors Alan Bailey (University of Texas at San Antonio), Zvi Bodie (Boston University), Jack Francis (Baruch College), David Griswold (Boston University), Carl Hudson (Auburn University), Robert Kleiman (Oakland University), Mindy Nitkin (Simmons College), Steve Rich (Baylor University), Tim Smaby (Penn State University), Charles Trzcinka (Indiana University), Sorin Tuluca (Fairleigh Dickinson University), Marilyn Wiley (Florida Atlantic University), and Chad Zutter (University of Pittsburgh) for many thoughtful comments. I thank my graduate students Scott Marolf, Heath Eckert, Ryan Brewer, Ruslan Goyenko, Wendy Liu, and Wannie Park for careful error-checking. I thank Jim Finnegan and many other students for providing helpful comments. I thank my family, Kathryn, Diana, and Jimmy, for their love and support.

About The Author

CRAIG W. HOLDEN

Craig Holden is the Max Barney Faculty Fellow and Associate Professor of Finance at the Kelley School of Business at Indiana University. His M.B.A. and Ph.D. are from the Anderson School at UCLA. He is the winner of many teaching and research awards. His research on security trading and market making ("market microstructure") has been published in leading academic journals. He has written four books on **Excel Modeling and Estimation** in finance, which are published by Pearson / Prentice Hall and Chinese editions are published by China Renmin University Press. He has chaired sixteen dissertations, been a member or chair of 46 dissertations, served on the program committee of the *Western Finance Association* for nine years, and served as an associate editor of the *Journal of Financial Markets* for eleven years. He chaired the department undergraduate committee for eleven years, chaired three different schoolwide committees over six years, and is currently chairing the department doctoral committee. He has lead several major curriculum innovations in the finance department. More information is available at Craig's home page: **www.kelley.iu.edu/cholden**.

PART 1 BONDS / FIXED INCOME SECURITIES

Chapter 1 Bond Pricing

1.1 Annual Payments

Problem. On November 1, 2007, an 8 year Treasury Bond with a face value of $1,000.00, paying $45.00 in coupon payments per year had a discount rate per year (yield) of 4.26%. Consider a bond that paid a $45.00 coupon payment once per year. What is price of this annual payment bond?

Solution Strategy. We will calculate the bond price in three equivalent ways. First, we will calculate the bond price as the present value of the bond's cash flows. Second, we use a formula for the bond price. Third, we use Excel's PV function for a bond price.

FIGURE 1.1 Excel Model of Bond Pricing – Annual Payments.

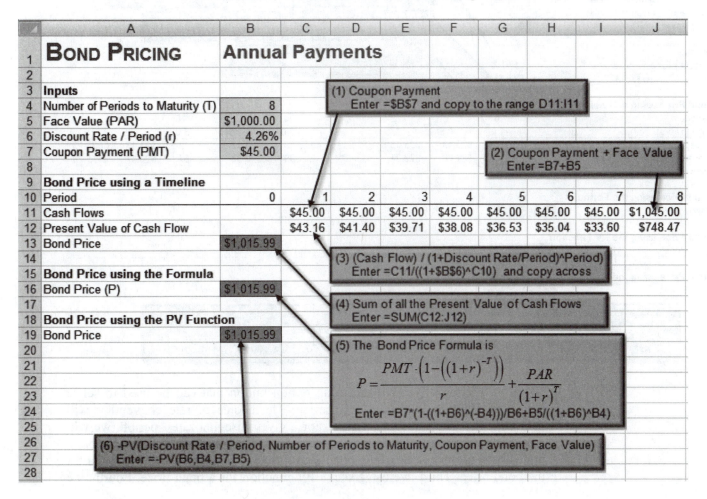

The resulting annual bond price is $1,015.99. Notice you get the same answer all three ways: using the cash flows, using the formula, or using the PV function!

1.2 EAR and APR

Problem. On November 1, 2007, a 4 year Treasury Bond with a face value of $1,000 and an annual coupon rate of 4.625% had a yield to maturity of 3.94%. This bond makes 2 (semi-annual) coupon payments per year and thus has 8 periods until maturity. What is price of this bond based on the Effective Annual Rate (EAR) convention? What is price of this bond based on the Annual Percentage Rate (APR) convention?

FIGURE 1.2 Excel Model of Bond Pricing – EAR and APR.

	A	B	C	D	E	F	G	H	I	J
1	**BOND PRICING**	**EAR and APR**			**Annual Percentage Rate**					
2										
3	**Inputs**									
4	Rate Convention	○ EAR ◉ APR	2	(1) If Rate Convention = EAR,						
5	Annual Coupon Rate	4.625%		Then (1+Yield To Maturity)^(1 / (Number of Payments / Year)) - 1						
6	Yield to Maturity (Annualized)	3.94%		Else (Yield To Maturity) / Number of Payment / Year)						
7	Number of Payments / Year	2		Enter =IF(C4=1,((1+B6)^(1/B7))-1,B6/B7)						
8	Number of Periods to Maturity (T)	8								
9	Face Value (PAR)	$1,000.00		(2) Coupon Rate * Face Value / (Number of Payments / Year)						
10				Enter =B5*B9/B7						
11	**Outputs**									
12	Discount Rate / Period (r)	1.97%		(3) Period / (Number of Payments / Year)						
13	Coupon Payment (PMT)	$23.13		Enter =B16/$B$7 and copy across						
14										
15	**Bond Price using a Timeline**									
16	Period	0	1	2	3	4	5	6	7	8
17	Time (Years)	0.0	0.5	1.0	1.5	2.0	2.5	3.0	3.5	4.0
18	Cash Flows		$23.13	$23.13	$23.13	$23.13	$23.13	$23.13	$23.13	$1,023.13
19	Present Value of Cash Flow		$22.68	$22.24	$21.81	$21.39	$20.98	$20.57	$20.17	$875.28
20	Bond Price	$1,025.12								
21										
22	**Bond Price using the Formula**									
23	Bond Price	$1,025.12								
24										
25	**Bond Price using the PV Function**									
26	Bond Price	$1,025.12								
27										
28	**Bond Price using the PRICE Function (under APR)**									
29	Bond Price	$1,025.12								
30										
31	(4) If Rate Convention = EAR, Then Blank,									
32	Else =PRICE(DATE(2000,1,1),DATE(2000 + Number of Periods to Maturity / (Number of Payments / Year),1,1),									
33	Coupon Rate, Yield To Maturity, 100, (Number of Payments / Year)) * Number of Periods to Maturity / 100)									
34	Enter =IF(C4=1,"",PRICE(DATE(2000,1,1),DATE(2000+B8/B7,1,1),B5,B6,100,B7)*B9/100)									

Solution Strategy. We will create an option button that can be used to select either the EAR or APR rate convention. The choice of rate convention will determine the discount rate / period. For a given discount rate / period, we will calculate the bond price in four equivalent ways. First, we will calculate the bond price as the present value of the bond's cash flows. Second, we use a formula for the bond price. Third, we use Excel's PV function for a bond price. Fourth, we use Excel's Analysis ToolPak Add-In PRICE function, which only works under the APR convention.

Excel's Analysis ToolPak contains several advanced bond functions, including the PRICE function which uses the APR convention. To access any of these functions, you need to install the Analysis ToolPak. Otherwise you will get the error message #NAME?.

Excel 2003 Equivalent

To install the Analysis ToolPak in Excel 2003, click on **Tools**, **Add-Ins**, check the **Analysis TookPak** checkbox on the Add-Ins dialog box, and click on **OK**.

To install the Analysis ToolPak, click on the **Office** button , click on the **Excel Options** button at the bottom of the drop-down window, click on **Add-Ins**, highlight the **Analysis ToolPak** in the list of Inactive Applications, click on **Go**, check the **Analysis ToolPak**, and click on **OK**.

The bond price function is =PRICE(Settlement Date, Maturity Date, Annual Coupon Rate, Yield To Maturity, Redemption Value, Number of Payments). The Settlement Date is the date when you exchange money to purchase the bond. Specifying the exact day of settlement and maturity allows a very precise calculation. For our purpose, we simple want the difference between the two dates to equal the (8 Periods To Maturity) / (2 Payments / Year) = 4 Years To Maturity. This is easily accomplished by the use of the DATE function. The DATE Function has the format =DATE(Year, Month, Day). We will enter an arbitrary starting date of 1/1/2000 for the Settlement Date and then specify a formula for 1/1/2000 plus T / NOP for the Maturity Date. We also add an IF statement to test for the rate convention being used.

The resulting semi-annual bond price is $1,025.12 under APR and $1,026.54 under EAR. Notice you get the same answer all ways: using the cash flows, using the formula, using the PV function, or using the PRICE function under APR!

1.3 By Yield To Maturity

What is the relationship between bond price and yield to maturity? We can construct a graph to find out.

FIGURE 1.3 Excel Model of Bond Pricing - By Yield To Maturity.

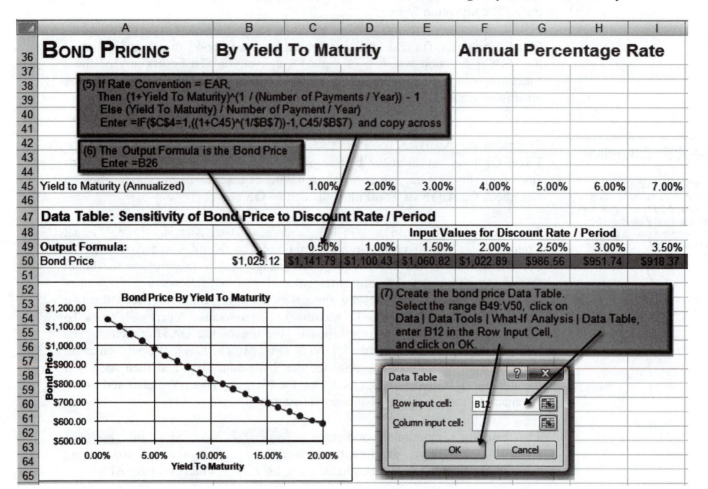

This graph shows the inverse relationship between bond price and yield to maturity. In other words, a higher discount rate (yield to maturity) lowers the present value of the bond's cash flows (price). The graph also shows that the relationship is curved (nonlinear) rather than being a straight line (linear).

Excel 2003 Equivalent

To call up a Data Table in Excel 2003. click on **Data | Table**

1.4 Dynamic Chart

If you increased the coupon rate of a bond, what would happen to its price? If you increased the yield to maturity of a bond, what would happen to its price? You can answer these questions and more by creating a *Dynamic Chart* using "spin button." Spin buttons are up-arrow / down-arrow buttons that allow you to easily change the inputs to the model with the click of a mouse. Then Excel recalculates the model and instantly redraws the model outputs on the graph.

FIGURE 1.4 Excel Model of Bond Pricing – Dynamic Chart.

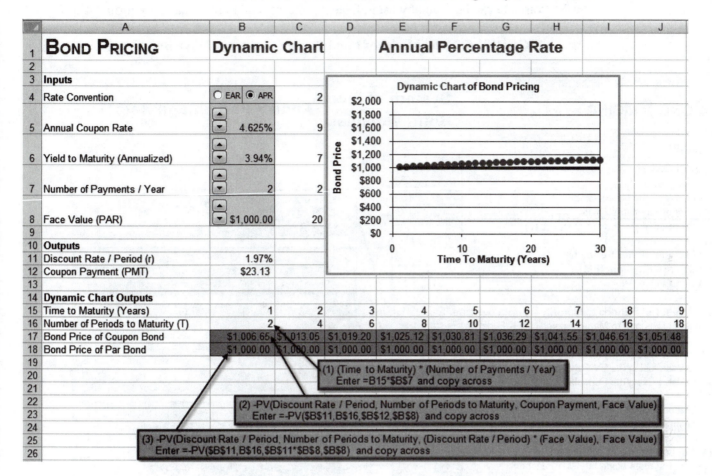

Your *Dynamic Chart* allows you to change the Bond Price inputs and instantly see the impact on a graph of the price of a coupon bond and par bond by time to maturity. This allows you to perform instant experiments on Bond Price. Below is a list of experiments that you might want to perform:

- What happens when the annual coupon rate is increased?
- What happens when the yield to maturity is increased?
- What happens when the number of payments / year is increased?
- What happens when the face value is increased?
- What is the relationship between the price of a par bond and time to maturity?
- What happens when the annual coupon rate is increased to the point that it equals the yield to maturity? What happens when it is increased further?

1.5 System of Five Bond Variables

There is a system of five bond variables: (1) Number of Periods to Maturity (T), (2) Face Value (PAR), (3) Discount Rate / Period (r), (4) Coupon Payments

(PMT), and (5) Bond Price (P). Given any four of these variables, the fifth variable can be found by using Excel functions (and in some cases by formulas).

FIGURE 1.5 Excel Model of Bond Pricing - System of Five Bond Variables.

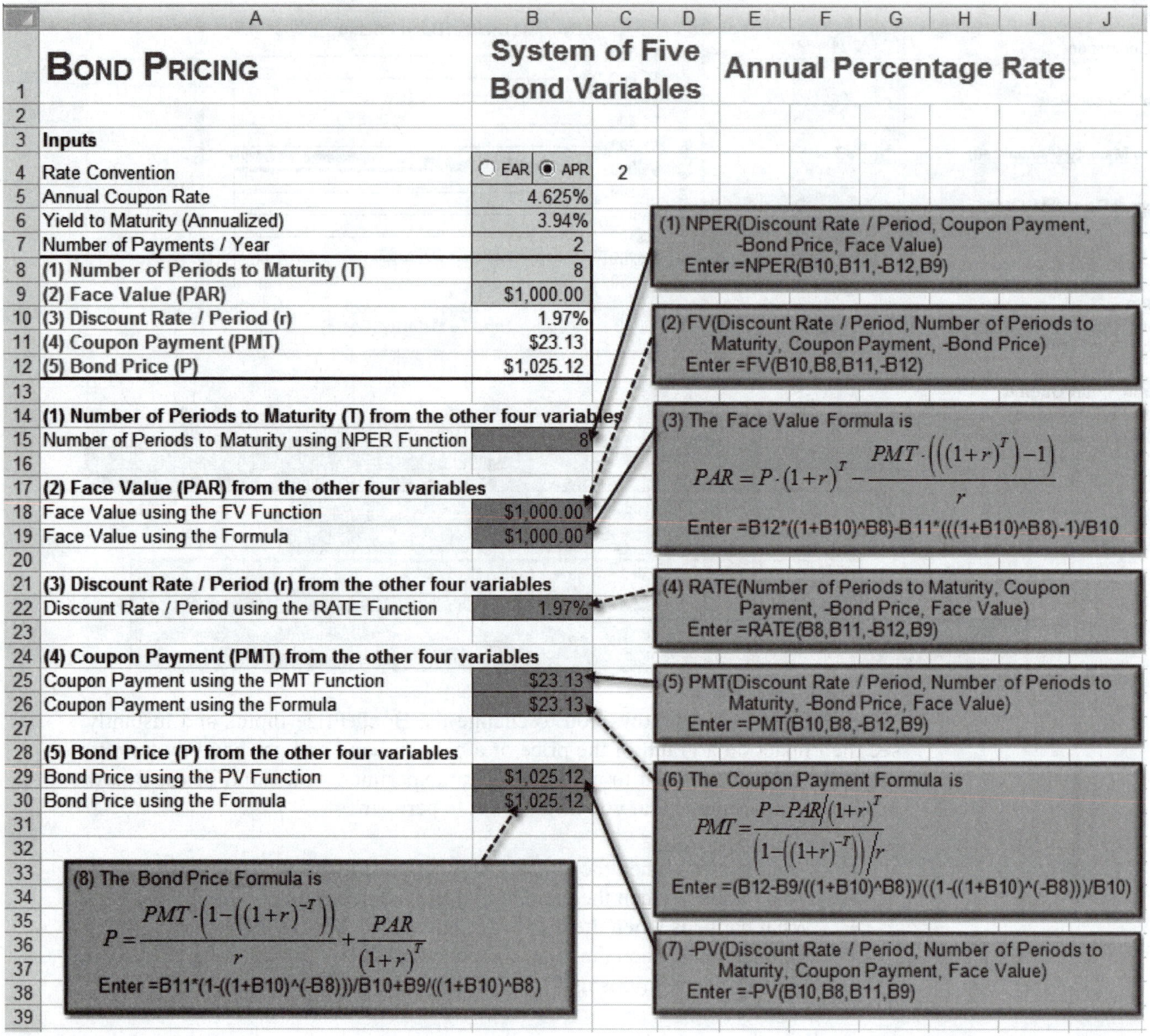

We see that the system of five bond variables is internally consistent. The five outputs in rows **15** through **30** (T=8, PAR=1000, r=1.97%, PMT=$23.13, P=$1,025.12) are identical to the five inputs in rows **8** through **12**. Thus, any of the five bond variables can be calculated from the other four in a fully consistent manner.

Problems

1. An annual bond has a face value of $1,000.00, makes an annual coupon payment of $12.00 per year, has a discount rate per year of 4.37%, and has 8 years to maturity. What is price of this bond?

2. A semi-annual bond has a face value of $1,000.00, an annual coupon rate of 4.60%, an yield to maturity of 8.12%, makes 2 (semi-annual) coupon payments per year, and 10 periods to maturity (or 5 years to maturity). Determine the price of this bond based on the Annual Percentage Rate (APR) convention and the price of this bond based on the Effective Annual Rate (EAR) convention.

3. Determine the relationship between bond price and yield to maturity by constructing a graph of the relationship.

4. Perform instant experiments on whether changing various inputs causes an increase or decrease in the Bond Price and by how much.

    (a.) What happens when the annual coupon rate is increased?
    (b.) What happens when the yield to maturity is increased?
    (c.) What happens when the number of payments / year is increased?
    (d.) What happens when the face value is increased?
    (e.) What is the relationship between the price of a par bond and time to maturity?
    (f.) What happens when the annual coupon rate is increased to the point that it equals the yield to maturity? What happens when it is increased further?

5. Given four of the bond variables, determine the fifth bond variable.

    (a.) Given Number of Periods to Maturity is 10, Face Value is $1,000.00, Discount Rate / Period is 3.27%, and Coupon Payment is $40.00, determine the Bond Price.

    (b.) Given Number of Periods to Maturity is 8, Face Value is $1,000.00, Discount Rate / Period is 4.54%, and the Bond Price is $880.00, determine the Coupon Payment.

    (c.) Given Number of Periods to Maturity is 6, Face Value is $1,000.00, Coupon Payment is $30.00, and the Bond Price is $865.00, determine Discount Rate / Period.

    (d.) Given Number of Periods to Maturity is 8, Discount Rate / Period is 3.81%, Coupon Payment is $45.00, and the Bond Price is $872.00, determine Face Value.

    (e.) Given Face Value is $1,000.00, Discount Rate / Period is 4.38%, Coupon Payment is $37.00, and the Bond Price is $887.00, determine the Number of Periods to Maturity.

Chapter 2 Bond Duration

2.1 Basics

Problem. On November 1, 2007, a 4 year Treasury Bond with a face value of $1,000 and an annual coupon rate of 4.625% had a yield to maturity of 3.94%. This bond makes 2 (semi-annual) coupon payments per year and thus has 8 periods until maturity. What is the duration and modified duration of this bond based on the Annual Percentage Rate (APR) convention? What is the duration and modified duration of this bond based on the Effective Annual Rate (EAR) convention? What is the intuitive interpretation of duration?

Solution Strategy. The choice of either the EAR or APR rate convention will determine the discount rate / period. For a given the discount rate / period, we will calculate duration and modified duration three equivalent ways. First, we will calculate duration as the weighted-average time to the bond's cash flows. This method illustrates the intuitive interpretation of duration. Second, we use a formula for duration. In both cases, modified duration is a simple adjustment of regular duration (also called Macaulay's Duration). Third, we use Excel's Analysis ToolPak Add-In **DURATION** and **MDURATION** functions, which only work under the APR convention.

FIGURE 2.1 Excel Model of Bond Duration - Basics.

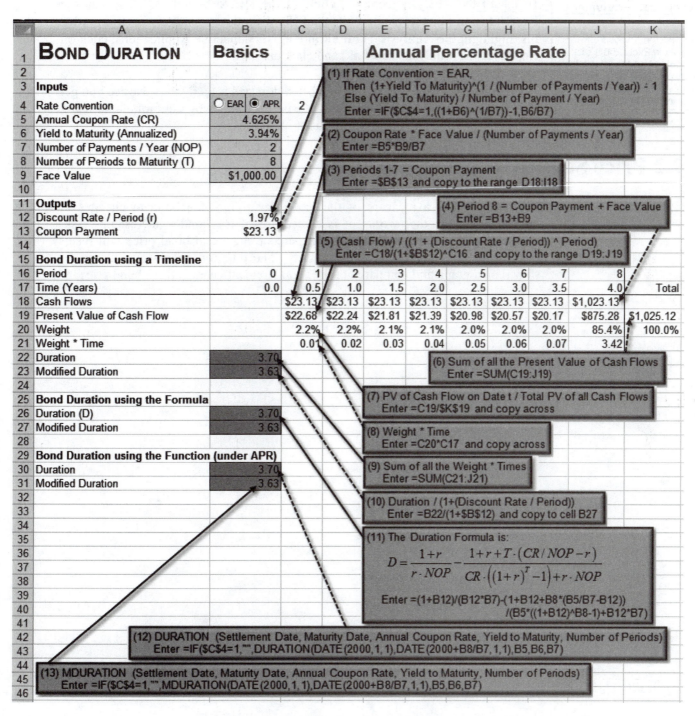

The timeline method of calculation directly illustrates the key intuition that (Macaulay's) duration is the weighted-average of the time until cash flows are received. The weights are based on the ratio of the present value of each cash flow over the present value of the total bond.

To install the Analysis ToolPak, click on the **Office** button [image], click on the
Excel Options button at the bottom of the drop-down window, click on **Add-Ins**, highlight the **Analysis ToolPak** in the list of Inactive Applications, click on **Go**, check the **Analysis ToolPak**, and click on **OK**.

The duration is 3.70 years and the modified duration is 3.63 years. Notice you get the same answer all three ways: using the cash flows, using the formula, or using the Analysis ToolPak Add-In function!

2.2 Price Sensitivity using Duration

Bond duration is a measure of the price sensitivity of a bond to changes in interest rates. In other words, it is a measure of the bond's interest rate risk. Duration tells you approximately what percent change in bond price will result from a given change in yield to maturity. The duration approximation can be shown on a graph and compared to the actual percent change in the bond price.

FIGURE 2.2 Excel Model of Bond Duration – Price Sensitivity using Duration.

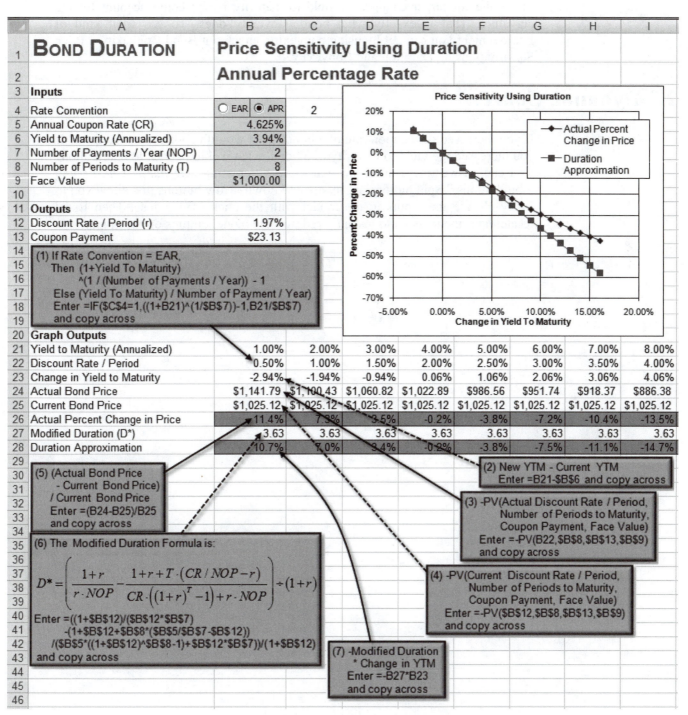

It is clear from the graph that duration does a very good job of approximating the price sensitivity of a bond. That is, the percent change in bond price from the duration approximation is very close to the actual percent change. This is especially true for relatively small changes in yield to maturity (say, plus or minus 3%). For larger changes in yield to maturity, there is a gap between the duration approximation and the actual percent change. The gap comes from the fact that the actual percent change is curved, whereas the duration approximation is a straight line. One could do a better job of approximating the price sensitivity of a bond for larger changes in yield to maturity if one could account for the curvature. That is exactly what bond convexity does. To see what kind of improvement you can get by using convexity, check out Bond Convexity – Price Sensitivity using Duration and Convexity.

2.3 Dynamic Chart

If you increased the coupon rate of a bond, what would happen to its duration? If you increased the yield to maturity of a bond, what would happen to its duration? You can answer these questions and more by creating a *Dynamic Chart* using "spin buttons." Spin buttons are up-arrow / down-arrow buttons that allow you to easily change the inputs to the model with the click of a mouse. Then Excel recalculates the model and instantly redraws the model outputs on the graph.

FIGURE 2.3 Excel Model of Bond Duration – Dynamic Chart.

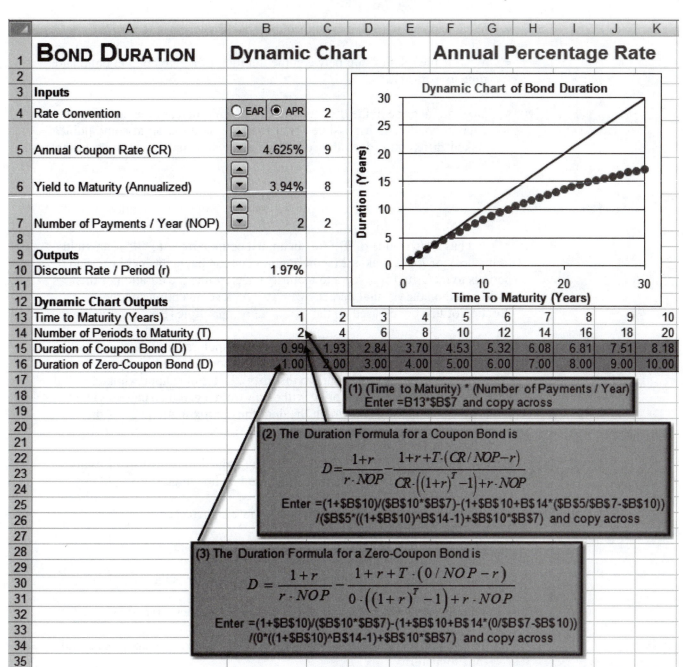

Your *Dynamic Chart* allows you to change the Bond Duration inputs and instantly see the impact on a graph of the duration of a coupon bond and zero coupon bond by time to maturity. This allows you to perform instant experiments on Bond Duration. Below is a list of experiments that you might want to perform:

- What happens when the annual coupon rate is increased?

- What happens when the yield to maturity is increased?

- What happens when the number of payments / year is increased?

- What happens when the annual coupon rate is decreased to zero?

- What is the relationship between the duration of a zero coupon bond and time to maturity?

- Does an increase in the time to maturity *always* increase the duration of a coupon bond or is it possible for it to decrease duration at some point? Asked differently, does the red curve always go up or can it be hump shaped?

Problems

1. A bond has a face value of $1,000, an annual coupon rate of 3.70%, an yield to maturity of 7.4%, makes 2 (semi-annual) coupon payments per year, and 6 periods to maturity (or 3 years to maturity). Determine the duration of this bond based on the Annual Percentage Rate (APR) convention and the duration of this bond based on the Effective Annual Rate (EAR) convention.

2. A bond has a face value of $1,000, an annual coupon rate of 6.50%, an yield to maturity of 9.2%, makes 2 (semi-annual) coupon payments per year, and 10 periods to maturity (or 5 years to maturity). Determine approximately what percent change in bond price will result from a given change in yield to maturity by comparing on a graph the duration approximation versus the actual percent change in the bond price.

3. Perform instant experiments on whether changing various inputs causes an increase or decrease in the Bond Duration and by how much.

    a. What happens when the annual coupon rate is increased?

    b. What happens when the yield to maturity is increased?

    c. What happens when the number of payments / year is increased?

    d. What happens when the annual coupon rate is decreased to zero?

    e. What is the relationship between the duration of a zero coupon bond and time to maturity?

    f. Does an increase in the time to maturity always increase the duration of a coupon bond or is it possible for it to decrease duration at some point? Asked differently, does the duration curve always go up or can it be hump shaped?

Chapter 3 Bond Convexity

3.1 Basics

Problem. On November 1, 2007, a 4 year Treasury Bond with a face value of $1,000 and an annual coupon rate of 4.625% had a yield to maturity of 3.94%. This bond makes 2 (semi-annual) coupon payments per year and thus has 8 periods until maturity. What is the convexity of this bond?

Solution Strategy. We will calculate convexity two equivalent ways. First, we will calculate convexity as the weighted-average (time-squared plus time) to the bond's cash flows. Second, we use a formula for convexity.

FIGURE 3.1 Excel Model of Bond Convexity - Basics.

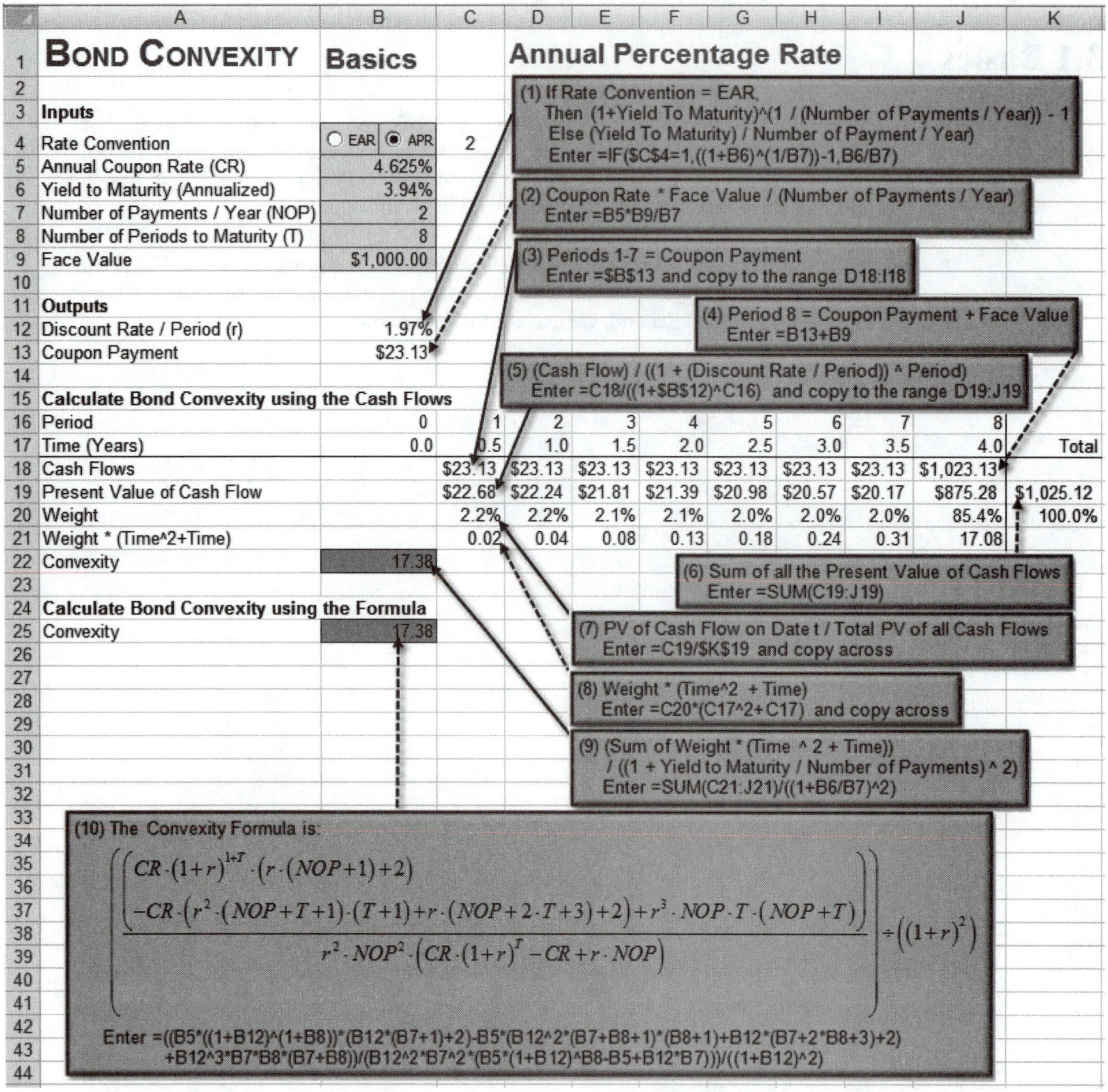

	A	B	C	D	E	F	G	H	I	J	K
1	**BOND CONVEXITY**	**Basics**		**Annual Percentage Rate**							
2											
3	**Inputs**										
4	Rate Convention	○ EAR ● APR	2								
5	Annual Coupon Rate (CR)	4.625%									
6	Yield to Maturity (Annualized)	3.94%									
7	Number of Payments / Year (NOP)	2									
8	Number of Periods to Maturity (T)	8									
9	Face Value	$1,000.00									
10											
11	**Outputs**										
12	Discount Rate / Period (r)	1.97%									
13	Coupon Payment	$23.13									
14											
15	**Calculate Bond Convexity using the Cash Flows**										
16	Period	0	1	2	3	4	5	6	7	8	
17	Time (Years)	0.0	0.5	1.0	1.5	2.0	2.5	3.0	3.5	4.0	Total
18	Cash Flows		$23.13	$23.13	$23.13	$23.13	$23.13	$23.13	$23.13	$1,023.13	
19	Present Value of Cash Flow		$22.68	$22.24	$21.81	$21.39	$20.98	$20.57	$20.17	$875.28	$1,025.12
20	Weight		2.2%	2.2%	2.1%	2.1%	2.0%	2.0%	2.0%	85.4%	100.0%
21	Weight * (Time^2+Time)		0.02	0.04	0.08	0.13	0.18	0.24	0.31	17.08	
22	Convexity	17.38									
23											
24	**Calculate Bond Convexity using the Formula**										
25	Convexity	17.38									

Callout notes:

(1) If Rate Convention = EAR,
Then (1+Yield To Maturity)^(1 / (Number of Payments / Year)) - 1
Else (Yield To Maturity) / Number of Payment / Year)
Enter =IF($C$4=1,((1+B6)^(1/B7))-1,B6/B7)

(2) Coupon Rate * Face Value / (Number of Payments / Year)
Enter =B5*B9/B7

(3) Periods 1-7 = Coupon Payment
Enter =$B$13 and copy to the range D18:I18

(4) Period 8 = Coupon Payment + Face Value
Enter =B13+B9

(5) (Cash Flow) / ((1 + (Discount Rate / Period)) ^ Period)
Enter =C18/((1+$B$12)^C16) and copy to the range D19:J19

(6) Sum of all the Present Value of Cash Flows
Enter =SUM(C19:J19)

(7) PV of Cash Flow on Date t / Total PV of all Cash Flows
Enter =C19/$K$19 and copy across

(8) Weight * (Time^2 + Time)
Enter =C20*(C17^2+C17) and copy across

(9) (Sum of Weight * (Time ^ 2 + Time))
/ ((1 + Yield to Maturity / Number of Payments) ^ 2)
Enter =SUM(C21:J21)/((1+B6/B7)^2)

(10) The Convexity Formula is:

$$\left(\frac{\begin{pmatrix}CR\cdot(1+r)^{1+T}\cdot\left(r\cdot(NOP+1)+2\right)\\-CR\cdot\left(r^2\cdot(NOP+T+1)\cdot(T+1)+r\cdot(NOP+2\cdot T+3)+2\right)+r^3\cdot NOP\cdot T\cdot(NOP+T)\end{pmatrix}}{r^2\cdot NOP^2\cdot\left(CR\cdot(1+r)^T-CR+r\cdot NOP\right)}\right)\div\left((1+r)^2\right)$$

Enter =((B5*((1+B12)^(1+B8))*(B12*(B7+1)+2)-B5*(B12^2*(B7+B8+1)*(B8+1)+B12*(B7+2*B8+3)+2)
+B12^3*B7*B8*(B7+B8))/(B12^2*B7^2*(B5*(1+B12)^B8-B5+B12*B7)))/((1+B12)^2)

The value of bond convexity is 17.38. Notice you get the same answer both ways: using the cash flows or using the formula!

3.2 Price Sensitivity Including Convexity

Bond convexity complements bond duration in measuring of the price sensitivity of a bond to changes in interest rates. In other words, duration and convexity combined give you a measure of the bond's interest rate risk. Adding convexity gives you a better approximation of what percent change in bond price will result from a given change in yield to maturity than you can get from duration alone. To get the overall picture we will compare all three on a graph: the duration approximation, the duration and convexity approximation, and the actual percent change in the bond price.

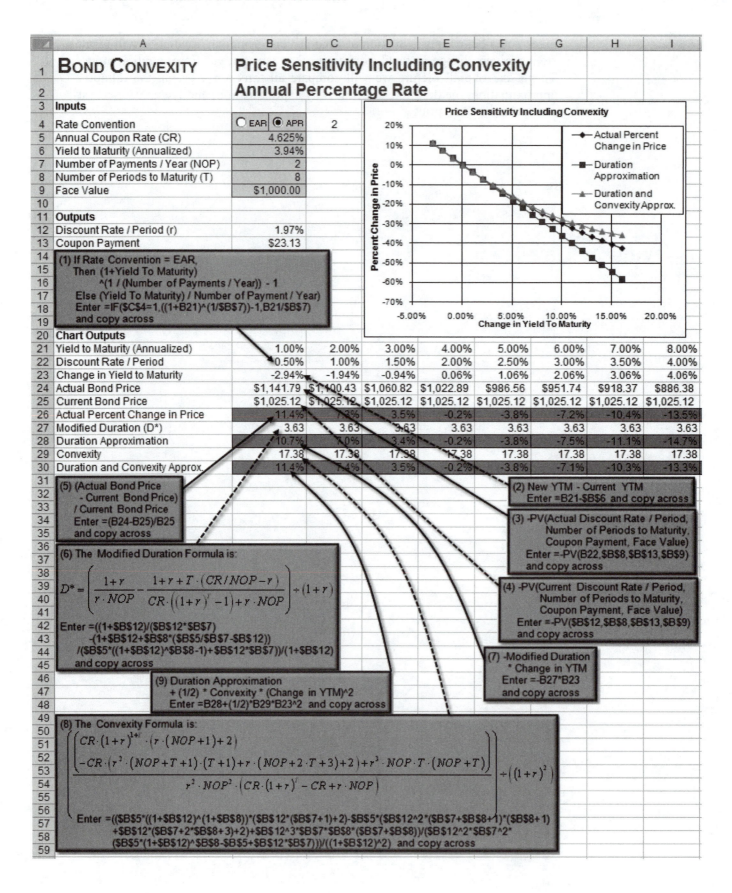

Bond Convexity

Price Sensitivity Including Convexity
Annual Percentage Rate

Inputs

Rate Convention	○ EAR ● APR	2	
Annual Coupon Rate (CR)	4.625%		
Yield to Maturity (Annualized)	3.94%		
Number of Payments / Year (NOP)	2		
Number of Periods to Maturity (T)	8		
Face Value	$1,000.00		

Outputs

Discount Rate / Period (r)	1.97%
Coupon Payment	$23.13

(1) If Rate Convention = EAR,
Then (1+Yield To Maturity)
^(1 / (Number of Payments / Year)) - 1
Else (Yield To Maturity) / Number of Payment / Year)
Enter =IF($C$4=1,((1+B21)^(1/$B$7))-1,B21/$B$7)
and copy across

Price Sensitivity Including Convexity

Chart legend:
- Actual Percent Change in Price
- Duration Approximation
- Duration and Convexity Approx.

(X-axis: Change in Yield To Maturity, −5.00% to 20.00%; Y-axis: Percent Change in Price, −70% to 20%)

Chart Outputs

	B	C	D	E	F	G	H	I
Yield to Maturity (Annualized)	1.00%	2.00%	3.00%	4.00%	5.00%	6.00%	7.00%	8.00%
Discount Rate / Period	0.50%	1.00%	1.50%	2.00%	2.50%	3.00%	3.50%	4.00%
Change in Yield to Maturity	-2.94%	-1.94%	-0.94%	0.06%	1.06%	2.06%	3.06%	4.06%
Actual Bond Price	$1,141.79	$1,100.43	$1,060.82	$1,022.89	$986.56	$951.74	$918.37	$886.38
Current Bond Price	$1,025.12	$1,025.12	$1,025.12	$1,025.12	$1,025.12	$1,025.12	$1,025.12	$1,025.12
Actual Percent Change in Price	11.4%	7.3%	3.5%	-0.2%	-3.8%	-7.2%	-10.4%	-13.5%
Modified Duration (D*)	3.63	3.63	3.63	3.63	3.63	3.63	3.63	3.63
Duration Approximation	10.7%	7.0%	3.4%	-0.2%	-3.8%	-7.5%	-11.1%	-14.7%
Convexity	17.38	17.38	17.38	17.38	17.38	17.38	17.38	17.38
Duration and Convexity Approx.	11.4%	7.4%	3.5%	-0.2%	-3.8%	-7.1%	-10.3%	-13.3%

(5) (Actual Bond Price
- Current Bond Price)
/ Current Bond Price
Enter =(B24-B25)/B25
and copy across

(2) New YTM - Current YTM
Enter =B21-$B$6 and copy across

(3) -PV(Actual Discount Rate / Period,
Number of Periods to Maturity,
Coupon Payment, Face Value)
Enter =-PV(B22,$B$8,$B$13,$B$9)
and copy across

(6) The Modified Duration Formula is:

$$D^* = \left(\frac{1+r}{r \cdot NOP} - \frac{1+r+T \cdot (CR/NOP-r)}{CR \cdot \left((1+r)^{T}-1\right)+r \cdot NOP} \right) \div (1+r)$$

Enter =((1+$B$12)/($B$12*$B$7)
-(1+$B$12+$B$8*($B$5/$B$7-$B$12))
/($B$5*((1+$B$12)^$B$8-1)+$B$12*$B$7))/(1+$B$12)
and copy across

(4) -PV(Current Discount Rate / Period,
Number of Periods to Maturity,
Coupon Payment, Face Value)
Enter =-PV($B$12,$B$8,$B$13,$B$9)
and copy across

(7) -Modified Duration
* Change in YTM
Enter =-B27*B23
and copy across

(9) Duration Approximation
+ (1/2) * Convexity * (Change in YTM)^2
Enter =B28+(1/2)*B29*B23^2 and copy across

(8) The Convexity Formula is:

$$\left(\frac{\begin{array}{l} CR \cdot (1+r)^{1+T} \cdot (r \cdot (NOP+1)+2) \\ -CR \cdot (r^2 \cdot (NOP+T+1) \cdot (T+1)+r \cdot (NOP+2 \cdot T+3)+2)+r^3 \cdot NOP \cdot T \cdot (NOP+T) \end{array}}{r^2 \cdot NOP^2 \cdot \left(CR \cdot (1+r)^{T} - CR+r \cdot NOP\right)} \right) \div (1+r)^2$$

Enter =((($B$5*((1+$B$12)^(1+$B$8))*($B$12*($B$7+1)+2)-$B$5*($B$12^2*($B$7+$B$8+1)*($B$8+1)
+$B$12*($B$7+2*$B$8+3)+2)+$B$12^3*$B$7*$B$8*($B$7+$B$8))/($B$12^2*$B$7^2*
($B$5*(1+$B$12)^$B$8-$B$5+$B$12*$B$7)))/((1+$B$12)^2) and copy across

The graph illustrates that duration and convexity approximation of the price sensitivity of a bond is better than the duration approximation alone. That is, the percent change in bond price from the duration and convexity approximation is very close to the actual percent change over a wide range of changes in yield to maturity (say, greater than +9.00%). Only for a very large change in yield to maturity is there any gap between the duration and convexity approximation and the actual percent change and the gap is pretty small. In approximating the actual percent change, duration alone does a good job of approximating the slope. Then convexity does a good job of adding the curvature. Together they do a great job of approximating the price sensitivity (i.e., interest rate risk) of a bond over a wide range of changes in yields.

3.3 Dynamic Chart

If you increased the coupon rate of a bond, what would happen to its convexity? If you increased the yield to maturity of a bond, what would happen to its convexity? You can answer these questions and more by creating a *Dynamic Chart* using "spin buttons." Spin buttons are up-arrow / down-arrow buttons that allow you to easily change the inputs to the model with the click of a mouse. Then Excel recalculates the model and instantly redraws the model outputs on the graph.

FIGURE 3.3 Excel Model of Bond Convexity – Dynamic Chart.

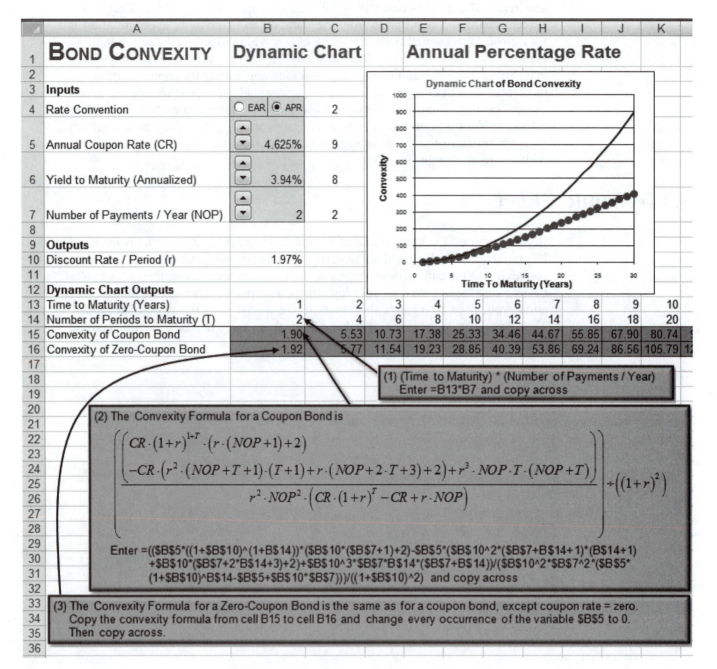

Your *Dynamic Chart* allows you to change the Bond Convexity inputs and instantly see the impact on a graph of the convexity of a coupon bond and zero coupon bond by time to maturity. This allows you to perform instant experiments on Bond Convexity. Below is a list of experiments that you might want to perform:

- What happens when the annual coupon rate is increased?

- What happens when the yield to maturity is increased?

- What happens when the number of payments / year is increased?

- What happens when the annual coupon rate is decreased to zero?

- Does an increase in the time to maturity *always* increase the convexity of a coupon bond or is it possible for it to decrease convexity at some point? Asked differently, does the red curve always go up or can it be hump shaped?

Problems

1. A bond has a face value of $1,000, an annual coupon rate of 2.30%, an yield to maturity of 8.9%, makes 2 (semi-annual) coupon payments per year, and 10 periods to maturity (or 5 years to maturity). Determine the convexity of this bond based on the Annual Percentage Rate (APR) convention and the convexity of this bond based on the Effective Annual Rate (EAR) convention.

2. A bond has a face value of $1,000, an annual coupon rate of 4.70%, an yield to maturity of 7.8%, makes 2 (semi-annual) coupon payments per year, and 8 periods to maturity (or 4 years to maturity). Determine approximately what percent change in bond price will result from a given change in yield to maturity by comparing on a graph the duration approximation, the duration and convexity approximation, and the actual percent change in the bond price.

3. Perform instant experiments on whether changing various inputs causes an increase or decrease in the Bond Convexity and by how much.

   a. What happens when the annual coupon rate is increased?

   b. What happens when the yield to maturity is increased?

   c. What happens when the number of payments / year is increased?

   d. What happens when the annual coupon rate is decreased to zero?

   e. Does an increase in the time to maturity always increase the convexity of a coupon bond or is it possible for it to decrease convexity at some point? Asked differently, does the convexity curve always go up or can it be hump shaped?

Chapter 4 US Yield Curve Dynamics

4.1 Dynamic Chart

How does the US yield curve change over time? What determines the volatility of changes in the yield curve? Are there differences in the volatility of short rates, medium rates, long rates, etc.? You can answer these questions and more using a *Dynamic Chart* of the yield curve, which is based on more than 37 years of monthly US zero-coupon, yield curve data. I update this Excel model each year with the latest yield curve data and make it available for free in the "Free Samples" section of www.excelmodeling.com.

The dynamic chart uses a vertical scroll bar in rows **3** to **5**. Clicking on the right arrow of the scroll bar moves the yield curve forward by one month. Clicking on the left arrow moves back by one month. Clicking right of the position bar, moves the yield curve forward by one *year*. Clicking left of the position bar moves back by one *year*. This allows you to see a dynamic "movie" or animation of the yield curve over time. Thus, you can directly observe the volatility of the yield curve and other dynamic properties. For details of what to look for, see the discussion below on "using the Excel model."

FIGURE 4.1 Excel Model of US Yield Curve Dynamics – Dynamic Chart.

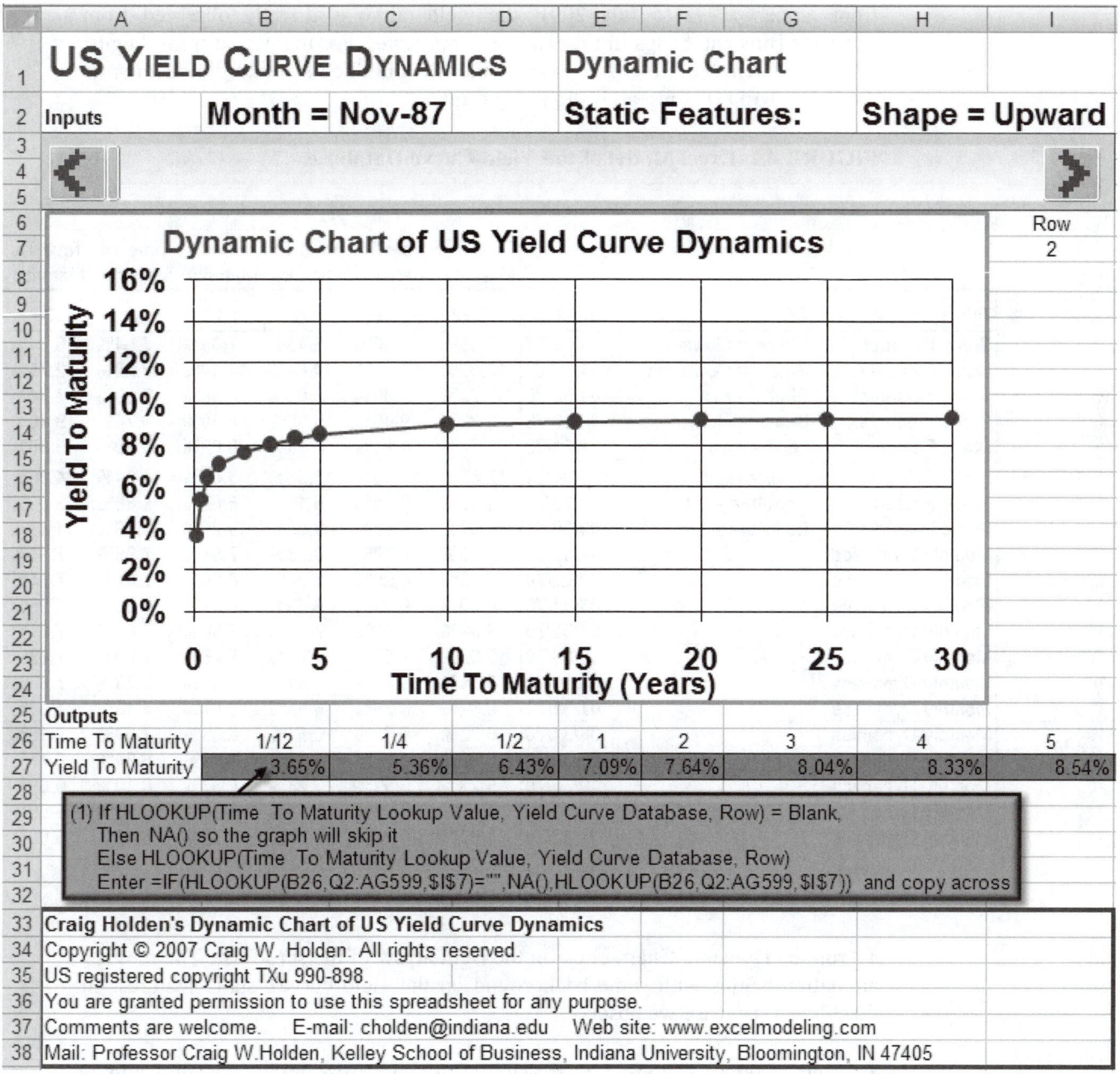

The yield curve database is located in columns **Q** to **AG**. Columns **Q, R,** and **S** contain three sets of titles for the dataset. Columns **T, U,** and **V** contain yield data for bond maturities of one month, three months, and six months (1/12, 1/4, and 1/2 years, respectively). Columns **W** through **AG** contain yield data for bond maturities of 1, 2, 3, 4, 5, 7, 10, 15, 20, 25, and 30 years. Rows **2** through **9** contain examples of static features of the yield curve that can be observed from actual data in a particular month. For example, the yield curve is sometimes upward sloping (as it was in Nov 87) or downward sloping (in Nov 80) or flat (in Jan 70) or hump shaped (in Dec 78). Rows **10** through **457** contain monthly US zero-coupon, yield curve data from January 1970 through March 2007. For the period from January 1970 through December 1991, the database is based on the Bliss (1992) monthly estimates of the zero-coupon, yield curve.[3] For the period from January 1992 to July 2001, the yield curve is directly observed from Treasury Bills and Strips in the *Wall Street Journal*. For the period from August 2001 to March 2007, the data is from the St Louis Fed's free online economic database FRED II at research.stlouisfed.org/fred2.

FIGURE 4.2 Excel Model of the Yield Curve Database.

	P	Q	R	S	T	U	V	W	X	Y
1					Time To Maturity	Time To Maturity	Time To Maturity	Time To Maturity	Time To Maturity	Time To Maturity
2		Title 1	Title 2	Title 3	1/12	1/4	1/2	1	2	3
3		Static Features:	Shape = Upward	11/30/87	3.65%	5.36%	6.43%	7.09%	7.64%	8.04%
4		Static Features:	Shape = Downward	11/28/80	14.83%	14.60%	14.64%	14.17%	13.22%	12.75%
5		Static Features:	Shape = Flat	01/30/70	7.73%	8.00%	8.03%	7.98%	7.95%	7.94%
6		Static Features:	Shape = Hump	12/29/78	8.82%	9.48%	9.99%	10.18%	9.76%	9.40%
7		Static Features:	Level = Low	12/31/70	4.62%	4.91%	4.95%	5.02%	5.40%	5.69%
8		Static Features:	Level = High	10/30/81	12.65%	13.13%	13.53%	13.85%	14.01%	14.06%
9		Static Features:	Curvature = Little	12/29/72	4.93%	5.24%	5.44%	5.62%	5.86%	6.01%
10		Static Features:	Curvature = Lot	09/30/82	6.67%	7.87%	9.05%	10.29%	11.16%	11.43%
11		Monthly Dynamics		01/30/70	7.73%	8.00%	8.03%	7.98%	7.95%	7.94%
12		Monthly Dynamics		02/27/70	6.23%	6.99%	6.97%	6.96%	7.02%	7.04%
13		Monthly Dynamics		03/31/70	6.33%	6.44%	6.53%	6.67%	6.85%	6.95%
14		Monthly Dynamics		04/30/70	6.48%	7.03%	7.35%	7.50%	7.60%	7.67%
15		Monthly Dynamics		05/29/70	6.22%	7.03%	7.28%	7.45%	7.58%	7.63%
16		Monthly Dynamics		06/30/70	6.14%	6.47%	6.81%	7.17%	7.43%	7.53%
17		Monthly Dynamics		07/31/70	6.32%	6.38%	6.55%	6.87%	7.19%	7.31%
18		Monthly Dynamics		08/31/70	6.22%	6.38%	6.57%	6.83%	7.07%	7.18%
19		Monthly Dynamics		09/30/70	5.32%	6.04%	6.49%	6.63%	6.64%	6.77%
20		Monthly Dynamics		10/30/70	5.23%	5.91%	6.23%	6.33%	6.50%	6.69%
21		Monthly Dynamics		11/30/70	4.86%	5.05%	5.11%	5.10%	5.29%	5.59%
22		Monthly Dynamics		12/31/70	4.62%	4.91%	4.95%	5.02%	5.40%	5.69%

Using The US Yield Curve Dynamic Chart.

To run the Dynamic Chart, click on the right arrow of the scroll bar. The movie / animation begins with some background on the yield curve's static features. In the 37 year database we observe:

- four different **shapes**: upward-sloping, downward-sloping, flat, and hump-shaped,
- the overall **level** of the yield curve ranges from low to high, and
- the amount of **curvature** at the short end ranges from a little to a lot.

---

[3] Bliss fits a parsimonious, nonlinear function that is capable of matching all of the empirically observed shapes of the zero-coupon, yield curve. For more details see Bliss, R., 1992, "Testing Term Structure Estimation Methods," Indiana University Discussion Paper #519.

Keep clicking on the right arrow of the scroll bar and you will get to the section of the Dynamic Chart covering 37 years of the US yield curve history. This section shows the yield curve on a month by month basis. For example, the figure below shows the US yield curve in November 1970.

FIGURE 4.3 Excel Model of Month By Month History – Dynamic Chart.

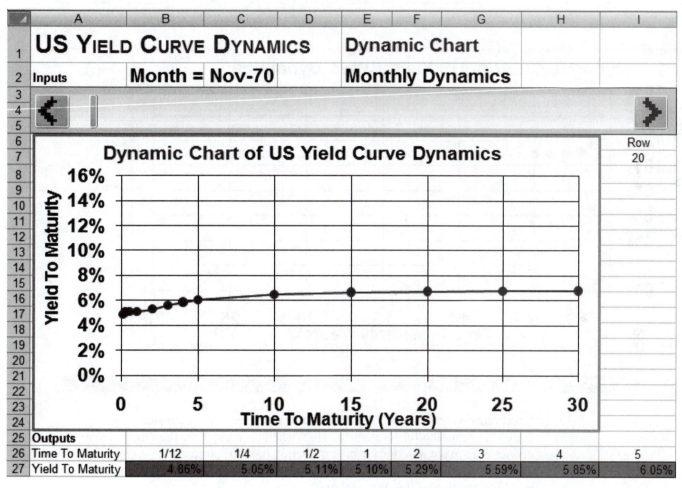

Keep clicking on the right arrow and you will see the yield curve move around over time. By observing this movie / animation, you should be able to recognize the following key **dynamic** properties of the yield curve:

- short rates (the 0 to 5 year piece of the yield curve) are more volatile than long rates (the 15 to 30 year piece),
- the overall volatility of the yield curve is higher when the level is higher (especially in the early 80's), and
- sometimes there are sharp reactions to government intervention.

As an example of the later, consider what happened in 1980. The figure below shows the yield curve in January 1980.

FIGURE 4.4 Excel Model Showing The Yield Curve in January 1980.

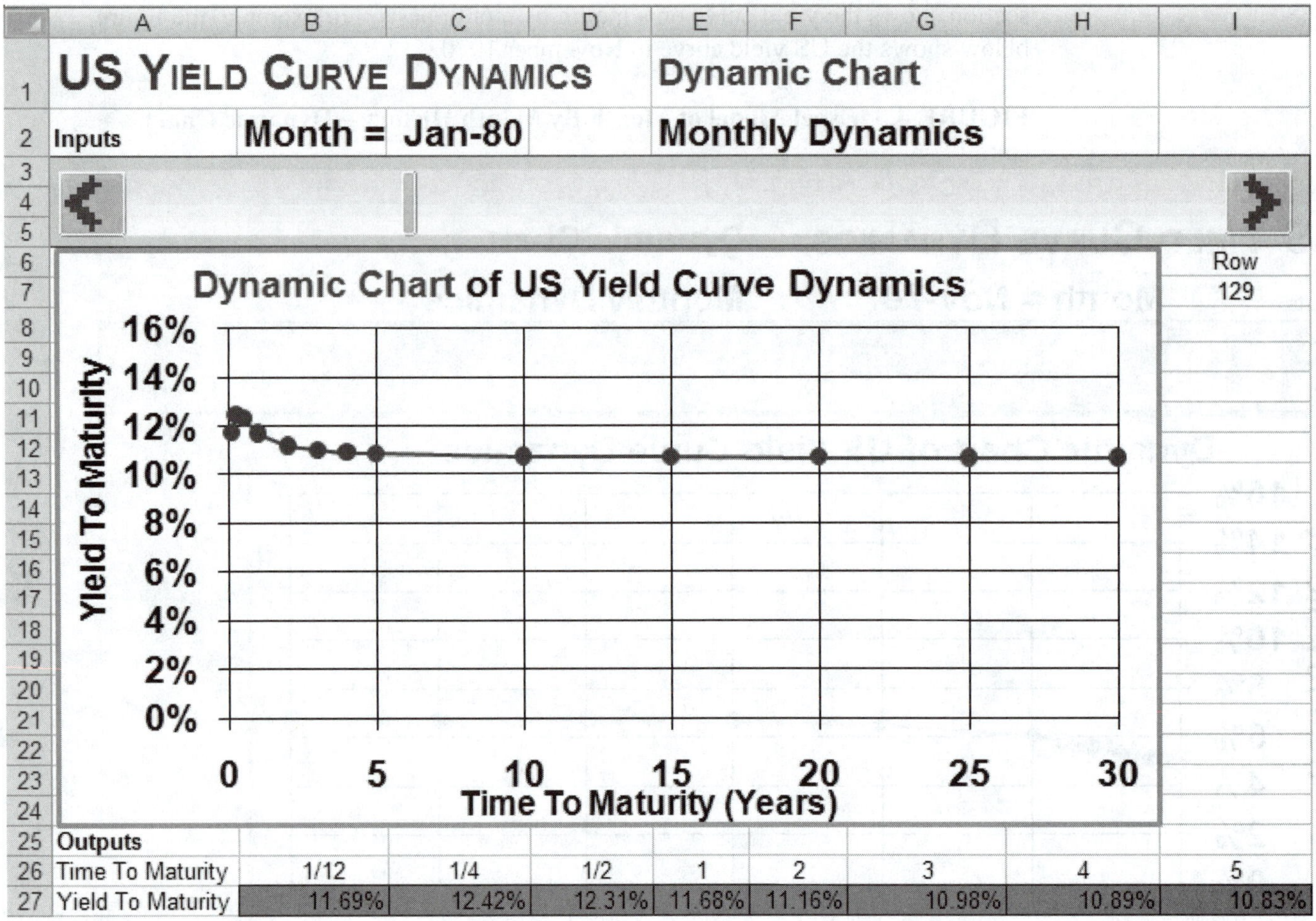

	A	B	C	D	E	F	G	H	I
1	US YIELD CURVE DYNAMICS				Dynamic Chart				
2	Inputs	Month =	Jan-80		Monthly Dynamics				
3									
4		◄							►
5									
6									Row
7		Dynamic Chart of US Yield Curve Dynamics							129

Dynamic Chart of US Yield Curve Dynamics

	A	B	C	D	E	F	G	H	I
25	Outputs								
26	Time To Maturity	1/12	1/4	1/2	1	2	3	4	5
27	Yield To Maturity	11.69%	12.42%	12 31%	11 68%	11.16%	10.98%	10.89%	10.83%

Short rates were around 12% and long rates were at 10.7%. President Jimmy Carter was running for re-election. He wished to manipulate the election year economy to make it better for his re-election bid. His strategy for doing this was to impose credit controls on the banking system. Click on the right arrow to see what the reaction of the financial market was.

FIGURE 4.5 Excel Model Showing The Yield Curve in March 1980.

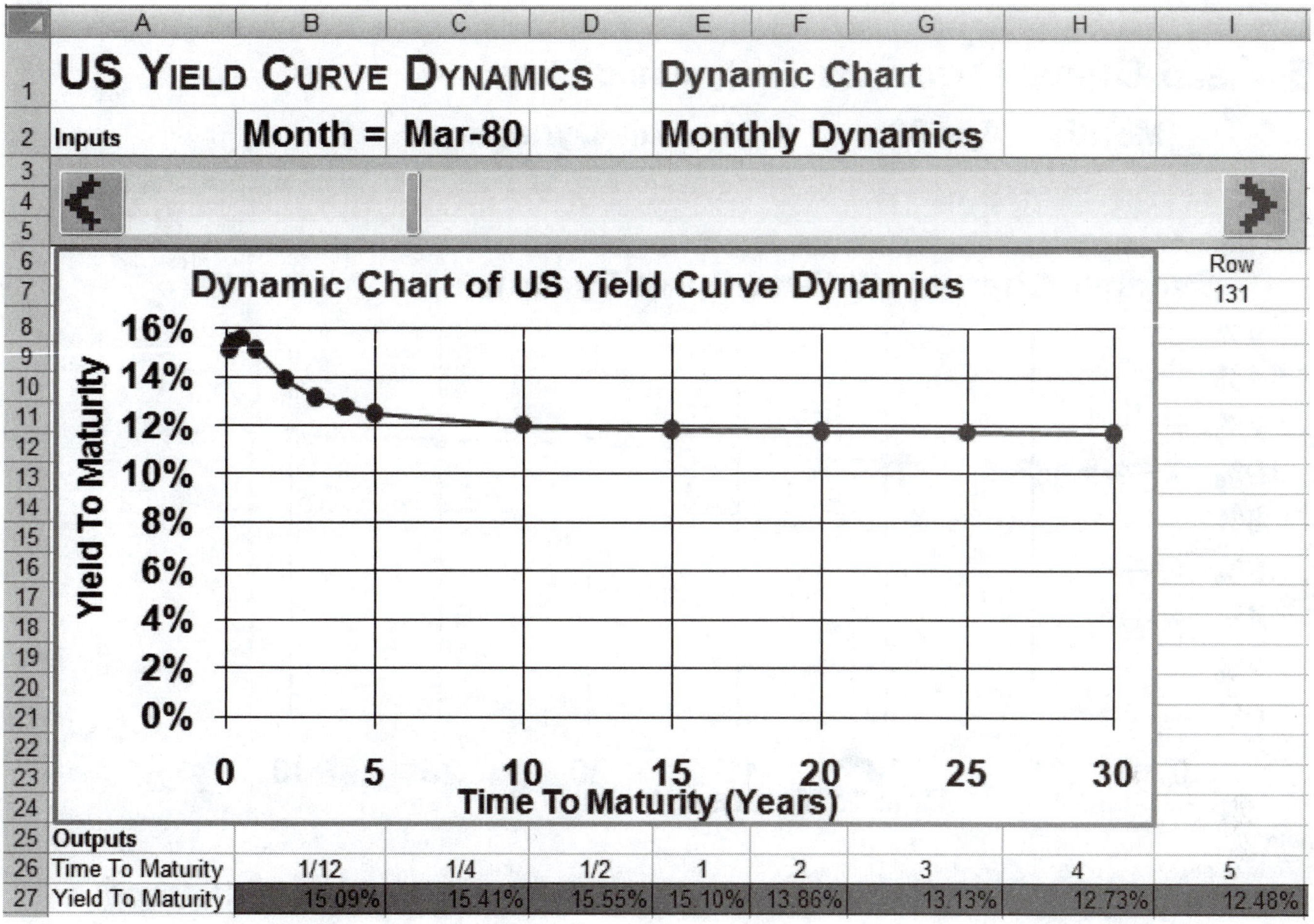

	A	B	C	D	E	F	G	H	I
1	US YIELD CURVE DYNAMICS				Dynamic Chart				
2	Inputs	Month = Mar-80			Monthly Dynamics				
3									
4									
5									
6									Row
7									131
25	Outputs								
26	Time To Maturity	1/12	1/4	1/2	1	2	3	4	5
27	Yield To Maturity	15.09%	15.41%	15.55%	15.10%	13.86%	13.13%	12.73%	12.48%

In two months time, the short rate when up to 15.5%, an increase of 3.5%! What a disaster! This was the opposite of the reaction the Carter had intended. Notice that long rates when up to 11.7%, an increase of only 1%. Apparently, the market expected that this intervention would only be a short-lived phenomenon. Carter quickly realized what a big political mistake he had made and announced that the credit controls were being dropped. Click on the right arrow to see what the reaction of the financial market was.

FIGURE 4.6 Excel Model Showing The Yield Curve in April 1980.

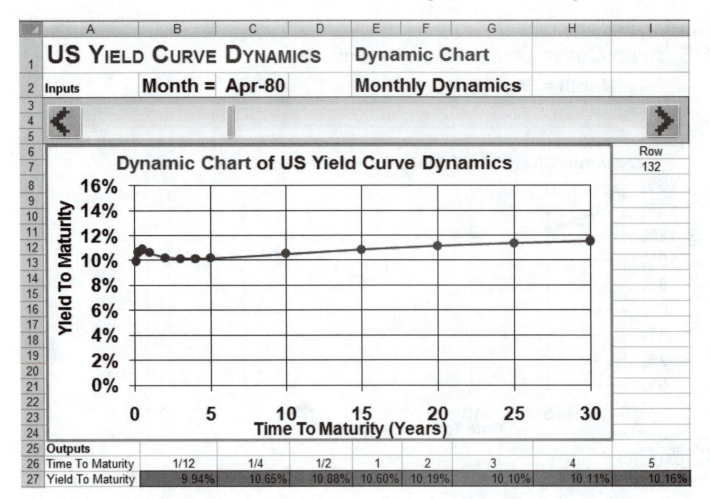

	A	B	C	D	E	F	G	H	I
1	US YIELD CURVE DYNAMICS				Dynamic Chart				
2	Inputs	Month =	Apr-80		Monthly Dynamics				
25	Outputs								
26	Time To Maturity	1/12	1/4	1/2	1	2	3	4	5
27	Yield To Maturity	9.94%	10.65%	10.88%	10.60%	10.19%	10.10%	10.11%	10.16%

Short rates dropped to 10.9%! A drop of 4.6% in one month! The high interest rates went away, but the political damage was done. This is the single biggest one month change in the yield curve in 37 years.

Problems

1. How volatile are short rates versus medium rates versus long rates?

    (a.) Get a visual sense of the answer to this question by clicking on the right arrow of the scroll bar to run through all of the years of US Yield Curve history in the database.

    (b.) Calculate the variance of the time series of: (i) one-month yields, (ii) five-year yields, (iii) fifteen-year yields, and (iv) thirty year yields. Use Excel's VAR function to calculate the variance of the yields in columns **T**, **AA**, **AD**, and **AG**.

2. Determine the relationship between the volatility of the yield curve and the level of the yield curve. Specifically, for each five year time period (70-74,

75-79, 80-84, etc.) calculate the variance and the average level of the time series of: (i) one-month yields, (ii) five-year yields, (iii) fifteen-year yields, and (iv) thirty year yields. Use Excel's VAR and AVERAGE functions to calculate the variance and the average of five-year ranges of the yields in columns **T**, **AA**, **AD**, and **AG**. For example:

o   The 70-74 time series of one-month yields is in the range **T11-T69**.
o   The 75-79 time series of one-month yields is in the range **T70-T129**.
o   The 80-84 time series of one-month yields is in the range **T130-T189**.
o   And so on.

Summarize what you have learned from this analysis.

PART 2 STOCKS / SECURITY ANALYSIS

Chapter 5 Portfolio Optimization

5.1 Two Risky Assets and a Riskfree Asset

Problem. The one-month riskfree rate is 0.40%. Risky Asset 1 has a mean return / month of 1.50% and a standard deviation of 10.00%. Risky Asset 2 has a mean return / month of 0.80% and a standard deviation of 5.0%. The correlation between Risky Asset 1 and 2 is 40.0%. An individual investor with a simple mean and variance utility function has a risk aversion of 2.2. Graph the Risky Opportunity Set, the Optimal Risky Portfolio, the Capital Allocation Line, the investor's Indifference Curve, and the Optimal Complete Portfolio.

Solution Strategy. The two-asset Risky Opportunity Set involves varying the proportion in the first asset and calculating the portfolio's standard deviation and expected return. The Optimal Risky Portfolio is computed using a formula for the optimal proportion in the first asset. The Capital Allocation Line comes from any two weights in the Optimal Risky Portfolio. The Optimal Complete Portfolio is computed from a formula for the utility maximizing standard deviation. Then, the Indifference Curve through the Optimal Complete Portfolio is computed.

FIGURE 5.1 Excel Model of Portfolio Optimization - Two Assets

	A	B	C	D	E
1	PORTFOLIO OPTIMIZATION				Two Risky Assets and a Riskfree Asset
2					
3	Inputs	Display on the Graph			
4	Display on the Graph	○ Risky Opportunity Set ○ + Capital Allocation Line ◉ + Indifference Curve		3	
5		Expected	Standard	Exp Ret	
6		Return/Mon	Deviation	- Riskless	
7		$E(r_i)$	σ_i	$E_i=E(r_i)-r_f$	
8	Riskfree Rate (r_f)	0.40%	0.00%	0.00%	
9	Risky Asset 1	1.50%	10.00%	1.10%	
10	Risky Asset 2	0.80%	5.00%	0.40%	
11	Correlation (ρ)		40.0%		
12	Risk Aversion	2.2			
13		4			
14		15	100		
15		8	50		
16			14		
17		22			

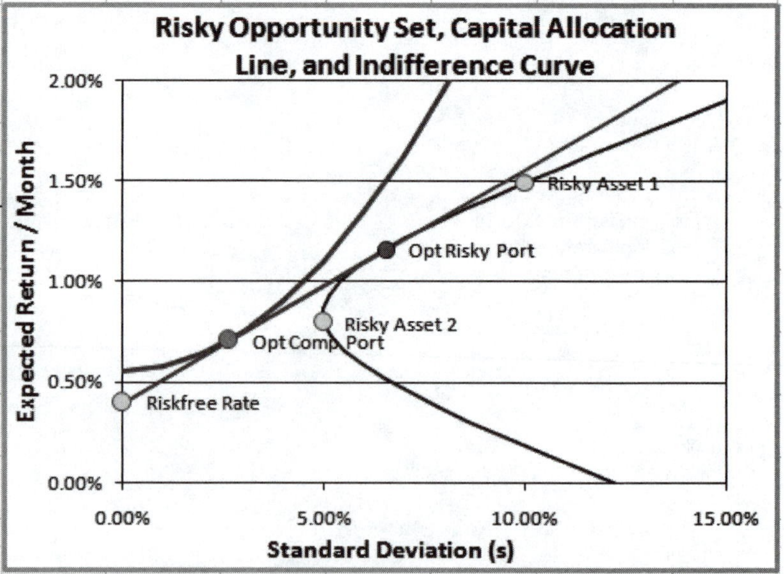

FIGURE 5.2 Excel Model of Portfolio Optimization - Two Assets

	A	B	C	D	E	F	G
19	**Outputs**			Risky Asset	Capital	Utility	Optimal
20		Proportion		Opp Set	Allocation	Indifference	Complete
21		in Risky	(x-axis)	Curve	Line	Curve	Portfolio
22		Asset 1 or	Standard	Expected	Expected	Expected	Expected
23		Opt Risky	Deviation	Ret / Mon	Ret / Mon	Ret / Mon	Ret / Mon
24	Opp Set Curve	-500.0%	46.9%	-2.7%			
25	Opp Set Curve	-150.0%	15.2%	-0.3%			
26	Opp Set Curve	-80.0%	9.3%	0.2%			
27	Opp Set Curve	-70.0%	8.6%	0.3%			
28	Opp Set Curve	-60.0%	7.8%	0.4%			
29	Opp Set Curve	-50.0%	7.2%	0.5%			
30	Opp Set Curve	-40.0%	6.5%	0.5%			
31	Opp Set Curve	-30.0%	6.0%	0.6%			
32	Opp Set Curve	-20.0%	5.5%	0.7%			
33	Opp Set Curve	-10.0%	5.2%	0.7%			
34	Opp Set Curve	0.0%	5.0%	0.8%			
35	Opp Set Curve	10.0%	5.0%	0.9%			
36	Opp Set Curve	20.0%	5.1%	0.9%			
37	Opp Set Curve	30.0%	5.4%	1.0%			
38	Opp Set Curve	40.0%	5.9%	1.1%			
39	Opp Set Curve	50.0%	6.4%	1.2%			
40	Opp Set Curve	60.0%	7.0%	1.2%			
41	Opp Set Curve	70.0%	7.7%	1.3%			
42	Opp Set Curve	80.0%	8.4%	1.4%			
43	Opp Set Curve	90.0%	9.2%	1.4%			
44	Opp Set Curve	100.0%	10.0%	1.5%			
45	Opp Set Curve	110.0%	10.8%	1.6%			
46	Opp Set Curve	120.0%	11.6%	1.6%			
47	Opp Set Curve	250.0%	23.0%	2.6%			
48	Opp Set Curve	750.0%	68.8%	6.1%			
49	Opt Risky Port	52.0%	6.5%		1.2%		
50	Cap Alloc Line	0.0%	0.0%		0.4%		
51	Cap Alloc Line	1000.0%	65.4%		8.0%		
52	Indifference Curve		0.0%			0.56%	
53	Indifference Curve		1.0%			0.58%	
54	Indifference Curve		2.0%			0.64%	
55	Indifference Curve		3.0%			0.75%	
56	Indifference Curve		4.0%			0.91%	
57	Indifference Curve		5.0%			1.11%	
58	Indifference Curve		6.0%			1.35%	
59	Indifference Curve		7.0%			1.63%	
60	Indifference Curve		8.0%			1.96%	
61	Indifference Curve		9.0%			2.34%	
62	Indifference Curve		10.0%			2.76%	
63	Indifference Curve		11.0%			3.22%	
64	Indifference Curve		12.0%			3.72%	
65	Indifference Curve		13.0%			4.27%	
66	Indifference Curve		14.0%			4.87%	
67	Indifference Curve		15.0%			5.51%	
68	Opt Comp Port		2.7%				0.7%
69							
70	Constant Utility Value		0.0056				

(1) The portfolio's standard deviation formula is

$$\sigma = \sqrt{w^2\sigma_1^2 + (1-w)^2\,\sigma_2^2 + 2w(1-w)\rho\sigma_1\sigma_2}$$

Enter =SQRT(B24^2*$C$9^2+(1-B24)^2*$C$10^2
+2*B24*(1-B24)*$C$11*$C$9*$C$10)
and copy to the range C25:C49

(2) The portfolio's expected return formula is

$$E(r) = wE(r_1) + (1-w)E(r_2)$$

Enter =B24*$B$9+(1-B24)*$B$10
and copy to the range D25:D49.
Then **Cut** the cell D49 and **Paste** it to E49.

(3) The optimal proportion in the first asset formula is

$$w_1 = \left(E_1\sigma_2^2 - E_2\rho\sigma_1\sigma_2\right)$$
$$/\left(E_1\sigma_2^2 + E_2\sigma_1^2 - (E_1 + E_2)\rho\sigma_1\sigma_2\right)$$

Enter =(D9*C10^2-D10*C11*C9*C10)
/(D9*C10^2+D10*C9^2-(D9+D10)*C11*C9*C10)

(4) (Portion in Opt Comb) * (Std Dev of Opt Comb)
Enter =B50*$C$49 and copy to cell C51

(5) If Display on Graph > Risky Opportunity Set
Then (Opt Comb Exp Ret) * (Portion in Opt Comb)
+ (Riskfree Rate) * (1 - Portion in Opt Comb)
Else -1
Enter =IF($D$4>1,$E$49*B50+$B$8*(1-B50),-1)
and copy to cell E51

(6) If Display on Graph = + Indifference Curve
Then Constant Utility Value
+ (Risk Aversion) * (Std Dev)^2
Else -1
Enter =IF($D$4=3,$C$70+$B$12*C52^2,-1)
and copy down

(7) (Exp Return of Optimal Risky Port - Riskfree Rate)
/ (2 * Risk Aversion * Std Dev of Opt Risky Port)
Enter =(E49-B8)/(2*B12*C49)

(8) If Display on Graph = + Indifference Curve
Then Riskfree Rate
+ ((Exp Ret of Optimal Risky Port - Riskfree Rate)
/ Std Dev of Optimal Risky Portfolio)
* (Std Dev of Optimal Complete Portfolio)
Else -1
Enter =IF($D$4=3,B8+((E49-B8)/C49)*C68,-1)

(9) Riskfree Rate + (1 / Risk Aversion) *
* ((Exp Ret of Opt Risky Port - Riskfree Rate)
/ (2 * Std Dev of Opt Risky Port))^2
Enter =B8+(1/B12)*((E49-B8)/(2*C49))^2

To focus on the two-asset Risky Opportunity Set, click on the **Risky Opportunity Set** option button. An interesting experiment is to click on the **Correlation** spin button to raise or lower the correlation.

FIGURE 5.3 Two Assets – Correlation of -20.0% and -100.0%

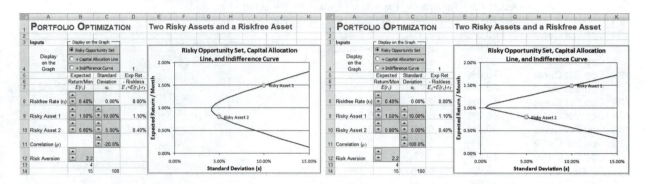

As the correlation is lowered, the Risky Opportunity Set shifts to the left permitting portfolios with lower standard deviations. At the extreme, a correlation of -100% permits a zero standard devivation (i.e., the Risky Opportunity Set should touch the y-axis). The graph would indeed touch y-axis if additional points in the vicinity were graphed.

FIGURE 5.4 Two Assets – Correlation of +70.0% and +100.0%

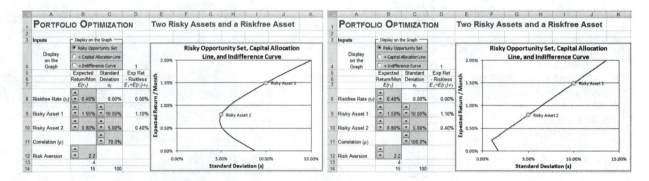

As the correlation is raised, the Risky Opportunity Set shifts to the right. At the other extreme, when the correlation is +100%, then the Risky Opportunity Set is a straight line.

Click on the **+Capital Allocation Line** option button to add the Capital Allocation Line and the Optimal Risky Portfolio. Click on the **+Indifference Curve** option button to add the Indifference Curve and the Optimal Complete Portfolio.

FIGURE 5.5 +Capital Allocation Line and +Indifference Curve

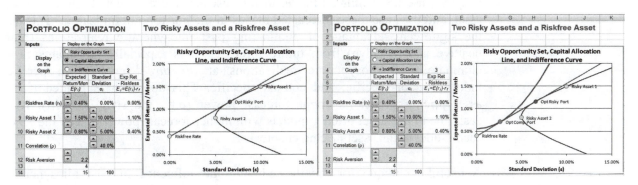

An interesting experiment is to click on the **Risk Aversion** down-arrow spin button to lower the investor's risk aversion.

FIGURE 5.6 Two Assets – Risk Aversion of 1.0 and 0.5

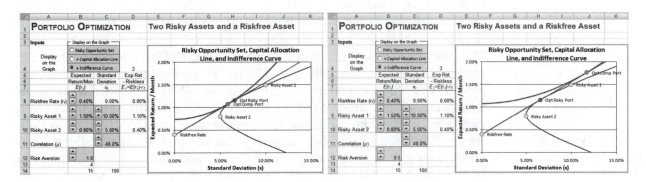

As risk aversion decreases, the Optimal Complete Portfolio slides up the Capital Allocation Line.

5.2 Descriptive Statistics

Mean-variance optimization is a very useful technique that can be used to find the optimal portfolio investment for any number of risky assets and any type of risky asset: stocks, corporate bonds, international bonds, real estate, commodities, etc. The key inputs required are the means, standard deviations, and correlations of the risky assets and the riskfree rate. Of course,these inputs must be estimated from historical data.

One approach to estimating the inputs is to use descriptive statistics. That is, use the sample means, sample standard deviations, and sample correlations. A serious limitation of this approach is that it assumes that past winners will be future winners and past losers will be future losers. Not surprisingly, the portfolio optimizer concludes that you should heavily buy past winners and heavily short-sell past losers. Given strong evidence that future returns are independent of past returns, then chasing past winners is a fruitless strategy.

A better approach is to estimate an asset pricing model (see the asset pricing chapter), use the estimated model to forecast the future expected return of each asset, and then use these forecasted means in the portfolio optimization. This has the significant advantage of eliminating past idiosyncratic realizations (both positive and negative) from future forecasts. It is especially advantageous to eliminate past idiosyncratic realizations at *all three levels*: firm-specific, industry/sector-specific, and country-specific. This approach is limited if the asset pricing model has poor forecast power (e.g., the static CAPM). It is desirable to use asset pricing models with higher forecast power (check the R^2 of each model in the asset pricing chapter).

A useful technique for greatly reducing the influence of past idiosyncratic realizations is to analyze portfolios. Therefore, we will use three asset types: individual stocks, broad U.S. portfolios, and country portfolios. The individual stocks include all idiosyncratic realizations. The broad U.S. portfolios have eliminated firm-specific realizations, but still have industry/sector-specific realizations and U.S.-specific realizations. The country portfolios have eliminated firm-specific realizations and mostly eliminated industry/sector-specific realizations, but each country portfolio still has own-country realizations.

The individual stocks are Barrick, Hanson, IBM, Nokia, Telephonos, and YPF. They were picked using 1996 (pre-sample) information to avoid selection bias. IBM was the highest volume US stock on the NYSE in 1996. The other five firms were the five highest volume foreign stocks cross-listed on the NYSE in 1996 after disallowing additional firms in the same industry. The US portfolios are six Fama-French portfolios formed by size and by book/market. For example, Small-Growth is an equally-weighted portfolio created from all NYSE/AMEX/NASDAQ firms that have both a small market capitalization and a low book value / market value ratio. Similarly, Big-Value is an equally-weighted portfolio of firms that have both a big market capitalization and a high book value / market value ratio. The country portfolios, created by Fama and French, are broadly-diversified portfolios of firms in each country. The six country portfolios are for Australia, Hong Kong, Italy, Japan, Norway, and the US. The monthly returns for all risky assets are computed from prices in US dollars that are adjusted for stock splits and dividends.

Problem. Given monthly returns for stocks, U.S. portfolios, and country portfolios, estimate the means, standard deviations, correlations, and variances/covariances among the risky assets. Given the U.S riskfree rate, compute the mean riskfree rate.

Solution Strategy. Monthly returns for 10 years are provided (see below). Each asset goes down a column. Use TRANSPOSE entered as an Excel matrix to transpose the monthly returns so that each asset goes across a row. This allows convenient computation of the correlation matrix. Specifically, you compute the correlation between one asset going down the column and another asset going across the row. The same approach works for the variance/covariance matrix. Compute the sample descriptive statistics using Excel's AVERAGE, STDEV, CORREL, and COVAR functions.

The starting point is the monthly returns for each asset.

FIGURE 5.7 Excel Model of Portfolio Optimization – Descriptive Statistics

	A	B	C	D	E	F	G	H	I	J
1	**PORTFOLIO OPTIMIZATION**					**Descriptive Statistics**				
2										
3										
4	**Returns**	Stock	Stock	Stock	Stock	Stock	Stock	US Portfolio	US Portfolio	US Portfolio
5	Month	Barrick	Hanson	IBM	Nokia	Telefonos	YPF	Small-Growth	Small-Neutral	Small-Value
6	Dec 2006	-3.50%	-0.24%	2.06%	8.76%	8.63%	0.50%	-0.59%	0.83%	2.08%
7	Nov 2006	-2.37%	4.88%	5.69%	0.51%	9.01%	-0.95%	2.58%	2.66%	3.08%
8	Oct 2006	1.79%	3.78%	-0.12%	1.70%	-1.08%	3.49%	5.87%	5.01%	5.17%
9	Sep 2006	0.92%	-3.49%	12.69%	0.93%	3.14%	7.02%	1.09%	1.11%	0.87%
10	Aug 2006	-8.23%	14.36%	1.20%	-5.68%	6.76%	-3.83%	3.22%	2.74%	2.38%
11	Jul 2006	8.68%	3.72%	5.00%	5.20%	3.02%	2.00%	-5.76%	-2.73%	-1.75%
12	Jun 2006	4.06%	0.88%	0.78%	-2.02%	12.51%	9.98%	-0.65%	0.27%	0.24%
13	May 2006	-3.30%	-0.32%	-3.86%	-5.67%	6.23%	0.03%	-7.71%	-4.48%	-4.00%
14	Apr 2006	0.80%	-8.40%	-2.61%	-5.23%	-9.99%	-17.69%	-0.80%	0.94%	1.51%
15	Mar 2006	11.90%	3.92%	-0.16%	9.38%	-2.17%	-3.07%	4.08%	5.49%	4.95%
16	Feb 2006	-0.48%	7.12%	2.78%	13.88%	1.21%	-2.81%	-0.42%	-0.36%	-0.65%
17	Jan 2006	-13.00%	5.15%	-1.05%	1.08%	-5.72%	0.89%	8.59%	9.37%	7.61%

For computational convenience, transpose the monthly returns.

FIGURE 5.8 Excel Model of Portfolio Optimization – Descriptive Statistics

	AB	AC	AD	AE	AF	AG
1		(1) TRANSPOSE(Monthly Returns Matrix) - enter as an				
2		Excel matrix (i.e., using Shift-Control-Enter) Select the range AB5:ES24				
3		Type =TRANSPOSE(A4:T125)				
4		Hold down the Shift and Control buttons and then press Enter				
5	**Returns**	Month	Dec 2006	Nov 2006	Oct 2006	Sep 2006
6	Stock	Barrick	-3.50%	-2.37%	1.79%	0.92%
7	Stock	Hanson	-0.24%	4.88%	3.78%	-3.49%
8	Stock	IBM	2.06%	5.69%	-0.12%	12.69%
9	Stock	Nokia	8.76%	0.51%	1.70%	0.93%
10	Stock	Telefonos	8.63%	9.01%	-1.08%	3.14%
11	Stock	YPF	0.50%	-0.95%	3.49%	7.02%
12	US Portfolio	Small-Growth	-0.59%	2.58%	5.87%	1.09%
13	US Portfolio	Small-Neutral	0.83%	2.66%	5.01%	1.11%
14	US Portfolio	Small-Value	2.08%	3.08%	5.17%	0.87%
15	US Portfolio	Big-Growth	0.43%	1.42%	3.14%	2.69%
16	US Portfolio	Big-Neutral	1.79%	2.83%	3.08%	2.16%
17	US Portfolio	Big-Value	2.79%	1.94%	4.78%	1.86%
18	Country Port	Australia	3.59%	3.38%	8.65%	-1.53%
19	Country Port	Hong Kong	6.23%	6.04%	1.10%	0.79%
20	Country Port	Italy	2.72%	5.74%	4.27%	0.67%
21	Country Port	Japan	2.40%	0.45%	1.94%	-1.88%
22	Country Port	Norway	5.39%	8.90%	8.84%	-7.52%
23	Country Port	US	1.08%	2.37%	3.71%	1.95%
24	US Riskfree	US Riskfree	0.40%	0.42%	0.41%	0.41%

Compute the sample average and sample standard deviation. Columns W to Y contain the forecasted expected return based on various asset pricing models (Static CAPM, Fama-French 3 Factor, and Macro 3 Factor). See the Asset Pricing chapter for details on how these forecasts were made.

FIGURE 5.9 Excel Model of Portfolio Optimization – Descriptive Statistics

	T	U	V	W	X	Y	Z
1	(2) Average(Monthly Returns for Asset i) Enter =AVERAGE(AD6:ES6) and copy down				Second Pass	Second Pass	
2				Second Pass	Fama-French	Macro	
3			Average	Static CAPM	3 Factor	3 Factor	
4	US Riskfree		Past	Expected	Expected	Expected	Standard
5	US Riskfree		Return	Return	Return	Return	Deviation
6	0.40%		0.70%	1.93%	2.07%	1.70%	10.31%
7	0.42%		1.17%	2.03%	2.37%	2.11%	10.00%
8	0.41%		1.26%	1.36%	0.72%	1.55%	9.39%
9	0.41%		2.44%	0.55%	1.99%	2.01%	13.74%
10	0.42%		2.08%	2.00%	1.71%	1.77%	9.09%
11	0.40%		1.56%	3.00%	3.88%	1.41%	10.34%
12	0.40%		0.71%	0.89%	0.56%	-1.07%	8.03%
13	0.43%		1.39%	1.28%	1.40%	1.32%	5.22%
14	0.36%		1.54%	1.31%	1.14%	-0.05%	5.03%
15	0.37%		0.72%	1.19%	0.75%	0.32%	4.83%
16	0.34%		1.01%	1.37%	0.94%	1.14%	4.36%
17	0.35%		0.99%	1.39%	1.91%	1.30%	4.39%
18	0.32%		1.15%	1.82%	1.99%	1.71%	5.00%
19	0.31%		0.79%	1.87%	2.20%	2.45%	7.83%
20	0.27%		1.36%	1.87%	1.76%	2.95%	6.33%
21	0.29%		0.42%	1.79%	1.73%	1.19%	5.91%
22	0.30%		1.40%	1.89%	2.87%	2.41%	6.78%
23	0.24%		0.82%	1.88%	1.57%	1.50%	4.60%
24	0.23%		0.30%				
25	0.24%			(3) Standard Deviation(Monthly Returns of Asset i) Enter =STDEV(AD6:ES6) and copy down			
26	0.21%						
27	0.21%						

FIGURE 5.10 Excel Model of Portfolio Optimization – Descriptive Statistics

	AB	AC	AD	AE	AF	AG	AH	AI
27				(4) CORREL(Returns for asset i, Returns for asset j)				
28				Enter =CORREL(B$6:B$125,$AD6:$ES6)				
29				and copy to the range AD33:AU50				
30								
31			Stock	Stock	Stock	Stock	Stock	Stock
32		**Correlations**	Barrick	Hanson	IBM	Nokia	Telefonos	YPF
33	Stock	Barrick	100.00%	26.80%	7.76%	11.99%	23.62%	28.47%
34	Stock	Hanson	26.80%	100.00%	19.97%	20.24%	19.26%	22.87%
35	Stock	IBM	7.76%	19.97%	100.00%	41.77%	38.50%	31.25%
36	Stock	Nokia	11.99%	20.24%	41.77%	100.00%	37.28%	20.37%
37	Stock	Telefonos	23.62%	19.26%	38.50%	37.28%	100.00%	38.68%
38	Stock	YPF	28.47%	22.87%	31.25%	20.37%	38.68%	100.00%
39	US Portfolio	Small-Growth	-17.34%	-10.62%	-1.62%	-8.86%	-0.10%	0.74%
40	US Portfolio	Small-Neutral	-16.18%	-7.91%	-3.39%	-16.26%	-6.74%	-7.56%
41	US Portfolio	Small-Value	-13.29%	-8.21%	-7.92%	-22.89%	-11.92%	-12.84%
42	US Portfolio	Big-Growth	-10.39%	-7.88%	-6.69%	-9.30%	-7.26%	9.46%
43	US Portfolio	Big-Neutral	-9.57%	-7.27%	-6.84%	-19.65%	-13.05%	-2.87%
44	US Portfolio	Big-Value	-3.58%	-4.78%	-11.95%	-13.16%	-10.45%	-1.66%
45	Country Port	Australia	-17.22%	5.20%	-8.09%	-15.02%	-14.71%	2.11%
46	Country Port	Hong Kong	3.57%	5.45%	6.31%	-13.11%	-2.42%	5.80%
47	Country Port	Italy	-2.93%	-8.35%	-11.36%	-8.29%	-18.51%	2.66%
48	Country Port	Japan	-18.33%	11.57%	-7.60%	-3.68%	-12.44%	1.91%
49	Country Port	Norway	-14.86%	-11.19%	-13.31%	-26.69%	-23.19%	-8.96%
50	Country Port	US	-13.43%	-9.18%	-6.22%	-13.49%	-8.30%	5.26%

FIGURE 5.11 Excel Model of Portfolio Optimization – Descriptive Statistics

	AB	AC	AD	AE	AF	AG	AH	AI
53								
54			(5) COVAR(Returns for asset i, Returns for asset j)					
55			Enter =COVAR(B$6:B$125,$AD6:$ES6)					
56			and copy to the range AD59:AU76					
57			Stock	Stock	Stock	Stock	Stock	Stock
58		**Covariances**	Barrick	Hanson	IBM	Nokia	Telefonos	YPF
59	Stock	Barrick	1.05%	0.27%	0.07%	0.17%	0.22%	0.30%
60	Stock	Hanson	0.27%	0.99%	0.19%	0.28%	0.17%	0.23%
61	Stock	IBM	0.07%	0.19%	0.87%	0.53%	0.33%	0.30%
62	Stock	Nokia	0.17%	0.28%	0.53%	1.87%	0.46%	0.29%
63	Stock	Telefonos	0.22%	0.17%	0.33%	0.46%	0.82%	0.36%
64	Stock	YPF	0.30%	0.23%	0.30%	0.29%	0.36%	1.06%
65	US Portfolio	Small-Growth	-0.14%	-0.08%	-0.01%	-0.10%	0.00%	0.01%
66	US Portfolio	Small-Neutral	-0.09%	-0.04%	-0.02%	-0.12%	-0.03%	-0.04%
67	US Portfolio	Small-Value	-0.07%	-0.04%	-0.04%	-0.16%	-0.05%	-0.07%
68	US Portfolio	Big-Growth	-0.05%	-0.04%	-0.03%	-0.06%	-0.03%	0.05%
69	US Portfolio	Big-Neutral	-0.04%	-0.03%	-0.03%	-0.12%	-0.05%	-0.01%
70	US Portfolio	Big-Value	-0.02%	-0.02%	-0.05%	-0.08%	-0.04%	-0.01%
71	Country Port	Australia	-0.09%	0.03%	-0.04%	-0.10%	-0.07%	0.01%
72	Country Port	Hong Kong	0.03%	0.04%	0.05%	-0.14%	-0.02%	0.05%
73	Country Port	Italy	-0.02%	-0.05%	-0.07%	-0.07%	-0.11%	0.02%
74	Country Port	Japan	-0.11%	0.07%	-0.04%	-0.03%	-0.07%	0.01%
75	Country Port	Norway	-0.10%	-0.08%	-0.08%	-0.25%	-0.14%	-0.06%
76	Country Port	US	-0.06%	-0.04%	-0.03%	-0.08%	-0.03%	0.02%

5.3 Many Risky Assets and a Riskfree Asset

Problem. An individual investor with a simple mean and variance utility function has a risk aversion of 2.8. This investor is considering investing in the given individual stocks, US portfolios, or country portfolios. This investor considers four methods to forecast expected returns: average past return, Static CAPM, Fama-French 3 Factor, or Macro 3 Factor. Determine the Portfolio Weights of the Optimal Risky Portfolio and the Optimal Complete Portfolio.

Solution Strategy. To compute the many-asset Risky Opportunity Set, vary the portfolio expected return from 0.00% to 3.00% in increments of 0.10%. Then compute the corresponding portfolio's standard deviation on the Risky Opportunity Set using the analytic formula. The Optimal Risky Portfolio is computed using a many-asset formula. The Capital Allocation Line comes from any two weights in the Optimal Risky Portfolio. The Optimal Complete Portfolio is computed from a many-asset formula for utility maximization. Then, the Indifference Curve through the Optimal Complete Portfolio is computed.

FIGURE 5.12 Excel Model of Portfolio Optimization - Many Assets

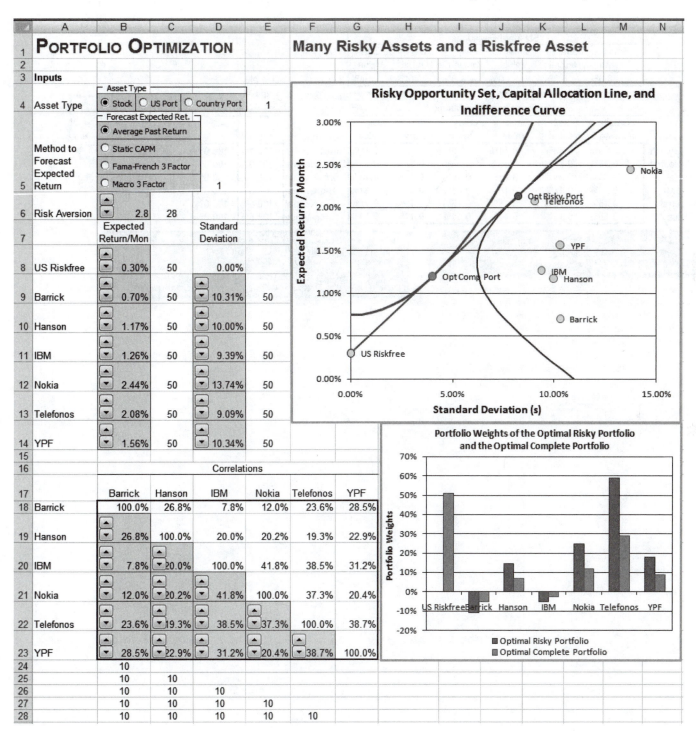

FIGURE 5.13 Excel Model of Portfolio Optimization - Many Assets

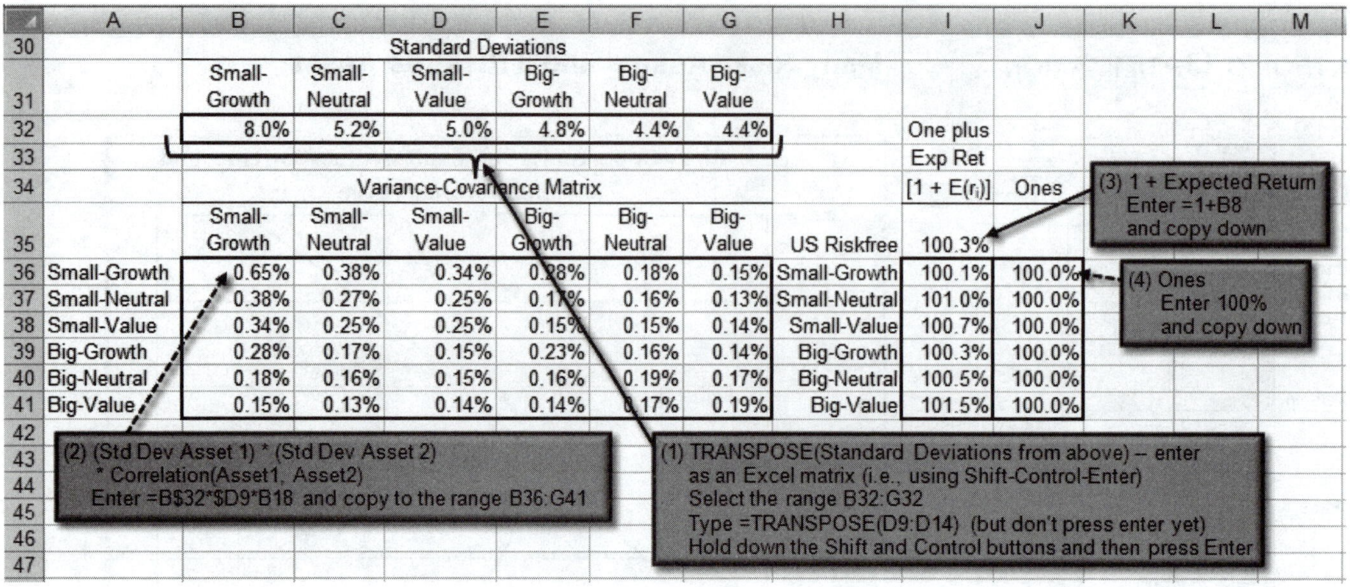

	A	B	C	D	E	F	G	H	I	J	K	L	M
30				Standard Deviations									
31		Small-Growth	Small-Neutral	Small-Value	Big-Growth	Big-Neutral	Big-Value		One plus				
32		8.0%	5.2%	5.0%	4.8%	4.4%	4.4%		Exp Ret				
33									Exp Ret				
34				Variance-Covariance Matrix					[1 + E(r$_i$)]	Ones			
35		Small-Growth	Small-Neutral	Small-Value	Big-Growth	Big-Neutral	Big-Value	US Riskfree	100.3%				
36	Small-Growth	0.65%	0.38%	0.34%	0.28%	0.18%	0.15%	Small-Growth	100.1%	100.0%			
37	Small-Neutral	0.38%	0.27%	0.25%	0.17%	0.16%	0.13%	Small-Neutral	101.0%	100.0%			
38	Small-Value	0.34%	0.25%	0.25%	0.15%	0.15%	0.14%	Small-Value	100.7%	100.0%			
39	Big-Growth	0.28%	0.17%	0.15%	0.23%	0.16%	0.14%	Big-Growth	100.3%	100.0%			
40	Big-Neutral	0.18%	0.16%	0.15%	0.16%	0.19%	0.17%	Big-Neutral	100.5%	100.0%			
41	Big-Value	0.15%	0.13%	0.14%	0.14%	0.17%	0.19%	Big-Value	101.5%	100.0%			
42													
43													
44													
45													
46													
47													

(3) 1 + Expected Return
Enter =1+B8
and copy down

(4) Ones
Enter 100%
and copy down

(2) (Std Dev Asset 1) * (Std Dev Asset 2)
    * Correlation(Asset1, Asset2)
    Enter =B$32*$D9*B18 and copy to the range B36:G41

(1) TRANSPOSE(Standard Deviations from above) – enter
    as an Excel matrix (i.e., using Shift-Control-Enter)
    Select the range B32:G32
    Type =TRANSPOSE(D9:D14) (but don't press enter yet)
    Hold down the Shift and Control buttons and then press Enter

FIGURE 5.14 Excel Model Details of Portfolio Optimization - Many Assets.

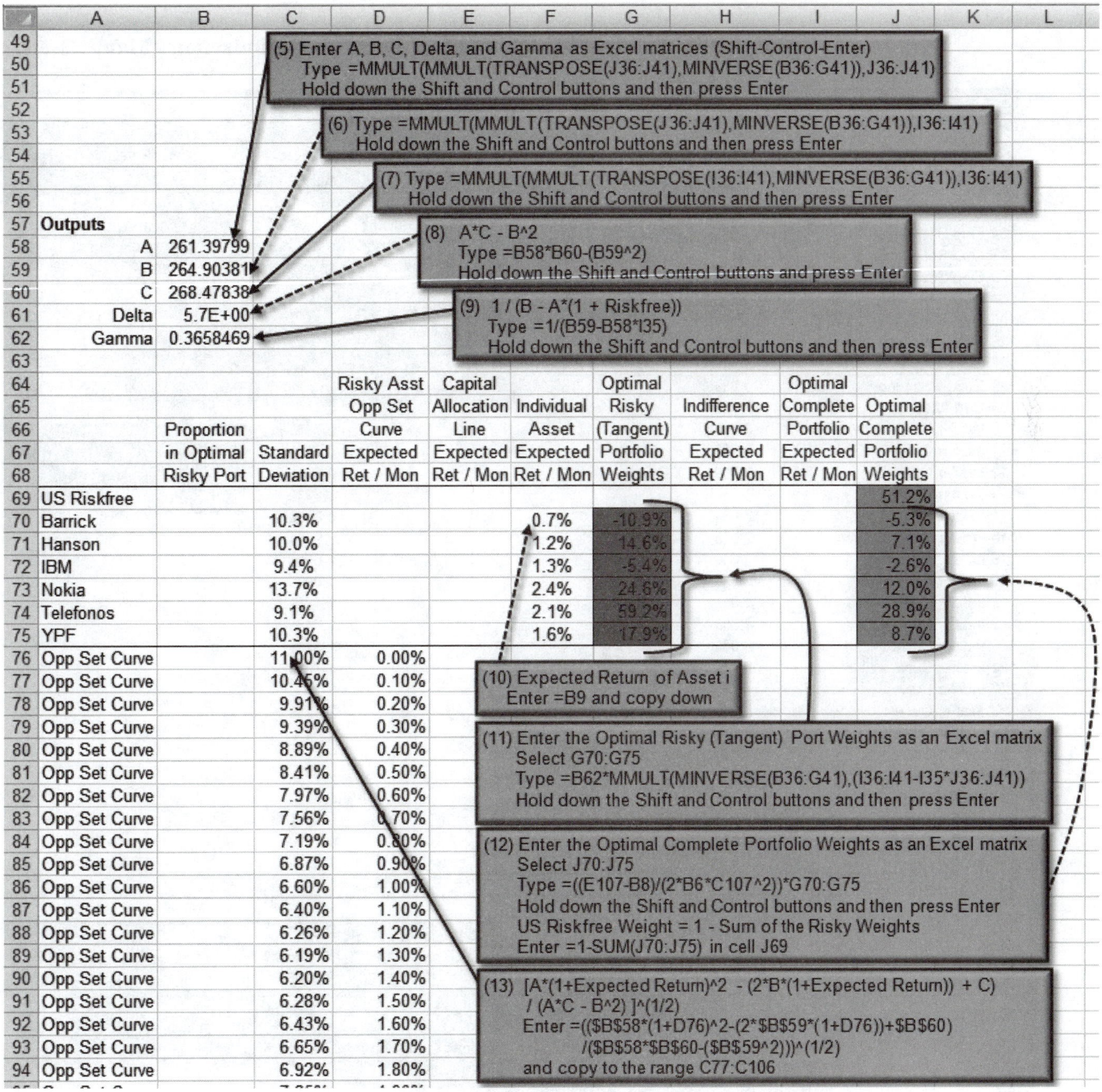

	A	B	C	D	E	F	G	H	I	J	K	L
49				(5) Enter A, B, C, Delta, and Gamma as Excel matrices (Shift-Control-Enter)							
50				Type =MMULT(MMULT(TRANSPOSE(J36:J41),MINVERSE(B36:G41)),J36:J41)							
51				Hold down the Shift and Control buttons and then press Enter							
52											
53				(6) Type =MMULT(MMULT(TRANSPOSE(J36:J41),MINVERSE(B36:G41)),I36:I41)							
54				Hold down the Shift and Control buttons and then press Enter							
55				(7) Type =MMULT(MMULT(TRANSPOSE(I36:I41),MINVERSE(B36:G41)),I36:I41)							
56				Hold down the Shift and Control buttons and then press Enter							
57	**Outputs**										
58	A	261.39799		(8) A*C - B^2							
59	B	264.90381		Type =B58*B60-(B59^2)							
60	C	268.47838		Hold down the Shift and Control buttons and press Enter							
61	Delta	5.7E+00		(9) 1 / (B - A*(1 + Riskfree))							
62	Gamma	0.3658469		Type =1/(B59-B58*I35)							
63				Hold down the Shift and Control buttons and then press Enter							
64				Risky Asst	Capital		Optimal		Optimal		
65				Opp Set	Allocation	Individual	Risky	Indifference	Complete	Optimal	
66		Proportion		Curve	Line	Asset	(Tangent)	Curve	Portfolio	Complete	
67		in Optimal	Standard	Expected	Expected	Expected	Portfolio	Expected	Expected	Portfolio	
68		Risky Port	Deviation	Ret / Mon	Ret / Mon	Ret / Mon	Weights	Ret / Mon	Ret / Mon	Weights	
69	US Riskfree									51.2%	
70	Barrick		10.3%			0.7%	-10.9%			-5.3%	
71	Hanson		10.0%			1.2%	14.6%			7.1%	
72	IBM		9.4%			1.3%	-5.4%			-2.6%	
73	Nokia		13.7%			2.4%	24.6%			12.0%	
74	Telefonos		9.1%			2.1%	59.2%			28.9%	
75	YPF		10.3%			1.6%	17.9%			8.7%	
76	Opp Set Curve		11.00%	0.00%							
77	Opp Set Curve		10.45%	0.10%	(10) Expected Return of Asset i						
78	Opp Set Curve		9.91%	0.20%	Enter =B9 and copy down						
79	Opp Set Curve		9.39%	0.30%	(11) Enter the Optimal Risky (Tangent) Port Weights as an Excel matrix						
80	Opp Set Curve		8.89%	0.40%	Select G70:G75						
81	Opp Set Curve		8.41%	0.50%	Type =B62*MMULT(MINVERSE(B36:G41),(I36:I41-I35*J36:J41))						
82	Opp Set Curve		7.97%	0.60%	Hold down the Shift and Control buttons and then press Enter						
83	Opp Set Curve		7.56%	0.70%							
84	Opp Set Curve		7.19%	0.80%	(12) Enter the Optimal Complete Portfolio Weights as an Excel matrix						
85	Opp Set Curve		6.87%	0.90%	Select J70:J75						
86	Opp Set Curve		6.60%	1.00%	Type =((E107-B8)/(2*B6*C107^2))*G70:G75						
87	Opp Set Curve		6.40%	1.10%	Hold down the Shift and Control buttons and then press Enter						
88	Opp Set Curve		6.26%	1.20%	US Riskfree Weight = 1 - Sum of the Risky Weights						
89	Opp Set Curve		6.19%	1.30%	Enter =1-SUM(J70:J75) in cell J69						
90	Opp Set Curve		6.20%	1.40%	(13) [A*(1+Expected Return)^2 - (2*B*(1+Expected Return)) + C]						
91	Opp Set Curve		6.28%	1.50%	/ (A*C - B^2)]^(1/2)						
92	Opp Set Curve		6.43%	1.60%	Enter =((\$B\$58*(1+D76)^2-(2*\$B\$59*(1+D76))+\$B\$60)						
93	Opp Set Curve		6.65%	1.70%	/(\$B\$58*\$B\$60-(\$B\$59^2)))^(1/2)						
94	Opp Set Curve		6.92%	1.80%	and copy to the range C77:C106						

Hyperbola Coefficients. In a Mean vs. Standard Deviation graph, the Risky Opportunity Set is a hyperbola. The exact location of the hyperbola is uniquely determined by three coefficients, usually called A, B, and C. The derivation of the formulas can be found in Merton (1972).[4]

FIGURE 5.15 Excel Model Details of Portfolio Optimization - Many Assets.

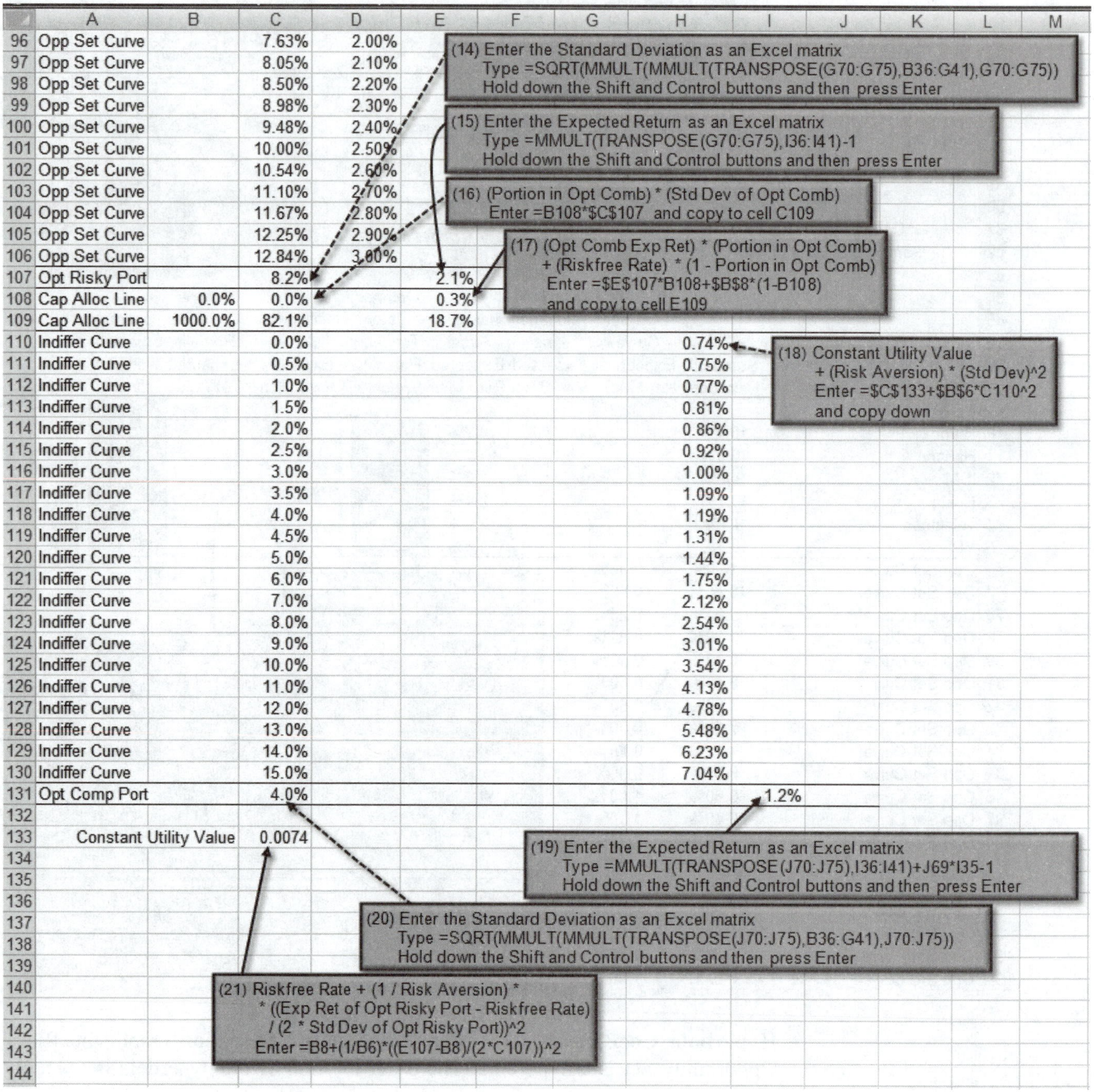

	A	B	C	D	E	F	G	H	I	J	K	L	M
96	Opp Set Curve		7.63%	2.00%									
97	Opp Set Curve		8.05%	2.10%									
98	Opp Set Curve		8.50%	2.20%									
99	Opp Set Curve		8.98%	2.30%									
100	Opp Set Curve		9.48%	2.40%									
101	Opp Set Curve		10.00%	2.50%									
102	Opp Set Curve		10.54%	2.60%									
103	Opp Set Curve		11.10%	2.70%									
104	Opp Set Curve		11.67%	2.80%									
105	Opp Set Curve		12.25%	2.90%									
106	Opp Set Curve		12.84%	3.00%									
107	Opt Risky Port		8.2%		2.1%								
108	Cap Alloc Line	0.0%	0.0%		0.3%								
109	Cap Alloc Line	1000.0%	82.1%		18.7%								
110	Indiffer Curve		0.0%					0.74%					
111	Indiffer Curve		0.5%					0.75%					
112	Indiffer Curve		1.0%					0.77%					
113	Indiffer Curve		1.5%					0.81%					
114	Indiffer Curve		2.0%					0.86%					
115	Indiffer Curve		2.5%					0.92%					
116	Indiffer Curve		3.0%					1.00%					
117	Indiffer Curve		3.5%					1.09%					
118	Indiffer Curve		4.0%					1.19%					
119	Indiffer Curve		4.5%					1.31%					
120	Indiffer Curve		5.0%					1.44%					
121	Indiffer Curve		6.0%					1.75%					
122	Indiffer Curve		7.0%					2.12%					
123	Indiffer Curve		8.0%					2.54%					
124	Indiffer Curve		9.0%					3.01%					
125	Indiffer Curve		10.0%					3.54%					
126	Indiffer Curve		11.0%					4.13%					
127	Indiffer Curve		12.0%					4.78%					
128	Indiffer Curve		13.0%					5.48%					
129	Indiffer Curve		14.0%					6.23%					
130	Indiffer Curve		15.0%					7.04%					
131	Opt Comp Port		4.0%							1.2%			
132													
133	Constant Utility Value		0.0074										
134													

Callout boxes in figure:

(14) Enter the Standard Deviation as an Excel matrix
Type =SQRT(MMULT(MMULT(TRANSPOSE(G70:G75),B36:G41),G70:G75))
Hold down the Shift and Control buttons and then press Enter

(15) Enter the Expected Return as an Excel matrix
Type =MMULT(TRANSPOSE(G70:G75),I36:I41)-1
Hold down the Shift and Control buttons and then press Enter

(16) (Portion in Opt Comb) * (Std Dev of Opt Comb)
Enter =B108*$C$107 and copy to cell C109

(17) (Opt Comb Exp Ret) * (Portion in Opt Comb)
+ (Riskfree Rate) * (1 - Portion in Opt Comb)
Enter =$E$107*B108+$B$8*(1-B108)
and copy to cell E109

(18) Constant Utility Value
+ (Risk Aversion) * (Std Dev)^2
Enter =$C$133+$B$6*C110^2
and copy down

(19) Enter the Expected Return as an Excel matrix
Type =MMULT(TRANSPOSE(J70:J75),I36:I41)+J69*I35-1
Hold down the Shift and Control buttons and then press Enter

(20) Enter the Standard Deviation as an Excel matrix
Type =SQRT(MMULT(MMULT(TRANSPOSE(J70:J75),B36:G41),J70:J75))
Hold down the Shift and Control buttons and then press Enter

(21) Riskfree Rate + (1 / Risk Aversion) *
* ((Exp Ret of Opt Risky Port - Riskfree Rate)
/ (2 * Std Dev of Opt Risky Port))^2
Enter =B8+(1/B6)*((E107-B8)/(2*C107))^2

---

[4] See Robert C. Merton, "An Analytic Derivation of the Efficient Portfolio Frontier," *Journal of Financial and Quantitative Analysis*, September 1972, pp. 1851-72. His article uses slightly different notation.

The graphs show several interesting things. First, click on **Stocks** and click on various option buttons for the **Method to Forecast Expected Return**.

FIGURE 5.16 Average Past Returns and Static CAPM

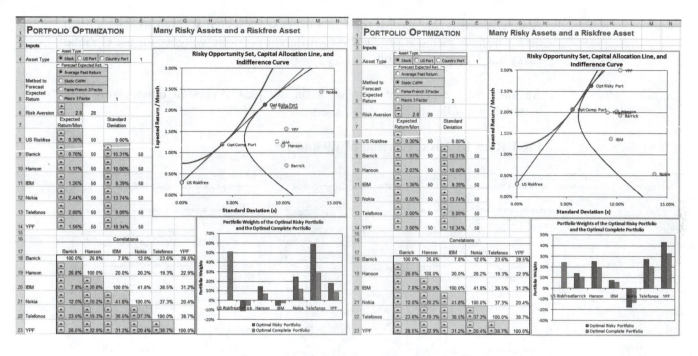

FIGURE 5.17 Fama-French 3 Factor and Macro 3 Factor

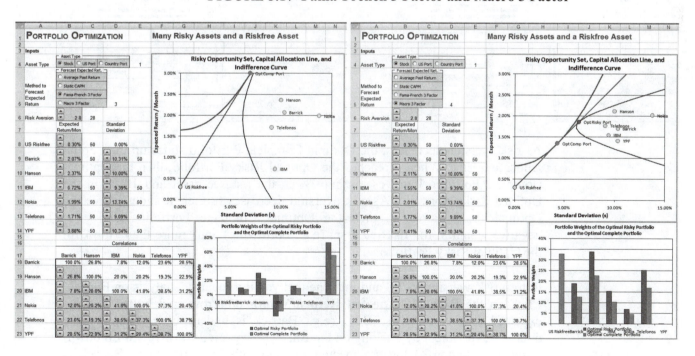

Barrick had a low average return from 1997 – 2006 (0.70%/month), so the Average Past Return method results in a negative portfolio weight on Barrick in the Optimal Risky and Complete Portfolios. However, the three methods based on asset pricing models forecast much higher returns for Barrick ranging from

1.20%/month to 2.07%/month. Hence all three asset pricing based methods result in positive portfolio weights on Barrick in the Optimal Risky and Complete Portfolios. This demonstrates that asset pricing based methods eliminate firm-specific past realizations, which are not generally predictive of future returns.

Another point is that the **Method to Forecast Expected Return** matters a great deal. The four methods produce very different portfolio weights for the Optimal Risky and Complete Portfolios.

An interesting experiment is to click on the **Risk Aversion** down-arrow spin button to lower the investor's risk aversion.

FIGURE 5.18 Risk Aversion of 1.9 and 1.3

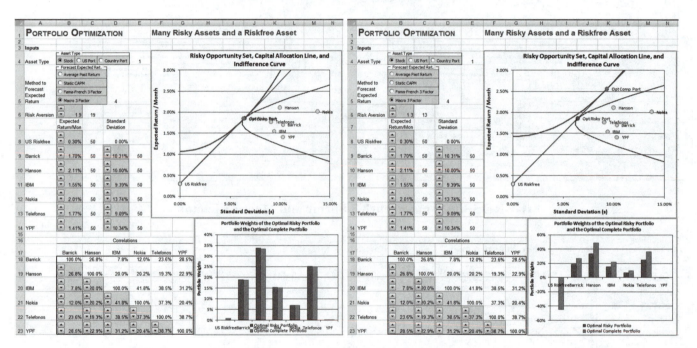

As risk aversion decreases, the Optimal Complete Portfolio slides up the Capital Allocation Line. When it reaches the Optimal Risky Portfolio, then the Optimal Complete Portfolio involves putting 0% in the riskfree asset and 100% in the Optimal Risky Portfolio. As risk aversion decreases further, it slides above the Optimal Risky Portfolio, then the Optimal Complete Portfolio involves a negative weigh in the riskfree asset (e.g., borrowing) and "more than 100%" in the Optimal Risky Portfolio.

Return risk aversion to 2.8 and imagine that you did security analysis on Barrick. Click on the **Barrick Expected Return/Month** up-arrow spin button to raise expected return/month to 2.30% (e.g., Barrick is underpriced). Then try the opposite experiment by clicking on the **Barrick Expected Return/Month** down-arrow spin button to lower expected return/month to 2.30% (e.g., Barrick is overpriced).

FIGURE 5.19 Barrick Expected Return/Month of 2.60% and 0.90%

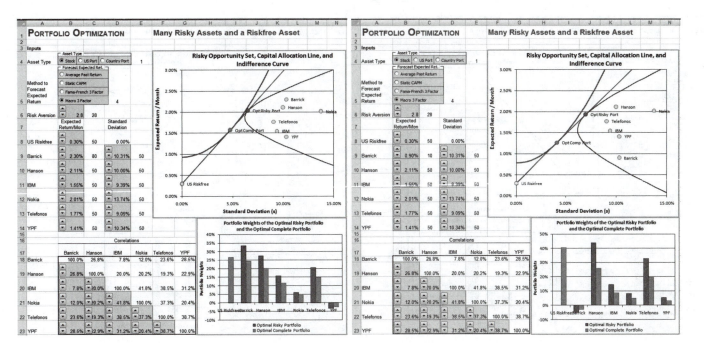

When Barrick's Expected Return/Month increases to 2.60%, the Optimal Risky Portfolio weight in Barrick rises dramatically (to 33.4%) to exploit this higher return. But also notice that the Optimal Risky Portfolio does NOT put 100% in Barrick even though it has the highest expected return of all assets considered. The Optimal Risky Portfolio maintains an investment in all five risk assets in order lower the portfolio standard deviation by diversification. Thus, the Optimal Risky Portfolio is always a trade-off between putting a higher weight in assets with higher returns vs. spreading out the investment to lower portfolio risk.

When Barrick's Expected Return/Month decreases to 0.90%, the Optimal Risky Portfolio weight in Barrick declines so far that it even goes negative (to -5.0%) to exploit this low return. A negative portfolio weight means short-selling. Putting a -5.0% in low return asset raises the overall portfolio return by allowing 105% to be invested in high return assets.

Return Barrick's Expected Return/Month to 1.70% and consider changes in Standard Deviation. Click on the **IBM Standard Deviation** down-arrow spin button to lower the standard deviation to 5.39%. Then try the opposite experiment by clicking on the **IBM Standard Deviation** up-arrow spin button to raise the standard deviation to 12.39%.

FIGURE 5.20 IBM Standard Deviation of 5.39% and 12.39%

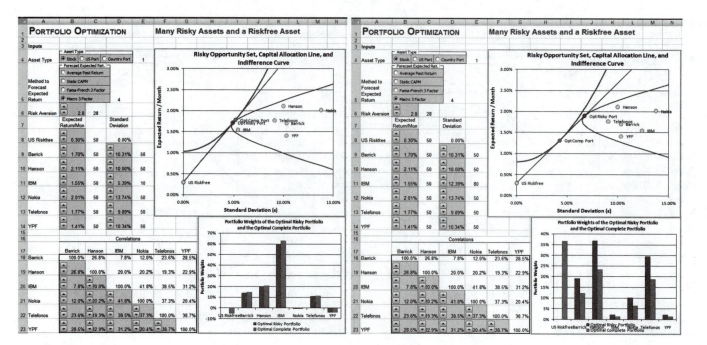

When IBM's Standard Deviation falls to 5.39%, the Optimal Risky Portfolio weight in IBM rises dramatically (to 59.9%) to exploit this low risk. But also notice that the Optimal Risky Portfolio does NOT put 100% in IBM even though it has the lowest standard deviation. It still pays to maintain some investment in all five risk assets in order lower the portfolio standard deviation by diversification. When IBM's Standard Deviation rises to 12.39%, the Optimal Risky Portfolio weight in IBM falls dramatically (to 2.2%) to avoid this high risk.

Return IBM's Standard Deviation to 9.39% and consider changes in Correlation. Click on the **Barrick/Telefonos Correlation** down-arrow spin button (in cell B22) to lower the correlation to -36.4%. Then try the opposite experiment by clicking on the **Barrick/Telefonos Correlation** up-arrow spin button to raise the correlation to 63.6%.

FIGURE 5.21 Barrick/Telefonos Correlation of -36.4% and 63.6%

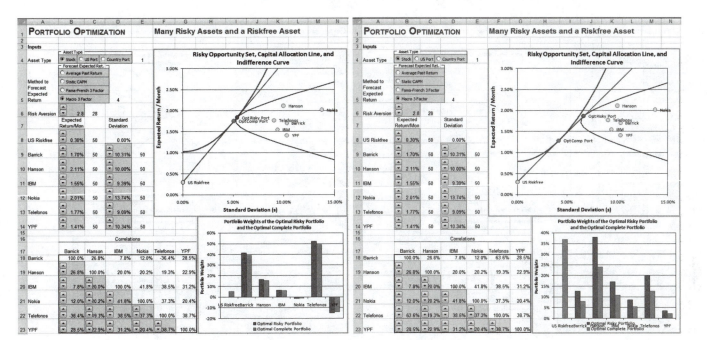

When Barrick/Telefonos' Correlation falls to -36.4%, the Optimal Risky Portfolio weight in both Barrick and Telefonos rises dramatically (Barrick to 41.4% and Telefonos to 52.1) to exploit this low correlation. When Barrick/Telefonos' Correlation rises to -63.6%, the Optimal Risky Portfolio weight in both Barrick and Telefonos falls dramatically (Barrick to 12.7% and Telefonos to 20.1) to avoid this high correlation.

Return Barrick/Telefonos' Correlation to 23.6% and consider changes in the Riskfree Rate. Click on the **US Riskfree Expected Return/Month** up-arrow spin button to raise the Riskfree Rate to 1.10%. Then try the opposite experiment by clicking on the **US Riskfree Expected Return/Month** down-arrow spin button to lower the Riskfree Rate to 0.02%.

FIGURE 5.22 US Riskfree Rate of 1.10% and 0.02%

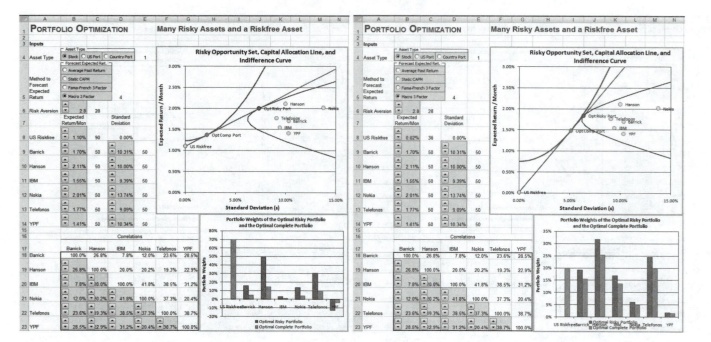

When the US Riskfree Rate increases to 1.10%, the Risky Opportunity Set (the blue curve) stays the same and Capital Allocation Line (the red line) slides up it, such that the Optimal Risky Portfolio (the purple dot) slides up the Risky Opportunity Set. This higher position means that Optimal Risky Portfolio increases the weights on high expected return assets like Hanson. When the US Riskfree Rate decreases to 0.02%, Capital Allocation Line slides down the Risky Opportunity Set, such that the Optimal Risky Portfolio slides down the Risky Opportunity Set. This lower position means that Optimal Risky Portfolio spreads its weights more evenly across all five assets.

Return the US Riskfree Rate to 0.30% and consider portfolios. Click on **Fama-French 3 Factor** and click on **US Port.** Next, click on **Country Port.**

FIGURE 5.23 US Portfolios and Country Portfolios

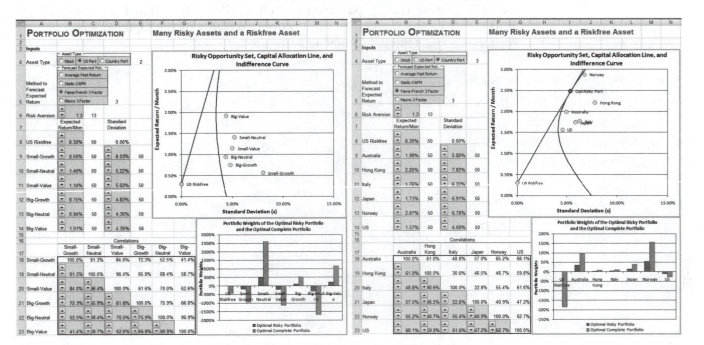

Notice that the Risky Opportunity Set shifts far to the left. This is because the standard deviations for US Portfolios and County Portfolios are much smaller than Individual Stocks. Roughly, the portfolio standard deviations are half as big as the individual stock standard deviations. This demonstrates the impact of portfolio diversification in eliminating firm-specific risk.

Again, using portfolios matters a great deal. The US Portfolios and County Portfolios produce very different portfolio weights for the Optimal Risky and Complete Portfolios than the Individual Stocks.

Problems

1. The one-month riskfree rate is 0.23%. Risky Asset 1 has a mean return / month of 2.10% and a standard deviation of 13.00%. Risky Asset 2 has a mean return / month of 1.30% and a standard deviation of 8.0%. The correlation between Risky Asset 1 and 2 is 20.0%. An individual investor with a simple mean and variance utility function has a risk aversion of 2.0. Graph the Risky Opportunity Set, the Optimal Risky Portfolio, the Capital Allocation Line, the investor's Indifference Curve, and the Optimal Complete Portfolio.

2. Download 10 years of monthly returns for stocks, U.S. portfolios, or country portfolios of your choice and estimate the means, standard deviations, correlations, and variances/covariances among the risky assets. Download 10 years of the U.S riskfree rate, compute the mean riskfree rate.

3. An individual investor with a simple mean and variance utility function has a risk aversion of 1.5. This investor is considering investing in the assets you

downloaded for problem 2. This investor considers four methods to forecast expected returns: average past return, Static CAPM, Fama-French 3 Factor, or Macro 3 Factor. Determine the Portfolio Weights of the Optimal Risky Portfolio and the Optimal Complete Portfolio.

Chapter 6 Constrained Portfolio Optimization

6.1 No Short Sales, No Borrowing, and Other Constraints

Problem. An individual investor with a simple mean and variance utility function has a risk aversion of 2.6. This investor is considering investing in the given individual stocks, US portfolios, or country portfolios. This investor considers four methods to forecast expected returns: average past return, Static CAPM, Fama-French 3 Factor, or Macro 3 Factor. The investor wishes to impose no short sales, no borrowing, and no portfolio weights great than 100%. Determine the Portfolio Weights of the Optimal Risky Portfolio and the Optimal Complete Portfolio.

Solution Strategy. There is no analytical solution, so the Constrained Risky Opportunity Set and the Constrained Complete Opportunity Set are found numerically using Excel **Solver**. Click on the Recalculation button

Click Here to Recalculate

in the range E2:G3 to run a macro which calls Solver 182 times. The "RepeatedlyRunSolver" macro takes about 4 minutes to run. With each call, Solver finds the portfolio weights which minimize the portfolio variance, subject to setting the portfolio expected return equal to a constant value and satisfying all constraints, (e.g., no short sales). When the weight in the Riskfree Asset *is constrained* to be exactly 0.00%, then you get the Constrained *Risky* Opportunity Set. When the weight in the Riskfree Asset is *not constrained*, then you get the Constrained *Complete* Opportunity Set. Computing the utility of each portfolio in the Constrained Complete Opportunity Set and rank ordering the utility values, identifies the *Optimal Complete* Portfolio. Zeroing out the weight in the riskfree asset and scaling up the weights in the risky assets determines the *Optimal Risky* Portfolio.

FIGURE 6.1 Excel Model of Constrained Portfolio Optimization – No Short Sales, No Borrowing, and Other Constraints

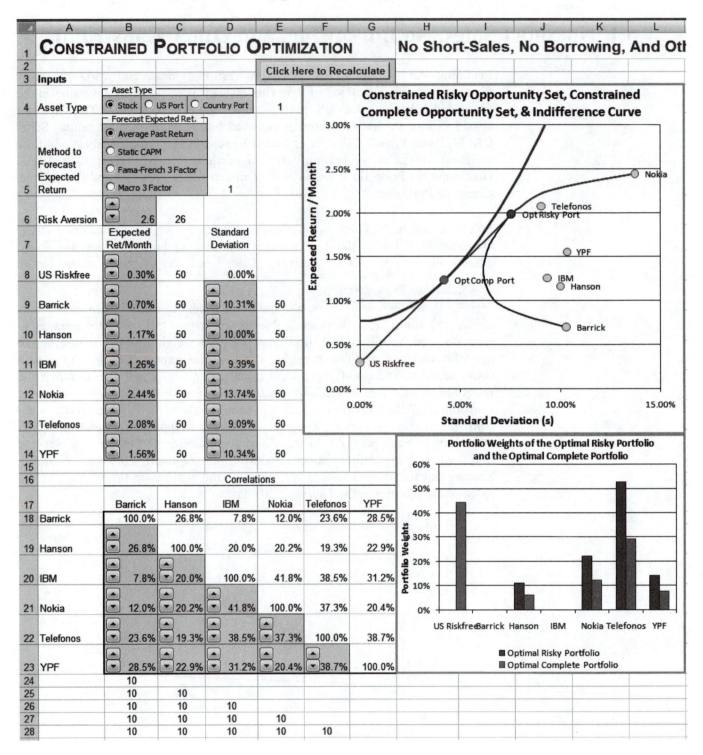

FIGURE 6.2 Excel Model of Constrained Portfolio Optimization – No Short Sales, No Borrowing, and Other Constraints

	A	B	C	D	E	F	G	H	I	J	K	L	M
30					Standard Deviations								
31		Barrick	Hanson	IBM	Nokia	Telefonos	YPF						
32		10.3%	10.0%	9.4%	13.7%	9.1%	10.3%						
33													
34					Variance-Covariance Matrix								
35		Barrick	Hanson	IBM	Nokia	Telefonos	YPF						
36	Barrick	1.06%	0.28%	0.08%	0.17%	0.22%	0.30%						
37	Hanson	0.28%	1.00%	0.19%	0.28%	0.17%	0.24%						
38	IBM	0.08%	0.19%	0.88%	0.54%	0.33%	0.30%						
39	Nokia	0.17%	0.28%	0.54%	1.89%	0.47%	0.29%						
40	Telefonos	0.22%	0.17%	0.33%	0.47%	0.83%	0.36%						
41	YPF	0.30%	0.24%	0.30%	0.29%	0.36%	1.07%						

(1) TRANSPOSE(Standard Deviations from above) -- enter as an Excel matrix (i.e., using Shift-Control-Enter)
Select the range B32:G32
Type =TRANSPOSE(D9:D14) (but don't press enter yet)
Hold down the Shift and Control buttons and then press Enter

(2) Covariance(Asset1, Asset2)
= (Std Dev1) * (Std Dev2) * Correlation(Asset1, Asset2)
Enter =B$32*$D9*B18 and copy to the range B36:G41

FIGURE 6.3 Excel Model of Constrained Portfolio Optimization – No Short Sales, No Borrowing, and Other Constraints

	N	O	P	Q	R	S	T	U	V	W	X
34	(3) Sum(Portfolio Weights) Enter =SUM(R48:X48)										
35											
36		(4) Matrix Multiply(Port Weights, Expected Returns) -- enter as an Excel matrix (Shift-Control-Enter) Type =MMULT(R48:X48, $B$8:$B$14) Hold down the Shift and Control buttons and then press Enter									
37											
38											
39											
40			(5) Square Root(MMULT(MMULT(Risky Port Weights, Variance-Covariance Matrix), TRANSPOSE(Risk Port Weights))) -- enter as an Excel matrix (Shift-Control-Enter) Type =SQRT(MMULT(MMULT(S48:X48, $B$36:$G$41), TRANSPOSE(S48:X48))) Hold down the Shift and Control buttons and then press Enter								
41											
42											
43											
44											
45	**Solver Analysis Area**										
46	Sum of	Portfolio	Portfolio	Solver				Portfolio Weights			
47	Portfolio Weights	Expected Ret/Mon.	Standard Deviation	Solution Code	US Riskfree	Barrick	Hanson	IBM	Nokia	Telefonos	YPF
48	100.00%	2.44%	13.74%	5	0.00%	0.00%	0.00%	0.00%	100.00%	0.00%	0.00%
49											
50											
51											
52	**Table of Problems and Solutions**										
53	Sum of	Portfolio	Portfolio	Solver				Portfolio Weights			
54	Portfolio Weights	Expected Ret/Mon	Standard Deviation	Solution Code	US Riskfree	Barrick	Hanson	IBM	Nokia	Telefonos	YPF
55	100.00%	0.70%	10.31%	5	0.00%	100.00%	0.00%	0.00%	0.00%	0.00%	0.00%
56	100.00%	0.70%	10.31%	5	0.00%	100.00%	0.00%	0.00%	0.00%	0.00%	0.00%
75	100.00%	0.70%	10.31%	5	0.00%	100.00%	0.00%	0.00%	0.00%	0.00%	0.00%
76	100.00%	0.70%	10.28%	0	0.00%	99.69%	0.00%	0.31%	0.00%	0.00%	0.00%
77	100.00%	0.73%	9.73%	0	0.00%	93.78%	0.00%	6.22%	0.00%	0.00%	0.00%
78	100.00%	0.77%	9.21%	0	0.00%	87.42%	2.59%	9.99%	0.00%	0.00%	0.00%
79	100.00%	0.80%	8.73%	0	0.00%	81.05%	5.42%	13.53%	0.00%	0.00%	0.00%
80	100.00%	0.83%	8.27%	0	0.00%	74.67%	8.25%	17.08%	0.00%	0.00%	0.00%
81	100.00%	0.87%	7.86%	0	0.00%	68.27%	11.09%	20.65%	0.00%	0.00%	0.00%
82	100.00%	0.90%	7.49%	0	0.00%	61.90%	13.91%	24.19%	0.00%	0.00%	0.00%
83	100.00%	0.93%	7.18%	0	0.00%	55.51%	16.75%	27.74%	0.00%	0.00%	0.00%
84	100.00%	0.97%	6.93%	0	0.00%	49.13%	19.58%	31.29%	0.00%	0.00%	0.00%
85	100.00%	1.00%	6.75%	0	0.00%	42.95%	22.20%	34.52%	0.00%	0.00%	0.33%
86	100.00%	1.03%	6.62%	0	0.00%	38.93%	22.62%	34.39%	0.00%	0.00%	4.06%
87	100.00%	1.07%	6.53%	0	0.00%	35.19%	22.97%	34.14%	0.00%	0.32%	7.39%
88	100.00%	1.10%	6.45%	0	0.00%	33.40%	22.77%	33.03%	0.00%	3.00%	7.79%
89	100.00%	1.13%	6.38%	0	0.00%	31.61%	22.57%	31.92%	0.00%	5.69%	8.20%
90	100.00%	1.17%	6.32%	0	0.00%	29.83%	22.38%	30.82%	0.00%	8.37%	8.61%
91	100.00%	1.20%	6.27%	0	0.00%	28.04%	22.18%	29.72%	0.00%	11.05%	9.02%
92	100.00%	1.23%	6.23%	0	0.00%	26.25%	21.98%	28.61%	0.00%	13.73%	9.42%
93	100.00%	1.27%	6.21%	0	0.00%	24.47%	21.78%	27.50%	0.00%	16.41%	9.83%
94	100.00%	1.30%	6.19%	0	0.00%	22.77%	21.57%	26.38%	0.19%	18.88%	10.22%
95	100.00%	1.33%	6.19%	0	0.00%	21.43%	21.29%	25.10%	1.16%	20.49%	10.53%
96	100.00%	1.37%	6.19%	0	0.00%	20.08%	21.01%	23.84%	2.14%	22.09%	10.83%
97	100.00%	1.40%	6.20%	0	0.00%	18.75%	20.73%	22.58%	3.11%	23.70%	11.14%
98	100.00%	1.43%	6.22%	0	0.00%	17.40%	20.45%	21.31%	4.08%	25.30%	11.45%
99	100.00%	1.47%	6.24%	0	0.00%	16.06%	20.17%	20.05%	5.06%	26.91%	11.75%
100	100.00%	1.50%	6.28%	0	0.00%	14.72%	19.89%	18.78%	6.04%	28.51%	12.06%
101	100.00%	1.53%	6.32%	0	0.00%	13.36%	19.61%	17.52%	7.00%	30.12%	12.38%
102	100.00%	1.57%	6.37%	0	0.00%	12.02%	19.32%	16.26%	7.98%	31.72%	12.70%
103	100.00%	1.60%	6.43%	0	0.00%	10.69%	19.03%	15.00%	8.95%	33.32%	13.02%

Rows 55 to 236 contain 182 problems for Solver to solve. Columns R through X contain the portfolio weights, which are the *choice variables* for each problem.

Columns Y through AN contain the constraint constants (sum of portfolio weights, target expected return, minimum portfolio weight, maximum portfolio weight) for each problem. Notice that the minimum portfolio weight for the risky assets (columns AB – AG) are 0.00%, which rules out negative weights (i.e., short-selling). The minimum portfolio weight for the riskfree asset (column AA) is 0.00%, which rules out a negative weight (i.e., borrowing). The maxium portfolio weight for the risky assets (columns AH – AN) are 100.00%, which rules out the most extremely undiversified positions.

Rows 55 to 145 contain 91 problems in which the weight in the Riskfree Asset is constrained to be exactly 0.00%. This is accomplished by setting minimum weight for the Riskfree Asset (column AA) to 0.00% and the maximum weight for the Riskfree Asset (column AH) to 0.00%. The solution to these problems yield the Constrained *Risky* Opportunity Set.

Rows 146 to 236 contain 91 problems in which the weight in the Riskfree Asset is NOT constrained to be exactly 0.00%. The maximum weight for the Riskfree Asset (column AH) is set to 100.00%. The solution to these problems yield the Constrained Complete Opportunity Set.

FIGURE 6.4 Excel Model of Constrained Portfolio Optimization – No Short Sales, No Borrowing, and Other Constraints

	Y	Z	AA	AB	AC	AD	AE	AF	AG	AH	AI	AJ	AK	AL	AM	AN
45								Constraints								
46	Sum of	Target				Minimum Portfolio Weights							Maximum Portfolio Weights			
47	Portfolio Weights	Expected Ret/Mon	US Riskfree	Barrick	Hanson	IBM	Nokia	Telefonos	YPF	US Riskfree	Barrick	Hanson	IBM	Nokia	Telefonos	YPF
48	100.00%	3.00%	0.00%	0.00%	0.00%	0.00%	0.00%	0.00%	0.00%	100.00%	100.00%	100.00%	100.00%	100.00%	100.00%	100.00%
49																
50																
51																
52								Constraints								
53	Sum of	Target				Minimum Portfolio Weights							Maximum Portfolio Weights			
54	Portfolio Weights	Expected Ret/Mon	US Riskfree	Barrick	Hanson	IBM	Nokia	Telefonos	YPF	US Riskfree	Barrick	Hanson	IBM	Nokia	Telefonos	YPF
55	100.00%	0.00%	0.00%	0.00%	0.00%	0.00%	0.00%	0.00%	0.00%	0.00%	100.00%	100.00%	100.00%	100.00%	100.00%	100.00%
56	100.00%	0.03%	0.00%	0.00%	0.00%	0.00%	0.00%	0.00%	0.00%	0.00%	100.00%	100.00%	100.00%	100.00%	100.00%	100.00%
75	100.00%	0.67%	0.00%	0.00%	0.00%	0.00%	0.00%	0.00%	0.00%	0.00%	100.00%	100.00%	100.00%	100.00%	100.00%	100.00%
76	100.00%	0.70%	0.00%	0.00%	0.00%	0.00%	0.00%	0.00%	0.00%	0.00%	100.00%	100.00%	100.00%	100.00%	100.00%	100.00%
77	100.00%	0.73%	0.00%	0.00%	0.00%	0.00%	0.00%	0.00%	0.00%	0.00%	100.00%	100.00%	100.00%	100.00%	100.00%	100.00%
78	100.00%	0.77%	0.00%	0.00%	0.00%	0.00%	0.00%	0.00%	0.00%	0.00%	100.00%	100.00%	100.00%	100.00%	100.00%	100.00%
79	100.00%	0.80%	0.00%	0.00%	0.00%	0.00%	0.00%	0.00%	0.00%	0.00%	100.00%	100.00%	100.00%	100.00%	100.00%	100.00%
80	100.00%	0.83%	0.00%	0.00%	0.00%	0.00%	0.00%	0.00%	0.00%	0.00%	100.00%	100.00%	100.00%	100.00%	100.00%	100.00%
81	100.00%	0.87%	0.00%	0.00%	0.00%	0.00%	0.00%	0.00%	0.00%	0.00%	100.00%	100.00%	100.00%	100.00%	100.00%	100.00%
82	100.00%	0.90%	0.00%	0.00%	0.00%	0.00%	0.00%	0.00%	0.00%	0.00%	100.00%	100.00%	100.00%	100.00%	100.00%	100.00%
83	100.00%	0.93%	0.00%	0.00%	0.00%	0.00%	0.00%	0.00%	0.00%	0.00%	100.00%	100.00%	100.00%	100.00%	100.00%	100.00%
84	100.00%	0.97%	0.00%	0.00%	0.00%	0.00%	0.00%	0.00%	0.00%	0.00%	100.00%	100.00%	100.00%	100.00%	100.00%	100.00%
85	100.00%	1.00%	0.00%	0.00%	0.00%	0.00%	0.00%	0.00%	0.00%	0.00%	100.00%	100.00%	100.00%	100.00%	100.00%	100.00%
86	100.00%	1.03%	0.00%	0.00%	0.00%	0.00%	0.00%	0.00%	0.00%	0.00%	100.00%	100.00%	100.00%	100.00%	100.00%	100.00%
87	100.00%	1.07%	0.00%	0.00%	0.00%	0.00%	0.00%	0.00%	0.00%	0.00%	100.00%	100.00%	100.00%	100.00%	100.00%	100.00%
88	100.00%	1.10%	0.00%	0.00%	0.00%	0.00%	0.00%	0.00%	0.00%	0.00%	100.00%	100.00%	100.00%	100.00%	100.00%	100.00%
89	100.00%	1.13%	0.00%	0.00%	0.00%	0.00%	0.00%	0.00%	0.00%	0.00%	100.00%	100.00%	100.00%	100.00%	100.00%	100.00%
90	100.00%	1.17%	0.00%	0.00%	0.00%	0.00%	0.00%	0.00%	0.00%	0.00%	100.00%	100.00%	100.00%	100.00%	100.00%	100.00%
91	100.00%	1.20%	0.00%	0.00%	0.00%	0.00%	0.00%	0.00%	0.00%	0.00%	100.00%	100.00%	100.00%	100.00%	100.00%	100.00%
92	100.00%	1.23%	0.00%	0.00%	0.00%	0.00%	0.00%	0.00%	0.00%	0.00%	100.00%	100.00%	100.00%	100.00%	100.00%	100.00%
93	100.00%	1.27%	0.00%	0.00%	0.00%	0.00%	0.00%	0.00%	0.00%	0.00%	100.00%	100.00%	100.00%	100.00%	100.00%	100.00%
94	100.00%	1.30%	0.00%	0.00%	0.00%	0.00%	0.00%	0.00%	0.00%	0.00%	100.00%	100.00%	100.00%	100.00%	100.00%	100.00%
95	100.00%	1.33%	0.00%	0.00%	0.00%	0.00%	0.00%	0.00%	0.00%	0.00%	100.00%	100.00%	100.00%	100.00%	100.00%	100.00%
96	100.00%	1.37%	0.00%	0.00%	0.00%	0.00%	0.00%	0.00%	0.00%	0.00%	100.00%	100.00%	100.00%	100.00%	100.00%	100.00%
97	100.00%	1.40%	0.00%	0.00%	0.00%	0.00%	0.00%	0.00%	0.00%	0.00%	100.00%	100.00%	100.00%	100.00%	100.00%	100.00%
98	100.00%	1.43%	0.00%	0.00%	0.00%	0.00%	0.00%	0.00%	0.00%	0.00%	100.00%	100.00%	100.00%	100.00%	100.00%	100.00%
99	100.00%	1.47%	0.00%	0.00%	0.00%	0.00%	0.00%	0.00%	0.00%	0.00%	100.00%	100.00%	100.00%	100.00%	100.00%	100.00%
100	100.00%	1.50%	0.00%	0.00%	0.00%	0.00%	0.00%	0.00%	0.00%	0.00%	100.00%	100.00%	100.00%	100.00%	100.00%	100.00%
101	100.00%	1.53%	0.00%	0.00%	0.00%	0.00%	0.00%	0.00%	0.00%	0.00%	100.00%	100.00%	100.00%	100.00%	100.00%	100.00%
102	100.00%	1.57%	0.00%	0.00%	0.00%	0.00%	0.00%	0.00%	0.00%	0.00%	100.00%	100.00%	100.00%	100.00%	100.00%	100.00%
103	100.00%	1.60%	0.00%	0.00%	0.00%	0.00%	0.00%	0.00%	0.00%	0.00%	100.00%	100.00%	100.00%	100.00%	100.00%	100.00%

FIGURE 6.5 Excel Model of Constrained Portfolio Optimization – No Short Sales, No Borrowing, and Other Constraints

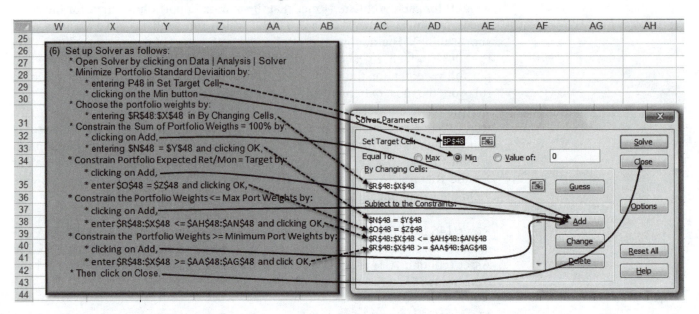

Excel 2003 Equivalent

To open Solver in Excel 2003, click on **Tools | Solver**.

Below we see rows 146 to 236, which contain the second set of 91 problems in which the weight in the Riskfree Asset is not constrained to be exactly 0.00%.

FIGURE 6.6 Excel Model of Constrained Portfolio Optimization – No Short Sales, No Borrowing, and Other Constraints

	N	O	P	Q	R	S	T	U	V	W	X
52	Table of Problems and Solutions										
53	Sum of	Portfolio	Portfolio	Solver				Portfolio Weights			
54	Portfolio Weights	Expected Ret/Mon	Standard Deviation	Solution Code	US Riskfree	Barrick	Hanson	IBM	Nokia	Telefonos	YPF
144	100.00%	2.44%	13.74%	5	0.00%	0.00%	0.00%	0.00%	100.00%	0.00%	0.00%
145	100.00%	2.44%	13.74%	5	0.00%	0.00%	0.00%	0.00%	100.00%	0.00%	0.00%
146	0.00%	0.00%	0.00%	5	0.00%	0.00%	0.00%	0.00%	0.00%	0.00%	0.00%
147	100.00%	0.30%	0.00%	5	100.00%	0.00%	0.00%	0.00%	0.00%	0.00%	0.00%
148	100.00%	0.30%	0.00%	5	100.00%	0.00%	0.00%	0.00%	0.00%	0.00%	0.00%
149	100.00%	0.30%	0.00%	5	100.00%	0.00%	0.00%	0.00%	0.00%	0.00%	0.00%
150	100.00%	0.30%	0.00%	5	100.00%	0.00%	0.00%	0.00%	0.00%	0.00%	0.00%
151	100.00%	0.30%	0.00%	5	100.00%	0.00%	0.00%	0.00%	0.00%	0.00%	0.00%
152	100.00%	0.30%	0.00%	5	100.00%	0.00%	0.00%	0.00%	0.00%	0.00%	0.00%
153	100.00%	0.30%	0.00%	5	100.00%	0.00%	0.00%	0.00%	0.00%	0.00%	0.00%
154	100.00%	0.30%	0.00%	5	100.00%	0.00%	0.00%	0.00%	0.00%	0.00%	0.00%
155	100.00%	0.30%	0.02%	0	99.73%	0.00%	0.03%	0.00%	0.06%	0.14%	0.04%
156	100.00%	0.33%	0.17%	0	97.76%	0.00%	0.25%	0.00%	0.49%	1.18%	0.31%
157	100.00%	0.37%	0.32%	0	95.78%	0.00%	0.47%	0.00%	0.93%	2.22%	0.59%
158	100.00%	0.40%	0.47%	0	93.81%	0.00%	0.69%	0.00%	1.36%	3.27%	0.87%
159	100.00%	0.43%	0.62%	0	91.83%	0.00%	0.91%	0.00%	1.80%	4.31%	1.15%
160	100.00%	0.47%	0.77%	0	89.86%	0.00%	1.13%	0.00%	2.23%	5.35%	1.43%
161	100.00%	0.50%	0.92%	0	87.88%	0.00%	1.35%	0.00%	2.67%	6.39%	1.70%
162	100.00%	0.53%	1.07%	0	85.91%	0.00%	1.57%	0.00%	3.10%	7.43%	1.98%
163	100.00%	0.57%	1.22%	0	83.93%	0.00%	1.79%	0.00%	3.54%	8.47%	2.26%
164	100.00%	0.60%	1.37%	0	81.96%	0.00%	2.02%	0.00%	3.97%	9.52%	2.54%
165	100.00%	0.63%	1.52%	0	79.98%	0.00%	2.24%	0.00%	4.41%	10.56%	2.81%
166	100.00%	0.67%	1.67%	0	78.01%	0.00%	2.46%	0.00%	4.84%	11.60%	3.09%
167	100.00%	0.70%	1.82%	0	76.03%	0.00%	2.69%	0.00%	5.28%	12.65%	3.35%
168	100.00%	0.73%	1.97%	0	74.06%	0.00%	2.91%	0.00%	5.71%	13.69%	3.63%
169	100.00%	0.77%	2.12%	0	72.09%	0.00%	3.12%	0.00%	6.15%	14.72%	3.92%
170	100.00%	0.80%	2.27%	0	70.11%	0.00%	3.34%	0.00%	6.59%	15.77%	4.20%
171	100.00%	0.83%	2.42%	0	68.14%	0.00%	3.56%	0.00%	7.02%	16.80%	4.48%
172	100.00%	0.87%	2.57%	0	66.16%	0.00%	3.78%	0.00%	7.46%	17.84%	4.76%
173	100.00%	0.90%	2.72%	0	64.18%	0.00%	4.00%	0.00%	7.89%	18.89%	5.04%
174	100.00%	0.93%	2.87%	0	62.21%	0.00%	4.22%	0.00%	8.32%	19.93%	5.32%
175	100.00%	0.97%	3.02%	0	60.23%	0.00%	4.44%	0.00%	8.75%	20.97%	5.60%
176	100.00%	1.00%	3.17%	0	58.25%	0.00%	4.66%	0.00%	9.19%	22.02%	5.88%
177	100.00%	1.03%	3.32%	0	56.28%	0.00%	4.88%	0.00%	9.62%	23.06%	6.16%
178	100.00%	1.07%	3.47%	0	54.30%	0.00%	5.10%	0.00%	10.06%	24.10%	6.43%
179	100.00%	1.10%	3.62%	0	52.33%	0.00%	5.32%	0.00%	10.49%	25.14%	6.71%
180	100.00%	1.13%	3.77%	0	50.36%	0.00%	5.54%	0.00%	10.93%	26.19%	6.99%
181	100.00%	1.17%	3.92%	0	48.38%	0.00%	5.76%	0.00%	11.36%	27.23%	7.26%
182	100.00%	1.20%	4.07%	0	46.41%	0.00%	5.99%	0.00%	11.80%	28.27%	7.54%
183	100.00%	1.23%	4.22%	0	44.43%	0.00%	6.22%	0.00%	12.24%	29.30%	7.81%
184	100.00%	1.27%	4.37%	0	42.46%	0.00%	6.41%	0.00%	12.67%	30.35%	8.09%
185	100.00%	1.30%	4.52%	0	40.48%	0.00%	6.65%	0.00%	13.11%	31.39%	8.37%
186	100.00%	1.33%	4.67%	0	38.52%	0.00%	6.87%	0.00%	13.55%	32.43%	8.64%
187	100.00%	1.37%	4.82%	0	36.54%	0.00%	7.09%	0.00%	13.98%	33.47%	8.92%
188	100.00%	1.40%	4.97%	0	34.57%	0.00%	7.31%	0.00%	14.42%	34.51%	9.20%
189	100.00%	1.43%	5.12%	0	32.59%	0.00%	7.53%	0.00%	14.84%	35.56%	9.49%
190	100.00%	1.47%	5.27%	0	30.62%	0.00%	7.76%	0.00%	15.31%	36.57%	9.75%
191	100.00%	1.50%	5.42%	0	28.64%	0.00%	7.97%	0.00%	15.73%	37.62%	10.03%
192	100.00%	1.53%	5.57%	0	26.66%	0.00%	8.19%	0.00%	16.16%	38.68%	10.31%
193	100.00%	1.57%	5.72%	0	24.69%	0.00%	8.41%	0.00%	16.58%	39.72%	10.59%
194	100.00%	1.60%	5.87%	0	22.71%	0.00%	8.63%	0.00%	17.03%	40.76%	10.88%

FIGURE 6.7 Excel Model of Constrained Portfolio Optimization – No Short Sales, No Borrowing, and Other Constraints

	Y	Z	AA	AB	AC	AD	AE	AF	AG	AH	AI	AJ	AK	AL	AM	AN
52			Constraints													
53	Sum of	Target	Minimum Portfolio Weights							Maximum Portfolio Weights						
54	Portfolio Weights	Expected Ret/Mon	US Riskfree	Barrick	Hanson	IBM	Nokia	Telefonos	YPF	US Riskfree	Barrick	Hanson	IBM	Nokia	Telefonos	YPF
144	100.00%	2.97%	0.00%	0.00%	0.00%	0.00%	0.00%	0.00%	0.00%	0.00%	100.00%	100.00%	100.00%	100.00%	100.00%	100.00%
145	100.00%	3.00%	0.00%	0.00%	0.00%	0.00%	0.00%	0.00%	0.00%	0.00%	100.00%	100.00%	100.00%	100.00%	100.00%	100.00%
146	100.00%	0.00%	0.00%	0.00%	0.00%	0.00%	0.00%	0.00%	0.00%	100.00%	100.00%	100.00%	100.00%	100.00%	100.00%	100.00%
147	100.00%	0.03%	0.00%	0.00%	0.00%	0.00%	0.00%	0.00%	0.00%	100.00%	100.00%	100.00%	100.00%	100.00%	100.00%	100.00%
148	100.00%	0.07%	0.00%	0.00%	0.00%	0.00%	0.00%	0.00%	0.00%	100.00%	100.00%	100.00%	100.00%	100.00%	100.00%	100.00%
149	100.00%	0.10%	0.00%	0.00%	0.00%	0.00%	0.00%	0.00%	0.00%	100.00%	100.00%	100.00%	100.00%	100.00%	100.00%	100.00%
150	100.00%	0.13%	0.00%	0.00%	0.00%	0.00%	0.00%	0.00%	0.00%	100.00%	100.00%	100.00%	100.00%	100.00%	100.00%	100.00%
151	100.00%	0.17%	0.00%	0.00%	0.00%	0.00%	0.00%	0.00%	0.00%	100.00%	100.00%	100.00%	100.00%	100.00%	100.00%	100.00%
152	100.00%	0.20%	0.00%	0.00%	0.00%	0.00%	0.00%	0.00%	0.00%	100.00%	100.00%	100.00%	100.00%	100.00%	100.00%	100.00%
153	100.00%	0.23%	0.00%	0.00%	0.00%	0.00%	0.00%	0.00%	0.00%	100.00%	100.00%	100.00%	100.00%	100.00%	100.00%	100.00%
154	100.00%	0.27%	0.00%	0.00%	0.00%	0.00%	0.00%	0.00%	0.00%	100.00%	100.00%	100.00%	100.00%	100.00%	100.00%	100.00%
155	100.00%	0.30%	0.00%	0.00%	0.00%	0.00%	0.00%	0.00%	0.00%	100.00%	100.00%	100.00%	100.00%	100.00%	100.00%	100.00%
156	100.00%	0.33%	0.00%	0.00%	0.00%	0.00%	0.00%	0.00%	0.00%	100.00%	100.00%	100.00%	100.00%	100.00%	100.00%	100.00%
157	100.00%	0.37%	0.00%	0.00%	0.00%	0.00%	0.00%	0.00%	0.00%	100.00%	100.00%	100.00%	100.00%	100.00%	100.00%	100.00%
158	100.00%	0.40%	0.00%	0.00%	0.00%	0.00%	0.00%	0.00%	0.00%	100.00%	100.00%	100.00%	100.00%	100.00%	100.00%	100.00%
159	100.00%	0.43%	0.00%	0.00%	0.00%	0.00%	0.00%	0.00%	0.00%	100.00%	100.00%	100.00%	100.00%	100.00%	100.00%	100.00%
160	100.00%	0.47%	0.00%	0.00%	0.00%	0.00%	0.00%	0.00%	0.00%	100.00%	100.00%	100.00%	100.00%	100.00%	100.00%	100.00%
161	100.00%	0.50%	0.00%	0.00%	0.00%	0.00%	0.00%	0.00%	0.00%	100.00%	100.00%	100.00%	100.00%	100.00%	100.00%	100.00%
162	100.00%	0.53%	0.00%	0.00%	0.00%	0.00%	0.00%	0.00%	0.00%	100.00%	100.00%	100.00%	100.00%	100.00%	100.00%	100.00%
163	100.00%	0.57%	0.00%	0.00%	0.00%	0.00%	0.00%	0.00%	0.00%	100.00%	100.00%	100.00%	100.00%	100.00%	100.00%	100.00%
164	100.00%	0.60%	0.00%	0.00%	0.00%	0.00%	0.00%	0.00%	0.00%	100.00%	100.00%	100.00%	100.00%	100.00%	100.00%	100.00%
165	100.00%	0.63%	0.00%	0.00%	0.00%	0.00%	0.00%	0.00%	0.00%	100.00%	100.00%	100.00%	100.00%	100.00%	100.00%	100.00%
166	100.00%	0.67%	0.00%	0.00%	0.00%	0.00%	0.00%	0.00%	0.00%	100.00%	100.00%	100.00%	100.00%	100.00%	100.00%	100.00%
167	100.00%	0.70%	0.00%	0.00%	0.00%	0.00%	0.00%	0.00%	0.00%	100.00%	100.00%	100.00%	100.00%	100.00%	100.00%	100.00%
168	100.00%	0.73%	0.00%	0.00%	0.00%	0.00%	0.00%	0.00%	0.00%	100.00%	100.00%	100.00%	100.00%	100.00%	100.00%	100.00%
169	100.00%	0.77%	0.00%	0.00%	0.00%	0.00%	0.00%	0.00%	0.00%	100.00%	100.00%	100.00%	100.00%	100.00%	100.00%	100.00%
170	100.00%	0.80%	0.00%	0.00%	0.00%	0.00%	0.00%	0.00%	0.00%	100.00%	100.00%	100.00%	100.00%	100.00%	100.00%	100.00%
171	100.00%	0.83%	0.00%	0.00%	0.00%	0.00%	0.00%	0.00%	0.00%	100.00%	100.00%	100.00%	100.00%	100.00%	100.00%	100.00%
172	100.00%	0.87%	0.00%	0.00%	0.00%	0.00%	0.00%	0.00%	0.00%	100.00%	100.00%	100.00%	100.00%	100.00%	100.00%	100.00%
173	100.00%	0.90%	0.00%	0.00%	0.00%	0.00%	0.00%	0.00%	0.00%	100.00%	100.00%	100.00%	100.00%	100.00%	100.00%	100.00%
174	100.00%	0.93%	0.00%	0.00%	0.00%	0.00%	0.00%	0.00%	0.00%	100.00%	100.00%	100.00%	100.00%	100.00%	100.00%	100.00%
175	100.00%	0.97%	0.00%	0.00%	0.00%	0.00%	0.00%	0.00%	0.00%	100.00%	100.00%	100.00%	100.00%	100.00%	100.00%	100.00%
176	100.00%	1.00%	0.00%	0.00%	0.00%	0.00%	0.00%	0.00%	0.00%	100.00%	100.00%	100.00%	100.00%	100.00%	100.00%	100.00%
177	100.00%	1.03%	0.00%	0.00%	0.00%	0.00%	0.00%	0.00%	0.00%	100.00%	100.00%	100.00%	100.00%	100.00%	100.00%	100.00%
178	100.00%	1.07%	0.00%	0.00%	0.00%	0.00%	0.00%	0.00%	0.00%	100.00%	100.00%	100.00%	100.00%	100.00%	100.00%	100.00%
179	100.00%	1.10%	0.00%	0.00%	0.00%	0.00%	0.00%	0.00%	0.00%	100.00%	100.00%	100.00%	100.00%	100.00%	100.00%	100.00%
180	100.00%	1.13%	0.00%	0.00%	0.00%	0.00%	0.00%	0.00%	0.00%	100.00%	100.00%	100.00%	100.00%	100.00%	100.00%	100.00%
181	100.00%	1.17%	0.00%	0.00%	0.00%	0.00%	0.00%	0.00%	0.00%	100.00%	100.00%	100.00%	100.00%	100.00%	100.00%	100.00%
182	100.00%	1.20%	0.00%	0.00%	0.00%	0.00%	0.00%	0.00%	0.00%	100.00%	100.00%	100.00%	100.00%	100.00%	100.00%	100.00%
183	100.00%	1.23%	0.00%	0.00%	0.00%	0.00%	0.00%	0.00%	0.00%	100.00%	100.00%	100.00%	100.00%	100.00%	100.00%	100.00%
184	100.00%	1.27%	0.00%	0.00%	0.00%	0.00%	0.00%	0.00%	0.00%	100.00%	100.00%	100.00%	100.00%	100.00%	100.00%	100.00%
185	100.00%	1.30%	0.00%	0.00%	0.00%	0.00%	0.00%	0.00%	0.00%	100.00%	100.00%	100.00%	100.00%	100.00%	100.00%	100.00%
186	100.00%	1.33%	0.00%	0.00%	0.00%	0.00%	0.00%	0.00%	0.00%	100.00%	100.00%	100.00%	100.00%	100.00%	100.00%	100.00%
187	100.00%	1.37%	0.00%	0.00%	0.00%	0.00%	0.00%	0.00%	0.00%	100.00%	100.00%	100.00%	100.00%	100.00%	100.00%	100.00%
188	100.00%	1.40%	0.00%	0.00%	0.00%	0.00%	0.00%	0.00%	0.00%	100.00%	100.00%	100.00%	100.00%	100.00%	100.00%	100.00%
189	100.00%	1.43%	0.00%	0.00%	0.00%	0.00%	0.00%	0.00%	0.00%	100.00%	100.00%	100.00%	100.00%	100.00%	100.00%	100.00%
190	100.00%	1.47%	0.00%	0.00%	0.00%	0.00%	0.00%	0.00%	0.00%	100.00%	100.00%	100.00%	100.00%	100.00%	100.00%	100.00%
191	100.00%	1.50%	0.00%	0.00%	0.00%	0.00%	0.00%	0.00%	0.00%	100.00%	100.00%	100.00%	100.00%	100.00%	100.00%	100.00%
192	100.00%	1.53%	0.00%	0.00%	0.00%	0.00%	0.00%	0.00%	0.00%	100.00%	100.00%	100.00%	100.00%	100.00%	100.00%	100.00%
193	100.00%	1.57%	0.00%	0.00%	0.00%	0.00%	0.00%	0.00%	0.00%	100.00%	100.00%	100.00%	100.00%	100.00%	100.00%	100.00%
194	100.00%	1.60%	0.00%	0.00%	0.00%	0.00%	0.00%	0.00%	0.00%	100.00%	100.00%	100.00%	100.00%	100.00%	100.00%	100.00%

FIGURE 6.8 Excel Model of Constrained Portfolio Optimization – No Short Sales, No Borrowing, and Other Constraints

(7) If Solver Solution Code = 0 (Solver found a solution)
Then Port Exp Return - (Risk Aversion) * (Port Std Dev)^2
Else -1
Enter =IF(Q55=0,O55-$B$6*P55^2,-1) and copy to the range L56:236

	H	I	J	K	L	M	N	O	P	Q
40										
41										
42										
43										
44										
45	Optimal	Optimal	Optimal				**Solver Analysis Area**			
46	Complete	Risky	Complete				Sum of	Portfolio	Portfolio	Solver
47	Expected Ret/Mon	Portfolio Weights	Portfolio Weights	Vlookup Column			Portfolio Weights	Expected Ret/Mon	Standard Deviation	Solution Code
48			64.2%	6			100.00%	2.44%	13.74%	5
49		0.0%	0.0%	7						
50		11.2%	4.0%	8						
51		0.0%	0.0%	9						
52		22.0%	7.9%	10			**Table of Problems and Solutions**			
53		52.7%	18.9%	11			Sum of	Portfolio	Portfolio	Solver
54		14.1%	5.0%	12	Investor Utility	Portfolio Ranking	Portfolio Weights	Expected Ret/Mon	Standard Deviation	Solution Code
55					-100.000%		100.00%	0.70%	10.31%	5
56					-100.000%		100.00%	0.70%	10.31%	5
75					-100.000%		100.00%	0.70%	10.31%	5
76					-3.529%		100.00%	0.70%	10.28%	0
77					-3.056%		100.00%	0.73%	9.73%	0
78					-2.629%		100.00%	0.77%	9.21%	0
79					-2.244%		100.00%	0.80%	8.72%	0
80					-1.901%		100.00%	0.83%	8.27%	0
81					-1.601%		100.00%	0.87%	7.85%	0
82					-1.344%		100.00%	0.90%	7.49%	0
83					-1.128%		100.00%	0.93%	7.18%	0
84					-0.955%		100.00%	0.97%	6.93%	0
85					-0.824%		100.00%	1.00%	6.75%	0
86					-0.722%		100.00%	1.03%	6.62%	0
87					-0.637%		100.00%	1.07%	6.53%	0
88					-0.562%		100.00%	1.10%	6.45%	0
89					-0.493%		100.00%	1.13%	6.38%	0
90					-0.430%		100.00%	1.17%	6.32%	0
91					-0.373%		100.00%	1.20%	6.27%	0
92					-0.321%		100.00%	1.23%	6.23%	0
93					-0.274%		100.00%	1.27%	6.21%	0
94					-0.233%		100.00%	1.30%	6.19%	0
95					-0.197%		100.00%	1.33%	6.19%	0
96					-0.165%		100.00%	1.37%	6.19%	0
97					-0.137%		100.00%	1.40%	6.20%	0
98					-0.113%		100.00%	1.43%	6.22%	0
99					-0.093%		100.00%	1.47%	6.24%	0
100					-0.077%		100.00%	1.50%	6.28%	0
101					-0.065%		100.00%	1.53%	6.32%	0
102					-0.057%		100.00%	1.57%	6.37%	0
103					-0.054%		100.00%	1.60%	6.43%	0
104					-0.054%		100.00%	1.63%	6.49%	0

FIGURE 6.9 Excel Model of Constrained Portfolio Optimization – No Short Sales, No Borrowing, and Other Constraints

	F	G	H	I	J	K	L	M	N	O	P	Q
52				22.0%	7.9%	10			Table of Problems and Solutions			
53				52.7%	18.9%	11			Sum of	Portfolio	Portfolio	Solver
54				14.1%	5.0%	12	Investor Utility	Portfolio Ranking	Portfolio Weights	Expected Ret/Mon	Standard Deviation	Solution Code
141							-100.000%		100.00%	2.44%	13.74%	5
142							-100.000%		100.00%	2.44%	13.74%	5
143							-100.000%		100.00%	2.44%	13.74%	5
144							-100.000%		100.00%	2.44%	13.74%	5
145							-100.000%		100.00%	2.44%	13.74%	5
146							-100.000%	66	100.00%	0.30%	0.00%	5
147							-100.000%	66	100.00%	0.30%	0.00%	5
148							-100.000%	66	100.00%	0.30%	0.00%	5
149							-100.000%	66	100.00%	0.30%	0.00%	5
150							-100.000%	66	100.00%	0.30%	0.00%	5
151							-100.000%	66	100.00%	0.30%	0.00%	5
152							-100.000%	66	100.00%	0.30%	0.00%	5
153							-100.000%	66	100.00%	0.30%	0.00%	5
154							-100.000%	66	100.00%	0.30%	0.00%	5
155							0.300%	37	100.00%	0.30%	0.02%	0
156							0.332%	35	100.00%	0.33%	0.17%	0
157							0.363%	33	100.00%	0.37%	0.32%	0
158							0.391%	31	100.00%	0.40%	0.47%	0
159							0.418%	29	100.00%	0.43%	0.62%	0
160							0.443%	27	100.00%	0.47%	0.77%	0
161							0.466%	25	100.00%	0.50%	0.92%	0
162							0.488%	23	100.00%	0.53%	1.07%	0
163							0.507%	21	100.00%	0.57%	1.22%	0
164							0.525%	19	100.00%	0.60%	1.37%	0
165							0.541%	17	100.00%	0.63%	1.52%	0
166							0.555%	15	100.00%	0.67%	1.67%	0
167							0.568%	13	100.00%	0.70%	1.82%	0
168							0.578%	11	100.00%	0.73%	1.97%	0
169							0.587%	9	100.00%	0.77%	2.12%	0
170							0.594%	7	100.00%	0.80%	2.27%	0
171							0.599%	5	100.00%	0.83%	2.42%	0
172							0.603%	3	100.00%	0.87%	2.57%	0
173							0.604%	1	100.00%	0.90%	2.72%	0
174							0.604%	2	100.00%	0.93%	2.87%	0
175							0.602%	4	100.00%	0.97%	3.02%	0
176							0.598%	6	100.00%	1.00%	3.17%	0
177							0.593%	8	100.00%	1.03%	3.32%	0
178							0.585%	10	100.00%	1.07%	3.47%	0
179							0.576%	12	100.00%	1.10%	3.62%	0
180							0.565%	14	100.00%	1.13%	3.77%	0
181							0.552%	16	100.00%	1.17%	3.92%	0
182							0.538%	18	100.00%	1.20%	4.07%	0
183							0.521%	20	100.00%	1.23%	4.22%	0
184							0.503%	22	100.00%	1.27%	4.37%	0
185							0.483%	24	100.00%	1.30%	4.52%	0
186							0.461%	26	100.00%	1.33%	4.67%	0
187							0.438%	28	100.00%	1.37%	4.82%	0
188							0.413%	30	100.00%	1.40%	4.97%	0
189							0.385%	32	100.00%	1.43%	5.12%	0
190							0.356%	34	100.00%	1.47%	5.27%	0

(8) RANK(Investor Utility from port i, Investor Utility from all portfolios) Enter =RANK(L146,$L$146:$L$236) and copy down

Column L contains the utility of each portfolio in the Constrained Complete Opportunity Set and column M contains rank ordering of these utility values. In this case, the portfolio in row 163 yields the highest utility value and is thus the *Optimal Complete* Portfolio.

FIGURE 6.10 Excel Model of Constrained Portfolio Optimization – No Short Sales, No Borrowing, and Other Constraints

	A	B	C	D	E	F	G	H	I	J	K
43	**Outputs**										
44			Constrd	Constrained							
45			Risky	Complete	Individual	Indiffer	Optimal	Optimal	Optimal	Optimal	
46			Opp Set	Opp Set	Asset	Curve	Risky	Complete	Risky	Complete	Vlookup
47		Standard Deviation	Expected Ret/Mon	Expected Ret/Mon	Expected Ret/Mon	Expected Ret/Mon	Expected Ret/Mon	Expected Ret/Mon	Portfolio Weights	Portfolio Weights	Column
48	US Riskfree	0.0%			0.3%					64.2%	6
49	Barrick	10.3%			0.7%				0.0%	0.0%	7
50	Hanson	10.0%			1.2%				11.2%	4.0%	8
51	IBM	9.4%			1.3%				0.0%	0.0%	9
52	Nokia	13.7%			2.4%				22.0%	7.9%	10
53	Telefonos	9.1%			2.1%				52.7%	18.9%	11
54	YPF	10.3%			1.6%				14.1%	5.0%	12
55	Constrd Risky	#N/A	0.00%								
56	Constrd Risky	#N/A	0.03%								
57	Constrd Risky	#N/A	0.07%								
58	Constrd Risky	#N/A	0.10%								
59	Constrd Risky	#N/A	0.13%								
60	Constrd Risky	#N/A	0.17%								
61	Constrd Risky	#N/A	0.20%								
62	Constrd Risky	#N/A	0.23%								
63	Constrd Risky	#N/A	0.27%								
64	Constrd Risky	#N/A	0.30%								
65	Constrd Risky	#N/A	0.33%								
66	Constrd Risky	#N/A	0.37%								
67	Constrd Risky	#N/A	0.40%								
68	Constrd Risky	#N/A	0.43%								
69	Constrd Risky	#N/A	0.47%								
70	Constrd Risky	#N/A	0.50%								
71	Constrd Risky	#N/A	0.53%								
72	Constrd Risky	#N/A	0.57%								
73	Constrd Risky	#N/A	0.60%								
74	Constrd Risky	#N/A	0.63%								
75	Constrd Risky	#N/A	0.67%								
76	Constrd Risky	10.28%	0.70%								
77	Constrd Risky	9.73%	0.73%								
78	Constrd Risky	9.21%	0.77%								
79	Constrd Risky	8.72%	0.80%								
80	Constrd Risky	8.27%	0.83%								
81	Constrd Risky	7.85%	0.87%								
82	Constrd Risky	7.49%	0.90%								
83	Constrd Risky	7.18%	0.93%								
84	Constrd Risky	6.93%	0.97%								

(9) Expected Return of Asset i
    Enter =B8 and copy down

(10) (Risky Weight i) / (Sum of the Risky Weights)
    Type =J49/(SUM($J$49:$J$54))
    and copy down

(11) VLOOKUP(#1 Utility Ranking, Complete Portfolio Range,Column,FALSE)
    Enter =VLOOKUP(1,$M$146:$X$236,K48,FALSE)
    and copy down

(12) If Solver Solution Code = 0   (Solver found a solution)
    Then Port Std Dev
    Else #N/A Error Code so it won't show up on the graph
    Enter =IF(Q55=0,P55,NA()) and copy to the range B56:B236

Column J shows the portfolio weights of the Optimal Complete Portfolio. In column I, the portfolio weight in the riskfree asset is zeroed out and the portfolio weights of the risky assets scaling up proportionally so that they add up to 100%. This yields the portfolio weights of the Optimal Risky Portfolio.

FIGURE 6.11 Excel Model of Constrained Portfolio Optimization – No Short Sales, No Borrowing, and Other Constraints

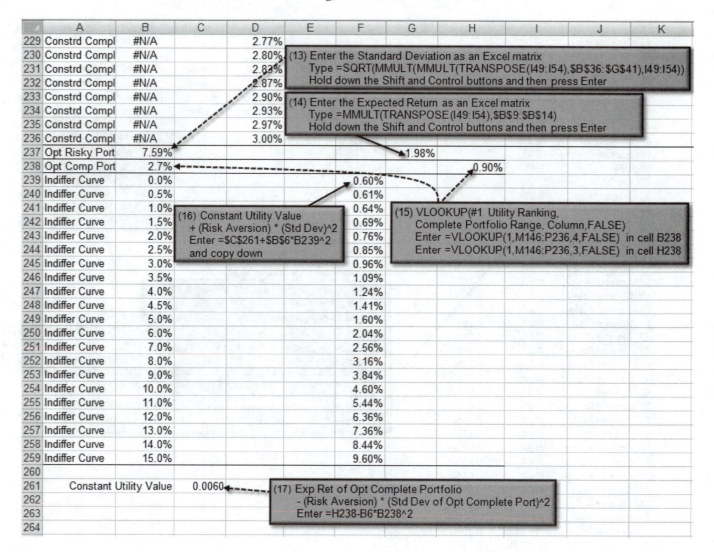

Once you have built the spreadsheet, you are ready to run the macro by clicking

on the Recalculation button **[Click Here to Recalculate]** in the range E2:G3. This button runs the macro "**RepeatedlyRunSolver.**"

To view the macro, click on **Developer | Code | Visual Basic** (see below). If the Developer tab is not visible, you can display it by clicking on the **Office** button , click on the **Excel Options** button at the bottom of the drop-down window, check the **Show Developer tab in the Ribbon** checkbox, and click **OK**.

> **Excel 2003 Equivalent**
>
> To view the macro in Excel 2003, click on **Tools | Macro | Visual Basic Editor**.

FIGURE 6.12 Excel Model of Constrained Portfolio Optimization – No Short Sales, No Borrowing, and Other Constraints

This opens the Visual Basic Development Environment. In the main window, you see the code for the "**RepeatedlyRunSolver**" macro. The macro is very straight-forward. It runs a big loop that solves each of the 182 problems from Rows 55 to 236. It starts at row 55 and copies the constraint constants Y55:AN55 to Y48:AN48. Row 48 is the **Solver Analysis Area**. Then it calls Solver and asks it solve the problem on Row

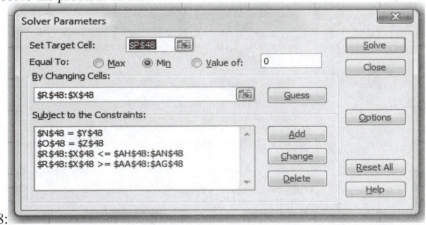

48:

Then it copies the results from N48:X48 (sum of port weights, portfolio expected return, portfolio standard deviation, Solver solution code, and portfolio weights) and pastes the result values to N55:X55. Then it repeats this process for Row 56, for Row 57, for Row 58, etc.

FIGURE 6.13 Excel Model of Constrained Portfolio Optimization – No Short Sales, No Borrowing, and Other Constraints

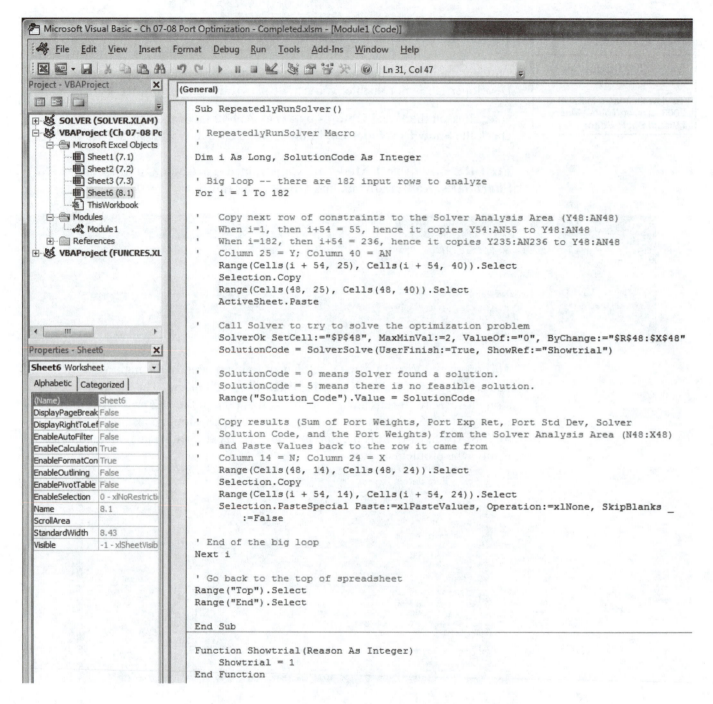

The macro code itself is in blue and black. The comments in green explain how macro works.

Now let's experiment with various inputs. First, click on **Stocks**, click on various option buttons for the **Method to Forecast Expected Return**, and then click the Recalculation button ⎡Click Here to Recalculate⎤. See the results below.

FIGURE 6.14 Average Past Returns and Static CAPM

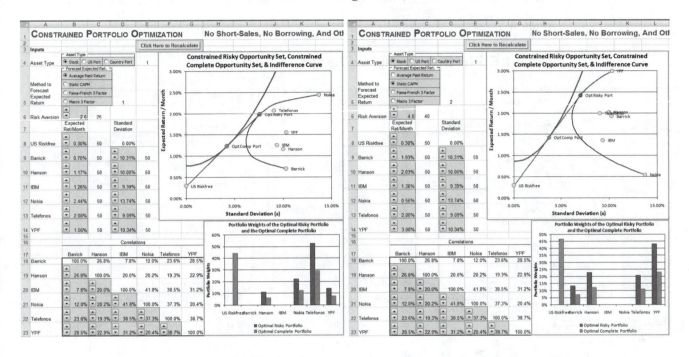

FIGURE 6.15 Fama-French 3 Factor and Macro 3 Factor

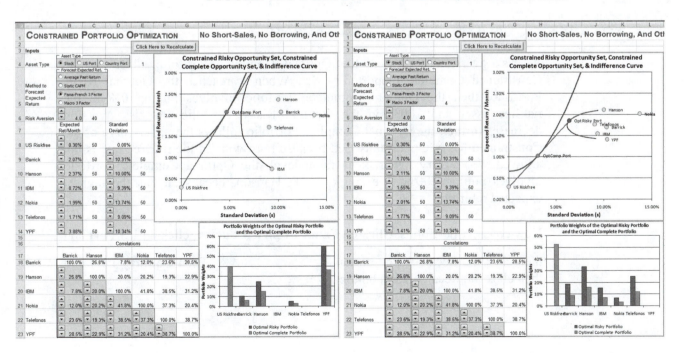

Again we see that the **Method to Forecast Expected Return** matters a great deal. The four methods produce very different portfolio weights for the Optimal Risky and Complete Portfolios.

An interesting experiment is to click on the **Risk Aversion** down-arrow spin button to lower the investor's risk aversion and then click the Recalculation button ⌈Click Here to Recalculate⌋.

FIGURE 6.16 Risk Aversion of 1.8 and 0.2

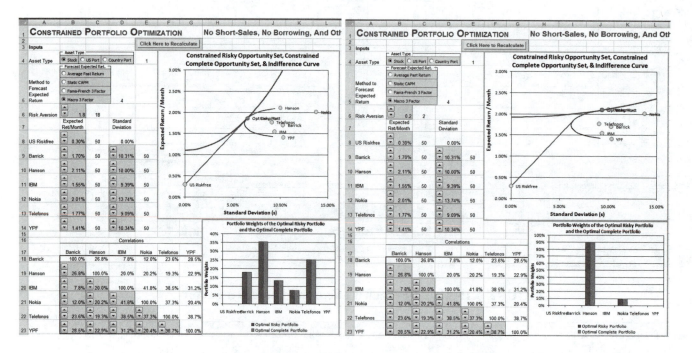

As risk aversion decreases, the Optimal Complete Portfolio slides up the Constrained Complete Opportunity Set. When it reaches the Optimal Risky Portfolio, then the Optimal Complete Portfolio involves putting 0% in the riskfree asset and 100% in the Optimal Risky Portfolio. As risk aversion decreases further, the Optimal Complete Portfolio follows the upper curve of the Constrained Risky Opportunity Set, because borrowing at the riskfree rate is not allowed. For a very low risk aversion level, the Optimal Complete Portfolio involves putting 100% in a single stock, Hanson, because it has the highest expected return.

Now consider portfolios. Click on **Fama-French 3 Factor**, click on **US Port** and then click the Recalculation button ⌈Click Here to Recalculate⌋. Then **Country Port** and then click the Recalculation button.

FIGURE 6.17 US Portfolios and Country Portfolios

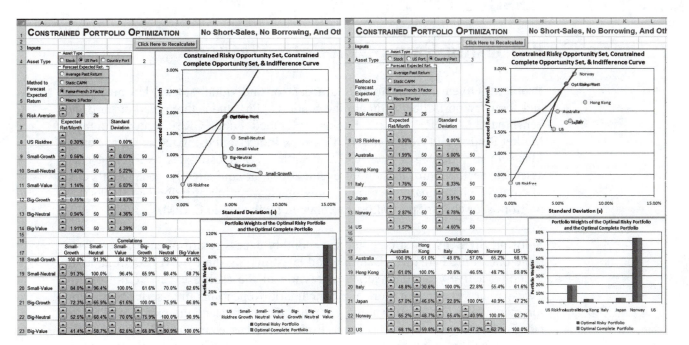

Again, we see that using portfolios matters a great deal. The Risky Opportunity Set has shifted far to the left, because portfolio diversification has eliminated firm-specific risk. The US Portfolios and County Portfolios produce very different portfolio weights for the Optimal Risky and Complete Portfolios than the Individual Stocks.

Problems

1. An individual investor with a simple mean and variance utility function has a risk aversion of 0.7. This investor is considering investing in the assets you downloaded for problem 2 of the prior chapter. This investor considers four methods to forecast expected returns: average past return, Static CAPM, Fama-French 3 Factor, or Macro 3 Factor. The investor wishes to impose no short sales, no borrowing, and no portfolio weights great than 100%. Determine the Portfolio Weights of the Optimal Risky Portfolio and the Optimal Complete Portfolio.

Chapter 7 Asset Pricing

7.1 Static CAPM Using Fama-MacBeth Method

Problem. Given monthly total return data on individual stocks, US portfolios, and country portfolios, estimate the Static CAPM under three market portfolio benchmarks (SPDR "Spider" Exchange Traded Fund, CRSP Value-Weighted Market Return, and Dow Jones World Stock Index) and using the standard Fama-MacBeth methodology. Then use the Static CAPM estimates to forecast each asset's expected return in the future (Jan 2007), or equivalently, each asset's cost of equity capital. Finally, determine how much variation of individual stocks, US portfolios, or country portfolios is explained by the Static CAPM.

Solution Strategy. First compute the monthly excess return of each asset. Then stage one of the Fama-MacBeth method is estimating the CAPM beta of an asset by doing a five-year, time-series regression of the asset's excess return on the excess return of a market portfolio benchmark. Repeat this time-series regression for many five-year windows and compute the average of the estimated CAPM betas. Then stage two of the Fama-Beth method is estimating the CAPM risk premium and intercept by doing a cross-sectional regression of the excess returns across assets in the following month on the CAPM beta from the immediately prior five-year window. Repeat this cross-sectional regression for many following months and compute the average of the estimated CAPM risk premium and intercept. Then use the estimated CAPM risk premium and intercept to forecast each asset's expected return, or equivalently, each asset's cost of equity capital. Finally, compute the R^2 ("explained variation") of both regressions.

FIGURE 7.1 Excel Model of Asset Pricing – Static CAPM Using Fama-MacBeth Method.

	A	B	C	D	E	F	G	H
1	ASSET PRICING		Static CAPM Using Fama-MacBeth Method					
2								
3	**Inputs**							
4	Market Portfolio Benchmark	Market Portfolio Benchmark ○ SPDR ETF ● CRSP VWMR ○ DJ World Stock			2			
5	Asset Type	Asset Type ○ Stock ● US Port ○ Country Port			2			
6								
7		Stock	Stock	Stock	Stock	Stock	Stock	US Portfolio
8		Barrick	Hanson	IBM	Nokia	Telefonos	YPF	Small-Growth
130				(1) Monthly Return(Asset i, Month t) - Riskfree Rate(Month t) Enter =B10-$AC10 and copy to B133:V252				
131								
132	**Monthly Excess Returns**							
133	Dec 2006	-3.90%	-0.64%	1.66%	8.36%	8.23%	0.10%	-0.99%
134	Nov 2006	-2.79%	4.46%	5.27%	0.09%	8.59%	-1.37%	2.16%
135	Oct 2006	1.38%	3.37%	-0.53%	1.29%	-1.49%	3.08%	5.46%
136	Sep 2006	0.51%	-3.90%	12.28%	0.52%	2.73%	6.61%	0.68%
137	Aug 2006	-8.65%	13.94%	0.78%	-6.10%	6.34%	-4.25%	2.80%
138	Jul 2006	8.28%	3.32%	4.60%	4.80%	2.62%	1.60%	-6.16%
139	Jun 2006	3.66%	0.48%	0.38%	-2.42%	12.11%	9.58%	-1.05%

FIGURE 7.2 Excel Model of Asset Pricing – Static CAPM Using Fama-MacBeth Method.

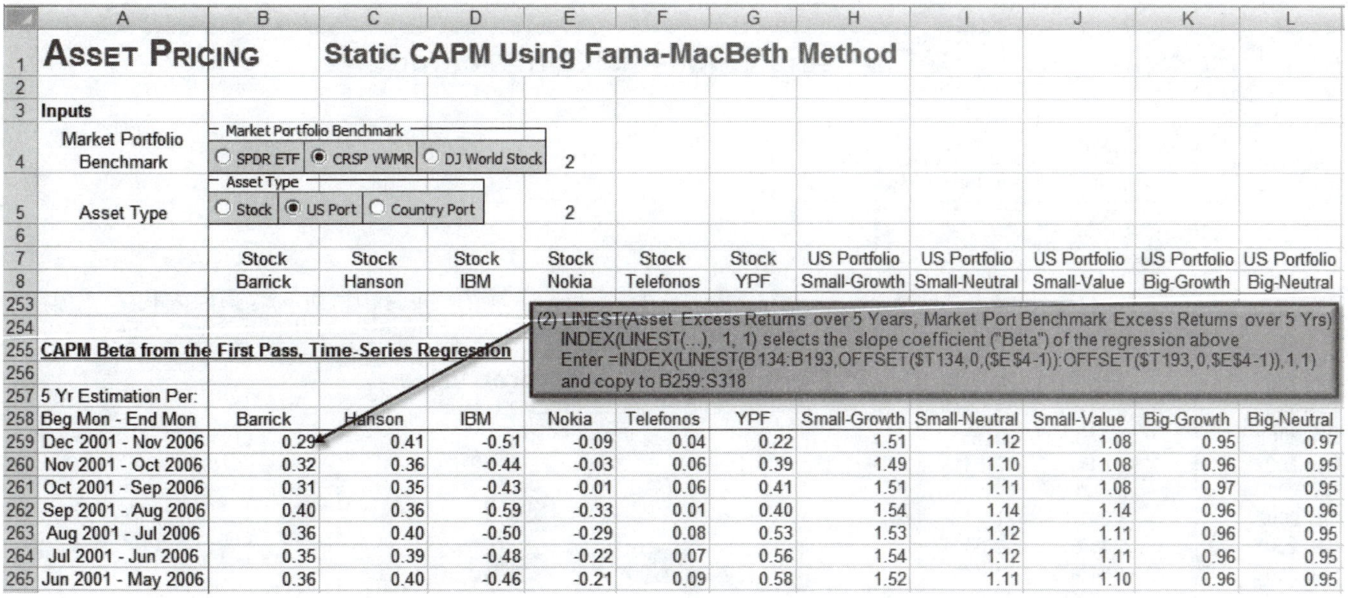

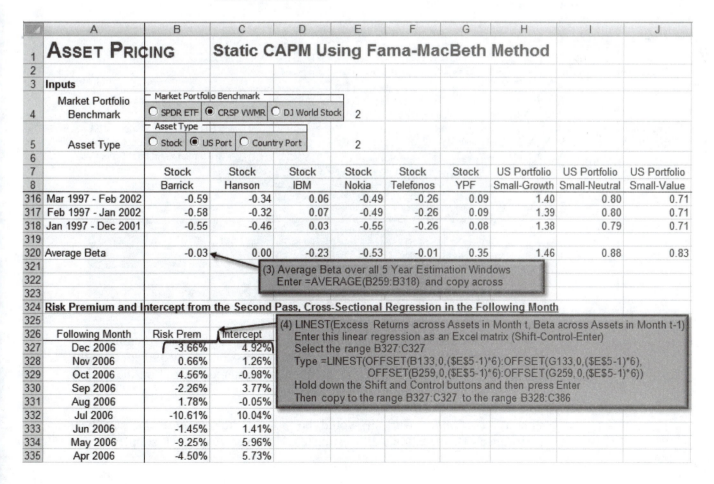

FIGURE 7.3 Excel Model of Asset Pricing – Static CAPM Using Fama-MacBeth Method.

FIGURE 7.4 Excel Model of Asset Pricing – Static CAPM Using Fama-MacBeth Method.

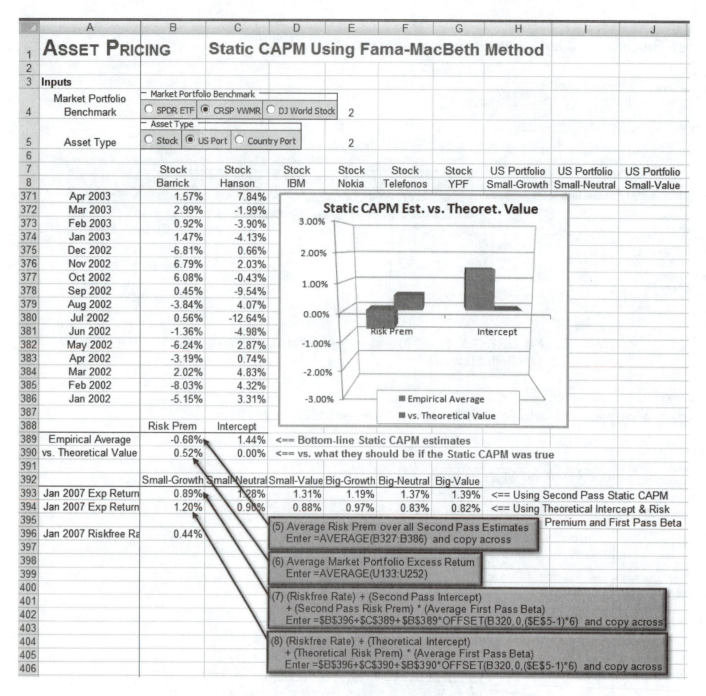

Row 389 contains the empirical average of the CAPM risk premium and intercept from the second-pass, cross-sectional regressions. Row 390 contains the theoretical value of the CAPM risk premium and intercept based on the CAPM beta from the first-pass, time-series regressions.

With a lot of extra work it would be possible to compute the statistical significance of the Static CAPM estimates. However, it is much simpler to just compare the empirical average and the theoretical value on a graph. It is clear at a glance that the empirical average and the theoretical value don't match very well.

It is interesting to make the same comparison for different market portfolio benchmarks by clicking on the option buttons in row 4 and for different asset types by clicking on the option buttons in row 5. Often the empirical average CAPM risk premium is negative, which doesn't make any economic sense. Often the empirical average of the CAPM intercept is far away from zero, which doesn't make any economic sense.

Row 393 contains the Static CAPM forecast of each asset's expected return in the future (Jan 2007), or equivalently, of each asset's cost of equity capital. This is a key output of this spreadsheet. However, given lack of economically sensible estimates for the Static CAPM, one should be very cautious about using the forecasts of each asset's expected return / cost of equity capital.

FIGURE 7.5 Excel Model of Asset Pricing – Static CAPM Using Fama-MacBeth Method.

	A	B	C	D	E	F	G	H	I	J
1	**ASSET PRICING**		**Static CAPM Using Fama-MacBeth Method**							
2										
3	**Inputs**									
4	Market Portfolio Benchmark	Market Portfolio Benchmark: ○ SPDR ETF ● CRSP VWMR ○ DJ World Stock			2					
5	Asset Type	Asset Type: ○ Stock ● US Port ○ Country Port			2					
6										
7		Stock	Stock	Stock	Stock	Stock	Stock	US Portfolio	US Portfolio	US Portfolio
8		Barrick	Hanson	IBM	Nokia	Telefonos	YPF	Small-Growth	Small-Neutral	Small-Value
408										
409		(9) LINEST(Asset Excess Returns over 5 Years, Market Port Benchmark Excess Returns over 5 Yrs)								
410		INDEX(LINEST(...), 3, 1) selects the R^2 of the regression above								
411		Enter =INDEX(LINEST(B134:B193,OFFSET($T134,0,($E$4-1)):OFFSET($T193,0,$E$4-1),,TRUE),3,1)								
412		and copy to B417:S476								
413	R^2 (Explained Variation as a Percentage of Total Variation) from the First Pass, Time-Series Regression									
414										
415	5 Yr Estimation Per:									
416	Beg Mon - End Mon	Barrick	Hanson	IBM	Nokia	Telefonos	YPF	Small-Growth	Small-Neutral	Small-Value
417	Dec 2001 - Nov 2006	1.5%	4.9%	4.9%	0.1%	0.1%	0.5%	81.7%	74.9%	65.5%
418	Nov 2001 - Oct 2006	1.9%	4.2%	4.0%	0.0%	0.2%	1.7%	82.0%	75.2%	66.7%
419	Oct 2001 - Sep 2006	1.8%	3.8%	3.7%	0.0%	0.2%	1.8%	80.3%	75.1%	66.6%
420	Sep 2001 - Aug 2006	3.3%	4.6%	7.5%	1.4%	0.0%	1.9%	82.5%	78.0%	70.5%
421	Aug 2001 - Jul 2006	2.8%	6.1%	5.7%	1.1%	0.3%	3.5%	82.8%	77.3%	69.5%
422	Jul 2001 - Jun 2006	2.6%	5.4%	5.3%	0.5%	0.2%	3.8%	82.7%	77.6%	69.7%
423	Jun 2001 - May 2006	2.8%	5.7%	4.8%	0.5%	0.4%	4.1%	79.7%	75.2%	69.2%
424	May 2001 - Apr 2006	2.4%	5.5%	5.2%	0.7%	0.6%	3.6%	79.3%	74.6%	68.1%
425	Apr 2001 - Mar 2006	2.3%	6.4%	5.4%	1.4%	0.5%	3.8%	80.0%	73.3%	66.8%

FIGURE 7.6 Excel Model of Asset Pricing – Static CAPM Using Fama-MacBeth Method.

	A	B	C	D	E	F	G	H	I	J	K
1	**ASSET PRICING**		**Static CAPM Using Fama-MacBeth Method**								
2											
3	**Inputs**										
4	Market Portfolio Benchmark	◯ SPDR ETF ◉ CRSP VWMR ◯ DJ World Stock			2						
5	Asset Type	◯ Stock ◉ US Port ◯ Country Port			2						
6											
7		Stock	Stock	Stock	Stock	Stock	Stock	US Portfolio	US Portfolio	US Portfolio	US Portfolio
8		Barrick	Hanson	IBM	Nokia	Telefonos	YPF	Small-Growth	Small-Neutral	Small-Value	Big-Growth
474	Mar 1997 - Feb 2002	7.5%	3.4%	0.1%	2.6%	1.5%	0.2%	60.4%	55.9%	52.2%	95.2%
475	Feb 1997 - Jan 2002	7.0%	3.1%	0.1%	2.7%	1.5%	0.3%	60.1%	55.8%	52.1%	95.2%
476	Jan 1997 - Dec 2001	6.5%	4.1%	0.0%	3.4%	1.5%	0.2%	59.9%	55.8%	52.6%	95.2%
477											
478	Average R^2	2.8%	1.7%	2.0%	3.4%	0.4%	2.5%	69.6%	62.0%	56.1%	95.4%
479											
480			(10) Average R^2 over all 5 Year Estimation Windows								
481			Enter =AVERAGE(B417:B476) and copy across								
482			(11) LINEST(Excess Returns across Assets in Month t, Beta across Assets in Month t)								
483			INDEX(LINEST(…), 3, 1) selects the R^2 of the regression above								
484			Enter =INDEX(LINEST(OFFSET(B133,0,($E$5-1)*6):OFFSET(G133,0,($E$5-1)*6),								
485			OFFSET(B259,0,($E$5-1)*6):OFFSET(G259,0,($E$5-1)*6),,TRUE),3,1)								
486			and copy down								
487											
488											
489	R^2 (Explained Variation as a Percentage of Total Variation) from the Second Pass, Cross-sectional Regression in the Following Month										
490											
491	Following Month	R^2									
492	Dec 2006	36.1%									
493	Nov 2006	4.3%									
494	Oct 2006	64.9%									
495	Sep 2006	46.0%									
496	Aug 2006	14.0%									
497	Jul 2006	73.8%									
498	Jun 2006	14.0%									

The Average R^2 of the first-pass, time-series regression tells us how much of the fluctuation in an asset's excess return can be explained by market portfolio's excess return. An R^2 of 0% means the two variables are unrelated vs. an R^2 of 100% means the two variables are move together perfectly. With single-digit R^2s, the individual stocks are poorly explained. By contrast, the US portfolios are pretty well-explained by US benchmarks and country portfolios are pretty well-explained by a world benchmark.

FIGURE 7.7 Excel Model of Asset Pricing – Static CAPM Using Fama-MacBeth Method.

	A	B	C	D	E	F	G	H	I
1	**ASSET PRICING**		**Static CAPM Using Fama-MacBeth Method**						
2									
3	**Inputs**								
4	Market Portfolio Benchmark	Market Portfolio Benchmark ○ SPDR ETF ● CRSP VWMR ○ DJ World Stock			2				
5	Asset Type	Asset Type ○ Stock ● US Port ○ Country Port			2				
6									
7		Stock	Stock	Stock	Stock	Stock	Stock	US Portfolio	US Portfolio
8		Barrick	Hanson	IBM	Nokia	Telefonos	YPF	Small-Growth	Small-Neutral
547	May 2002	62.8%							
548	Apr 2002	4.9%							
549	Mar 2002	6.2%							
550	Feb 2002	69.5%							
551	Jan 2002	34.3%							
552									
553	Average R^2	30.8%							
554									
555			(12) Average R^2 over all Following Months in Second Pass Regressions						
556			Enter =AVERAGE(B492:B551)						
557									

The Average R^2 of the second-pass, cross-sectional regression tells us how much of the fluctuation in the excess returns across assets in the following month can be explained by the CAPM beta from the immediately prior five-year window. With an Average R^2 of around 30%, the individual stocks and US portfolios are modestly explained by their CAPM betas. With an Average R^2 of below 20%, the country portfolio are very modestly explained by their CAPM betas.

7.2 APT or Intertemporal CAPM Using Fama-McBeth Method

Problem. Given monthly total return data on individual stocks, US portfolios, and country portfolios, estimate the APT or Intertemporal CAPM (ICAPM) under two sets of factors (Fama-French 3 factors and 3 macro factors) and using the standard Fama-MacBeth methodology. Then use the APT or ICAPM estimates from Jan 1997 – Dec 2006 data to forecast each asset's expected return in the future (Jan 2007), or equivalently, each asset's cost of equity capital. Finally, determine how much variation of individual stocks, US portfolios, or country portfolios is explained by the APT or ICAPM.

Solution Strategy. First carry over the monthly excess return of each asset from the other sheet. Then stage one of the Fama-MacBeth method is estimating the APT or ICAPM factor betas of an asset by doing a five-year, time-series regression of the asset's excess return on sets of APT or ICAPM factors. Repeat this time-series regression for many five-year windows and compute the average of the estimated APT or ICAPM factor betas. Then stage two of the Fama-Beth method is estimating the APT or ICAPM factor risk premia and intercept by doing a cross-sectional regression of the excess returns across assets in the following month on the APT or ICAPM factor betas from the immediately prior five-year window. Repeat this cross-sectional regression for many following months and compute the average of the estimated APT or ICAPM factor risk premia and intercept. Then use the estimated APT or ICAPM factor risk premia and intercept to forecast each asset's expected return in the future (Jan 2007), or equivalently, each asset's cost of equity capital. Finally, compute the R^2 ("explained variation") of both regressions.

FIGURE 7.8 Excel Model of Asset Pricing – APT or Intertemporal CAPM Using Fama-MacBeth Method.

	A	B	C	D	E	F	G	H	I
1	**ASSET PRICING APT or Intertemporal CAPM Using Fama-MacBeth Method**								
2									
3	**Inputs**								
4	APT or ICAPM Factors	APT or ICAPM Factors ● Fama-French 3 Factors ○ 3 Macro Factors			1				
5	Asset Type	Asset Type ● Stock ○ US Port ○ Country Port			1				
6						(1) Monthly Return from Sheet 9.1 Enter ='9.1'!B10 and copy to D10:AE129			
7				Stock	Stock	Stock	Stock	Stock	Stock
8				Barrick	Hanson	IBM	Nokia	Telefonos	YPF
9	**Monthly Returns**								
10	Dec 2006			-3.50%	-0.24%	2.06%	8.76%	8.63%	0.50%
11	Nov 2006			-2.37%	4.88%	5.69%	0.51%	9.01%	-0.95%
12	Oct 2006			1.79%	3.78%	-0.12%	1.70%	-1.08%	3.49%
13	Sep 2006			0.92%	-3.49%	12.69%	0.93%	3.14%	7.02%
14	Aug 2006			-8.23%	14.36%	1.20%	-5.68%	6.76%	-3.83%
15	Jul 2006			8.68%	3.72%	5.00%	5.20%	3.02%	2.00%
16	Jun 2006			4.06%	0.88%	0.78%	-2.02%	12.51%	9.98%

FIGURE 7.9 Excel Model of Asset Pricing – APT or Intertemporal CAPM Using Fama-MacBeth Method.

	A	B	C	D	E	F	G	H	I
1	**ASSET PRICING** APT or Intertemporal CAPM Using Fama-MacBeth Method								
2									
3	**Inputs**								
4	APT or ICAPM Factors	APT or ICAPM Factors ⦿ Fama-French 3 Factors ○ 3 Macro Factors		1					
5	Asset Type	Asset Type ⦿ Stock ○ US Port ○ Country Port		1					
6									
7				Stock	Stock	Stock	Stock	Stock	Stock
8				Barrick	Hanson	IBM	Nokia	Telefonos	YPF
130	(2) LINEST(Asset Returns over 5 Years, 3 Factor Innovations over 5 Yrs)								
131	Enter this linear regression as an Excel matrix (Shift-Control-Enter)								
132	Select D143:D145								
133	Type =TRANSPOSE(LINEST(OFFSET(D$11,$B143,0):OFFSET(D$70,$B143,0),								
134	OFFSET($Y$11,$B143,($E$4-1)*3):OFFSET($AA$70,$B143,($E$4-1)*3)))								
135	Hold down the Shift and Control buttons and then press Enter								
136	Then copy to the range D143:D145 to the range E143:U145; Then copy the range D143:U145 to the range D146:U148;								
137	Then copy the doubled range D143:U148 to the range D149:U154; Keep doubling until row 322 is reached.								
138									
139	**Three Factor Betas from the First Pass, Time-Series Regression**								
140									
141	5 Yr Estimation Per:	Row							
142	Beg Mon - End Mon	Offset	Factors	Barrick	Hanson	IBM	Nokia	Telefonos	YPF
143	Dec 2001 - Nov 2006	0	FF HML	-0.10	-0.67	-0.95	-1.12	-0.64	-1.84
144			FF SMB	0.15	0.16	0.11	-1.31	-0.35	-0.95
145			FF Mkt-RF	0.24	0.27	-0.67	0.05	0.03	0.17
146	Nov 2001 - Oct 2006	1	FF HML	-0.09	-0.69	-0.90	-1.09	-0.62	-1.74
147			FF SMB	0.14	0.18	0.07	-1.33	-0.37	-1.04
148			FF Mkt-RF	0.27	0.23	-0.59	0.11	0.06	0.38
149	Oct 2001 - Sep 2006	2	FF HML	0.06	-0.41	-0.93	-1.38	-0.48	-1.69
150			FF SMB	0.06	0.04	0.08	-1.19	-0.44	-1.07
151			FF Mkt-RF	0.30	0.28	-0.59	0.05	0.09	0.39
152	Sep 2001 - Aug 2006	3	FF HML	0.08	-0.43	-0.91	-1.45	-0.49	-1.68
153			FF SMB	0.14	0.01	0.01	-1.45	-0.46	-1.02
154			FF Mkt-RF	0.37	0.29	-0.73	-0.14	0.06	0.43
155	Aug 2001 - Jul 2006	4	FF HML	0.05	-0.40	-0.98	-1.50	-0.51	-1.84
156			FF SMB	0.20	-0.04	-0.08	-1.43	-0.53	-1.11
157			FF Mkt-RF	0.31	0.35	-0.64	-0.16	0.14	0.53

FIGURE 7.10 Excel Model of Asset Pricing – APT or Intertemporal CAPM Using Fama-MacBeth Method.

	A	B	C	D	E	F	G	H	I
1	**ASSET PRICING APT or Intertemporal CAPM Using Fama-MacBeth Method**								
2									
3	**Inputs**								
4	APT or ICAPM Factors	APT or ICAPM Factors ⦿ Fama-French 3 Factors ○ 3 Macro Factors			1				
5	Asset Type	Asset Type ⦿ Stock ○ US Port ○ Country Port			1				
6									
7					Stock	Stock	Stock	Stock	Stock	Stock
8					Barrick	Hanson	IBM	Nokia	Telefonos	YPF
314	Mar 1997 - Feb 2002	57	FF HML	-0.19	-0.23	0.02	-1.14	-0.48	-0.64
315			FF SMB	-0.47	-0.37	0.09	-0.37	0.04	-0.46
316			FF Mkt-RF	-0.60	-0.40	0.05	-1.09	-0.56	-0.20
317	Feb 1997 - Jan 2002	58	FF HML	-0.27	-0.26	-0.02	-1.14	-0.50	-0.65
318			FF SMB	-0.48	-0.37	0.08	-0.37	0.04	-0.46
319			FF Mkt-RF	-0.63	-0.40	0.04	-1.10	-0.56	-0.20
320	Jan 1997 - Dec 2001	59	FF HML	-0.30	-0.14	0.05	-1.04	-0.49	-0.64
321			FF SMB	-0.51	-0.23	0.14	-0.29	0.04	-0.45
322			FF Mkt-RF	-0.63	-0.50	0.02	-1.12	-0.56	-0.21
323									
324		Average Factor Betas		Barrick	Hanson	IBM	Nokia	Telefonos	YPF
325			FF HML	0.17	-0.05	-0.46	-1.23	-0.31	-1.19
326			FF SMB	-0.07	-0.23	-0.04	-0.94	-0.16	-0.95
327			FF Mkt-RF	0.06	0.04	-0.41	-0.87	-0.12	0.07
328									
329									
330		(3) LINEST(Returns across Assets in Month t, Factor Betas across Assets in Month t)							
331		Enter this linear regression as an Excel matrix (Shift-Control-Enter)							
332		Select the range D340:G340							
333		Type =LINEST(OFFSET(D10,0,($E$5-1)*6):OFFSET(I10,0,($E$5-1)*6), OFFSET($D$143,B340,($E$5-1)*6):OFFSET($I$145,B340,($E$5-1)*6))							
334		Hold down the Shift and Control buttons and then press Enter							
335		Then copy to the range D340:G340 to the range D341:G399							
336									
337	**Factor Risk Premia and Intercept from the Second Pass, Cross-Sectional Regression in the Following Month**								
338		Row							
339	Following Month	Offset		FF Mkt-RF	FF SMB	FF HML	Intercept		
340	Dec 2006	0		-6.62%	-8.45%	4.84%	4.02%		
341	Nov 2006	3		-5.84%	1.49%	-0.50%	3.39%		
342	Oct 2006	6		5.94%	3.89%	-3.74%	-0.29%		
343	Sep 2006	9		-5.56%	6.75%	-8.17%	0.26%		
344	Aug 2006	12		1.43%	3.74%	0.43%	2.87%		
345	Jul 2006	15		-1.00%	1.79%	0.38%	5.82%		
346	Jun 2006	18		4.59%	-7.84%	4.70%	4.24%		

FIGURE 7.11 Excel Model of Asset Pricing – APT or Intertemporal CAPM Using Fama-MacBeth Method.

	A	B	C	D	E	F	G	H	I	J
1	**ASSET PRICING** APT or Intertemporal CAPM Using Fama-MacBeth Method									
2										
3	**Inputs**									
4	APT or ICAPM Factors	APT or ICAPM Factors ⊙ Fama-French 3 Factors ○ 3 Macro Factors			1					
5	Asset Type	Asset Type ⊙ Stock ○ US Port ○ Country Port			1					
6										
7				Stock	Stock	Stock	Stock	Stock	Stock	US Portfolio
8				Barrick	Hanson	IBM	Nokia	Telefonos	YPF	Small-Growth
397	Mar 2002	171		-27.27%	-18.35%	36.97%	-10.99%			
398	Feb 2002	174		2.53%	-2.98%	4.97%	8.79%			
399	Jan 2002	177		-4.61%	-16.37%	13.76%	-2.55%			
400										
401				FF Mkt-RF	FF SMB	FF HML				
402	Factor Premia			Premium	Premium	Premium	Intercept			
403	Average			1.95%	-2.89%	0.56%	1.21%	<= Bottom-line APT or Intertemporal		
404								CAPM estimates		
405	Expected Return using APT or ICAPM Est.			Barrick	Hanson	IBM	Nokia	Telefonos	YPF	
406	Jan 2007	Fama-French 3 Factors		2.07%	2.37%	0.72%	1.99%	1.71%	3.88%	
407										
408		Jan 2007 Riskfree Rate		0.44%						
409						(4) Average Factor Risk Prem over all Second Pass Estimates Enter =AVERAGE(D340:D399) and copy across				
410										
411				(5) (Riskfree Rate) + (Second Pass Intercept)						
412				+ (Second Pass Factor 1 Risk Prem) * (First Pass Factor 1 Beta)						
413				+ (Second Pass Factor 2 Risk Prem) * (First Pass Factor 2 Beta)						
414				+ (Second Pass Factor 3 Risk Prem) * (First Pass Factor 3 Beta)						
415				Enter =$D$408+$G$403+$D$403*OFFSET(D327,0,($E$5-1)*6)						
416				+$E$403*OFFSET(D326,0,($E$5-1))						
417				+$F$403*OFFSET(D325,0,($E$5-1)*6) and copy across						
418										

Row 403 contains the empirical average of the APT or ICAPM factor risk premia and intercept from the second-pass, cross-sectional regressions. Given the wide flexibility in specifying APT or ICAPM factors in terms of either long positions or short positions, it is legitimately possible that risk premia could be either positive or negative.

Row 406 contains the APT or ICAPM forecast of each asset's expected return in the future (Jan 2007), or equivalently, of each asset's cost of equity capital. This is a key output of this spreadsheet.

FIGURE 7.12 Excel Model of Asset Pricing – APT or Intertemporal CAPM Using Fama-MacBeth Method.

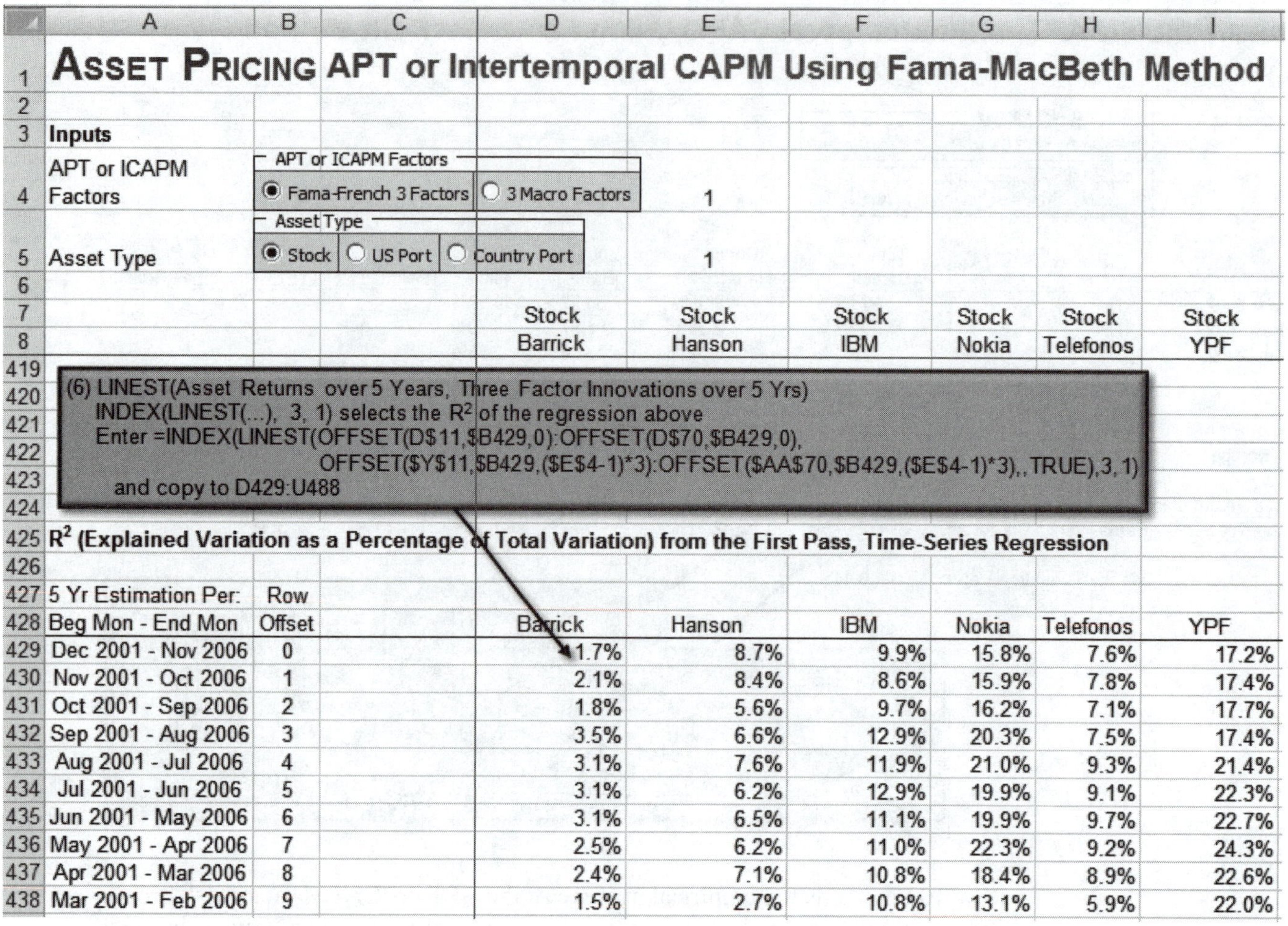

	A	B	C	D	E	F	G	H	I
1	**ASSET PRICING** APT or Intertemporal CAPM Using Fama-MacBeth Method								
2									
3	**Inputs**								
4	APT or ICAPM Factors	APT or ICAPM Factors: ⦿ Fama-French 3 Factors ◯ 3 Macro Factors		1					
5	Asset Type	Asset Type: ⦿ Stock ◯ US Port ◯ Country Port		1					
6									
7				Stock	Stock	Stock	Stock	Stock	Stock
8				Barrick	Hanson	IBM	Nokia	Telefonos	YPF
419									
420	(6) LINEST(Asset Returns over 5 Years, Three Factor Innovations over 5 Yrs)								
421	INDEX(LINEST(...), 3, 1) selects the R^2 of the regression above								
422	Enter =INDEX(LINEST(OFFSET(D$11,$B429,0):OFFSET(D$70,$B429,0),								
423	OFFSET($Y$11,$B429,($E$4-1)*3):OFFSET($AA$70,$B429,($E$4-1)*3),,TRUE),3, 1)								
424	and copy to D429:U488								
425	R^2 **(Explained Variation as a Percentage of Total Variation) from the First Pass, Time-Series Regression**								
426									
427	5 Yr Estimation Per:	Row							
428	Beg Mon - End Mon	Offset		Barrick	Hanson	IBM	Nokia	Telefonos	YPF
429	Dec 2001 - Nov 2006	0		1.7%	8.7%	9.9%	15.8%	7.6%	17.2%
430	Nov 2001 - Oct 2006	1		2.1%	8.4%	8.6%	15.9%	7.8%	17.4%
431	Oct 2001 - Sep 2006	2		1.8%	5.6%	9.7%	16.2%	7.1%	17.7%
432	Sep 2001 - Aug 2006	3		3.5%	6.6%	12.9%	20.3%	7.5%	17.4%
433	Aug 2001 - Jul 2006	4		3.1%	7.6%	11.9%	21.0%	9.3%	21.4%
434	Jul 2001 - Jun 2006	5		3.1%	6.2%	12.9%	19.9%	9.1%	22.3%
435	Jun 2001 - May 2006	6		3.1%	6.5%	11.1%	19.9%	9.7%	22.7%
436	May 2001 - Apr 2006	7		2.5%	6.2%	11.0%	22.3%	9.2%	24.3%
437	Apr 2001 - Mar 2006	8		2.4%	7.1%	10.8%	18.4%	8.9%	22.6%
438	Mar 2001 - Feb 2006	9		1.5%	2.7%	10.8%	13.1%	5.9%	22.0%

FIGURE 7.13 Excel Model of Asset Pricing – APT or Intertemporal CAPM Using Fama-MacBeth Method.

	A	B	C	D	E	F	G	H	I	J
1	**ASSET PRICING** APT or Intertemporal CAPM Using Fama-MacBeth Method									
2										
3	**Inputs**									
4	APT or ICAPM Factors		APT or ICAPM Factors: ⦿ Fama-French 3 Factors ○ 3 Macro Factors			1				
5	Asset Type		Asset Type: ⦿ Stock ○ US Port ○ Country Port			1				
6										
7				Stock	Stock	Stock	Stock	Stock	Stock	US Portfolio
8				Barrick	Hanson	IBM	Nokia	Telefonos	YPF	Small-Growth
486	Mar 1997 - Feb 2002	57		11.0%	6.0%	0.3%	7.6%	4.7%	5.3%	97.8%
487	Feb 1997 - Jan 2002	58		10.2%	5.8%	0.4%	7.7%	4.9%	5.5%	97.9%
488	Jan 1997 - Dec 2001	59		10.1%	4.8%	0.4%	7.8%	4.8%	5.1%	98.2%
489										
490	Average R^2			5.2%	4.1%	4.5%	13.4%	4.0%	17.1%	97.4%

(7) Average R^2 over all 5 Year Estimation Windows
Enter =AVERAGE(D429:D488) and copy across

(8) LINEST(Returns across Assets in Month t, Factor Betas across Assets in Month t)
INDEX(LINEST(…), 3, 1) selects the R^2 of the regression above
Enter =INDEX(LINEST(OFFSET(D10,0,($E$5-1)*6):OFFSET(I10,0,($E$5-1)*6),
OFFSET($D$143,B340,($E$5-1)*6):OFFSET($I$145,B340,($E$5-1)*6),,TRUE),3,1)
and copy down

R^2 (Explained Variation as a Percentage of Total Variation) from the Second Pass, Cross-sectional Regression in the Following Month

	A	D
503	Following Month	R^2
504	Dec 2006	60.5%
505	Nov 2006	29.7%
506	Oct 2006	76.1%
507	Sep 2006	65.1%
508	Aug 2006	10.4%
509	Jul 2006	36.2%
510	Jun 2006	32.8%
511	May 2006	40.0%

The Average R^2 of the first-pass, time-series regression tells us how much of the fluctuation in an asset's excess return can be explained by the APT or ICAPM factors. An R^2 of 0% means the two variables are unrelated vs. an R^2 of 100% means the two variables are move together perfectly. With single-digit R^2s, the individual stocks are poorly explained. With an R^2 over 90%, the US portfolios are extremely well-explained by US-based APT or ICAPM factors. With an R^2 around 50%, country portfolios are somewhat-explained by US-based APT or ICAPM factors.

FIGURE 7.14 Excel Model of Asset Pricing – APT or Intertemporal CAPM Using Fama-MacBeth Method.

	A	B	C	D	E	F	G	H	I
1	**ASSET PRICING APT or Intertemporal CAPM Using Fama-MacBeth Method**								
2									
3	**Inputs**								
4	APT or ICAPM Factors	APT or ICAPM Factors: ◉ Fama-French 3 Factors ○ 3 Macro Factors		1					
5	Asset Type	Asset Type: ◉ Stock ○ US Port ○ Country Port		1					
6									
7				Stock	Stock	Stock	Stock	Stock	Stock
8				Barrick	Hanson	IBM	Nokia	Telefonos	YPF
559	May 2002			94.3%					
560	Apr 2002			93.0%					
561	Mar 2002			79.5%					
562	Feb 2002			29.4%					
563	Jan 2002			54.9%					
564									
565	Average R^2			63.4%					
566									
567				(9) Average R^2 over all Following Months in Second Pass Regressions					
568				Enter =AVERAGE(D504:D563)					
569									

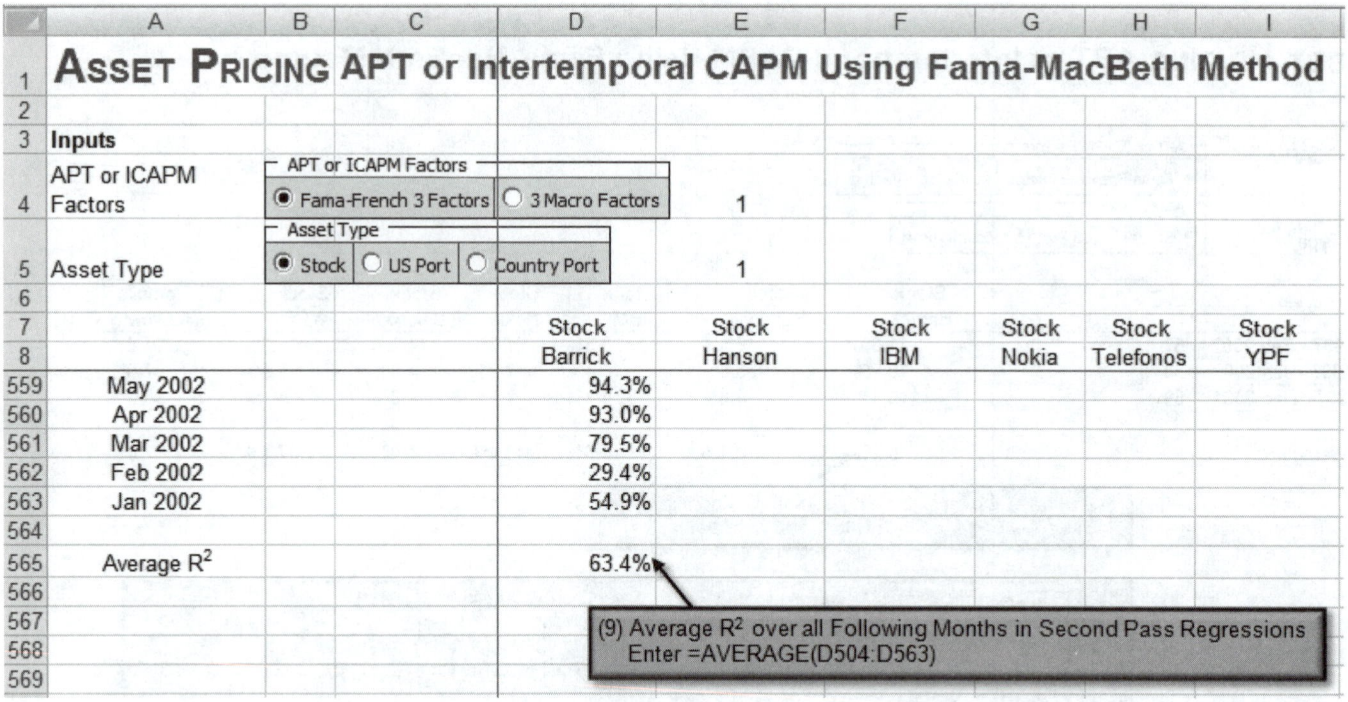

The Average R^2 of the second-pass, cross-sectional regression tells us how much of the fluctuation in the excess returns across assets in the following month can be explained by the APT or ICAPM factor betas from the immediately prior five-year window. With an Average R^2 of 50% - 70%, the individual stocks, US portfolios, and country portfolios are pretty well-explained by their APT or ICAPM factors.[5]

Problems

1. Download ten years of monthly total return data for individual stocks, US portfolios, and country portfolios. Then use that data to estimate the Static CAPM under three market portfolio benchmarks (SPDR "Spider" Exchange Traded Fund, CRSP Value-Weighted Market Return, and Dow Jones World Stock Index) and using the standard Fama-MacBeth methodology. Then use the Static CAPM estimates to forecast each asset's expected return in the

---

[5] Lewellen, Nagel and Shaken (2007) suggest that apparently high cross-sectional R^2 provide quite weak support for an asset pricing model. They offer a number of suggestions for improving empirical asset pricing tests, include expanding the set of assets tested to include industry portfolios and using Generalized Least Squares (GLS) R^2, rather than regular regression (OLS) R^2. They test seven popular asset pricing models, including the Static CAPM and the Fama-French 3 Factor model. They find that for an expanded set of assets which includes industry portfolios, the GLS R^2 is less than 10% for all seven asset pricing models. See Lewellen, J., S. Nagel, and J. Shaken, 2007, A Skeptical Appraisal of Asset-Pricing Tests, Emory working paper.

next future month, or equivalently, each asset's cost of equity capital. Finally, determine how much variation of individual stocks, US portfolios, or country portfolios is explained by the Static CAPM.

2. Download ten years of monthly total return data for individual stocks, US portfolios, and country portfolios. Then use that data to estimate the APT or Intertemporal CAPM (ICAPM) under two sets of factors (Fama-French 3 factors and 3 macro factors) and using the standard Fama-MacBeth methodology. Then use the APT or ICAPM estimates to forecast each asset's expected return in the next future month, or equivalently, each asset's cost of equity capital. Finally, determine how much variation of individual stocks, US portfolios, or country portfolios is explained by the APT or ICAPM.

Chapter 8 Trading Simulations using @RISK

8.1 Trader Simulation

Purpose. The purpose of this simulation is:

- To permit the scientific analysis of a wide variety of security trader problems, including differences in requested volume ratio, average volume, trader patience, trader penalty, trader information, and performance metric.
- For each trading problem, to permit the scientific analysis of wide variety of order submission strategies – with either static or dynamic submission of many order types, sizes, and limit prices.
- To give you hands-on security trading experience.
- To add to your knowledge of Excel and @RISK.

How To Access @RISK And The Project File.

The basic platform we will use is an Excel add-in program for doing simulations called @RISK. Consult your instructor for how access to @RISK on your campus.

Launch **Excel 2007**. Click on the **Office** button ![Office button], click on the **Excel Options** button at the bottom of the drop-down window, click on **Trust Center** in the left column ![Trust Center], click on the **Trust Center Settings** button ![Trust Center Settings...], click on **Macro Settings** in the left column ![Macro Settings], click on **Enable all macros (not recommended; potentially dangerous code can run)** in the **Macro Settings** section ⦿ Enable all macros (not recom, click on **OK** two times. Exit **Excel 2007**. (When you are done working on the project, follow the same steps to restore the Macro Settings to **Disable all macros with notification**)

Launch **@RISK**. Now open **Ch 10 Trader Simulation.xlsm**, if asked click on **Yes** open a new simulation file based on the @RISK settings in Trader Simulation.xlsm, and click on **No** to save the old simulation. Then, click on **F9** to recalculate the spreadsheet and you're ready to go!

The Setting

You work at the Order Desk of a major institutional trader and your job is to make various fund managers as happy as possible by doing the best job of implementing their trading requests. For example, suppose that a fund manager just asked you to buy a Requested Volume Ratio equal to 90% of the Average Volume of a particular stock and suppose that the Average Volume of that stock was 300 round lots (30,000 shares). Then the Requested Volume = (90%) * (300 round lots) = 270 round lots (27,000 shares). The fund manager wants you to buy the Requested Volume within a certain timeframe (reflecting the fund manager's degree of patience) and indicates how upset he/she would be for failure to purchase the desired number of lots (the fund manager's "penalty"). Your goal is to find the optimal order submission strategy that minimizes the fund manager's disutility (or "unhappiness"), which is given by:

*Fund Manager's Disutility = (Total Cost of Trading) * (Scale Factor)*

*+ (Penalty Coefficient) *(Absolute Value of Lots Over/Under) * (Scale Factor)*

where *Total Cost of Trading = Summation over all trades: (Cost of Trading / Lot) * (Lots In Each Trade)*

where $Cost\ of\ Trading\ /\ Lot = \begin{cases} Trade\ Price - Trade\ Midpoint & \text{for buys} \\ Trade\ Midpoint - Trade\ Price & \text{for sells.} \end{cases}$

and where *Scale Factor = 20.*

The performance metric used to measure your results may be based on the effective spread (as shown above) or based on implementation shortfall as show below:

$Cost\ of\ Trading\ /\ Lot = \begin{cases} Trade\ Price - Initial\ Midpoint & \text{for buys} \\ Initial\ Midpoint - Trade\ Price & \text{for sells} \end{cases}$

*+ Opportunity Cost = (Ending Midpoint – Initial Midpoint) * (Lots Not Bought).*

Fund managers can have a wide range of patience. The highest patience fund manager has all 80 periods (the entire trading day) to trade. Whereas the lowest patience fund manager only has 10 periods to trade. Intermediate degrees of patience are 30 periods or 60 periods.

Fund managers can have a wide range of penalty. The highest penalty fund manager has a penalty of .03. Whereas the lowest penalty fund manager has a zero penalty and thus acts as a pseudo-market maker. Intermediate degrees of penalty are .01 or .02.

Fund managers can have different degrees of information. Uninformed fund managers have no private information about the direction of the stock. High info fund managers are highly bullish about this stock. That is, they expect (correctly as it turns out) that the stock price will increase a lot on average over the trading day. In the intermediate cases, medium info and low info the stock price will increase a medium amount and low amount, respectively, on average over the trading day.

You have rich set of orders to choose from:

o   market orders or limit orders

- o any limit order price
- o each order can be any number of lots
- o limit orders can be cancelled at any time.

Explanation of the Project File

The project file **Trader Simulation.xlsm** is shown in Figure 8.1.

Figure 8.1 The Project File.

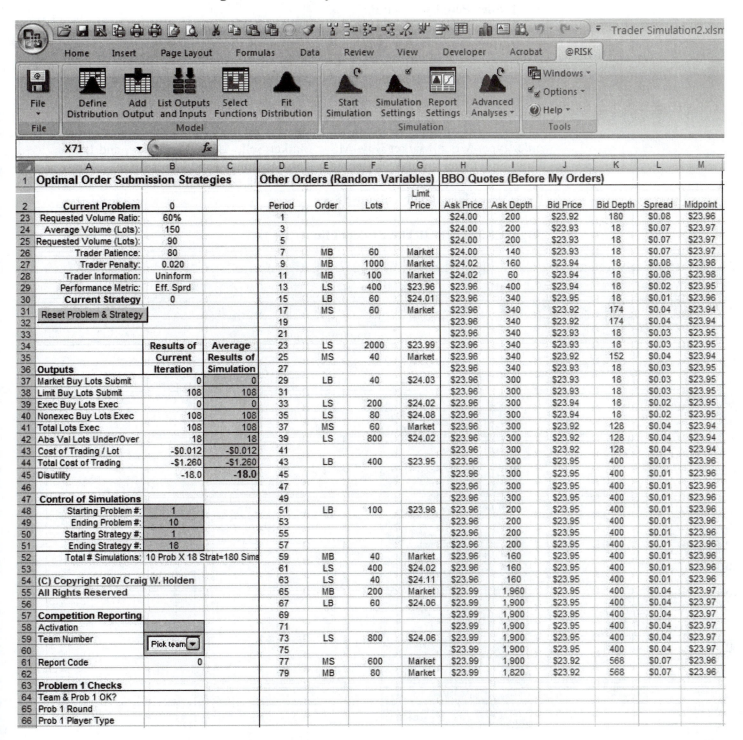

The **Current Problem** section displays the current value of:

- **Requested Volume Ratio** in cell B23,
- **Average Volume (Lots)** in cell B24,
- **Requested Volume (Lots)** in cell B25,

- **Trader Patience** in cell B26,
- **Trader Penalty** in cell B27,
- **Trader Information** in cell B28, , and
- **Performance Metric** in cell B29.

The **Other Orders (Random Variables)** section shows a sequence of events, which are generated by random variables. Events happen in odd numbered **Periods** (column D). One type of event is the arrival of an order submitted by other security traders. When an order arrives, **Order** (column E) indicates the order type: MB = Market Buy, MS = Market Sell, LB = Limit Buy, and LS = Limit Sell. Order information includes **Lots** (column F) and **Limit Price** (column G). The other type of event is the passage of clock time with no activity. More of the project file is shown in Figure 8.2.

Figure 8.2 More Of The Project File.

Left section — **Optimal Order Submission Strategies**

	B	C
Current Problem	0	
Requested Volume Ratio:	60%	
Average Volume (Lots):	150	
Requested Volume (Lots):	90	
Trader Patience:	80	
Trader Penalty:	0.020	
Trader Information:	Uniform	
Performance Metric:	Eff. Sprd	
Current Strategy	0	
Reset Problem & Strategy		
	Results of Current Iteration	Average Results of Simulation
Outputs		
Market Buy Lots Submit	0	0
Limit Buy Lots Submit	108	108
Exec Buy Lots Exec	0	0
Nonexec Buy Lots Exec	108	108
Total Lots Exec	108	108
Abs Val Lots Under/Over	18	18
Cost of Trading / Lot	-$0.012	-$0.012
Total Cost of Trading	-$1.260	-$1.260
Disutility	-18.0	-18.0
Control of Simulations		
Starting Problem #:	1	
Ending Problem #:	10	
Starting Strategy #:	1	
Ending Strategy #:	18	
Total # Simulations:	10 Prob X 18 Strat=180 Sims	
(C) Copyright 2007 Craig W. Holden		
All Rights Reserved		
Competition Reporting		
Activation		
Team Number	Pick team ▼	
Report Code	0	
Problem 1 Checks		
Team & Prob 1 OK?		
Prob 1 Round		
Prob 1 Player Type		

Right section — **My Orders (Choice Variables)** (N–S), **My Executable Buy Trades** (T–W), **My Nonexec Buy Trades** (X–AA)

Period	Order	Lots	Limit Price	Cancel Order Number	Order Number	Incremental Lots	Price	Cost of Trading	Cumulative Lots	Incremental Lots	Price	Cost of Trading	Cumulative Lots
2	LB	18	$23.93		28	0			0	0			0
4						0			0	0			0
6						0			0	0			0
8	LB	18	$23.94		70	0			0	0			0
10						0			0	0			0
12						0			0	0			0
14	LB	18	$23.95		112	0			0	0			0
16						0			0	54	$23.94	-$0.01	54
18						0			0	0			54
20	LB	18	$23.93	28	154	0			0	0			54
22						0			0	0			54
24						0			0	18	$23.93	-$0.02	72
26	LB	18	$23.93	70	196	0			0	0			72
28						0			0	0			72
30						0			0	0			72
32	LB	18	$23.94	112	238	0			0	0			72
34						0			0	0			72
36						0			0	36	$23.94	-$0.01	108
38		0	$23.93	154		0			0	0			108
40						0			0	0			108
42						0			0	0			108
44		0	$23.96	196		0			0	0			108
46						0			0	0			108
48						0			0	0			108
50		0	$23.96	238		0			0	0			108
52						0			0	0			108
54						0			0	0			108
56		0	$23.96			0			0	0			108
58						0			0	0			108
60						0			0	0			108
62		0	$23.96			0			0	0			108
64						0			0	0			108
66						0			0	0			108
68		0	$23.96			0			0	0			108
70						0			0	0			108
72						0			0	0			108
74		0	$23.96			0			0	0			108
76						0			0	0			108
78						0			0	0			108
80		0	$23.93			0			0	0			108

Strat 1, except LB price = bid - .01

Title bar: Trader Simulation2.xlsm - Microsoft Excel

The **My Orders (Choice Variables)** section with light blue-shaded cells is where you specify your order submission strategy. A strategy includes four columns: **Order** (column O), **Lots** (column P), **Limit Price** (column Q), and **Cancel Order Number** (column R). You may submit orders in even numbered

Event Time Periods (column N). An event time period is *immediately after* an event happens (see the next section).

This is a pure limit order market. So nonexecutable limit orders from anyone go on the Limit Order Book. Executable orders (market orders or executable limit orders) from anyone cross with limit orders on the book.

The **Outputs** section shows the **Results of the Current Iteration** (range B37:B45) as follows:

- **Market Buy Lots Submit** in cell B37,
- **Limit Buy Lots Submit** in cell B38,
- **Exec Buy Lots Exec** in cell B39,
- **Limit Buy Lots Exec** in cell B40,
- **Total Lots Exec** in cell B41,
- **Abs Val Lots Under/over** = Abs Value of [(Requested Volume) − (Total Lots Executed)]   in cell B42,
- **Cost of Trading / Lot** = Cost of Trading / Lot on average for all lots bought in cell B43,
- **Total Cost of Trading** = (Cost of Trading / Lot) * (Lots Bought) in cell B44, and
- **Disutility** = (Total Cost of Trading) − (Trader Penalty) * (Abs Value of Lots Under/over) in cell B45.

The **Average Results of the Simulation** with light green-shaded cells (range C37:C45) contains the average results over all iterations in a given simulation. Cell C37 shows the mean of cell B37. Cell C38 shows the mean of cell B38. And so on. The key bottom line is the **Average Disutility** with **bold highlighting** in cell C45. The goal of this project is to find order submission strategies which minimize the average disutility.

The **Control of Simulations** section allows you to automate running multiple simulations. You do this by specifying the starting problem, ending problem, starting strategy, and ending strategy. In this example, 10 different problems are being tested using 18 different strategies for a total of 180 simulations in a single run.

Entering Orders

Let's look in detail at how you enter orders. Suppose the fund manager has requested that you buy 450 round lots. By fiat, you are *not allowed to sell*, because this might permit price manipulation strategies. Thus, you are allowed to use market buys and/or limit buys. Entering the value "MB" (or a formula that produces "MB" under certain conditions) in the **Order** column yields a market buy. Similarly, the value or formula result "LB" in the **Order** column yields a limit buy. For each order, you need to supply a value or formula for the number of lots in the **Lots** column. For limit buys, you need to supply a value or formula for the price in the **Limit Price** column. For example, consider row 26 in Figure 8.2. It contains formulas which generate a limit buy for 90 lots at $34.59 which is submitted in event period 8. Limit prices must be "reasonably near" the bid-ask midpoint. Limit prices that are more than $0.50 above or below the midpoint are automatically reset to be inside the bracket.

Notice that this limit buy generates an "order number" of 70 in cell S26 of the **Order Number** column. This order number identifies this particular limit and thus allows it to be cancelled on a future date. To cancel this order, simply reference cell S26 in the **Cancel Order Number** column. For example, cell R35 has the formula "=S26", which yields the order number 70. Thus in event period 26, any remaining portion of the limit buy submitted in event period 8 is cancelled.

Formulas can refer to any information in Columns D – M on the same row or higher and to any information in Columns S – AA on higher rows, since this is *past* information that is known. For example in Figure 8.2, the cell G35 in the **Limit Price** column contains the formula =J35-.01. This formula looks at the bid price on the same row (which comes from the previous period) and subtracts one cent to obtain the limit buy price. Formulas may NOT refer to any information from a lower row, since this is *future* information that hasn't happened yet. It you enter a function that depends on future information, then it will generate a circular reference. If this happens to you by accident, just click **Edit | Undo**. If you run @RISK and get an odd error message, check the Status Bar at the bottom of Excel to see if you have circular reference.

Order submission strategies can depend on many things. For example, you could test if the bid-ask spread (in column L) was wide or narrow and only submit market orders when the spread was narrow. As another example, you could see how large the ask depth (in column I) is and set the number of lots equal to the ask depth so as to avoid walking up the book. As a third example, you could submit a limit order early on, then near the end of time available you could sum the number of lots purchased so far, cancel any unexecuted limit orders, and submit market orders for the remaining lots required. As a fourth example, if the ask price (in column H) and the bid price (in column J) have risen such that a previously submitted limit buy has become far behind the market, then you could cancel that order and submit a new limit buy at a more competitive price. The possibilities are endless.

A minor technicality is that occasionally the limit order book is empty. If there are no limit sell orders on the book, then the ask price (in column H) is set equal to a dummy value of $1,000 and the midpoint is carried down from the last period. Similarly, if there are no limit buy orders, the bid price (in column J) is set equal to a dummy value of $0 and the midpoint is carried down from the last period. This means that (limit price) formulas tied to the midpoint will always work, but formulas tied to the ask must test if the ask is less than $1,000 and formulas tied to the bid must test if the bid is greater than $0.

Storing Strategies

Space is provided to store up to 40 strategies in rows 285 – 2080. The easiest way to store a strategy is to first enter the orders into the light blue-shaded cells of the range O23:R62. Then enter a short description of the strategy in cell O63. Then copy the whole range O23:R63 to the storage area for Strategy 1. This is done by selecting the entire range O23:R63, clicking on **Home | Clipboard | Copy**, select the cell O285, and clicking on **Home | Clipboard | Paste**. See the figure below.

Figure 8.3 Storing Strategies.

	A	B	C	N	O	P	Q	R
1	Optimal Order Submission Strategies			My Orders (Choice Variables)				
2	Current Problem	0		Period	Order	Lots	Limit Price	Cancel Order Number
282								
283				My Orders (Choice Variables)				
284		Strategy 1		Period	Order	Lots	Limit Price	Cancel Order Number
285				2	LB	90	-$0.01	
286				4				
287				6				
288				8	LB	90	-$0.01	
289				10				
290				12				
291				14	LB	90	-$0.01	
292				16				
293				18				
294				20	LB	90	-$0.01	0
295				22				
296				24				
297				26	LB	90	-$0.01	0
298				28				
299				30				
300				32	LB	90	-$0.01	0
301				34				
302				36				
303				38	LB	90	-$0.01	0
304				40				
305				42				
306				44	LB	90	-$0.01	0
307				46				
308				48				
309				50	LB	90	-$0.01	0
310				52				
311				54				
312				56	LB	90	-$0.01	0
313				58				
314				60				
315				62	LB	90	-$0.01	0
316				64				
317				66				
318				68	LB	90	-$0.01	0
319				70				
320				72				
321				74	LB	90	-$0.01	0
322				76				
323				78				
324				80	LB	90	-$0.01	0
325				Description:	LBs at bid -.01; 9 period cancel & resub			

To store a second strategy, enter it in the light blue-shaded cells of the range O23:R62and copy it to the storage area for Strategy 2 (pasting it to cell O330). Follow the same procedure to store as many as 40 strategies.

Selecting Problems

Problems are selected clicking the spin buttons in rows 70 – 75. The spreadsheet is setup to allow you to test as many as 10 different problems in a single run. Each problem has its own column. For example, Problem 1 is in column N, Problem 2 is in column O, etc. You specify Problem 1 by selecting the six inputs in the range N70:N75. In particular, you specify Problem 1 by clicking the spin button in cell N70 to select the Requested Volume Ratio, clicking the spin button in cell N71 to select the Average Volume, . . . , and clicking the spin button in cell N75 to select the Performance Metric.

Figure 8.4 Selecting Problems.

	A	B	C	N	O	P	Q	R	S	T	U	V	W
1	Optimal Order Submission Strategies			My Orders (Choice Variables)						My Executable Buy Trades			
2	Current Problem	0		Period	Order	Lots	Limit Price	Cancel Order Number	Order Number	Incremental Lots	Price	Cost of Trading	Cumulative Lots
68													
69	Average Results By Problem & By Strat			Problem 1	Problem 2	Problem 3	Problem 4	Problem 5	Problem 6	Problem 7	Problem 8	Problem 9	Problem 10
70		Requested Volume Ratio:		60%	60%	60%	60%	30%	30%	10%	30%	60%	90%
71		Average Volume:		150	150	150	150	300	300	30	30	30	30
72		Trader Patience:		60	60	60	60	10	80	30	30	30	30
73		Trader Penalty:		0.000	0.010	0.020	0.030	0.020	0.020	0.010	0.010	0.010	0.010
74		Trader Information:		Uninform	Uninform	Uninform	Uninform	High Info	High Info	Med Info	Med Info	Med Info	Med Info
75		Performance Metric:		Eff. Sprd	Eff. Sprd	Eff. Sprd	Eff. Sprd	Impl Shrt	Impl Shrt	Eff. Sprd	Eff. Sprd	Eff. Sprd	Eff. Sprd

It is helpful to create *Problem Sets* of two to four problems, where all items are held constant except for one item. For example, in Figure 8.4, Problems 1 – 4 are a Problem Set. All items are held constant, except for Trader Penalty which varies from 0.0 in Problem 1 up to 0.03 in Problem 4. Another example, in Figure 8.4, Problems 6 and 6 are a set based on looking at opposite extremes. All items are held constant, except for Trader Patience which varies from the low extreme of 10 to the high extreme of 80. Also in Figure 8.4, Problems 7 – 10 are a Problem Set. All items are held constant, except for Requested Volume Ratio which varies from 10% to 90%. Analyzing problems in sets allows you to isolate cause and effect. That is, holding everything else constant, how does a change in one item cause optimal strategies to change?

Figure 8.5 Strategy Sets.

76	Strategy:	Description		
77	Strategy 01:	LBs at bid -.01		
78	Strategy 02:	Strat 1, except LB price = bid		
79	Strategy 03:	Strat 1, except LB price = bid + .01		
80	Strategy 04:	One large MB		
81	Strategy 05:	Strat 4, except many smaller MBs		
82	Strategy 06:	Strat 4, except tiny MBs every period		
83	Strategy 07:	LBs with no cancel & resub		
84	Strategy 08:	Strat 7, except cancel & resub =12 per		
85	Strategy 09:	Strat 7, except cancel & resub = 3 per		
86	Strategy 10:	MBs with no condition; rest at end		
87	Strategy 11:	Strat 10, except MB when spread<.06		
88	Strategy 12:	Strat 10, except MB when spread<.04		
89	Strategy 13:	LBs with no time pattern		
90	Strategy 14:	Strat 13, except more aggressive early		
91	Strategy 15:	Strat 13, except more aggressive late		
92	Strategy 16:	LBs with base quantity		
93	Strategy 17:	Strat 16, except 2 X quantity		
94	Strategy 18:	Strat 16, except 4 X quantity		

It is helpful to create *Strategy Sets* of two to four strategies, where most of the strategy is held constant, but one characteristic is varied. For example, Figure 8.5 shows six Strategy Sets which explore six different dimensions of trading strategy:

- Strategies 1-3 are LBs tied to the bid with **varying price aggressiveness**,
- Strategies 4-6 are MBs with **varying time concentration** (one big order, many smaller orders, tiny orders every period),
- Strategies 7-9 are LBs with **varying cancellation and resubmit policies** (no cancellation, 12 period cancel and resubmit, 3 period cancel and resubmit),
- Strategies 10-12 are MBs with **varying spread conditions** (no condition, submit when spread is less than 6 cents, submit when spread is less than 4 cents),
- Strategies 13-15 are LBs with **varying time when more aggressive** (no time pattern, more aggressive earlier in the trading day, more aggressive later in the trading day), and
- Strategies 16-18 are LBs with **varying quantities** (base quantity, 2 times the base quantity, 4 times the base quantity).

Analyzing strategies in sets allows you to pin down what specific aspect of a strategy makes a difference.

Strategies that attempt to "game" the simulation are not allowed. At the instructor's discretion, such strategies will be disqualified.

Running Simulations

Suppose you want to do 10 problems x 40 strategies in one run. Enter **1** for the Starting Problem # in cell B48, **10** for the Ending Problem # in cell B49, **1** for the Starting Strategy # in cell B50, and **40** for the Ending Strategy # in cell B51.

The   cell   C52   shows   that   this   is   400   simulations.

	A	B	C
47	**Control of Simulations**		
48	Starting Problem #:	1	
49	Ending Problem #:	10	
50	Starting Strategy #:	1	
51	Ending Strategy #:	40	
52	Total # Simulations:	10 Prob X 40 Strat=400 Sims	

To set up @RISK, click on the @RISK tab and then click on the "**Simulation**

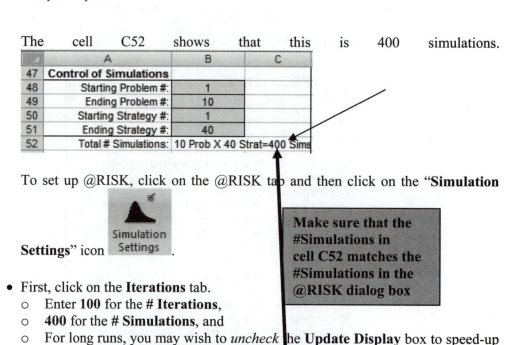

Settings" icon   .

Make sure that the
#Simulations in
cell C52 matches the
#Simulations in the
@RISK dialog box

- First, click on the **Iterations** tab.
  - o Enter **100** for the **# Iterations**,
  - o **400** for the **# Simulations**, and
  - o For long runs, you may wish to *uncheck* the **Update Display** box to speed-up

the run.

- Second, click on the **Sampling** tab,
  - o Under **Sampling Type**, click on **Latin Hypercube**,
  - o Under **Random Generator Seed**, click on **Choose Randomly**,
  - o Under **Standard Recalc**, click on **Monte Carlo**,
  - o Under   **Collect   Distribution   Samples**,   click   on   **None**.

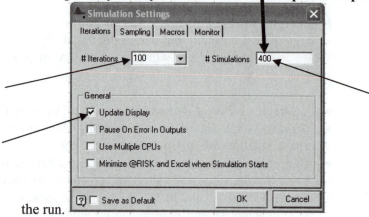

- Third, click on the **Macros** tab.
  - ○ Verify that **Before Each Simulation** is checked,
  - ○ Verify that a macro called **Before** is entered in the corresponding **Macro Name** box,
  - ○ Verify that **After Each Simulation** is checked,
  - ○ Verify that a macro called **After** is entered in the corresponding **Macro**

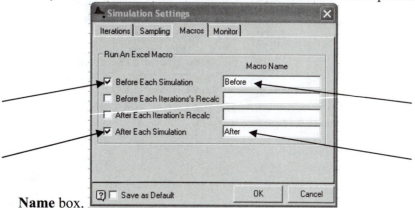

Name box.
- Then click on **OK**.

Then, click on the "**Report Settings**" icon , uncheck the box for **Show Interactive @RISK Results Window**, and click on **OK**.

Close any other Excel files that you have open. If more than one Excel file is left open, then @RISK may get "confused" about what to do and generate strange results.

Verify that the **Current Problem** in cell B2 is **0** and the **Current Strategy** in cell B30 is **0**. If either one or both of these cells are not zero, then fix this by clicking on the **Reset Problem and Strategy** button 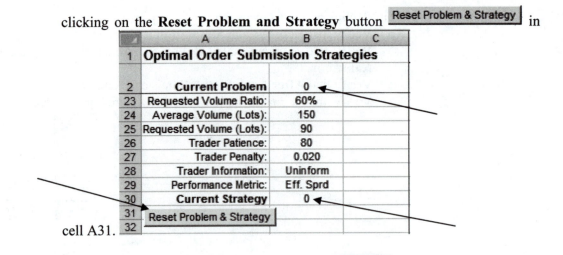 in

	A	B	C
1	**Optimal Order Submission Strategies**		
2	**Current Problem**	0	
23	Requested Volume Ratio:	60%	
24	Average Volume (Lots):	150	
25	Requested Volume (Lots):	90	
26	Trader Patience:	80	
27	Trader Penalty:	0.020	
28	Trader Information:	Uninform	
29	Performance Metric:	Eff. Sprd	
30	**Current Strategy**	0	
31	Reset Problem & Strategy		
32			

cell A31.

Finally, click on the "**Start Simulation**" icon [Start Simulation].

Here is how the whole process works:

- The **Before** Macro copies a particular Trader Strategy from one of the storage areas down below (Strategy 1, Strategy 2, etc.) up to the working area in rows 23 – 63.
- Then a complete simulation is performed using the Number of Trails that you requested.
- The **After** Macro copies the average results of the simulation to the **Saved Results** section in rows 2085 – 2522. Importantly, the average results are *saved as values*. This is very important, because if you just save the @RISK spreadsheet under a different name, then live results in the light green-shaded cells will reset next time you open it and your results will be lost.
- The three steps above repeat for all of the problems and all of the strategies that you requested.

A bird's eye view of the average results is displayed in the **Average Results By Problem and Strategy** section in rows 69 – 116. In Figure 8.6, we see the **Average Disutility** results for the 10 problems x 10 strategies.

Figure 8.6 Average Results By Problem and Strategy.

			Period	Order	Lots	Limit Price	Cancel Order Number	Order Number	Incremental Lots	Price	Cost of Trading	Cumulative Lots
Optimal Order Submission Strategies			**My Orders (Choice Variables)**						**My Executable Buy Trades**			
Current Problem	0											
Average Results By Problem & By Strat			Problem 1	Problem 2	Problem 3	Problem 4	Problem 5	Problem 6	Problem 7	Problem 8	Problem 9	Problem 10
	Requested Volume Ratio:		60%	60%	60%	60%	30%	30%	10%	30%	60%	90%
	Average Volume:		150	150	150	150	300	300	30	30	30	30
	Trader Patience:		60	60	60	60	10	80	30	30	30	30
	Trader Penalty:		0.000	0.010	0.020	0.030	0.020	0.020	0.010	0.010	0.010	0.010
	Trader Information:		Uninform	Uninform	Uninform	Uninform	High Info	High Info	Med Info	Med Info	Med Info	Med Info
	Performance Metric:		Eff. Sprd	Eff. Sprd	Eff. Sprd	Eff. Sprd	Impl Shrt	Impl Shrt	Eff. Sprd	Eff. Sprd	Eff. Sprd	Eff. Sprd
Strategy: Description			**Average Disutility**									
Strategy 01: LBs at bid -.01			-20.1	-53.8	-183.4	-536.5	35.2	-40.2	0.1	0.6	1.3	3.0
Strategy 02: Strat 1, except LB price = bid			-101.7	-45.4	-33.9	-2425.1	34.7	-5736.0	-0.2	0.2	0.7	2.0
Strategy 03: Strat 1, except LB price = bid + .01			-5083.8	-206.4	-178.6	-5076.7	24.0	-453.2	-1.3	-2.1	-3.1	-2.4
Strategy 04: One large MB			67.5	67.7	67.2	67.2	67.0	67.3	2.2	6.8	13.8	20.7
Strategy 05: Strat 4, except many smaller MBs			6252.8	67.8	59.1	211.6	41.5	67.2	2.8	5.4	12.4	16.3
Strategy 06: Strat 4, except tiny MBs every period			578.4	68.2	64.2	742.5	42.9	1227.2	0.6	1.8	11.0	12.2
Strategy 07: LBs with no cancel & resub			-4644.0	-215.2	-366.7	-1601.4	21.0	-509.0	-1.8	-2.6	-6.2	-6.3
Strategy 08: Strat 7, except cancel & resub =12 per			-451.7	-49.1	-59.1	-45.4	21.5	-37.8	-1.4	-2.8	-4.1	-4.2
Strategy 09: Strat 7, except cancel & resub = 3 per			-408.9	-52.2	-838.1	-1864.4	21.8	-259.3	-1.3	-2.6	-4.1	-4.1
Strategy 10: MBs with no condition; rest at end			77.3	79.8	176.3	80.0	40.8	85.2	0.6	5.9	9.9	15.7
Strategy 11: Strat 10, except MB when spread<.06			16.8	25.6	33.9	42.2	35.9	2174.4	0.6	2.1	4.2	6.4
Strategy 12: Strat 10, except MB when spread<.04			8.7	19.5	31.2	42.0	35.5	6944.3	0.6	1.9	3.7	5.7
Strategy 13: LBs with no time pattern			-510.3	-35.3	-53.2	-146.1	34.9	-27636.0	0.6	0.6	1.3	2.4
Strategy 14: Strat 13, except more aggressive early			-307.3	-53.5	-38.1	-78.3	18.6	-7706.4	-1.5	-2.6	-4.8	-5.3
Strategy 15: Strat 13, except more aggressive late			-682.6	-789.8	-4195.1	-151.2	35.6	-22556.4	0.6	0.9	1.1	3.7
Strategy 16: LBs with base quantity			-534.5	-1514.8	-1728.3	-1153.6	29.0	-10920.1	0.6	-0.8	-1.4	0.1
Strategy 17: Strat 16, except 2 X quantity			-36.8	-1297.5	-37.8	-247.8	20.7	-288.4	-1.1	-2.0	-3.9	-4.6
Strategy 18: Strat 16, except 4 X quantity			-14489.9	-351.8	-261.5	-13.2	6.8	162.9	-1.6	-3.4	-6.5	-6.9

The first step is to find the optimal trader strategy, highlighted by the **green-shaded cell**, for each problem. For example, for Problem 1 we look down column N and see that the **lowest** Average Disutility is **-14489.9** produced by Strategy 18. For Problem 2, we look down column O and see that the **lowest** Average Disutility is **-1514.8** produced by Strategy 16. And so on.

The second step to analyze a Problem Set to see how a change in a problem item causes a change in the optimal trader strategy. For example, the Problem Set 1 – 4 yields the following principle and intuition:

Principle: *As Trader Penalty increases from .00 to .03, the optimal trader strategy changes from Limit Buys Submitted in Large Quantities (Strategy 18) to Limit Buys with Base Quantity (Strategy 16) to Limit Buys Submitted With A More Aggressive Price Late in the Day (Strategy 15) to Limit Buys at an Aggressive Price All The Time (Strategy 3).*

Intuition: *An increase in trader penalty causes an increase in the penalty that is assessed for buying less than the requested volume, which makes it important to be more aggressive on prices in order to buy a larger volume.*

A good way to do a large number of simulations is to set up a large number of problems and strategies, start it running late evening, let it run overnight, and save the results in the morning. Another way to do it is to go to a computer lab during off-peak hours and run different simulations on many computers at the same time.

A word of caution is that each simulation takes quite a while to calculate. It is best to start doing simulations early on so that you don't run out of time.

Scientific Analysis

The overall goal is to scientifically analyze a wide range of fund manager problems and determine the optimal order submission strategy for each problem. To do this, you need to design a series of experiments to perform on the simulation. Here is the recommended approach.

1. Specify a variety of problems to be analyzed (at least 50 to 100 problems). Each problem is a combination of six items: requested volume ratio, average volume, trader patience, trader penalty, trader information, and performance metric. Remember to form problem sets with all items held constant, except for one item which is varied.
2. Specify a variety of strategies to be tested. Each strategy describes a set of orders to be submitted on a static basis (fixed values) or on a dynamic basis (as functions of spread, depth, executions, etc.). In other words, a strategy describes what you put in columns O – R. Initially, you may wish to consider some simple, pure-case strategies. As you gain experience, consider more complex, combined strategies.
3. For each problem, look down the corresponding column of the Average Disutility table to determine the optimal strategy (highlighted by the **green-shaded cell**) that yields the lowest average disutility.
4. Analyze each problem set to determine the *principle* (how a change in a problem item causes a change in the optimal trader strategy) and the *intuition* (why this principle makes sense). Examine comparisons such as Average Absolute Value of Lots Over/Under, Average Cost of Trading / Lot, etc. to figure out and convincingly explain the intuition underlying each principle.
5. Compile a list of principles and intuitions from all of your problem sets. Figure out the *big picture* of how they all fit together. Try to synthesize a short list of *general principles* that characterize optimal trader strategy.

Here are two cautions:

- **You can NOT compare disutility values across different levels of Trader Patience, Trader Penalty, or Trader information.** Different values of Patience, Penalty, and Information effectively represent different Fund Managers and their disutility values can NOT be compared. Why not? Ask yourself are you more happy or less happy than one of your fellow students? It is hard to say because happiness (or unhappiness) is a subjective state of being. Disutility is intended to represent the degree of unhappiness of a particular fund manager. Formally speaking, the scale of a utility (or disutility) function is completely arbitrary and thus it can NOT be compared across <u>different fund managers</u>. However, you can compare the disutility generated by <u>different strategies</u> for the <u>same fund manager</u>!

- **In general, it is not interesting to compare disutility values across problems.** It is not surprising that more difficult problems yield worse disutility values. Instead, you want to focus on how the *optimal trader strategy* changes as one problem item is changed.

Here is a hint about strategies. When Trader Penalty = 0, then submitting no orders yields a disutility of zero. In this extreme case, you only want to execute orders that contribute negative disutility (= profit).

Security Trader Competition

You are asked to participate in a Dealer Competition to a computer lab. Please bring your project files to the computer lab.

The competition will determine which group can do the best job of minimizing the **Average Disutility** for several rounds of trading. Each round of trading will involve different combinations of **Requested Volume Ratio, Average Volume, Trader Patience, Trader Penalty, Trader Information, and Performance Metric** that will be announced on the spot. We will do as many rounds as time permits.

Average cumulative disutility scores for each member of each group will be reported electronically. After the competition, a rank ordering of the score that each member achieves in each round will be determined. Then, the average ranking that each group achieves across all members and over all rounds will be computed. The average ranking for each group will determine how many competition points each group gets.

If you analyze more problems and more strategies, then you will have more "weapons in your arsenal" by which to win the competition. Historically, there is a positive correlation between the number of problems and strategies analyzed and competition performance.

The Findings Summary

The format of the findings summary is a two page executive summary and an unlimited-length appendix for tables and graphs. All tables and graphs should be clearly labeled and professional in appearance. This format will require you condense your explanation into a clear and concise form.

The findings summary should:

1. Introduce and motivate the overall questions that you seek to answer.
2. Specify the set of problems analyzed and how they form problem sets.
3. Specify the strategies tested and how they form strategy sets.
4. Explain the *principle* (how a change in a problem item causes a change in the optimal trader strategy) and the *intuition* (why this principle makes sense) for each problem set. Support the principles with well-labeled tables of your results. Support the intuitions with well-labeled 2D or 3D graphs of any

comparisons (such as Average Absolute Value of Lots Over/Under, Average Cost of Trading / Lot, etc.) that are helpful in understanding the intuitions.

5. Explain the *big picture* of how all of the principles and intuitions fit together. Explain a short list of *general principles* that characterize optimal trader strategy.

"Sales Presentation" to Fund Managers

Designated groups will make a *thirteen minute*, PowerPoint "sales presentation" to the class to summarize their findings. The class will play the role of fund managers who are looking to outsource the order desk function by hiring one of the candidate groups to perform the order desk function. Each group will play the role of a candidate group to be hired and will explain why they would do the best job of picking order submission strategies to minimize the fund managers' disutility.

Following each presentation, there will be a *two minute* opportunity for audience questions. Audience members are encouraged to ask skeptical questions and to deflate exaggerated or incorrect claims. All time limits will be strictly observed in order to be fair to everyone.

Finally, each audience member will evaluate all of the group presentations (except their own) and subjectively evaluate the merits of the presented strategies. Each group will be rated on a scale from 1 to 9, where 1 is poor, 5 is average, and 9 is outstanding.

8.2 Dealer Simulation

Purpose. The purpose of this simulation is:

- To permit the scientific analysis of a wide variety of dealer problems, including differences in volume, stock, overnight volatility, risk aversion, and order processing cost.
- For each dealer problem, to permit the scientific analysis of wide variety of dealer strategies for setting bid price, ask price, bid depth, ask depth, and executing full vs. quoted.
- To give you hands-on market making experience.
- To add to your knowledge of Excel and @RISK.

How To Access @RISK And The Project File.

The basic platform we will use is an Excel add-in program for doing simulations called @RISK. Consult your instructor for how access to @RISK on your campus.

Launch **Excel 2007**. Click on the **Office** button 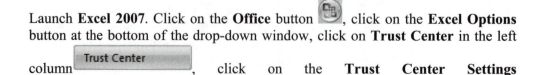, click on the **Excel Options** button at the bottom of the drop-down window, click on **Trust Center** in the left column, click on the **Trust Center Settings** button Trust Center Settings... , click on **Macro** **Settings** in the left column Macro Settings , click on **Enable all macros (not recommended; potentially dangerous code can run)** in the **Macro Settings** section ⊙ Enable all macros (not recom , click on **OK** two times. Exit **Excel 2007**. (When you are done working on the project, follow the same steps to restore the Macro Settings to **Disable all macros with notification**)

Launch **@RISK**. Now open **Ch 10 Dealer Simulation.xlsm**, if asked click on **Yes** open a new simulation file based on the @RISK settings in Dealer Simulation.xlsm, and click on **No** to save the old simulation. Then, click on **F9** to recalculate the spreadsheet and you're ready to go!

The Setting

You are a dealer in a dealer market. You need to compete with other dealers to attract order flow. In odd periods, other dealer's set their ask price, bid price, ask depth, and bid depth. In even periods, you set your ask price, bid price, ask depth, and bid depth. Then orders arrive. Some will come to you and others will go to other dealers. You also get to choose whether to execute the full quantity or quoted quantity of any orders you receive. The trades you do in even periods enable you to gain utility (or "happiness") based on that period's profit and suffer disutility (or "unhappiness") based on that period's inventory risk. For each market making problem, the goal is to develop optimal strategies that maximize your average terminal utility, which is the average of cumulative utility over all trading periods.

Explanation of the Project File

The project file **Dealer Simulation.xlsm** is shown in Figure 8.7.

Figure 8.7 The Project File.

Left section — Optimal Dealer Strategies

A	B	C
Optimal Dealer Strategies		
Current Problem	0	
Volume:	0.25	
Adverse Selection:	0.4	
Risk Aversion:	0.2	
Daytime Volatility:	0.0045	
Overnight Volatility:	5	
Order Proc Cost:	0.012	
Current Strategy	0	
Reset Problem & Strategy		
	Results of	**Average**
	Current	**Results of**
Outputs	**Iteration**	**Simulation**
Gross Profits	0.56	0.56
Order Proc Costs	0.18	0.18
Net Profits	0.38	0.38
Chg in Inv Value	1.58	1.58
Total Profits	1.96	1.96
Disutility of Inv Risk	-0.21	-0.21
Utility	34.92	**34.92**
Control of Simulations		
Starting Problem #:	1	
Ending Problem #:	10	
Starting Strategy #:	1	
Ending Strategy #:	15	
Total # Simulations:	10 Prob X 15 Strat = 150 Sims	

Right section — Other Dealer Strategies

Day	Time	Period	Best Other Bid Price	Best Other Ask Price	Ave Bid Depth	Ave Ask Depth	# of Others at Best Bid	# of Others at Best Ask	Spread	Midpoint
1	10:00 AM	1	46.82	46.92	15	9	2	2	0.10	46.870
1	10:30 AM	3	46.80	46.90	17	15	2	2	0.10	46.850
1	11:00 AM	5	46.65	46.74	16	10	2	2	0.09	46.695
1	11:30 AM	7	46.75	46.83	17	17	2	2	0.08	46.790
1	12:00 PM	9	46.91	47.00	15	12	2	2	0.09	46.955
1	12:30 PM	11	46.90	47.01	6	7	2	2	0.11	46.955
1	1:00 PM	13	46.90	47.01	12	5	2	2	0.11	46.955
1	1:30 PM	15	46.74	46.84	15	11	2	2	0.10	46.790
1	2:00 PM	17	46.76	46.85	10	15	2	2	0.09	46.805
1	2:30 PM	19	46.75	46.86	20	18	2	2	0.11	46.805
1	3:00 PM	21	46.74	46.85	12	18	2	2	0.11	46.795
1	3:30 PM	23	46.89	46.98	17	16	2	2	0.09	46.935
1	4:00 PM	25	46.89	46.99	5	20	2	2	0.10	46.940
2	9:30 AM	27	46.88	46.98	15	15	2	2	0.10	46.930
2	10:00 AM	29	46.83	46.95	19	9	2	2	0.12	46.890
2	10:30 AM	31	46.73	46.84	14	10	2	2	0.11	46.785
2	11:00 AM	33	46.90	47.00	17	8	2	2	0.10	46.950
2	11:30 AM	35	46.89	46.98	10	8	2	2	0.09	46.935
2	12:30 PM	37	46.89	46.99	10	15	2	2	0.10	46.940
2	1:00 PM	39	46.76	46.85	19	9	2	2	0.09	46.805
2	1:30 PM	41	46.76	46.87	14	15	2	2	0.11	46.815
2	2:00 PM	43	46.76	46.87	5	15	2	2	0.11	46.815
2	2:30 PM	45	46.76	46.86	17	14	2	2	0.10	46.810
2	3:00 PM	47	46.77	46.85	10	15	2	2	0.08	46.810
2	3:30 PM	49	46.85	46.93	6	11	2	2	0.08	46.890
2	4:00 PM	51	46.71	46.80	13	8	2	2	0.09	46.755
3	9:30 AM	53	46.70	46.82	14	14	2	2	0.12	46.760
3	10:00 AM	55	46.70	46.81	15	11	2	2	0.11	46.755
3	10:30 AM	57	46.71	46.81	14	8	2	2	0.10	46.760
3	11:00 AM	59	46.65	46.76	17	16	2	2	0.11	46.705
3	11:30 AM	61	46.66	46.75	20	15	2	2	0.09	46.705
3	12:30 PM	63	46.73	46.84	11	17	2	2	0.11	46.785
3	1:00 PM	65	46.73	46.83	8	20	2	2	0.10	46.780
3	1:30 PM	67	46.74	46.83	15	8	2	2	0.09	46.785
3	2:00 PM	69	46.73	46.82	19	10	2	2	0.09	46.775
3	2:30 PM	71	46.72	46.82	12	20	2	2	0.10	46.770
3	3:00 PM	73	46.68	46.80	14	15	2	2	0.12	46.740
3	3:30 PM	75	46.63	46.73	17	7	2	2	0.10	46.680
3	4:00 PM	77	46.71	46.79	18	5	2	2	0.08	46.750
4	9:30 AM	79	46.71	46.81	7	5	2	2	0.10	46.760

The **Current Problem** section displays the current value of:

- **Volume** in cell B3,
- **Adverse Selection** in cell B4,
- **Risk Aversion** in cell B5,
- **Daytime Volatility** in cell B6,
- **Overnight Volatility** the in cell B7,
- **Order Processing Cost** in cell B8.

Figure 8.8 More of The Project File.

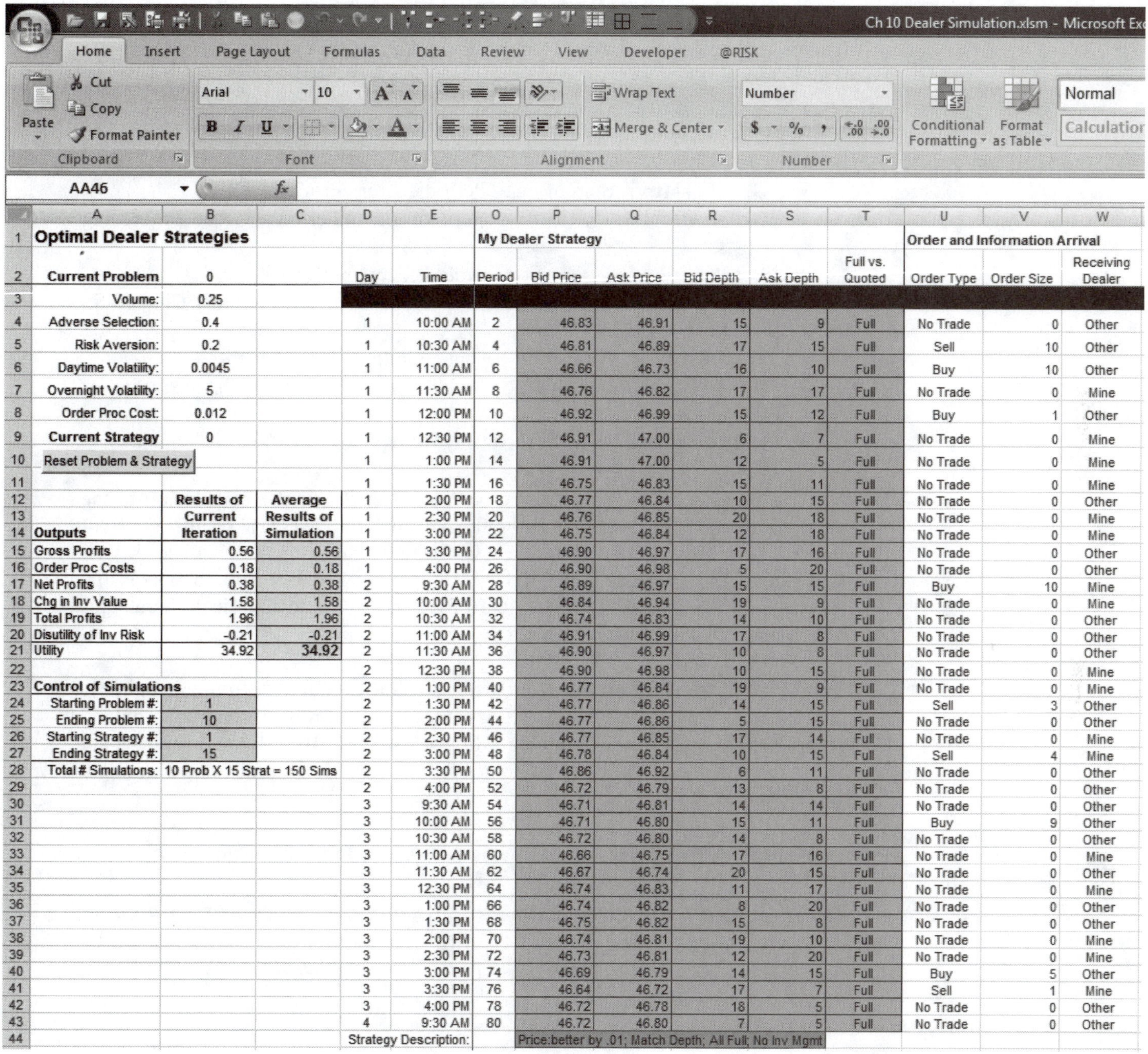

	A	B	C	D	E	O	P	Q	R	S	T	U	V	W
1	**Optimal Dealer Strategies**					**My Dealer Strategy**						**Order and Information Arrival**		
2	**Current Problem**	0		Day	Time	Period	Bid Price	Ask Price	Bid Depth	Ask Depth	Full vs. Quoted	Order Type	Order Size	Receiving Dealer
3	Volume:	0.25												
4	Adverse Selection:	0.4		1	10:00 AM	2	46.83	46.91	15	9	Full	No Trade	0	Other
5	Risk Aversion:	0.2		1	10:30 AM	4	46.81	46.89	17	15	Full	Sell	10	Other
6	Daytime Volatility:	0.0045		1	11:00 AM	6	46.66	46.73	16	10	Full	Buy	10	Other
7	Overnight Volatility:	5		1	11:30 AM	8	46.76	46.82	17	17	Full	No Trade	0	Mine
8	Order Proc Cost:	0.012		1	12:00 PM	10	46.92	46.99	15	12	Full	Buy	1	Other
9	**Current Strategy**	0		1	12:30 PM	12	46.91	47.00	6	7	Full	No Trade	0	Mine
10	Reset Problem & Strategy			1	1:00 PM	14	46.91	47.00	12	5	Full	No Trade	0	Mine
11				1	1:30 PM	16	46.75	46.83	15	11	Full	No Trade	0	Mine
12		**Results of**	**Average**	1	2:00 PM	18	46.77	46.84	10	15	Full	No Trade	0	Other
13		**Current**	**Results of**	1	2:30 PM	20	46.76	46.85	20	18	Full	No Trade	0	Mine
14	**Outputs**	**Iteration**	**Simulation**	1	3:00 PM	22	46.75	46.84	12	18	Full	No Trade	0	Mine
15	Gross Profits	0.56	0.56	1	3:30 PM	24	46.90	46.97	17	16	Full	No Trade	0	Other
16	Order Proc Costs	0.18	0.18	1	4:00 PM	26	46.90	46.98	5	20	Full	No Trade	0	Other
17	Net Profits	0.38	0.38	2	9:30 AM	28	46.89	46.97	15	15	Full	Buy	10	Mine
18	Chg in Inv Value	1.58	1.58	2	10:00 AM	30	46.84	46.94	19	9	Full	No Trade	0	Mine
19	Total Profits	1.96	1.96	2	10:30 AM	32	46.74	46.83	14	10	Full	No Trade	0	Other
20	Disutility of Inv Risk	-0.21	-0.21	2	11:00 AM	34	46.91	46.99	17	8	Full	No Trade	0	Other
21	Utility	34.92	34.92	2	11:30 AM	36	46.90	46.97	10	8	Full	No Trade	0	Other
22				2	12:30 PM	38	46.90	46.98	10	15	Full	No Trade	0	Mine
23	**Control of Simulations**			2	1:00 PM	40	46.77	46.84	19	9	Full	No Trade	0	Mine
24	Starting Problem #:	1		2	1:30 PM	42	46.77	46.86	14	15	Full	Sell	3	Other
25	Ending Problem #:	10		2	2:00 PM	44	46.77	46.86	5	15	Full	No Trade	0	Other
26	Starting Strategy #:	1		2	2:30 PM	46	46.77	46.85	17	14	Full	No Trade	0	Mine
27	Ending Strategy #:	15		2	3:00 PM	48	46.78	46.84	10	15	Full	Sell	4	Mine
28	Total # Simulations:	10 Prob X 15 Strat = 150 Sims		2	3:30 PM	50	46.86	46.92	6	11	Full	No Trade	0	Other
29				2	4:00 PM	52	46.72	46.79	13	8	Full	No Trade	0	Other
30				3	9:30 AM	54	46.71	46.81	14	14	Full	No Trade	0	Other
31				3	10:00 AM	56	46.71	46.80	15	11	Full	Buy	9	Other
32				3	10:30 AM	58	46.72	46.80	14	8	Full	No Trade	0	Other
33				3	11:00 AM	60	46.66	46.75	17	16	Full	No Trade	0	Mine
34				3	11:30 AM	62	46.67	46.74	20	15	Full	No Trade	0	Other
35				3	12:30 PM	64	46.74	46.83	11	17	Full	No Trade	0	Mine
36				3	1:00 PM	66	46.74	46.82	8	20	Full	No Trade	0	Other
37				3	1:30 PM	68	46.75	46.82	15	8	Full	No Trade	0	Other
38				3	2:00 PM	70	46.74	46.81	19	10	Full	No Trade	0	Mine
39				3	2:30 PM	72	46.73	46.81	12	20	Full	No Trade	0	Mine
40				3	3:00 PM	74	46.69	46.79	14	15	Full	Buy	5	Other
41				3	3:30 PM	76	46.64	46.72	17	7	Full	Sell	1	Mine
42				3	4:00 PM	78	46.72	46.78	18	5	Full	No Trade	0	Other
43				4	9:30 AM	80	46.72	46.80	7	5	Full	No Trade	0	Other
44				Strategy Description:			Price:better by .01; Match Depth; All Full; No Inv Mgmt							

The **My Dealer Strategy** section with light blue-shaded cells allows you to specify your dealer strategy. It has five columns: **Bid Price** (column P), **Ask Price** (column Q), **Bid Depth** (column R), **Ask Depth** (column S), and **Full Vs. Quoted** (column T).

The **Other Dealer Strategies** section reports the strategies set by other dealers. The columns show their Best Bid Price, Best Ask Price, Average Bid Depth at the Best Bid, Average Ask Depth at the Best Ask, Number of Other Dealers at the Best Bid, Number of Other Dealers at the Best Ask, Other Dealer Spread, and

Other Dealer Midpoint. The information in these columns is updated by random variables.

This is a pure dealer market. Hence, all market orders execute against a dealer and there aren't any limit orders.

The **Outputs** section shows the **Results of the Current Iteration** as follows:

- **Gross Profits** = Sum of Each Period's Gross Profits,
- **Order Processing Costs** = Sum of Each Period's Order Processing Costs,
- **Net Profits** = Gross Profits – Order Processing Costs,
- **Change in Inventory Value** = Sum of Each Periods Change in Inventory Value,
- **Total Profits** = Net Profits + Change in Inventory Value,
- **Disutility of Inventory Risk** = Sum of Each Period's Disutility of Inventory Risk
- **Utility** = (Total Profits + Disutility of Inventory Risk) * (Scale Factor).

The **Outputs** section also shows the **Average Results of the Simulation** in the area with light green-shaded cells. It contains the average results over all iterations in a given simulation. Cell C15 shows the average of cell B15. Cell C16 shows the average of cell B16. And so on. The key bottom line is the **Average Utility** in cell C21. The goal of this project is to find dealer strategies which maximize Average Utility for any given problem.

The **Control of Simulations** section allows you to automate running multiple simulations. You do this by specifying the starting problem, ending problem, starting strategy, and ending strategy. In this example, 10 different problems are being tested using 15 different strategies for a total of 150 simulations in a single run.

In the **My Profits** section, the following is calculated for each even date t:

$$This\ Period's\ GrossProfit_t = (Trade\ Quantity_t) * (Trade\ Price_t - Midpoint_t) \quad for\ Dealer\ Sells = Cust\ Buys$$

$$= (Trade\ Quantity_t) * (Midpoint_t - Trade\ Price_t) \quad for\ Dealer\ Buys = Cust\ Sells$$

$$where \quad Midpoint_t = (Best\ Other\ Bid\ Price_t + Best\ Other\ Ask\ Price_t) / 2$$

$$This\ Period's\ Order\ Processing\ Cost_t = (Trade\ Quantity_t) * (Order\ Processing\ Cost)$$

$$This\ Period's\ Net\ Proft_t = This\ Period's\ Gross\ Profit_t - This\ Period's\ Order\ Processing\ Cost_t$$

In the **My Risk** section, the following is calculated for each even date t:

$$Change\ in\ Inventory\ Value_t = (Inventory_{t-1}) * (Midpoint_t - Midpoint_{t-1})$$

$$This\ Period's\ Total\ Profit_t = This\ Period's\ Net\ Profit_t + This\ Period's\ Change\ in\ Inventory\ Value_t$$

Disutility of Inventory Risk$_t$ =- (Risk Aversion)*(Absolute Value of Inventory$_{t-1}$)*(Volatility$_t$).

In the **My Utility** section, the following is calculated for each even date *t*:

This Period's Utility Gain$_t$ = This Period's Total Profit$_t$ + Disutility of Inventory Risk$_t$

In the **Results of the Current Iteration** section (column B), your cumulative results over all of the even periods are:

$$Profit_{80} = \sum_{t=1}^{40} This\ Period's\ Profit_{2t}$$

$$Disutility\ of\ Inventory\ Risk_{80} = \sum_{t=1}^{40} This\ Period's\ Disutility\ of\ Inventory\ Risk_{2t}$$

$$Utility_{80} = \left(\sum_{t=1}^{40} This\ Period's\ Utility\ Gain_{2t}\right) * \left(Scale\ Factor\right)$$

where *Scale Factor = 20.*

Entering Dealer Strategies

Let's look in detail at how you enter dealer strategies. Start with bid prices at 10:00 am (row 4). The best bid price from the other dealers is $46.97. You can match that price by entering the formula =G4 in cell P4. This causes your bid price = $46.97. Alternatively, you can beat that price by a penny by entering =G4+.01 in cell P4. Your bid price = $46.98. Having the best bid price by a penny means that a sell order will come to you and you get to make profitable trade. Conversely, match the bid price means that a sell order randomly comes either to you or one of the other dealers. If you get the order, then you will make a larger profit, but often you will not get the order. Another possibility is to set your bid price be one penny worse than the other dealers by entering =G4-.01 in cell P4. You will not get orders very often, but when you do you will make an even larger profit.

Now consider bid depth. One way set bid depth would be enter a fixed value. For example, you could enter **18** in cell R4. This would set you bid depth = 18 round lots. Alternatively, you could add or subtract to the average bid depth of other dealers. For example, you could enter =I4+5 in cell R4. Since the average bid depth of other dealers = 16 round lots, then your bid depth = 21 round lots. Bid depth has two effects. First, it specifies the minimum size sell order that you have committed to trade at your bid price. Second, in the case of a tie for the best bid price, it helps determine if you get the sell order. That is, a larger bid depth will give you a larger probability of getting the sell order (vs. the other tied dealers) when there is a tie for the best bid price.

Now consider full vs. quoted. Suppose your bid depth is 15 round lots and a sell order for 40 round lots is routed to you. You now have a choice of whether to execute the full sell order for 40 round lots or execute the quoted bid depth of 15 round lots only (and route the remainder of the order to another dealer). Executing a larger quantity will contribute to your profits. However, if this sell order moves your inventory *away from zero*, then it will increase your risk (which hurts your utility). But if this sell order moves your inventory *towards zero*, then if will decrease your risk (which helps your utility). Thus, there are some circumstances under which you will want to execute the full quantity and other circumstances under which you will want to execute the quoted quantity only. As an example of this, you could enter **=IF(AND(AD3>20,U4="Sell"),"Quoted",IF(AND(AD3<-20,U4="Buy"),"Quoted","Full"))** in cell T4. The first IF & AND combination checks if the prior period inventory is greater than 20 round lots and if the arriving order is a Sell (causing the dealer to buy and increase inventory) and then executes quoted. The second IF & AND combination checks if the prior period inventory is less than -20 round lots and if the arriving order is a Buy (causing the dealer to sell and decrease inventory) and then executes quoted. If both conditions are not true, then it executes full. A more elaborate formula might take it consideration the size of the arriving order in cell V4.

Notice that the formulas shown so far depend on *past* information. It you enter a function that depends on *future* information, then it will generate a circular reference. If this happens to you by accident, just click **Undo** on the Quick Access Toolbar. If you run @RISK and get an odd error message, check to Status Bar at the bottom of Excel to see if you have circular reference.

Information and Inventory Management

A key element in market making is information. There are two news agencies are available: Reuters and CNBC. Both news agencies report information relevant to the given stock. Some of the new events are:

- *public* information events being reported as soon as they happen
- the eventually public revelation of previously *private* information events that privately informed traders have already traded on for several periods.

The other dealers in the simulation will adjust their quotes automatically to both the CNBC and Reuters new items. However, both you and the other dealers have no direct knowledge of any unrevealed private information that currently exists. You can partially infer this private info from order imbalances (that is, more buys than sells or vice versa). You have the opportunity to respond to these order imbalances, but the other dealers are programmed to act in a naïve way and ignore the pattern of order imbalances.

Another key element in market making is inventory management. If your risk aversion is high then the price risk of any nonzero inventory will significantly reduce your inventory. This makes it critical to keep your inventory close to zero. Inventory management can be done three ways: (1) by price, (2) by depth, and by execution strategy. These three methods can be done separately or combined. For example, suppose that you have a large positive inventory. This implies that you should encourage customer buy orders (so you can sell) and discourage customer sell orders. Inventory management by price means having a competitive ask price and a non-competitive bid price. Inventory management by depth means having a large ask depth and a small bid depth. Inventory management by execution strategy means executing *full* for buys and executing *quoted* for sells. Conversely, if you have a large negative inventory, then you should do the opposite – encourage sells and discourage buys. This can be done by price, by depth, or by execution strategy – just do the opposite of what is mentioned above.

Storing Strategies

Space is provided to store up to 40 strategies in rows 345 – 2179. The easiest way to store a strategy is to first enter the orders into the light blue-shaded cells of the range P4:T43. Then enter a description of the strategy in cell P44. Then copy the whole range P4:T44 to the storage area for Strategy 1. This is done by selecting the entire range P4:T44, clicking on **Home | Copy**, select the cell G346, and clicking on **Home | Paste**. See the figure below.

Figure 8.9 Storing Strategies.

	A	B	C	D	E	O	P	Q	R	S	T
1	**Optimal Dealer Strategies**					My Dealer Strategy					
2	Current Problem	0		Day	Time	Period	Bid Price	Ask Price	Bid Depth	Ask Depth	Full vs. Quoted
342											
343		**Strategy 1**				My Dealer Strategy					
344				Day	Time	Period	Bid Price	Ask Price	Bid Depth	Ask Depth	Full vs. Quoted
345				1	9:30 AM						
346				1	10:00 AM	2	0.01	-0.01	0	0	Full
347				1	10:30 AM	4	0.01	-0.01	0	0	Full
348				1	11:00 AM	6	0.01	-0.01	0	0	Full
349				1	11:30 AM	8	0.01	-0.01	0	0	Full
350				1	12:00 PM	10	0.01	-0.01	0	0	Full
351				1	12:30 PM	12	0.01	-0.01	0	0	Full
352				1	1:00 PM	14	0.01	-0.01	0	0	Full
353				1	1:30 PM	16	0.01	-0.01	0	0	Full
354				1	2:00 PM	18	0.01	-0.01	0	0	Full
355				1	2:30 PM	20	0.01	-0.01	0	0	Full
356				1	3:00 PM	22	0.01	-0.01	0	0	Full
357				1	3:30 PM	24	0.01	-0.01	0	0	Full
358				1	4:00 PM	26	0.01	-0.01	0	0	Full
359				2	9:30 AM	28	0.01	-0.01	0	0	Full
360				2	10:00 AM	30	0.01	-0.01	0	0	Full
361				2	10:30 AM	32	0.01	-0.01	0	0	Full
362				2	11:00 AM	34	0.01	-0.01	0	0	Full
363				2	11:30 AM	36	0.01	-0.01	0	0	Full
364				2	12:30 PM	38	0.01	-0.01	0	0	Full
365				2	1:00 PM	40	0.01	-0.01	0	0	Full
366				2	1:30 PM	42	0.01	-0.01	0	0	Full
367				2	2:00 PM	44	0.01	-0.01	0	0	Full
368				2	2:30 PM	46	0.01	-0.01	0	0	Full
369				2	3:00 PM	48	0.01	-0.01	0	0	Full
370				2	3:30 PM	50	0.01	-0.01	0	0	Full
371				2	4:00 PM	52	0.01	-0.01	0	0	Full
372				3	9:30 AM	54	0.01	-0.01	0	0	Full
373				3	10:00 AM	56	0.01	-0.01	0	0	Full
374				3	10:30 AM	58	0.01	-0.01	0	0	Full
375				3	11:00 AM	60	0.01	-0.01	0	0	Full
376				3	11:30 AM	62	0.01	-0.01	0	0	Full
377				3	12:30 PM	64	0.01	-0.01	0	0	Full
378				3	1:00 PM	66	0.01	-0.01	0	0	Full
379				3	1:30 PM	68	0.01	-0.01	0	0	Full
380				3	2:00 PM	70	0.01	-0.01	0	0	Full
381				3	2:30 PM	72	0.01	-0.01	0	0	Full
382				3	3:00 PM	74	0.01	-0.01	0	0	Full
383				3	3:30 PM	76	0.01	-0.01	0	0	Full
384				3	4:00 PM	78	0.01	-0.01	0	0	Full
385				4	9:30 AM	80	0.01	-0.01	0	0	Full
386				Strategy Description:		Price:better by .01; Match Depth; All Full; No Inv Mgmt					

To store a second strategy, enter it in the light blue-shaded cells and copy it to the storage area for Strategy 2 (pasting it to cell P392). Follow the same procedure to store as many as 40 strategies.

Selecting Problems

Problems are selected clicking the spin buttons in rows 49 – 54. The spreadsheet is setup to allow you to test as many as 10 different problems in a single run. Each problem has its own column. For example, Problem 1 is in column P, Problem 2 is in column Q, etc. You specify Problem 1 by selecting the six inputs in the range P49:P54. In particular, you specify Problem 1 by clicking the spin button in cell P49 to select the Volume, clicking the spin button in cell P50 to select the Adverse Selection, . . . , and clicking the spin button in cell P54 to select the Order Processing Cost.

Figure 8.10 Selecting Problems.

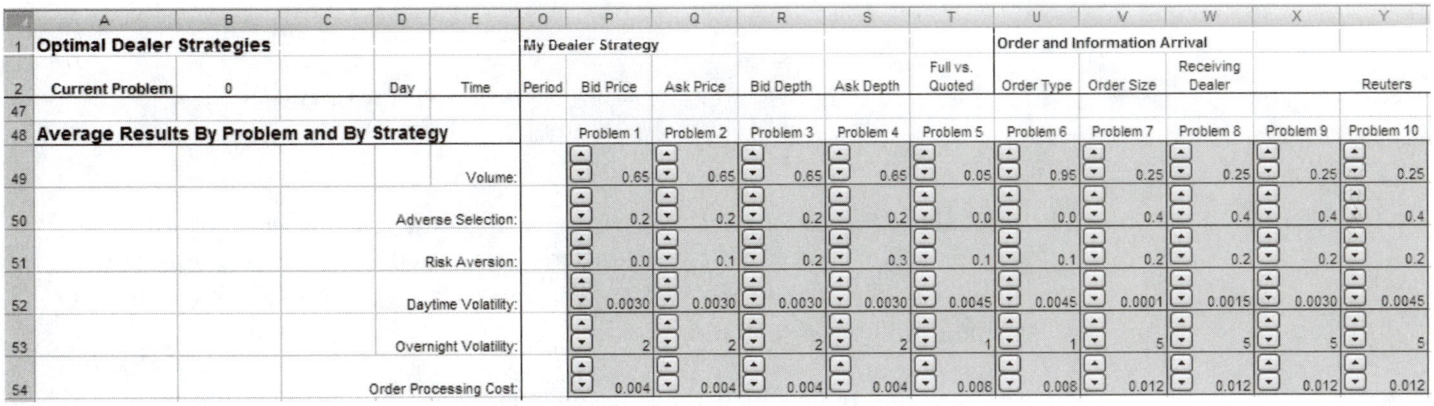

	A	B	C	D	E	O	P	Q	R	S	T	U	V	W	X	Y
1	**Optimal Dealer Strategies**					My Dealer Strategy						Order and Information Arrival				
2	Current Problem	0		Day	Time	Period	Bid Price	Ask Price	Bid Depth	Ask Depth	Full vs. Quoted	Order Type	Order Size	Receiving Dealer		Reuters
47																
48	**Average Results By Problem and By Strategy**						Problem 1	Problem 2	Problem 3	Problem 4	Problem 5	Problem 6	Problem 7	Problem 8	Problem 9	Problem 10
49					Volume:		0.65	0.65	0.65	0.65	0.05	0.95	0.25	0.25	0.25	0.25
50					Adverse Selection:		0.2	0.2	0.2	0.2	0.0	0.0	0.4	0.4	0.4	0.4
51					Risk Aversion:		0.0	0.1	0.2	0.3	0.1	0.1	0.2	0.2	0.2	0.2
52					Daytime Volatility:		0.0030	0.0030	0.0030	0.0030	0.0045	0.0045	0.0001	0.0015	0.0030	0.0045
53					Overnight Volatility:		2	2	2	2	1	1	5	5	5	5
54					Order Processing Cost:		0.004	0.004	0.004	0.004	0.008	0.008	0.012	0.012	0.012	0.012

It is helpful to create *Problem Sets* of two to five problems, where all items are held constant except for one item. For example, in Figure 8.10 Problems 1 – 54 are a Problem Set. All items are held constant, except for Risk Aversion which varies from 0 in Problem 1 up to 0.3 in Problem 4. Another example, in Figure 8.10, Problems 5 and s are a set based on looking at opposite extremes. All items are held constant, except for Volume which varies from the low extreme of 0.05 to the high extreme of 0.95. Also in Figure 8.10, Problems 7 – 10 are a Problem Set. All items are held constant, except for Daytime Volatility which varies from 0.0001 to 0.0045. Analyzing problems in sets allows you to isolate cause and effect. That is, holding everything else constant, how does a change in one item cause a change in the optimal dealer strategy?

Figure 8.11 Strategy Sets.

55	Strategy	Description			
56	Strategy 1	Price:better by .01; Match Depth; All Full; No Inv Mgmt			
57	Strategy 2	Strat 1, except price = match			
58	Strategy 3	Strat 1, except price = match and depth = +10			
59	Strategy 4	Strat 1, except price = worse by .01			
60	Strategy 5	Inventory Management in Price; Cutoffs = 10			
61	Strategy 6	Inventory Management in Price; Cutoffs = 30			
62	Strategy 7	Inventory Management in Depth; Cutoffs = 20			
63	Strategy 8	Inventory Management in Depth; Cutoffs = 40			
64	Strategy 9	Inventory Management in Execution; Cutoffs = 10			
65	Strategy 10	Inventory Management in Execution; Cutoffs = 30			
66	Strategy 11	Inv Mgmt in Price from 2:30 - 4:00 PM; Cutoff = 20			
67	Strategy 12	Inv Mgmt in Price from 2:30 - 4:00 PM; Cutoff = 40			
68	Strategy 13	Infer private info:Better/Mat/Wor: 3Sells/Other/3Buys			
69	Strategy 14	Infer private info:Better/Mat/Wor: 4Sells/Other/4Buys			
70	Strategy 15	Do nothing			

It is helpful to create *Strategy Sets* of two to five strategies, where most of the strategy is held constant, but one characteristic is varied. For example, in Figure 8.11, Strategies 1 – 4 are a Strategy Set. All aspects of the strategy are held constant, except for:

- the limit price which varies from better by .01 in Strategy 1 to worse by .01 in Strategy 4 and
- the depth which varies from matching other dealers' depth to being match + 10 lots in Strategy 3.

Another example, in Figure 8.11, Strategies 5 – 6. Strategy 5 implements inventory management in price with cutoffs at 10. Strategy 6 implements inventory management using only price with cutoffs at 30. Strategies 7-8 implement inventory management in depth and with cutoffs at 20 and 40, respectively. Strategies 9-10 implement inventory management in ex and with cutoffs at 20 and 40, respectively. Strategies 11-12 implements inventory management using only price, but only from 2:30 – 4:00 pm so as to "go home flat" and avoid overnight volatility. Analyzing strategies in sets allows you to pin down what specific aspect of a strategy makes a difference.

Two other interesting strategies are illustrated in Figure 8.11. Strategies 13-14 attempt to infer the private information of arriving traders by looking for sustained order arrival patterns. Upon three (or four) buys in a row, dealer buying is encouraged by setting the bid competitively and the ask uncompetitively. Conversely, upon three (or four) sells in a row, dealer selling is encouraged by setting the ask competitively and the bid uncompetitively. Strategy 15 is a "do nothing" strategy accomplished by setting both the bid and ask at uncompetitive prices. This strategy always yields an average utility of zero. Therefore, any other strategy which yields *negative* average utility is dominated by a do nothing strategy.

Strategies that attempt to "game" the simulation are not allowed. At the instructor's discretion, such strategies will be disqualified.

Running Simulations

Suppose you want to do 10 problems x 40 strategies in one run. Enter **1** for the Starting Problem # in cell B24, **10** for the Ending Problem # in cell B25, **1** for the Starting Strategy # in cell B26, and **40** for the Ending Strategy # in cell B27. The range B28:C28 shows that this is 400 simulations.

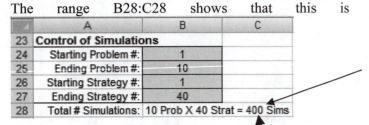

	A	B	C
23	**Control of Simulations**		
24	Starting Problem #:	1	
25	Ending Problem #:	10	
26	Starting Strategy #:	1	
27	Ending Strategy #:	40	
28	Total # Simulations:	10 Prob X 40 Strat = 400 Sims	

To set up @RISK, click on the @RISK tab and then click on the "**Simulation**

Settings" icon Simulation Settings .

Make sure that the #Simulations in cell C28 matches the #Simulations in the @RISK dialog box

- First, click on the **Iterations** tab.
  - o Enter **400** for the # **Iterations**,
  - o **400** for the # **Simulations**, and
  - o For long runs, you may wish to *uncheck* the **Update Display** box to speed-up

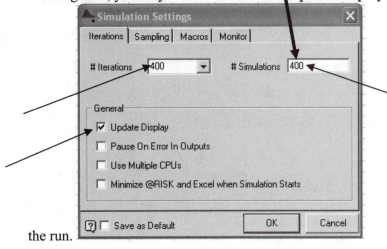

the run.

- Second, click on the **Sampling** tab,
  - Under **Sampling Type**, click on **Latin Hypercube**,
  - Under **Random Generator Seed**, click on **Choose Randomly**,
  - Under **Standard Recalc**, click on **Monte Carlo**,
  - Under **Collect Distribution Samples**, click on **None**.

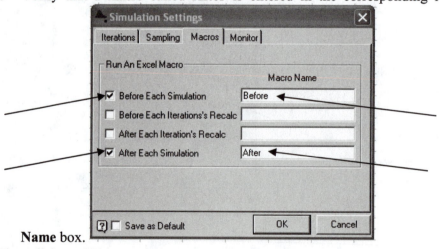

- Third, click on the **Macros** tab.
  - Verify that **Before Each Simulation** is checked,
  - Verify that a macro called **Before** is entered in the corresponding **Macro Name** box,
  - Verify that **After Each Simulation** is checked,
  - Verify that a macro called **After** is entered in the corresponding **Macro Name** box.
- Then click on **OK**.

Then, click on the "**Report Settings**" icon , uncheck the box for **Show Interactive @RISK Results Window**, and click on **OK**.

Close any other Excel files that you have open. If more than one Excel file is left open, then @RISK may get "confused" about what to do and generate strange results.

Verify that the **Current Problem** in cell B2 is **0** and the **Current Strategy** in cell B9 is **0**. If either one or both of these cells are not zero, then fix this by clicking on the **Reset Problem and Strategy** button Reset Problem & Strategy in

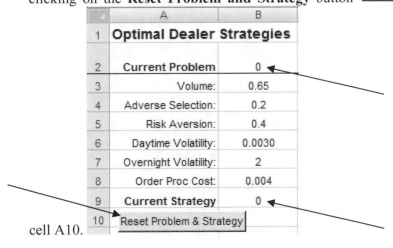

cell A10.

Finally, click on the "**Start Simulation**" icon .

Here is how the whole process works:

- The **Before** Macro copies a particular Dealer Strategy from one of the storage areas down below (Strategy 1, Strategy 2, etc.) up to the working area in rows 4 – 44.
- Then a complete simulation is performed using the number of iterations that you requested.
- The **After** Macro copies the average results of the simulation to the **Saved Results** section in rows 2184 – 2619. Importantly, the average results are *saved as values*. This is very important, because if you just save the @RISK spreadsheet under a different name, then live results in the light green-shaded cells will reset next time you open it and your results will be lost.
- The three steps above repeat for all of the problems and all of the strategies that you requested.

A bird's eye view of the average results is displayed in the **Average Results By Problem and Strategy** section in rows 48 – 95. In Figure 8.12, we see the Average Disutility results for the 10 problems x 15 strategies.

Figure 8.12. Average Results By Problem and Strategy.

	A	B	C	D	E	P	Q	R	S	T	U	V	W	X	Y
1	**Optimal Dealer Strategies**					aler Strategy					Order and Information Arrival				
2	**Current Problem**	0		Day	Time	Bid Price	Ask Price	Bid Depth	Ask Depth	Full vs. Quoted	Order Type	Order Size	Receiving Dealer		Reuters
47															
48	**Average Results By Problem and By Strategy**					Problem 1	Problem 2	Problem 3	Problem 4	Problem 5	Problem 6	Problem 7	Problem 8	Problem 9	Problem 10
49					Volume:	0.65	0.65	0.65	0.65	0.05	0.95	0.25	0.25	0.25	0.25
50					Adverse Selection:	0.2	0.2	0.2	0.2	0.0	0.0	0.4	0.4	0.4	0.4
51					Risk Aversion:	0.0	0.1	0.2	0.3	0.1	0.1	0.2	0.2	0.2	0.2
52					Daytime Volatility:	0.0030	0.0030	0.0030	0.0030	0.0045	0.0045	0.0001	0.0015	0.0030	0.0045
53					Overnight Volatility:	2	2	2	2	1	1	5	5	5	5
54					Order Processing Cost:	0.004	0.004	0.004	0.004	0.008	0.008	0.012	0.012	0.012	0.012
55	Strategy	Description				**Average Utility**									
56	Strategy 1	Price:better by .01; Match Depth; All Full; No Inv Mgmt				-7.3	-11.3	-15.3	-19.3	-3.7	-8.8	2.0	-0.6	-4.6	-16.5
57	Strategy 2	Strat 1, except price = match				5.2	1.2	-2.8	-6.8	-2.8	8.6	9.2	6.6	2.6	-9.2
58	Strategy 3	Strat 1, except price = match and depth = +10				0.3	-4.9	-10.0	-15.1	-2.0	7.3	12.1	4.3	-3.5	-20.1
59	Strategy 4	Strat 1, except price = worse by .01				2.6	2.0	1.4	0.8	0.2	8.1	2.0	2.2	1.9	0.8
60	Strategy 5	Inventory Management in Price; Cutoffs = 10				11.0	8.2	5.4	2.6	-2.7	7.6	6.9	6.9	5.1	-4.5
61	Strategy 6	Inventory Management in Price; Cutoffs = 30				8.3	4.7	1.1	-2.5	-2.7	8.7	8.6	6.7	3.5	-7.3
62	Strategy 7	Inventory Management in Depth; Cutoffs = 20				6.4	3.3	0.1	-3.0	-2.7	11.5	9.1	6.2	3.1	-8.0
63	Strategy 8	Inventory Management in Depth; Cutoffs = 40				5.5	1.8	-1.9	-5.7	-2.8	11.5	9.3	7.0	3.7	-7.9
64	Strategy 9	Inventory Management in Execution; Cutoffs = 10				10.2	6.6	3.0	-0.7	-2.8	12.7	9.1	8.0	6.3	-5.8
65	Strategy 10	Inventory Management in Execution; Cutoffs = 30				7.8	3.9	0.0	-3.9	-2.8	12.5	9.3	7.8	4.6	-6.9
66	Strategy 11	Inv Mgmt in Price from 2:30 - 4:00 PM; Cutoff = 20				6.4	2.7	-1.1	-4.9	-2.8	6.6	8.8	7.4	4.1	-7.4
67	Strategy 12	Inv Mgmt in Price from 2:30 - 4:00 PM; Cutoff = 40				6.2	2.2	-1.7	-5.6	-2.8	8.0	9.1	6.3	2.2	-9.7
68	Strategy 13	Infer private info:Better/Mat/Wor: 3Sells/Other/3Buys				-2.0	-6.6	-11.1	-15.7	-3.2	-2.2	9.6	1.0	-6.8	-23.2
69	Strategy 14	Infer private info:Better/Mat/Wor: 4Sells/Other/4Buys				-1.5	-6.2	-10.8	-15.5	-3.2	-2.6	9.6	0.5	-7.8	-24.5
70	Strategy 15	Do nothing				0.0	0.0	0.0	0.0	0.0	0.0	0.0	0.0	0.0	0.0

The first step is to find the optimal dealer strategy, highlighted by the **green-shaded cell**, for each problem. For example, for Problem 1 we look down column P and see that the **highest** Average Utility is **11.0** produced by Strategy 5. For Problem 5, we look down column T and see that the **highest** Average Utility is **0.2** produced by Strategy 4. And so on.

The second step is to analyze a Problem Set by seeing how a change in a problem item causes a change in the optimal dealer strategy. For example, the Problem Set 7 – 10 yields the following principle and intuition:

Principle: *As Daytime Volatility increases from 0 to 0.4, the optimal dealer strategy changes from Matching on Price With No Inventory Management (strategy 3) to Inventory Management in Depth (strategy 9) and then to a Wide Spread (strategy 4) .*

Intuition: *An increase in risk aversion causes an increase in the disutility of inventory risk, which makes aggressive inventory management more attractive to hold-down the disutility of inventory risk. For very high values of daytime volatility, the disutility of inventory risk from matching other dealers becomes so high that one must set a wide spread to avoid negative utility.*

A good way to do a large number of simulations is to set up a large number of problems and strategies, start it running late evening, let it run overnight, and save the results in the morning. Another way to do it is to go to a computer lab during off-peak hours and run different simulations on many computers at the same time.

Scientific Analysis

The overall goal is to scientifically analyze a wide range of dealer problems and determine the optimal dealer strategy for each problem. To do this, you need to design a series of experiments to perform on the simulation. Here is the recommended approach.

1. Specify a variety of problems to be analyzed (at least 50 to 100 problems). Each problem is a combination of six items: volume, adverse selection, risk aversion, daytime volatility, overnight volatility multiple, and order processing cost. It is helpful to form problem sets with all items held constant, except for one item which is varied.

2. Specify a variety of strategies to be tested. Each strategy describes a set of dealer actions (bid price, ask price, bid depth, ask depth, full vs. quoted) to be take on a static basis (fixed values) or on a dynamic basis (as functions of best other dealer bid, best other dealer ask, average bid depth, average ask depth, etc.). It is helpful to form strategy sets with most of the strategy is held constant, except for one characteristic which is varied. Initially, you may wish to consider simple, pure-case strategies. As you gain experience, consider more complex, combined strategies.

3. For each problem, look down the corresponding column of the Average Utility table to determine the optimal strategy (highlighted by the **green-shaded cell**) that yields the highest average utility.

4. Analyze each problem set to determine the *principle* (how a change in a problem item causes a change in the optimal dealer strategy) and the *intuition* (why this principle makes sense). Examine comparisons such as Average Total Profits, Average Disutility of Inventory Risk, etc. to help figure out and convincingly explain the intuition underlying each principle.

5. Compile a list of principles and intuitions from all of your problem sets. Figure out the *big picture* of how they all fit together. Try to synthesize a short list of *general principles* that characterize optimal dealer strategy.

Here are two cautions:

- **You can NOT compare utility values across different levels of Risk Aversion.** Different values of Risk Aversion effectively represent different Dealers and their utility values can NOT be compared. Why not? Ask yourself are you more happy or less happy than one of your fellow students? It is hard to say because happiness is a subjective state of being. Utility is intended to represent the degree of happiness of a particular dealer. Formally speaking, the scale of a utility function is completely arbitrary and thus it can NOT be compared across <u>different dealers</u>. However, you can compare the utility generated by <u>different strategies</u> for the <u>same dealer</u>!
- **In general, it is not interesting to compare utility values across problems.** It is not surprising that easier problems yield higher utility values. Instead, you want to focus on how the *optimal dealer strategy* changes as one problem item is changed.

Dealer Competition

You are asked to participate in a Dealer Competition to a computer lab. Please bring your project files to the computer lab.

The competition will determine which group can do the best job of maximizing the Average Utility for several rounds of trading. Each round of trading will involve different combinations of **Volume, Adverse Selection, Risk Aversion, Daytime Volatility, Overnight Volatility, and Order Processing Cost** that will be announced on the spot. We will do as many rounds as time permits.

Average cumulative utility scores for each member of each group will be reported electronically. After the competition, a rank ordering of the score that each member achieves in each round will be determined. Then, the average ranking that each group achieves across all members and over all rounds will be computed. The average ranking for each group will determine how many competition points each group gets.

If you analyze more problems and more strategies, then you will have more "weapons in your arsenal" by which to win the competition. Historically, there is a positive correlation between the number of problems and strategies analyzed and competition performance.

The Findings Summary

The format of the findings summary is a two page executive summary and an unlimited-length appendix for tables and graphs. All tables and graphs should be clearly labeled and professional in appearance. This format will require you condense your explanation into a clear and concise form.

The findings summary should:

1. Introduce and motivate the overall questions that you seek to answer.

2. Specify the set of problems analyzed and how they form problem sets.

3. Specify the simple, pure-case strategies tested and the more complex, combined strategies tested.

4. Explain the *principle* (how a change in a problem item causes a change in the optimal dealer strategy) and the *intuition* (why this principle makes sense) for each problem set. Support the principles with well-labeled tables of your results. Support the intuitions with well-labeled 2D or 3D graphs of any comparisons (such as Average Total Profits, Average Disutility of Inventory Risk, etc.) that are helpful in understanding the intuitions.

5. Explain the *big picture* of how all of the principles and intuitions fit together. Explain a short list of *general principles* that characterize optimal dealer strategy.

"Sales Presentation" to Big Dealer Firms

Designated groups will make a *thirteen minute*, PowerPoint "sales presentation" to the class to summarize their findings. The class will play the role of big dealer firms (potential bidders) who are looking to expand by paying an attractive takeover premium to acquire small dealer firms. Each group will play the role of a smaller dealer firm (potential targets) and will explain why they would do the best job of picking quote and execution strategies to maximize the dealer's utility.

Following each presentation, there will be a *two minute* opportunity for audience questions. Audience members are encouraged to ask skeptical questions and to deflate exaggerated or incorrect claims. All time limits will be strictly observed in order to be fair to everyone.

Finally, each audience member will evaluate all of the group presentations (except their own) and subjectively evaluate the merits of the presented strategies. Each group will be rated on a scale from 1 to 9, where 1 is poor, 5 is average, and 9 is outstanding. The average evaluation of each group will determine how many presentation points each group gets.

Chapter 9 Portfolio Diversification Lowers Risk

9.1 Basics

Problem. For simplicity, suppose that all risky assets have a standard deviation of 30% and all pairs of risky assets have a correlation coefficient of 40%. In this simple setting, consider a portfolio diversification strategy of investing in equally-weighted portfolios (e.g., put an equal amount in each risky asset). As you increase the number of assets in your portfolio (that you are diversifying across), how much does this lower the risk of your portfolio?

Solution Strategy. Calculate the portfolio standard deviation of an equally-weighted portfolio as the number of assets increases. As a benchmark, compare with the portfolio standard deviation in the limiting case as the number of assets goes to infinity.

FIGURE 9.1 Excel Model of Portfolio Diversification Lowers Risk - Basics.

	A	B	C	D	E	F	G	H	I	J
1	**PORTFOLIO DIVERSIFICATION LOWERS RISK**					**Basics and International**				
2										
3	Inputs									
4	Standard Deviation	30%	6							
5	Correlation Coefficient	40%	14							
6										
21	Number of Assets	1	2	3	4	5	6	7	8	9
22	Portfolio Std Dev	30.00%	25.10%	23.24%	22.25%	21.63%	21.21%	20.91%	20.68%	20.49%
23	Minimum Std Dev	18.97%	18.97%	18.97%	18.97%	18.97%	18.97%	18.97%	18.97%	18.97%

Chart: **Portfolio Diversification Lowers Risk** — Portfolio Standard Deviation (y-axis 0% to 40%) versus Number of Assets (x-axis 0 to 60).

(1)
$$\left(\sqrt{\frac{1+(\text{Number of assets}-1)\cdot \text{Correlation Coefficient}}{\text{Number of assets}}} \right)$$
$$\cdot (\text{Standard Deviation})$$
Enter =SQRT((1+(B21-1)*$B$5)/B21)*$B$4
and copy across

(2)
$$\left(\sqrt{\text{Correlation Coefficient}} \right)(\text{Standard Deviation})$$
Enter =SQRT($B$5)*$B$4 and copy across

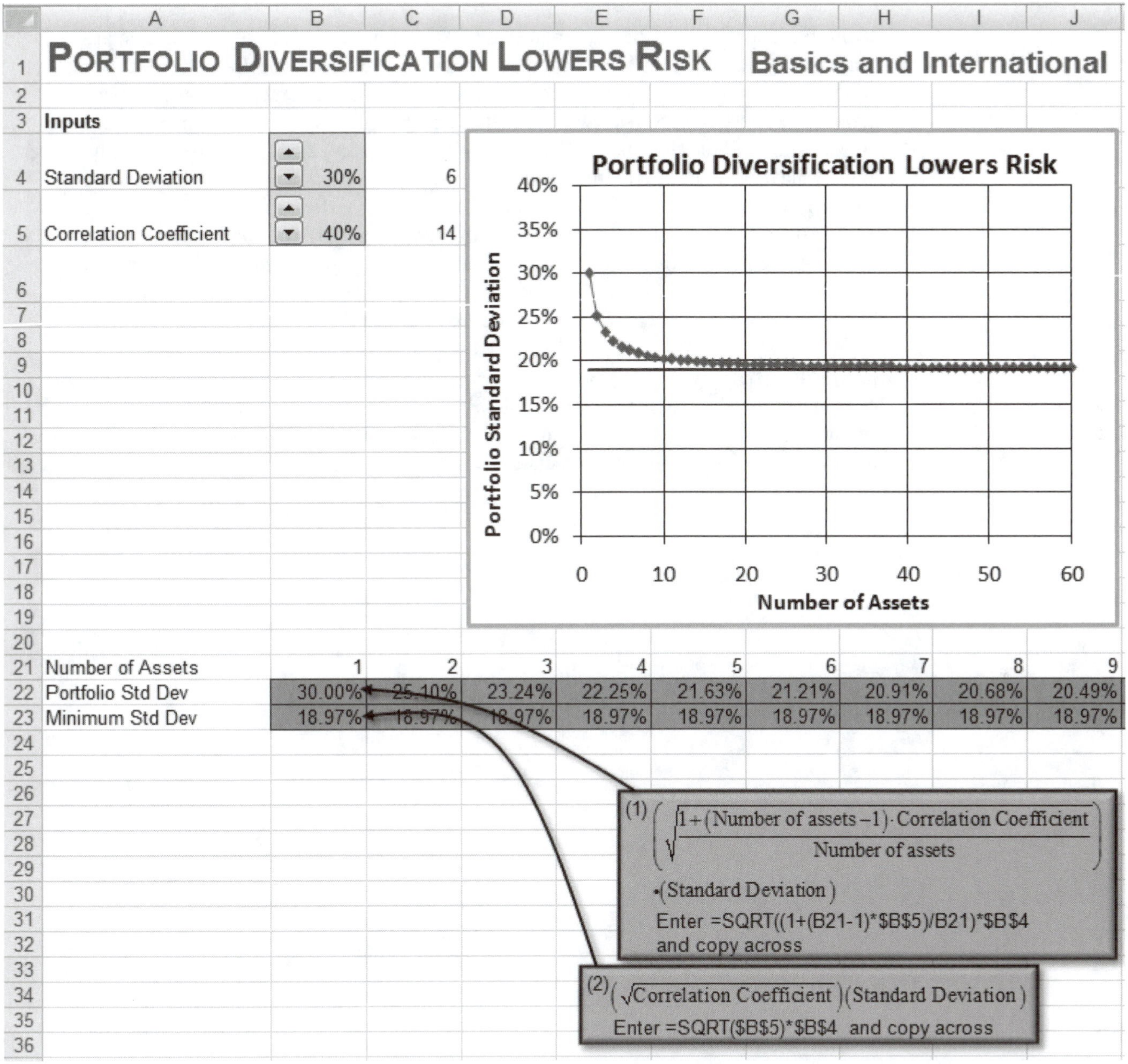

This graph shows how diversifying across many assets can reduce risk from 30% to as low as 18.97%. Most of the risk reduction is accomplished with a relatively small number of assets. Increasing the number of assets from one to ten accomplishes more that 85% of the potential risk reduction. Increasing to thirty assets accomplishes more than 95% of the potential risk reduction. In summary, very significant risk reduction can be accomplished by diversifying across thirty assets, but relatively little risk reduction is accomplished by increasing the number of assets further.

9.2 International

Problem. There is a lot of evidence that international correlation coefficients are dramatically lower than local (same country) correlation coefficients. We can explore the benefits of international diversification by extending the Basics example. Suppose there are two countries and all risky assets in both countries have a standard deviation of 30%. All pairs of risky assets *within* the same country have a local correlation coefficient of 40%, but all pairs of risky assets *between* countries have an international correlation coefficient of 10%. Consider an international diversification strategy of investing half of your money in an equally-weighted portfolio in country 1 and the other half in an equally-weighted portfolio in country 2. As you increase the number of assets in your total portfolio, how much does this lower the risk of your portfolio?

Solution Strategy. Calculate the portfolio standard deviation of the internationally diversified portfolio as the number of assets increases. As a benchmark, compare with the international portfolio standard deviation in the limiting case as the number of assets goes to infinity.

FIGURE 9.2   Excel Model of Portfolio Diversification Lowers Risk - International.

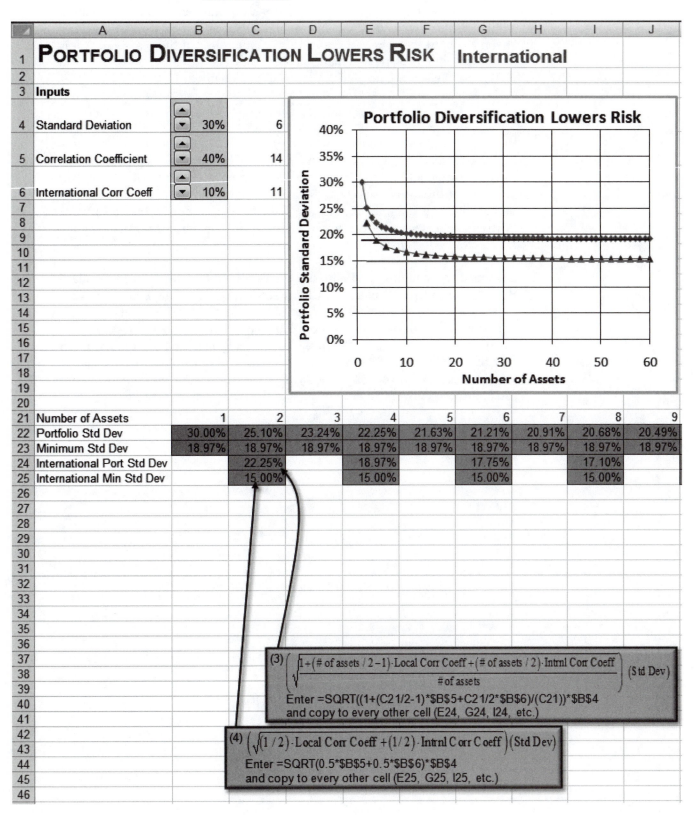

This graph shows how international diversification can significantly reduce risk beyond local (one country) diversification. In this example, local diversification reduces risk from 30.00% to as low as 18.97%, but international diversification can reduce risk as low as 15.00%. International diversification works by getting rid of some country-specific sources of risk. Again, most of the risk reduction is accomplished with a relatively small number of assets. Beyond 30 assets (15 in each country), there is not much risk reduction potential left.

Problems

1. All risky assets have a standard deviation of 50% and all pairs of risky assets have a correlation coefficient of 60%. Consider a portfolio diversification strategy of investing in equally-weighted portfolios (e.g., put an equal amount in each risky asset). As you increase the number of assets in your portfolio (that you are diversifying across), how much does this lower the risk of your portfolio?

2. There are two countries and all risky assets in both countries have a standard deviation of 50%. All pairs of risky assets *within* the same country have a local correlation coefficient of 60%, but all pairs of risky assets *between* countries have an international correlation coefficient of 20%. Consider an international diversification strategy of investing half of your money in an equally-weighted portfolio in country 1 and the other half in an equally-weighted portfolio in country 2. As you increase the number of assets in your total portfolio, how much does this lower the risk of your portfolio?

Chapter 10 Life-Cycle Financial Planning

10.1 Basics

Problem. Suppose that you are currently 30 years old and expect to earn a constant real salary of $80,000 starting next year. You are planning to retire at age 70. You currently have $0 in financial capital. You are limited to investing in the riskfree asset. The real riskfree rate is 2.8%. Develop a financial plan for real savings and real consumption over your lifetime.

Solution Strategy. Develop a financial plan on a year-by-year basis over an entire lifetime. During your working years, divide your salary each year between current consumption and savings to provide for consumption during your retirement years. Put savings in a retirement fund that is invested at the riskfree rate. During your retirement years, your salary is zero, but you are able to consume each year by withdrawing money from your retirement fund. Calculate a constant level of real consumption that can be sustained in both working years and retirement years. Since there is substantial uncertainty about how long you will actually live and since it's not a good idea to run out of money, calculate real consumption based on infinite annuity. This level of real consumption can be sustained indefinitely. Finally, analyze human capital, financial capital, and total wealth over your lifetime.

Life Expectancy. How long will you live? For the US in 2004, the average age of death ("life expectancy at birth") was 78. Also in 2004, the average age of death by those 65 or older ("life expectancy at 65") was 84. Life expectancy at birth and at age 65 have both increased by approximately 1 year over the prior 5 years due to medical and health progress. By simply extrapolating this trend into the future, the next 60 years would add 12 years to life expectancy. So life expectancy at birth would rise to 90 and life expectancy at 65 would rise to 96. So averaging between those two figures, today's typical 30 year old might expect to live to 93. This is a very conservative forecast in the sense that medical and health progress is likely to accelerate, rather than just maintain the current rate of improvement.

To determine your individual life expectancy, add to (or subtract from) 93 based on your individual health-conscious practices. Not smoking adds nine years. Aerobic exercising and getting seven to eight hours of sleep per night adds three years. A healthy diet and maintaining a desirable weight based on your height adds three years. A thorough annual medical exam to catch cancer and other health problems early adds two years. The following six items add one year each: (1) daily aspirin to reduce fatal heart attacks, (2) preventing high blood pressure, (3) avoiding accidents, (4) getting immunized against pneumonia and influenza, (5) avoiding suicide and AIDS, and (6) avoiding heavy alcohol consumption. For more information on the factors effecting longevity and the long-run impact of scientific and medical progress, visit George Webster's web site at: www.george-webster.com.

FIGURE 10.1 Excel Model of Life-Cycle Financial Planning - Basics.

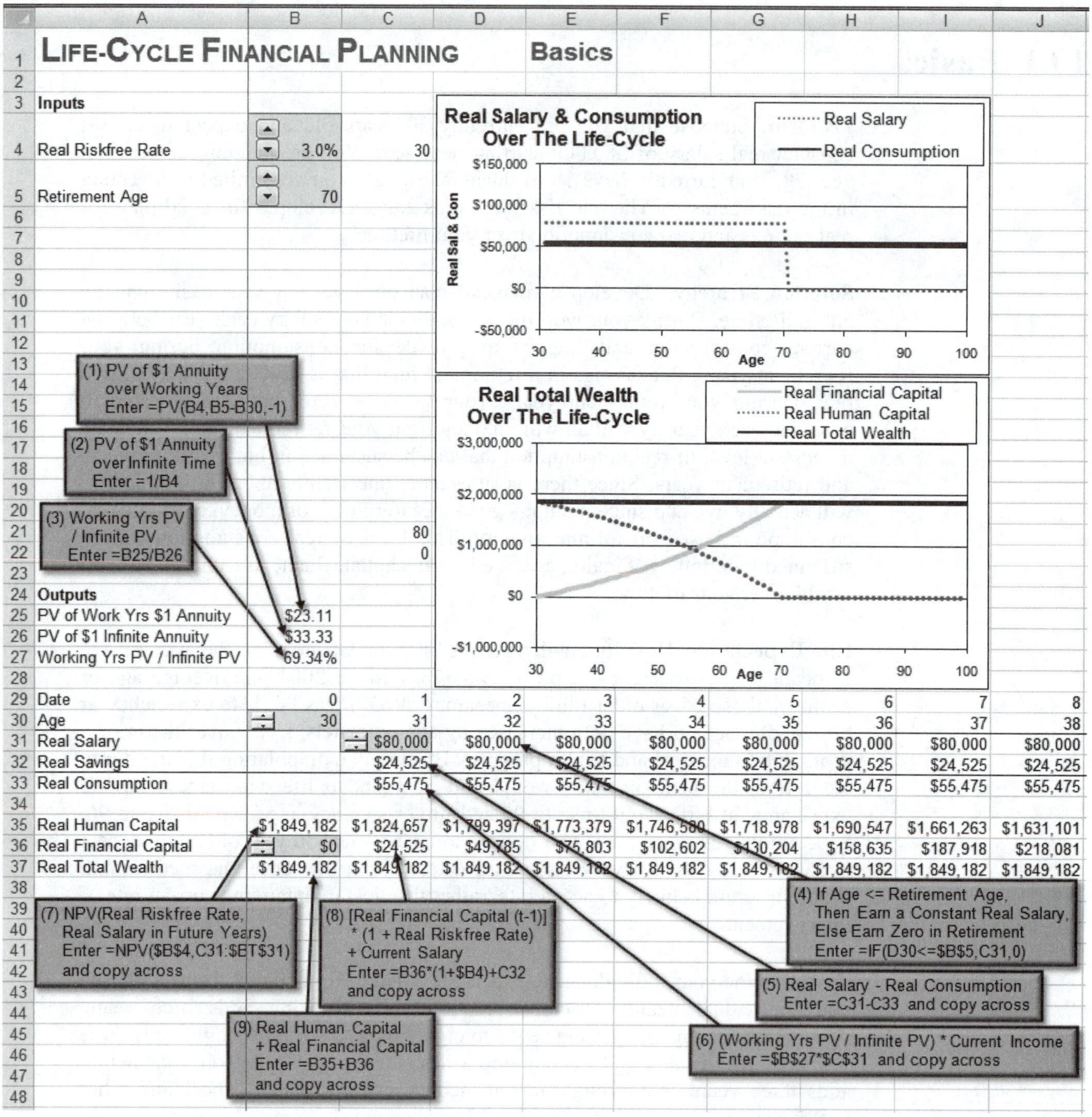

	A	B	C	D	E	F	G	H	I	J
1	**LIFE-CYCLE FINANCIAL PLANNING**				**Basics**					
2										
3	**Inputs**									
4	Real Riskfree Rate	3.0%	30							
5	Retirement Age	70								
6										
7										
8										
9										
10										
11										
12										
13		(1) PV of $1 Annuity								
14		over Working Years								
15		Enter =PV(B4,B5-B30,-1)								
16										
17		(2) PV of $1 Annuity								
18		over Infinite Time								
19		Enter =1/B4								
20		(3) Working Yrs PV								
21		/ Infinite PV	80							
22		Enter =B25/B26	0							
23										
24	**Outputs**									
25	PV of Work Yrs $1 Annuity	$23.11								
26	PV of $1 Infinite Annuity	$33.33								
27	Working Yrs PV / Infinite PV	69.34%								
28										
29	Date	0	1	2	3	4	5	6	7	8
30	Age	30	31	32	33	34	35	36	37	38
31	Real Salary		$80,000	$80,000	$80,000	$80,000	$80,000	$80,000	$80,000	$80,000
32	Real Savings		$24,525	$24,525	$24,525	$24,525	$24,525	$24,525	$24,525	$24,525
33	Real Consumption		$55,475	$55,475	$55,475	$55,475	$55,475	$55,475	$55,475	$55,475
34										
35	Real Human Capital	$1,849,182	$1,824,657	$1,799,397	$1,773,379	$1,746,580	$1,718,978	$1,690,547	$1,661,263	$1,631,101
36	Real Financial Capital	$0	$24,525	$49,785	$75,803	$102,602	$130,204	$158,635	$187,918	$218,081
37	Real Total Wealth	$1,849,182	$1,849,182	$1,849,182	$1,849,182	$1,849,182	$1,849,182	$1,849,182	$1,849,182	$1,849,182
38										

Real Salary & Consumption Over The Life-Cycle — Real Salary, Real Consumption

Real Total Wealth Over The Life-Cycle — Real Financial Capital, Real Human Capital, Real Total Wealth

(4) If Age <= Retirement Age, Then Earn a Constant Real Salary, Else Earn Zero in Retirement Enter =IF(D30<=$B$5,C31,0)

(5) Real Salary - Real Consumption Enter =C31-C33 and copy across

(6) (Working Yrs PV / Infinite PV) * Current Income Enter =$B$27*$C$31 and copy across

(7) NPV(Real Riskfree Rate, Real Salary in Future Years) Enter =NPV($B$4,C31:$ET$31) and copy across

(8) [Real Financial Capital (t-1)] * (1 + Real Riskfree Rate) + Current Salary Enter =B36*(1+$B$4)+C32 and copy across

(9) Real Human Capital + Real Financial Capital Enter =B35+B36 and copy across

FIGURE 10.2 Transition from Working Years to Retirement Years.

	A	AN	AO	AP	AQ	AR
29	Date	38	39	40	41	42
30	Age	68	69	70	71	72
31	Real Salary	$80,000	$80,000	$80,000	$0	$0
32	Real Savings	$24,525	$24,525	$24,525	-$55,475	-$55,475
33	Real Consumption	$55,475	$55,475	$55,475	$55,475	$55,475
34						
35	Real Human Capital	$153,078	$77,670	$0	$0	$0
36	Real Financial Capital	$1,696,104	$1,771,512	$1,849,182	$1,849,182	$1,849,182
37	Real Total Wealth	$1,849,182	$1,849,182	$1,849,182	$1,849,182	$1,849,182

From the first graph, we see that your Real Salary from working years only is used to support a constant level of Real Consumption over an "infinite" lifetime. By using this approach, the same level of Real Consumption can be sustained even if you end up living much longer than originally anticipated. From the second graph, we see that Real Total Wealth is constant over a lifetime. At date 0, Real Total Wealth comes entirely from Real Human Capital, which is the present value of all future Real Salary. Over time Real Human Capital declines and Real Financial Capital builds up. After retirement, Real Total Wealth comes entirely from Real Financial Capital.

10.2 Full-Scale Estimation

Problem. Suppose that you are currently 30 years old and expect to earn a constant real salary of $80,000 starting next year. You are planning to retire at age 70. You currently have $0 in financial capital. You can invest in the riskfree asset or a broad stock portfolio. The inflation rate is 2.1% and the real riskfree rate is 2.8%. A broad stock portfolio offers an average real return of 6.0% and a standard deviation of 17.0%. Suppose that federal income taxes have six brackets with the following rates: 10.0%, 15.0%, 25.0%, 28.0%, 33.0%, and 35.0%. For current year, the upper cutoffs on the first five brackets are $7,550, $30,650, $74,200, $154,800, and $336,550 and these cutoffs are indexed to inflation. The state tax rate is 3.0%, federal FICA-SSI tax rate on salary up to $97,500 is 6.2%, and the federal FICA-Medicare tax rate on any level of salary is 1.45%. The current level of social security benefits is $34,368 per year and this is indexed to inflation. Develop a financial plan for real savings and real consumption over your lifetime.

Solution Strategy. The full-scale Excel model of life-cycle financial planning adds consideration of inflation, taxes, social security, and the opportunity to invest in a broad stock index. It is assumed that your savings are put in a tax-deferred retirement fund. You pay zero taxes on contributions to the retirement fund during your working years. But you have to pay taxes on withdrawals from the retirement fund during your retirement years. This Excel model includes several *choice variables*. You need to choose your Real Growth Rate in Salary. You need to choose your Taxable Income / Total Wealth. Specifying taxable income as a percentage of total wealth indirectly determines your consumption and savings as a percentage of total wealth. You also need to choose your Asset Allocation: Stock Portfolio %, that is, what percentage of your savings to invest in the broad stock portfolio. Investing in the broad stock portfolio will give you higher average returns than the riskfree asset, but also more risk. The balance of your savings will be invested in the riskfree asset and will grow at the riskfree rate.

FIGURE 10.3 Excel Model of Life-Cycle Fin Plan – Full-Scale Estimation.

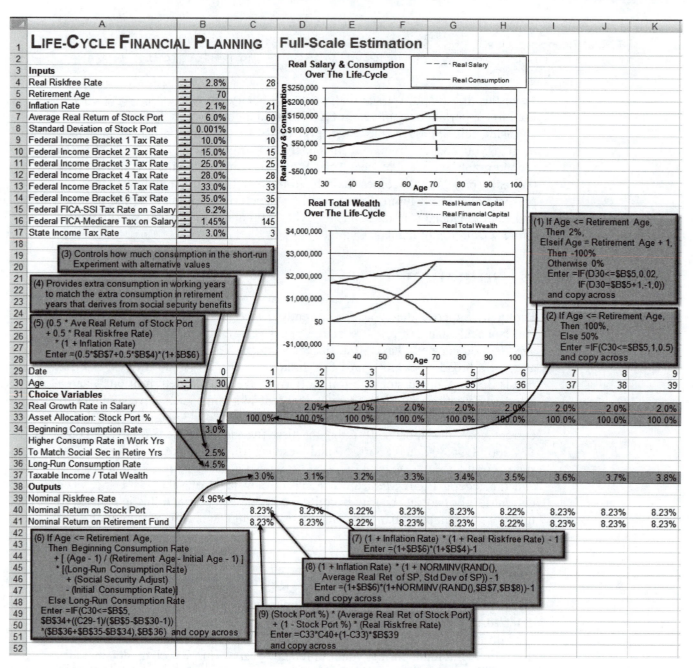

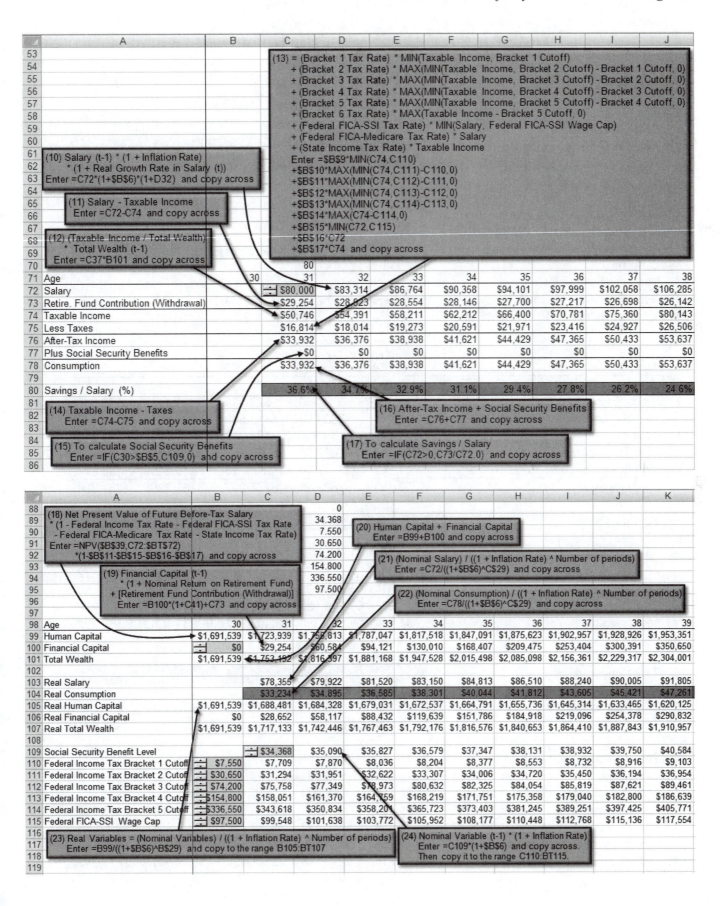

(13) = (Bracket 1 Tax Rate) * MIN(Taxable Income, Bracket 1 Cutoff)
+ (Bracket 2 Tax Rate) * MAX(MIN(Taxable Income, Bracket 2 Cutoff) - Bracket 1 Cutoff, 0)
+ (Bracket 3 Tax Rate) * MAX(MIN(Taxable Income, Bracket 3 Cutoff) - Bracket 2 Cutoff, 0)
+ (Bracket 4 Tax Rate) * MAX(MIN(Taxable Income, Bracket 4 Cutoff) - Bracket 3 Cutoff, 0)
+ (Bracket 5 Tax Rate) * MAX(MIN(Taxable Income, Bracket 5 Cutoff) - Bracket 4 Cutoff, 0)
+ (Bracket 6 Tax Rate) * MAX(Taxable Income - Bracket 5 Cutoff, 0)
+ (Federal FICA-SSI Tax Rate) * MIN(Salary, Federal FICA-SSI Wage Cap)
+ (Federal FICA-Medicare Tax Rate) * Salary
+ (State Income Tax Rate) * Taxable Income
Enter =$B$9*MIN(C74,C110)
+$B$10*MAX(MIN(C74,C111)-C110,0)
+$B$11*MAX(MIN(C74,C112)-C111,0)
+$B$12*MAX(MIN(C74,C113)-C112,0)
+$B$13*MAX(MIN(C74,C114)-C113,0)
+$B$14*MAX(C74-C114,0)
+$B$15*MIN(C72,C115)
+$B$16*C72
+$B$17*C74 and copy across

(10) Salary (t-1) * (1 + Inflation Rate)
* (1 + Real Growth Rate in Salary (t))
Enter =C72*(1+$B$6)*(1+D32) and copy across

(11) Salary - Taxable Income
Enter =C72-C74 and copy across

(12) (Taxable Income / Total Wealth)
* Total Wealth (t-1)
Enter =C37*B101 and copy across

		30	31	32	33	34	35	36	37	38
71	Age		31	32	33	34	35	36	37	38
72	Salary		$80,000	$83,314	$86,764	$90,358	$94,101	$97,999	$102,058	$106,285
73	Retire. Fund Contribution (Withdrawal)		$29,254	$28,823	$28,554	$28,146	$27,700	$27,217	$26,698	$26,142
74	Taxable Income		$50,746	$54,391	$58,211	$62,212	$66,400	$70,781	$75,360	$80,143
75	Less Taxes		$16,814	$18,014	$19,273	$20,591	$21,971	$23,416	$24,927	$26,506
76	After-Tax Income		$33,932	$36,376	$38,938	$41,621	$44,429	$47,365	$50,433	$53,637
77	Plus Social Security Benefits		$0	$0	$0	$0	$0	$0	$0	$0
78	Consumption		$33,932	$36,376	$38,938	$41,621	$44,429	$47,365	$50,433	$53,637
79											
80	Savings / Salary (%)		36.6%	34.7%	32.9%	31.1%	29.4%	27.8%	26.2%	24.6%

(14) Taxable Income - Taxes
Enter =C74-C75 and copy across

(16) After-Tax Income + Social Security Benefits
Enter =C76+C77 and copy across

(15) To calculate Social Security Benefits
Enter =IF(C30>$B$5,C109,0) and copy across

(17) To calculate Savings / Salary
Enter =IF(C72>0,C73/C72,0) and copy across

(18) Net Present Value of Future Before-Tax Salary
* (1 - Federal Income Tax Rate - Federal FICA-SSI Tax Rate
- Federal FICA-Medicare Tax Rate - State Income Tax Rate)
Enter =NPV($B$39,C72:$BT$72)
*(1-$B$11-$B$15-$B$16-$B$17) and copy across

(20) Human Capital + Financial Capital
Enter =B99+B100 and copy across

(19) Financial Capital (t-1)
* (1 + Nominal Return on Retirement Fund)
+ [Retirement Fund Contribution (Withdrawal)]
Enter =B100*(1+C41)+C73 and copy across

(21) (Nominal Salary) / ((1 + Inflation Rate) ^ Number of periods)
Enter =C72/((1+$B$6)^C$29) and copy across

(22) (Nominal Consumption) / ((1 + Inflation Rate) ^ Number of periods)
Enter =C78/((1+$B$6)^C$29) and copy across

			0
89			34.368
90			7.550
91			30.650
92			74.200
93			154.800
94			336.550
95			97.500

		30	31	32	33	34	35	36	37	38	39
98	Age	30	31	32	33	34	35	36	37	38	39
99	Human Capital	$1,691,539	$1,723,939	$1,758,813	$1,787,047	$1,817,518	$1,847,091	$1,875,623	$1,902,957	$1,928,926	$1,953,351
100	Financial Capital	$0	$29,254	$60,584	$94,121	$130,010	$168,407	$209,475	$253,404	$300,391	$350,650
101	Total Wealth	$1,691,539	$1,753,192	$1,816,897	$1,881,168	$1,947,528	$2,015,498	$2,085,098	$2,156,361	$2,229,317	$2,304,001
102											
103	Real Salary		$78,355	$79,922	$81,520	$83,150	$84,813	$86,510	$88,240	$90,005	$91,805
104	Real Consumption		$33,234	$34,895	$36,585	$38,301	$40,044	$41,812	$43,605	$45,421	$47,261
105	Real Human Capital	$1,691,539	$1,688,481	$1,684,328	$1,679,031	$1,672,537	$1,664,791	$1,655,736	$1,645,314	$1,633,465	$1,620,125
106	Real Financial Capital	$0	$28,652	$58,117	$88,432	$119,639	$151,786	$184,918	$219,096	$254,378	$290,832
107	Real Total Wealth	$1,691,539	$1,717,133	$1,742,446	$1,767,463	$1,792,176	$1,816,576	$1,840,653	$1,864,410	$1,887,843	$1,910,957
108											
109	Social Security Benefit Level		$34,368	$35,090	$35,827	$36,579	$37,347	$38,131	$38,932	$39,750	$40,584
110	Federal Income Tax Bracket 1 Cutoff	$7,550	$7,709	$7,870	$8,036	$8,204	$8,377	$8,553	$8,732	$8,916	$9,103
111	Federal Income Tax Bracket 2 Cutoff	$30,650	$31,294	$31,951	$32,622	$33,307	$34,006	$34,720	$35,450	$36,194	$36,954
112	Federal Income Tax Bracket 3 Cutoff	$74,200	$75,758	$77,349	$78,973	$80,632	$82,325	$84,054	$85,819	$87,621	$89,461
113	Federal Income Tax Bracket 4 Cutoff	$154,800	$158,051	$161,370	$164,759	$168,219	$171,751	$175,358	$179,040	$182,800	$186,639
114	Federal Income Tax Bracket 5 Cutoff	$336,550	$343,618	$350,834	$358,201	$365,723	$373,405	$381,245	$389,251	$397,425	$405,771
115	Federal FICA-SSI Wage Cap	$97,500	$99,548	$101,638	$103,772	$105,952	$108,177	$110,448	$112,768	$115,136	$117,554

(23) Real Variables = (Nominal Variables) / ((1 + Inflation Rate) ^ Number of periods)
Enter =B99/((1+$B$6)^B$29) and copy to the range B105:BT107

(24) Nominal Variable (t-1) * (1 + Inflation Rate)
Enter =C109*(1+$B$6) and copy across.
Then copy it to the range C110:BT115.

FIGURE 10.5 Transition From Working To Retirement Years.

	A	AN	AO	AP	AQ	AR
29	Date	38	39	40	41	42
30	Age	68	69	70	71	72
31	**Choice Variables**					
32	Real Growth Rate in Salary	2.0%	2.0%	2.0%	-100.0%	0.0%
33	Asset Allocation: Stock Port %	100.0%	100.0%	100.0%	50.0%	50.0%
34	Beginning Consumption Rate					
35	Higher Consump Rate in Work Yrs To Match Social Sec in Retire Yrs					
36	Long-Run Consumption Rate					
37	Taxable Income / Total Wealth	6.8%	6.9%	7.0%	4.5%	4.5%
38	**Outputs**					
39	Nominal Riskfree Rate					
40	Nominal Return on Stock Port	8.23%	8.23%	8.23%	8.23%	8.22%
41	Nominal Return on Retirement Fund	8.23%	8.23%	8.23%	6.59%	6.59%
42						
70						
71	Age	68	69	70	71	72
72	Salary	$359,128	$374,003	$389,494	$0	$0
73	Retire. Fund Contribution (Withdrawl)	-$15,466	-$19,060	-$23,015	-$274,181	-$279,940
74	Taxable Income	$374,594	$393,063	$412,509	$274,181	$279,940
75	Less Taxes	$123,841	$130,364	$137,242	$71,706	$73,212
76	After-Tax Income	$250,753	$262,698	$275,267	$202,475	$206,727
77	Plus Social Security Benefits	$0	$0	$0	$78,919	$80,577
78	Consumption	$250,753	$262,698	$275,267	$281,395	$287,304
79						
80	Savings / Salary (%)	-4.3%	-5.1%	-5.9%	0.0%	0.0%
81						
97						
98	Age	68	69	70	71	72
99	Human Capital	$456,816	$238,798	$0	$0	$0
100	Financial Capital	$5,247,985	$5,660,592	$6,103,227	$6,231,408	$6,362,232
101	Total Wealth	$5,704,801	$5,899,390	$6,103,227	$6,231,408	$6,362,232
102						
103	Real Salary	$163,031	$166,292	$169,618	$0	$0
104	Real Consumption	$113,833	$116,803	$119,874	$120,022	$120,022
105	Real Human Capital	$207,378	$106,176	$0	$0	$0
106	Real Financial Capital	$2,382,398	$2,516,853	$2,657,846	$2,657,852	$2,657,837
107	Real Total Wealth	$2,589,777	$2,623,029	$2,657,846	$2,657,852	$2,657,837
108						
109	Social Security Benefit Level	$74,149	$75,706	$77,296	$78,919	$80,577
110	Federal Income Tax Bracket 1 Cutoff	$16,631	$16,981	$17,337	$17,701	$18,073
111	Federal Income Tax Bracket 2 Cutoff	$67,516	$68,934	$70,382	$71,860	$73,369
112	Federal Income Tax Bracket 3 Cutoff	$163,449	$166,881	$170,386	$173,964	$177,617
113	Federal Income Tax Bracket 4 Cutoff	$340,996	$348,157	$355,468	$362,933	$370,555
114	Federal Income Tax Bracket 5 Cutoff	$741,358	$756,926	$772,822	$789,051	$805,621
115	Federal FICA-SSI Wage Cap	$214,775	$219,285	$223,890	$228,591	$233,392

As you adapt this model to your own situation, it is not necessary to go from full-time work to zero work. You could consider retiring to part-time work and then gradually tapering off. For example, you could drop to half-time work by setting your Real Growth in Salary to **-50%** in your first retirement year and then set your Real Growth in Salary to **-100.0%** in the year that you stop working entirely.

It is assumed that the Real Return on Broad Stock Portfolio is normally distributed with the average return given in cell **B7** and the standard deviation given in cell **B8**. The Excel function **RAND()** generates a random variable with a uniform distribution over the interval from 0 to 1 (that is, with an equal chance of getting any number between 0 and 1). To transform this uniformly distributed random variable into a normally distributed one, just place **RAND()** inside the Excel function **NORMINV**.[6]

The Human Capital computation make a fairly rough adjustment for taxes, but the year-by-year cash flow analysis has a more sophisticated calculation of taxes. The reason for doing it this way (as opposed to present valuing the After-Tax Income row) is that this approach avoids generating circular references

It doesn't make any sense to live like a king in your working years and the live in poverty in your retirement years. Similarly, it doesn't make sense to live in poverty in your working years and live like a king in your retirement years. The key idea is that you want to have a smooth pattern of real consumption over the life-cycle. Setting Taxable Income as a percentage of Total Wealth does a good job of delivering a smooth pattern. The only tricky part is when social security kicks in. Looking at the graph of Real Consumption, you should see a smooth pattern with no jump up or down at your retirement date. Notice that Taxable Income / Total Wealth is 7.0% in cell **AP37** and 4.5% the next year in cell **AQ37**, which is an adjustment of 2.5%. In other words, the drop in Taxable Income is offset by addition of Social Security Benefits (which are NOT taxable). Notice that Real Consumption transitions smoothly from $119,874 in cell **AP104** to $120,022 in cell **AQ104**. The Higher Consumption in Working Years of 2.5% in cell **B35** works well for the default input values of this Excel model. When you change input values, you may need to change the adjustment. Manually adjust the value in cell **B35** in small increments until the graph of Real Consumption shows a smooth pattern with no jump at the retirement date.

Since the standard deviation (risk) in cell **B8** is virtually zero, the results we see in the two graphs are based on *average returns*. Starting with the second graph,

---

[6] The "Transformation Method" for converting a uniform random variable x into some other random variable y based on a cumulative distribution F is $y(x) = F^{-1}(x)$. See Press, W., B. Flannery, S. Teukolsky, and W. Vetterling, 1987, Numerical Recopies: The Art of Scientific Computing, Cambridge University Press, chapter on Random Numbers, subsection on the Transformation Method, page 201.

we see that Real Human Capital starts at $1.7 million and declines smoothly to $0 at retirement. Real Financial Capital starts at $0, rises smoothly to $2.7 million at retirement, and then stays constant at that level. Turning to the first graph, Real Consumption starts at $33,234, rises smoothly to $120,022 at retirement, and then stays constant at that level.

How much saving does it take to reach such a comfortable lifestyle? Savings starts at 36.6% of salary at age 31 and gradually tapers off. Clearly, a lot of saving is required to live so well in retirement.

Now let's consider the risk involved. Change the standard deviation to a realistic figure. Enter **17.000%** in cell **B8**. The random variables in rows **40** and **41** spring to life and the graph of real consumption over the life-cycle reflect the high or low realizations of the broad stock portfolio. Press the function key **F9** and the Excel model is recalculated. You see a new realization of real consumption on the first graph. The three figures below show: (a) a low real consumption case due to low stock returns, (b) a medium real consumption case due to medium stock returns, and (c) a high real consumption case due to high stock returns.

FIGURE 10.6 Low Real Consumption Due To Low Stock Returns.

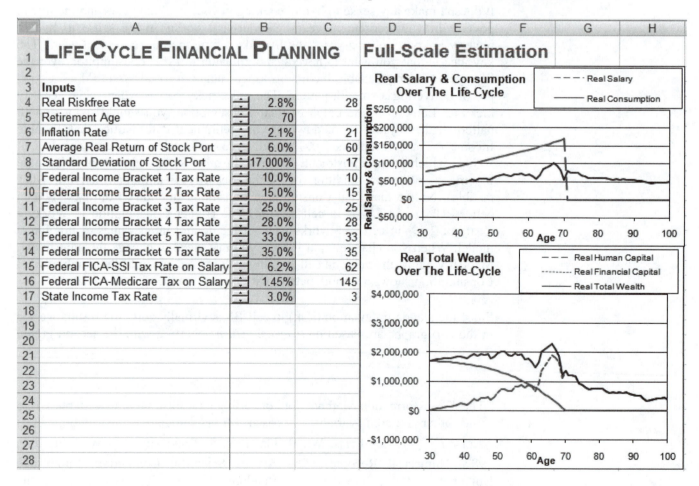

FIGURE 10.7 Medium Real Consumption Due To Medium Stock Returns.

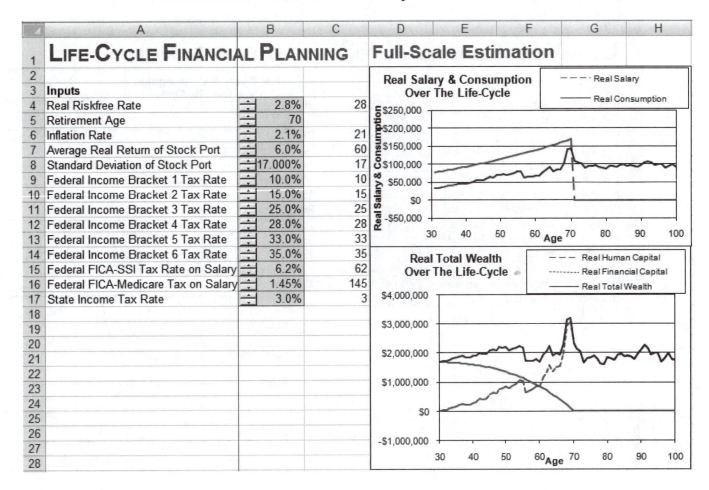

FIGURE 10.8 High Real Consumption Due To High Stock Returns.

	A	B	C	D	E	F	G	H
1	LIFE-CYCLE FINANCIAL PLANNING			Full-Scale Estimation				
2								
3	Inputs							
4	Real Riskfree Rate	2.8%	28					
5	Retirement Age	70						
6	Inflation Rate	2.1%	21					
7	Average Real Return of Stock Port	6.0%	60					
8	Standard Deviation of Stock Port	17.000%	17					
9	Federal Income Bracket 1 Tax Rate	10.0%	10					
10	Federal Income Bracket 2 Tax Rate	15.0%	15					
11	Federal Income Bracket 3 Tax Rate	25.0%	25					
12	Federal Income Bracket 4 Tax Rate	28.0%	28					
13	Federal Income Bracket 5 Tax Rate	33.0%	33					
14	Federal Income Bracket 6 Tax Rate	35.0%	35					
15	Federal FICA-SSI Tax Rate on Salary	6.2%	62					
16	Federal FICA-Medicare Tax on Salary	1.45%	145					
17	State Income Tax Rate	3.0%	3					
18								
19								
20								
21								
22								
23								
24								
25								
26								
27								
28								

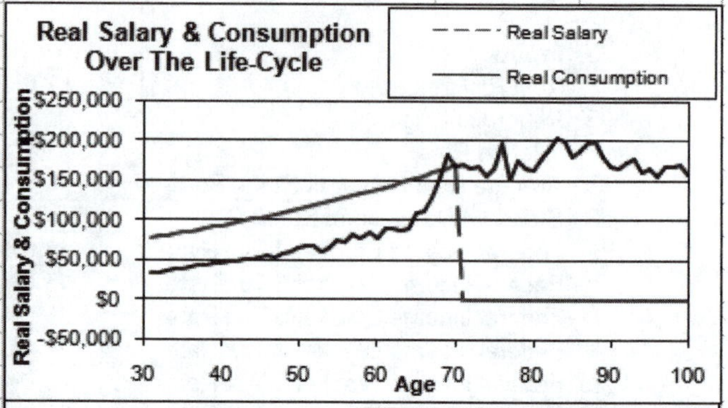

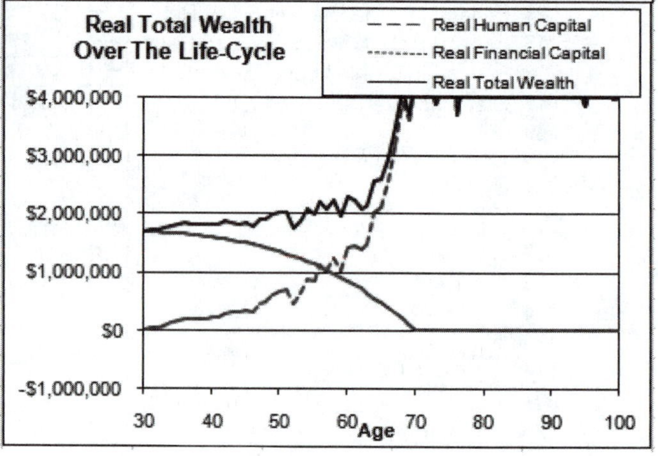

These three graphs are "representative" of the risk you face from being heavily investing in the broad stock portfolio. In the low case, real consumption drops to about $50,000. In the medium case, real consumption fluctuates around $100,000. In the high case, real consumption fluctuates between $150,000 and $200,000. Clearly, there is substantial risk from being so heavily exposed to the broad stock portfolio.

Now that we have completed the Excel model, it is time for you to explore. Click on the spin buttons to change the inputs and/or edit the values of the choice variables and see the implications for lifetime real consumption and real total wealth. For example, if you are uncomfortable with the amount of risk implied by the three figures above, consider more conservative strategies. Many investors reduce stock exposure in retirement years to little or nothing.

A key driver in the model is the Beginning Consumption Rate in cell **B34**. Raise this value and there will be more real consumption in early working years and less real consumption retirement years. Lower this value and it will tilt in the opposite direction.

Play around with the choice variables and have fun exploring your lifetime opportunities. Enjoy!

Problems

1. Suppose that you are currently 28 years old and expect to earn a constant real salary of $64,000 starting next year. You are planning to work for 32 years and then retire. You currently have $0 in financial capital. You are limited to investing in the riskfree asset. The real riskfree rate is 2.8%. Develop a financial plan for real savings and real consumption over your lifetime.

2. Suppose that you are currently 32 years old and expect to earn a constant real salary of $85,000 starting next year. You are planning to work for 25 years and then retire. You currently have $10,000 in financial capital. You can invest in the riskfree asset or a broad stock portfolio. The inflation rate is 3.4% and the real riskfree rate is 2.5%. A broad stock portfolio offers an average real return of 7.3% and a standard deviation of 25.0%. Suppose that federal income taxes have six brackets with the following rates: 10.0%, 15.0%, 27.0%, 30.0%, 35.0%, and 38.6%. For current year, the upper cutoffs on the first five brackets are $6,000, $27,950, $67,700, $141,250, and $307,050 and these cutoffs are indexed to inflation. The state tax rate is 4.5%, federal FICA-SSI tax rate on salary up to $87,000 is 6.2%, and the federal FICA-Medicare tax rate on any level of salary is 1.45%. You will start receiving social security benefits at age 66. The current level of social security benefits is $24,204 per year and this is indexed to inflation. Develop a financial plan for real savings and real consumption over your lifetime.

Chapter 11 Dividend Discount Models

11.1 Dividend Discount Model

Problem. Currently a stock pays a dividend per share of $6.64. A security analyst projects the future dividend growth rate over the next five years to be 12.0%, 11.0%, 10.0%, 9.0%, 8.0% and then 7.0% each year thereafter to infinity. The levered cost of equity capital for the firm is 12.0% per year. What is the stock's value / share?

Solution Strategy. Construct a two-stage discounted dividend model. In stage one, explicitly forecast the firm's dividend over a five-year horizon. In stage two, forecast the firm's dividend from year six to infinity and calculate its continuation value as the present value of this infinitely growing annuity. Then, discount the future dividends and the date 5 continuation value back to the present to get the stock's value.

FIGURE 11.1 Excel Model for Stock Valuation – Dividend Discount Model.

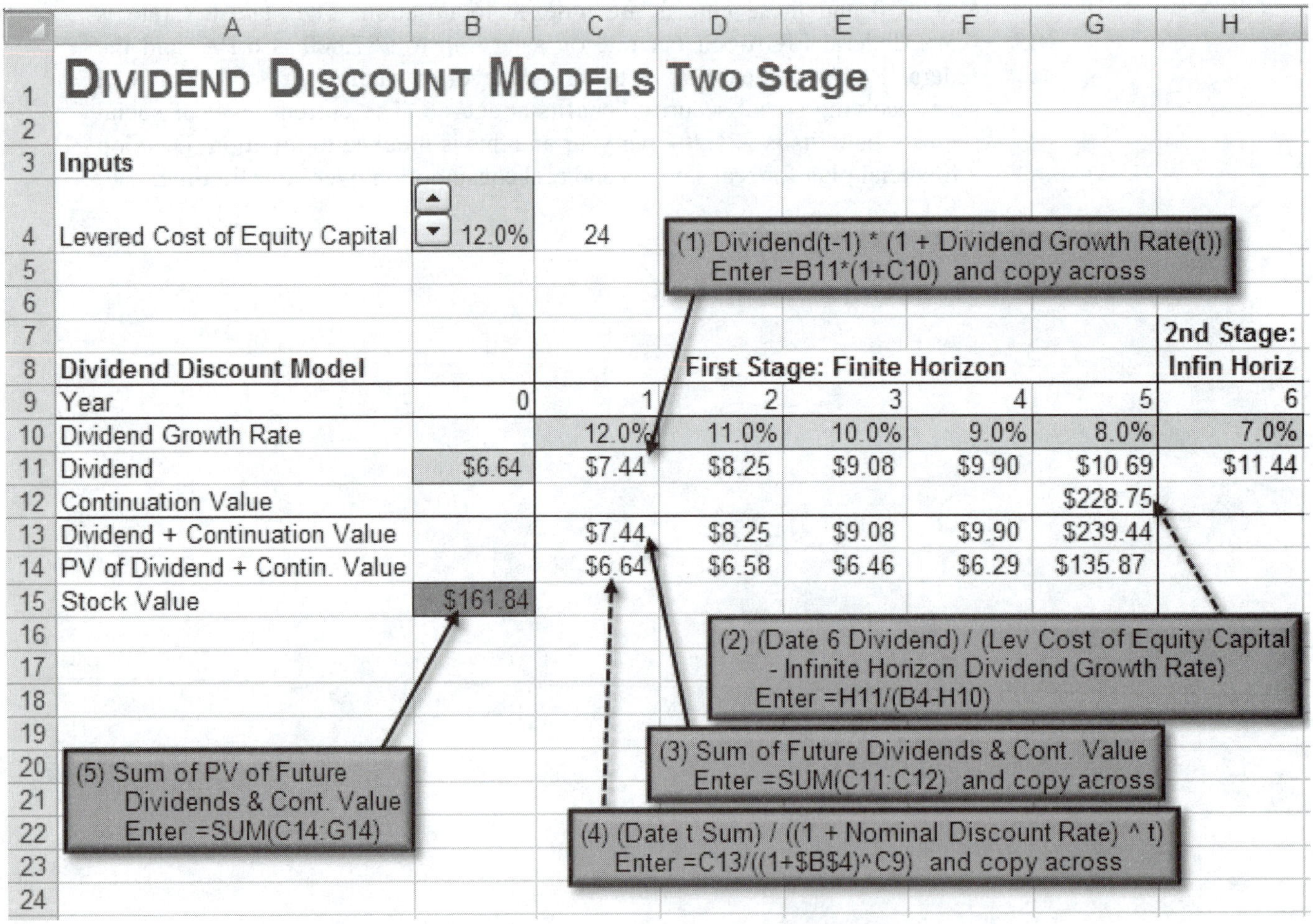

	A	B	C	D	E	F	G	H
1	DIVIDEND DISCOUNT MODELS Two Stage							
2								
3	Inputs							
4	Levered Cost of Equity Capital	12.0%	24					
5								
6								
7								2nd Stage:
8	Dividend Discount Model			First Stage: Finite Horizon				Infin Horiz
9	Year	0	1	2	3	4	5	6
10	Dividend Growth Rate		12.0%	11.0%	10.0%	9.0%	8.0%	7.0%
11	Dividend	$6.64	$7.44	$8.25	$9.08	$9.90	$10.69	$11.44
12	Continuation Value						$228.75	
13	Dividend + Continuation Value		$7.44	$8.25	$9.08	$9.90	$239.44	
14	PV of Dividend + Contin. Value		$6.64	$6.58	$6.46	$6.29	$135.87	
15	Stock Value	$161.84						

(1) Dividend(t-1) * (1 + Dividend Growth Rate(t))
Enter =B11*(1+C10) and copy across

(2) (Date 6 Dividend) / (Lev Cost of Equity Capital - Infinite Horizon Dividend Growth Rate)
Enter =H11/(B4-H10)

(3) Sum of Future Dividends & Cont. Value
Enter =SUM(C11:C12) and copy across

(4) (Date t Sum) / ((1 + Nominal Discount Rate) ^ t)
Enter =C13/((1+$B$4)^C9) and copy across

(5) Sum of PV of Future Dividends & Cont. Value
Enter =SUM(C14:G14)

The stock value is estimated to be $161.84.

Problems

1. Currently a stock pays a dividend per share of $43.37. A security analyst projects the future dividend growth rate over the next five years to be 21.0%, 18.0%, 15.0%, 13.5%, 11.5% and then 11.0% each year thereafter to infinity. The levered cost of equity capital for the firm is 13.4% per year. What is the stock's value / share?

PART 3 OPTIONS / FUTURES / DERIVATIVES

Chapter 12 Option Payoffs and Profits

12.1 Basics

Problem. A call option has an exercise price of $40.00 and an option price of $5.00. A put option has the same exercise price and option price. Graph the option payoffs and profits for buying or selling a call option and for buying or selling a put option.

Solution Strategy. For a range of stock prices at maturity, calculate option payoffs and profits. Then graph it.

FIGURE 12.1 Excel Model of Option Payoffs and Profits - Basics.

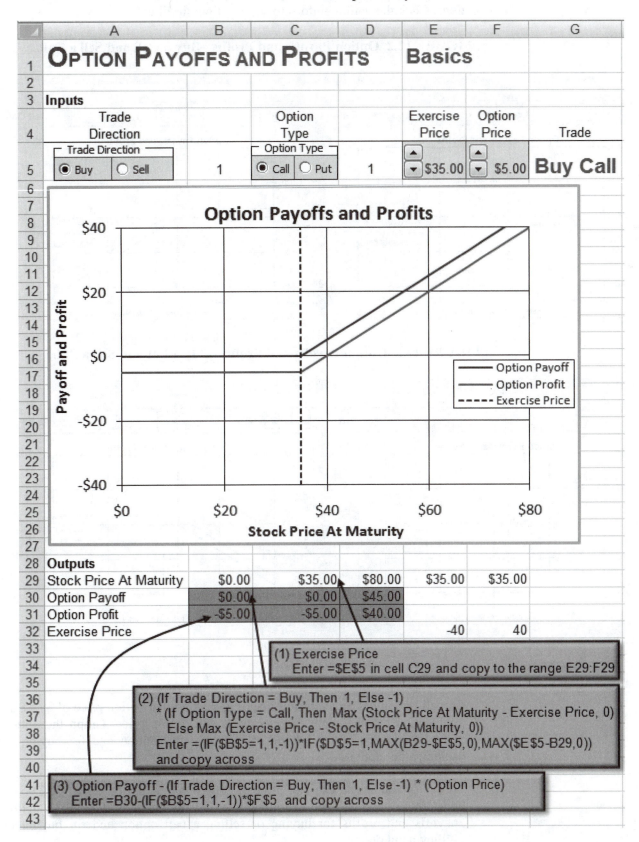

The graph displays the "hockey stick" payoffs and profits that characterize options. Click the option buttons to see all of possibilities.

FIGURE 12.2 Option Payoffs and Profits –Buy a Call and Sell a Call.

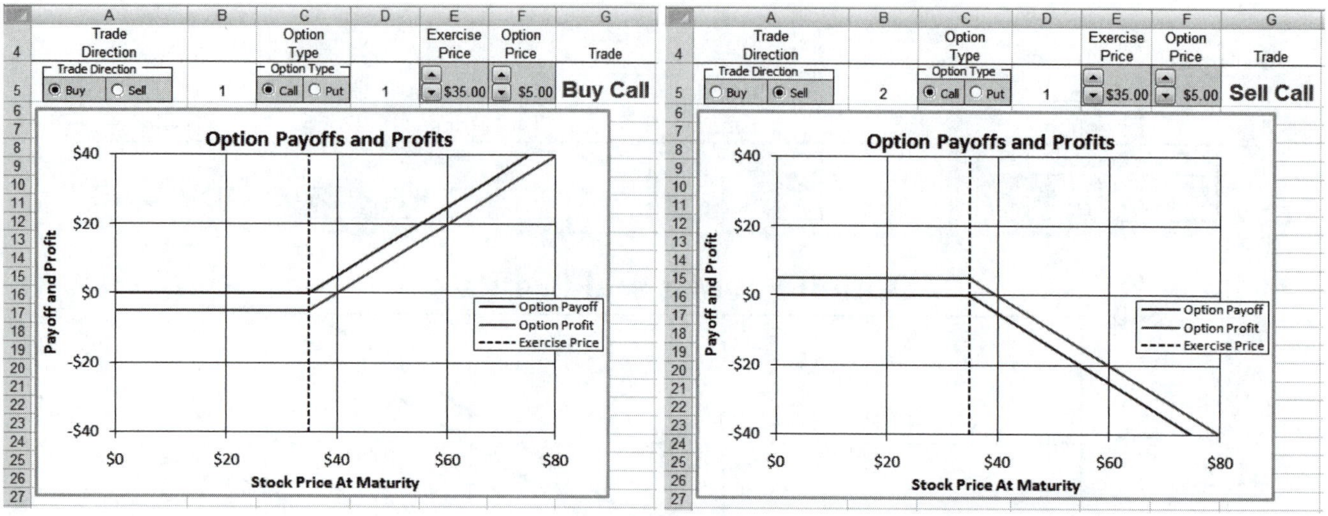

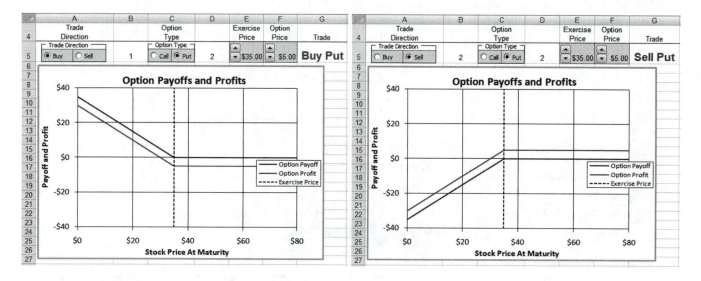

FIGURE 12.3 Option Payoffs and Profits –Buy a Put and Sell a Put.

Problems

1. A call option has an exercise price of $32.54 and an option price of $4.71. A put option has the same exercise price and option price. Graph the option payoffs and profits for buying or selling a call option and for buying or selling a put option.

2. A call option has an exercise price of $18.23 and an option price of $2.96. A put option has the same exercise price and option price. Graph the option payoffs and profits for buying or selling a call option and for buying or selling a put option.

Chapter 13 Option Trading Strategies

13.1 Two Assets

Problem. There are three types of trading strategies involving options: (1) strategies involving a single option and a stock, (2) spreads involving options of one type (i.e., two or more calls or two or more puts), and (3) combinations involving both call(s) and put(s). Construct a chart that can show all of the trading strategies involving two assets.

Solution Strategy. We will create ranges for first asset inputs and for second asset inputs. Then calculate first asset profit, second asset profit, total profit, exercise price lines, and graph them.

FIGURE 13.1 Excel Model of Option Trading Strategies - Two Assets.

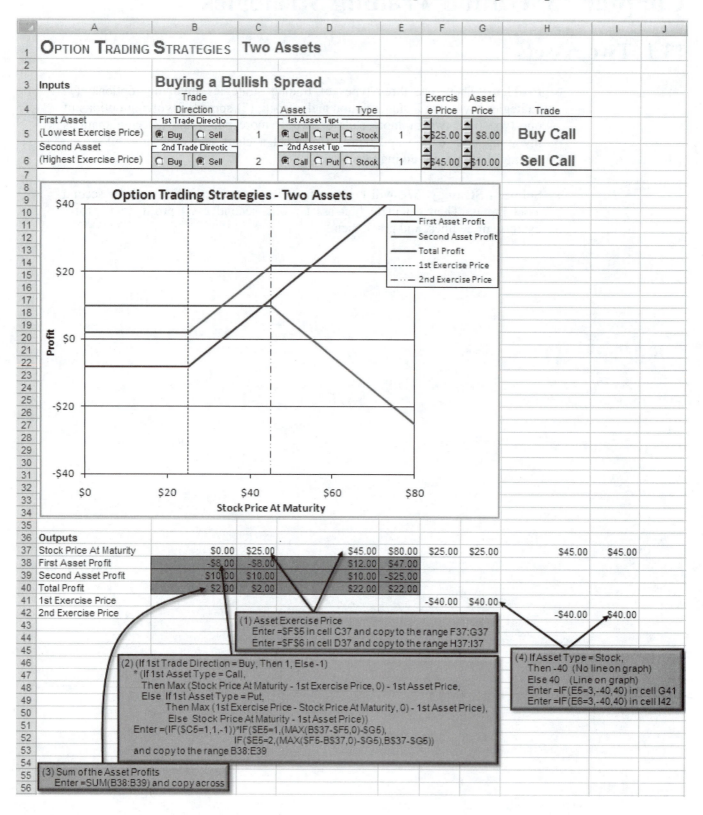

FIGURE 13.2 Table of Option Trading Strategies.

	J	K	L	M
4	Trades Listed From Asset 1 to Asset 2 (Lowest To Highest Exercise Price)			
5	Buy Call, Sell Call			
6				
7				
8	Test	Two-Asset Strategies	Description (Lowest To Highest Exercise Price)	Type
9	Yes	Buying a Bullish Spread	"Buy Call, Sell Call" or "Buy Put, Sell Put"	Spread
10	No	Buying a Bearish Spread	"Sell Call, Buy Call" or "Sell Put, Buy Put"	Spread
11	No	Buying a Straddle	"Buy Call, Buy Put" or "Buy Put, Buy Call" at the same exercise price	Combination
12	No	Writing a Straddle	"Sell Call, Sell Put" or "Sell Put, Sell Call" at the same exercise price	Combination
13	No	Buying a Strangle	"Buy Put, Buy Call"	Combination
14	No	Writing a Strangle	"Sell Put, Sell Call"	Combination
15	No	Buying a Covered Call	"Buy Stock, Sell Call" or "Sell Call, Buy Stock"	N.A.
16	No	Writing a Covered Call	"Sell Stock, Buy Call" or "Buy Call, Sell Stock"	N.A.
17	No	Buying a Protective Put	"Buy Stock, Buy Put" or "Buy Put, Buy Stock"	N.A.
18	No	Writing a Protective Put	"Sell Stock, Sell Put" or "Sell Put, Sell Stock"	N.A.
19	No	Other Strategies		
20				
21	Note: Writing a Bullish Spread = Buying a Bearish Spread			
22		Writing a Bearish Spread = Buying a Bullish Spread		

FIGURE 13.3 Buying a Bullish Spread using Calls and Buying a Bullish Spread using Puts.

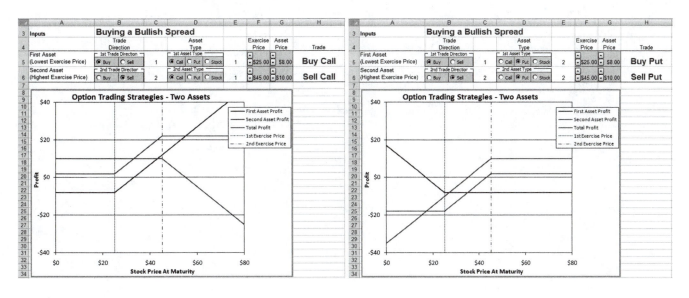

FIGURE 13.4 Buying a Bearish Spread using Calls and Buying a Bearish Spread using Puts.

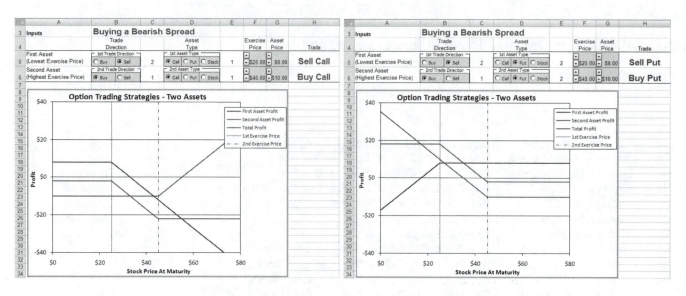

FIGURE 13.5 Buying a Straddle and Writing a Straddle.

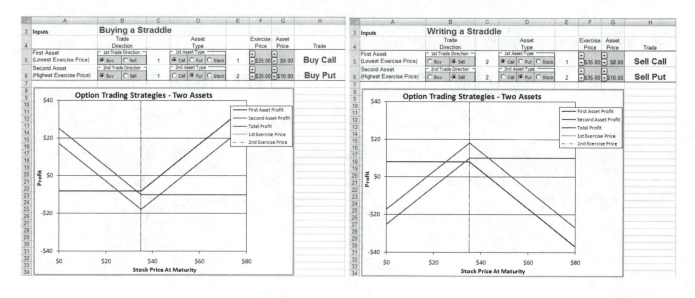

FIGURE 13.6 Buying a Strangle and Writing a Strangle.

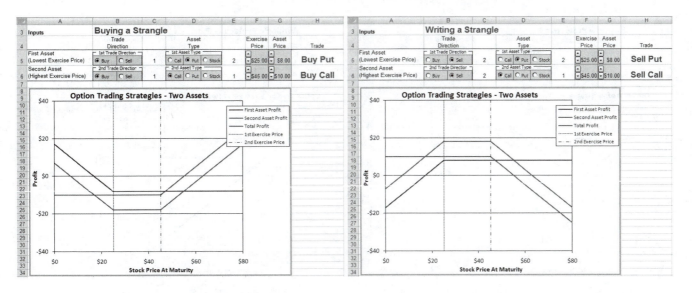

FIGURE 13.7 Buying a Covered Call and Writing a Covered Call.

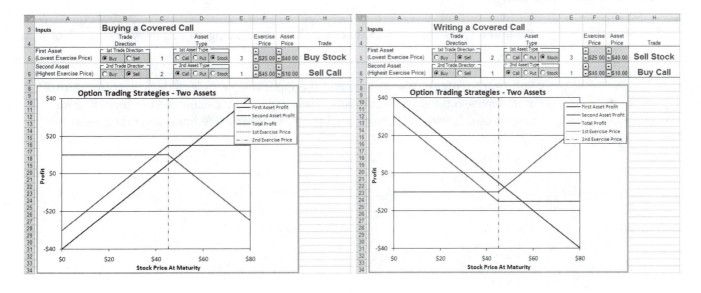

FIGURE 13.8 Buying a Protective Put and Writing a Protective Put.

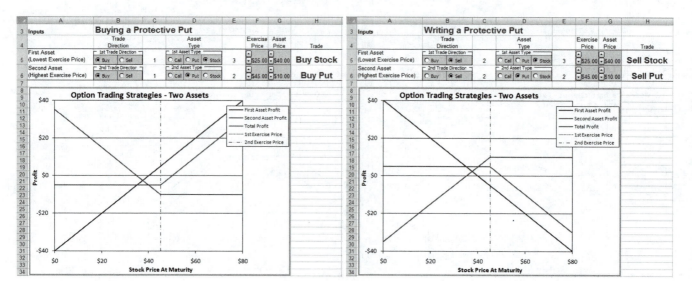

13.2 Four Assets

Problem. Construct a chart that can show the trading strategies which involve four assets.

Solution Strategy. We will expand the input ranges to include a place for third asset inputs and fourth asset inputs. Then expand the calculations to include third asset profit, fourth asset profit, total profit, exercise price lines, and graph them.

FIGURE 13.9 Excel Model of Option Trading Strategies - Four Assets.

	A	B	C	D	E	F	G	H
1	OPTION TRADING STRATEGIES Four Assets					Buying a Butterfly Spread		
2								
3	**Inputs**							
4		Trade Direction			Asset Type		Exercise Price	Asset Price	Trade
5	First Asset (Lowest Exercise Price)	1st Trade Direction ● Buy ○ Sell	1	1st Asset Type ● Call ○ Put ○ Stock	1	$25.00	$8.00	**Buy Call**
6	Second Asset (Med-Low Exercise Price)	2nd Trade Direction ○ Buy ● Sell	2	2nd Asset Type ● Call ○ Put ○ Stock	1	$35.00	$10.00	**Sell Call**
7	Third Asset (Med-High Exercise Price)	3rd Trade Direction ○ Buy ● Sell	2	3rd Asset Type ● Call ○ Put ○ Stock	1	$35.00	$4.00	**Sell Call**
8	Fourth Asset (Highest Exercise Price)	4th Trade Direction ● Buy ○ Sell	1	4th Asset Type ● Call ○ Put ○ Stock	1	$45.00	$10.00	**Buy Call**

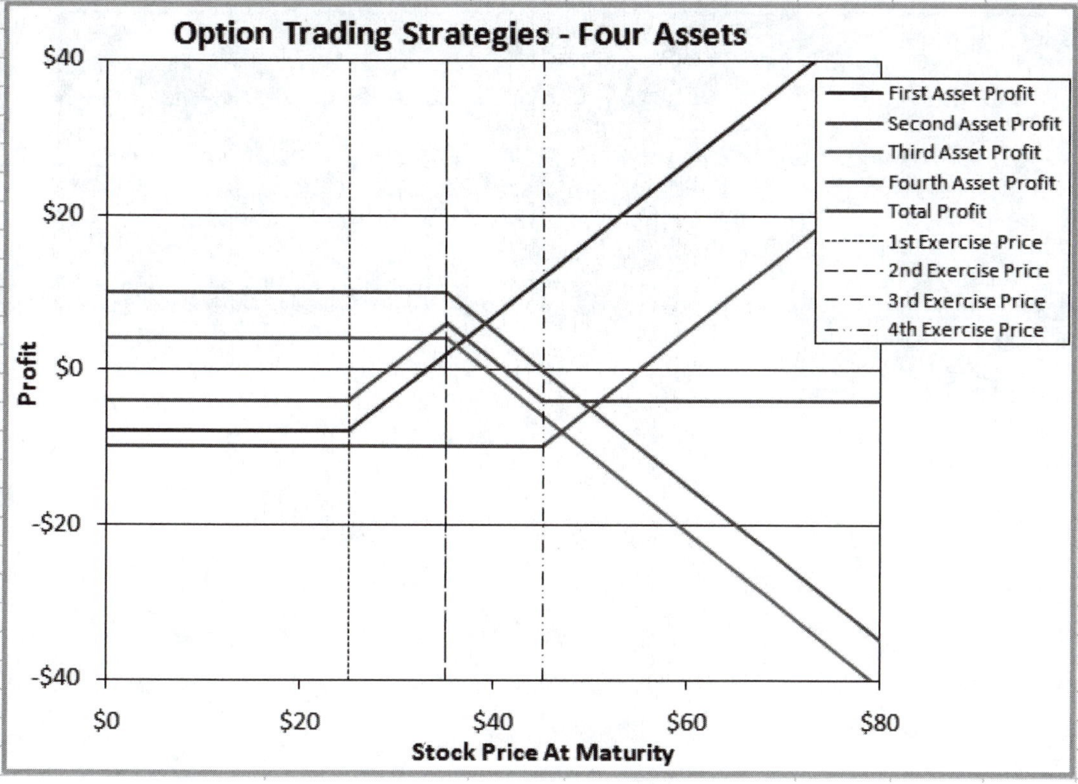

Option Trading Strategies - Four Assets

Legend:
- First Asset Profit
- Second Asset Profit
- Third Asset Profit
- Fourth Asset Profit
- Total Profit
- 1st Exercise Price
- 2nd Exercise Price
- 3rd Exercise Price
- 4th Exercise Price

Y-axis: Profit ($40, $20, $0, -$20, -$40)
X-axis: Stock Price At Maturity ($0, $20, $40, $60, $80)

FIGURE 13.10 Excel Model of Option Trading Strategies - Four Assets.

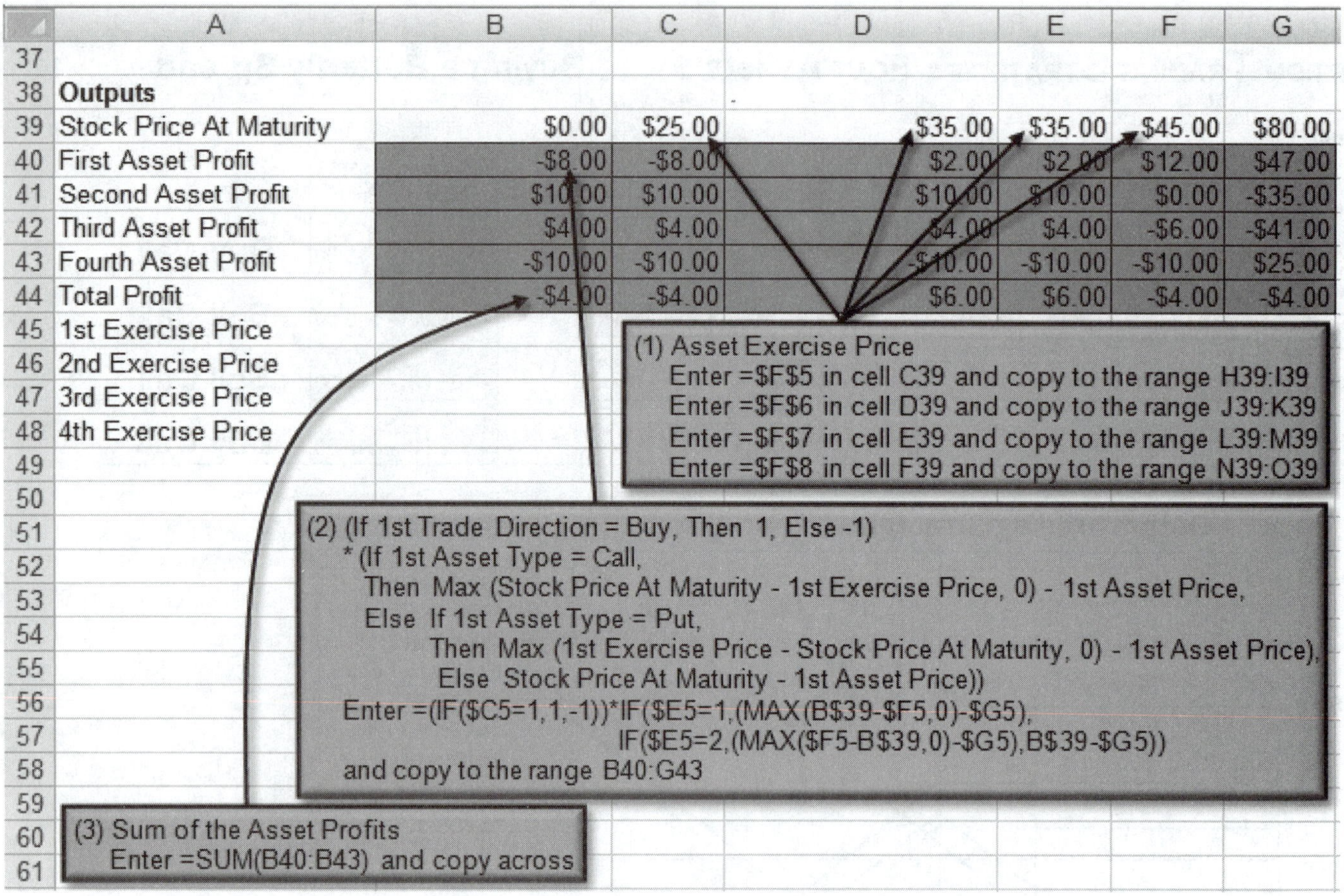

	A	B	C	D	E	F	G
37							
38	**Outputs**						
39	Stock Price At Maturity	$0.00	$25.00	$35.00	$35.00	$45.00	$80.00
40	First Asset Profit	-$8.00	-$8.00	$2.00	$2.00	$12.00	$47.00
41	Second Asset Profit	$10.00	$10.00	$10.00	$10.00	$0.00	-$35.00
42	Third Asset Profit	$4.00	$4.00	$4.00	$4.00	-$6.00	-$41.00
43	Fourth Asset Profit	-$10.00	-$10.00	-$10.00	-$10.00	-$10.00	$25.00
44	Total Profit	-$4.00	-$4.00	$6.00	$6.00	-$4.00	-$4.00
45	1st Exercise Price						
46	2nd Exercise Price						
47	3rd Exercise Price						
48	4th Exercise Price						

(1) Asset Exercise Price
    Enter =$F$5 in cell C39 and copy to the range H39:I39
    Enter =$F$6 in cell D39 and copy to the range J39:K39
    Enter =$F$7 in cell E39 and copy to the range L39:M39
    Enter =$F$8 in cell F39 and copy to the range N39:O39

(2) (If 1st Trade Direction = Buy, Then 1, Else -1)
     * (If 1st Asset Type = Call,
        Then Max (Stock Price At Maturity - 1st Exercise Price, 0) - 1st Asset Price,
      Else If 1st Asset Type = Put,
            Then Max (1st Exercise Price - Stock Price At Maturity, 0) - 1st Asset Price),
            Else Stock Price At Maturity - 1st Asset Price))
     Enter =(IF($C5=1,1,-1))*IF($E5=1,(MAX(B$39-$F5,0)-$G5),
                          IF($E5=2,(MAX($F5-B$39,0)-$G5),B$39-$G5))
     and copy to the range B40:G43

(3) Sum of the Asset Profits
     Enter =SUM(B40:B43) and copy across

FIGURE 13.11 Excel Model of Option Trading Strategies - Four Assets.

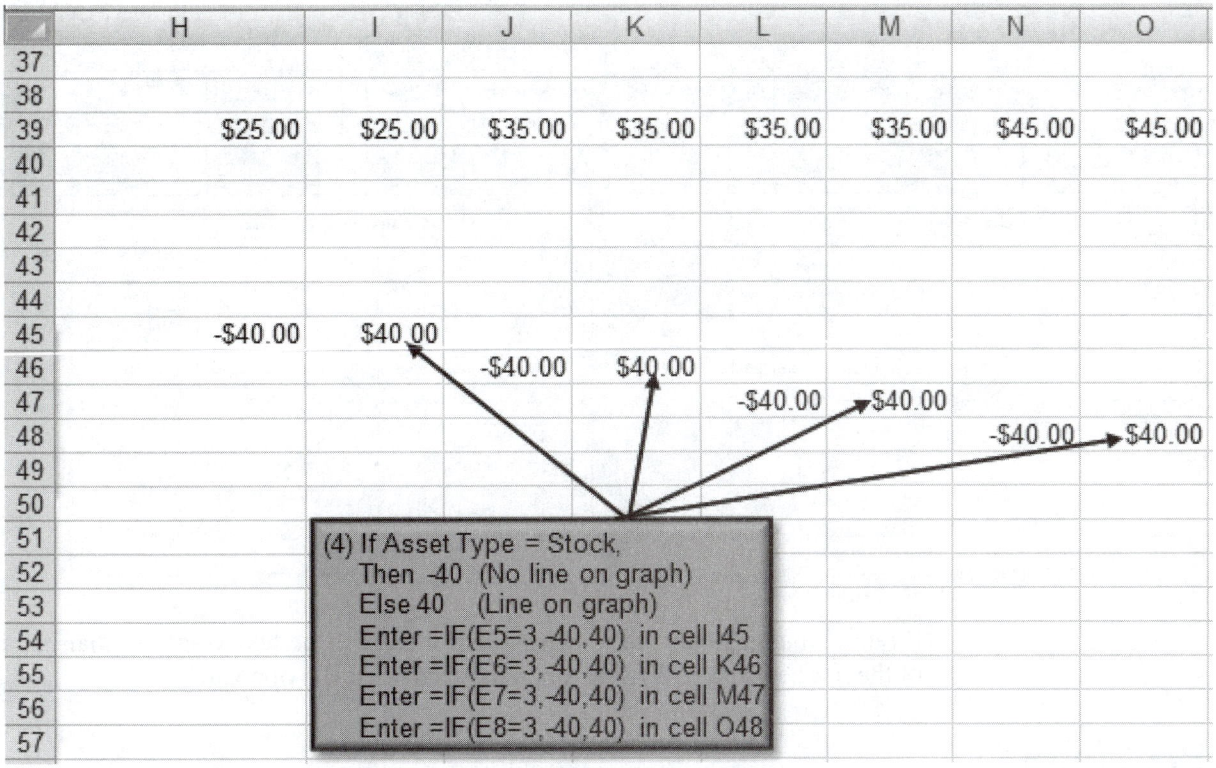

	H	I	J	K	L	M	N	O
37								
38								
39	$25.00	$25.00	$35.00	$35.00	$35.00	$35.00	$45.00	$45.00
40								
41								
42								
43								
44								
45	-$40.00	$40.00						
46			-$40.00	$40.00				
47					-$40.00	$40.00		
48							-$40.00	$40.00
49								
50								
51			(4) If Asset Type = Stock,					
52			Then -40 (No line on graph)					
53			Else 40 (Line on graph)					
54			Enter =IF(E5=3,-40,40) in cell I45					
55			Enter =IF(E6=3,-40,40) in cell K46					
56			Enter =IF(E7=3,-40,40) in cell M47					
57			Enter =IF(E8=3,-40,40) in cell O48					

FIGURE 13.12 Table of Option Trading Strategies.

	J	K	L	M	N	O	P	Q	R	S	T	U	V
4	Trades Listed From Asset 1 to Asset 4 (Lowest To Highest Exercise Price)												
5	Buy Call, Sell Call, Sell Call, Buy Call												
6													
7													
8													
9													
10	Test	Four-Asset Strategies			Description (Trades Listed By Assets Having The Lowest To Highest Exercise Price)								Type
11	Yes	Buying a Butterfly Spread			"Buy Call, Sell Call, Sell Call, Buy Call" or "Buy Put, Sell Put, Sell Put, Buy Put"								Spread
12					with Assets 2 and 3 at the same exercise price								
13	No	Writing a Butterfly Spread			"Sell Call, Buy Call, Buy Call, Sell Call" or "Sell Put, Buy Put, Buy Put, Sell Put"								Spread
14					with Assets 2 and 3 at the same exercise price								
15	No	Other Strategies											

FIGURE 13.13 Buying a Butterfly Spread and Writing a Butterfly Spread.

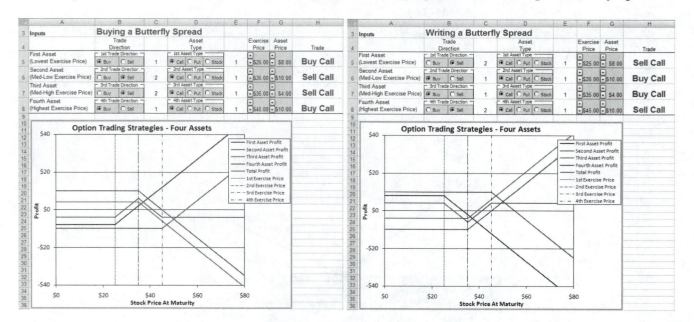

Buying a butterfly spread is betting that there will be less volatility than the rest of the market thinks. Writing a butterfly spread is the opposite.

Problems

1. There are three types of trading strategies involving options: (1) strategies involving a single option and a stock, (2) spreads involving options of one type (i.e., two or more calls or two or more puts), and (3) combinations involving both call(s) and put(s). Graph all of the trading strategies involving two assets. In particular, show the following strategies:

   a. <u>First asset:</u> Buy a call with an exercise price of $24.12 for a call price of $5.31 and
   <u>Second asset:</u> Sell a call with an exercise price of $38.34 for a call price of $3.27 = Buying a bullish spread = Writing a bearish spread.

   b. <u>First asset:</u> Sell a call with an exercise price of $18.92 for a call price of $7.39 and
   <u>Second asset:</u> Buy a call with an exercise price of $45.72 with a call price of $3.78 = Buying a bearish spread = Writing a bullish spread.

   c. <u>First asset:</u> Buy a call with an exercise price of $41.29 for a call price of $3.81 and
   <u>Second asset:</u> Buy a put with an exercise price of $41.29 for a put price of $4.94 = Buying a straddle.

   d. <u>First asset:</u> Sell a call with an exercise price of $38.47 for a call price of $2.93 and
   <u>Second asset:</u> Sell a put with an exercise price of $38.47 for a put price of $5.63 = Writing a straddle.

e. <u>First asset:</u>   Buy a call with an exercise price of $42.72 for a call price of $2.93 and
    <u>Second asset:</u> Buy a put with an exercise price of $36.44 for a put price of $5.63 = Buying a strangle.

f. <u>First asset:</u>   Sell a call with an exercise price of $46.18 for a call price of $3.58 and
    <u>Second asset:</u> Sell a put with an exercise price of $38.50 for a put price of $6.39 = Writing a strangle.

g. <u>First asset:</u>   Buy a stock for a stock price (asset price) of $41.25 and
    <u>Second asset:</u> Sell a call with an exercise price of $47.39 for a call price of $5.83 = Buying a covered call.

h. <u>First asset:</u>   Sell a stock for a stock price (asset price) of $36.47 and
    <u>Second asset:</u> Buy a call with an exercise price of $32.83 for a call price of $6.74 = Writing a covered call.

i. <u>First asset:</u>   Buy a stock for a stock price (asset price) of $43.72 and
    <u>Second asset:</u> Buy a put with an exercise price of $47.87 for a put price of $7.31 = Buying a protective put.

j. <u>First asset:</u>   Sell a stock for a stock price (asset price) of $36.93 and
    <u>Second asset:</u> Sell a put with an exercise price of $33.29 for a put price of $6.36 = Writing a protective put.

2. Graph all of the trading strategies involving four assets. In particular, show:

k. <u>First asset:</u>   Buy a call with an exercise price of $25.73 for a call price of $7.92 and
    <u>Second asset:</u> Sell a call with an exercise price of $34.07 for a call price of $10.15
    <u>Third asset:</u>   Sell a call with an exercise price of $34.07 for a call price of $3.96 and
    <u>Fourth asset:</u>   Buy a call with an exercise price of $41.83 for a call price of $9.23 = Buying a butterfly spread using calls.

l. <u>First asset:</u>   Sell a call with an exercise price of $23.84 for a call price of $5.39 and
    <u>Second asset:</u> Buy a call with an exercise price of $36.19 for a call price of $6.98
    <u>Third asset:</u>   Buy a call with an exercise price of $36.19 for a call price of $3.36 and
    <u>Fourth asset:</u>   Sell a call with an exercise price of $47.28 for a call price of $8.34 = Writing a butterfly spread using calls.

m. <u>First asset:</u>   Buy a put with an exercise price of $29.33 for a put price of $4.59 and
    <u>Second asset:</u> Sell a put with an exercise price of $39.54 for a put price of $2.87
    <u>Third asset:</u>   Sell a put with an exercise price of $39.54 for a put price of

$4.56 and

<u>Fourth asset:</u> Buy a put with an exercise price of $54.78 for a put price of $10.37 = Buying a butterfly spread using puts.

n. <u>First asset:</u>   Sell a put with an exercise price of $27.49 for a put price of $3.22 and

<u>Second asset:</u> Buy a put with an exercise price of $41.38 for a put price of $5.39

<u>Third asset:</u>   Buy a put with an exercise price of $41.38 for a put price of $2.74 and

<u>Fourth asset:</u>   Sell a put with an exercise price of $52.86 for a put price of $9.49 = Writing a butterfly spread using puts.

Chapter 14 Put-Call Parity

14.1 Basics

Problem. Consider a call option and put option on the same underlying stock with the same exercise price and time to maturity. The call price is $4.00, the underlying stock price is $43.00, the exercise price on both options is $40.00, the riskfree rate is 5.00%, the time to maturity on both options is 0.25 years, and the stock pays a $2.00 / share dividend in 0.10 years. What is the price of the put price now?

FIGURE 14.1 Excel Model of Put-Call Parity - Basics.

	A	B	C	D
1	**PUT-CALL PARITY** Basics			
2				
3	**Inputs**			
4	Call Price Now	$4.00		
5	Stock Price Now	$43.00		
6	Exercise Price	$40.00		
7	Riskfree Rate	5.00%		
8	Time To Maturity	0.25		
9	Dividend	$2.00		
10	Time To Dividend	0.10		
11				
12	**Outputs**			
13	Put Price Now	$2.51		
14				
15				
16	(1) Call Price Now - Stock Price Now			
17	+ Exercise Price / ((1 + Riskfree Rate)^(Time to Maturity))			
18	+ Dividend / ((+ Riskfree Rate)^(Time to Dividend))			
19	Enter =B4-B5+B6/((1+B7)^B8)+B9/((1+B7)^B10)			
20				

Put-Call Parity predicts the Put Price is $2.51.

14.2 Payoff Diagram

The Put-Call Parity equation claims that one Put Option is equivalent to a replicating portfolio consisting of one Call Option, short one Stock, and a Bond paying a face value equal to the exercise price of the put and call options. Construct a payoff diagram to determine if the payoff at maturity of the replicating portfolio is equivalent to the payoff at maturity of a put option.

FIGURE 14.2 Excel Model of Put-Call Parity - Payoff Diagram.

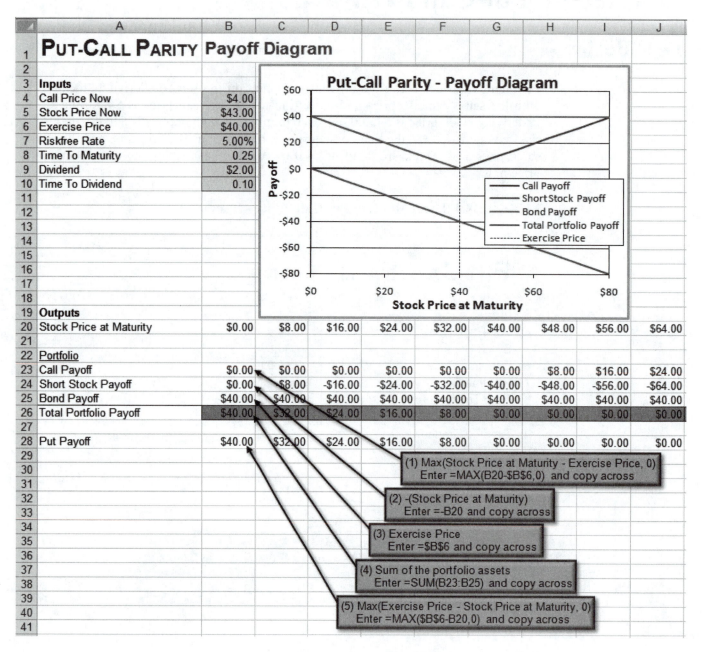

FIGURE 14.3 Excel Model of Put-Call Parity - Payoff Diagram.

	K	L	M	N
20	$72.00	$80.00	$40.00	$40.00
21				
22				
23	$32.00	$40.00		
24	-$72.00	-$80.00		
25	$40.00	$40.00		
26	$0.00	$0.00		
27			-$80.00	$60.00
28	$0.00	$0.00		
29				
30		(6) Exercise Price		
31		Enter =$B$6 and copy across		

Looking at the Total Portfolio Payoff (row **26**), we see that it matches the Put Payoff in row **28**. Looking at the Payoff Diagram we can see the payoff of each of the component of the replicating portfolio: (1) Call Payoff, (2) Short Stock Payoff, and (3) Bond Payoff. At each point on the X-axis, we vertically sum the three components to get the Total Payoff. The Payoff Diagram verifies that the Total Payoff has the same "hockey stick" payoff as a put option.

Problems

1. Consider a call option and put option on the same underlying stock with the same exercise price and time to maturity. The call price is $2.59, the underlying stock price is $28.63, the exercise price on both options is $26.18, the riskfree rate is 6.21%, the time to maturity on both options is 0.47 years, and the stock pays a $1.64 / share dividend in 0.28 years. Determine the price of the put price now.

2. The Put-Call Parity equation claims that one Put Option is equivalent to a replicating portfolio consisting of one Call Option, short one Stock, and a Bond paying a face value equal to the exercise price of the put and call options. Determine if the payoff at maturity of the replicating portfolio is equivalent to the payoff at maturity of a put option.

Chapter 15 Binomial Option Pricing

15.1 Estimating Volatility

The binomial option pricing model can certainly be used to price European calls and puts, but it can do much more. The Binomial Tree / Risk Neutral method can be extended to price *any* type of derivative security (European vs. American vs. other) on any underlying asset(s), with any underlying dividends or cash flows, with any derivative payoffs at maturity and/or payoffs before maturity. Indeed, it is one of the most popular techniques on Wall Street for pricing and hedging derivatives.

Problem. What is the annual standard deviation of Amazon.com stock based on continuous returns?

Solution Strategy. Download three months of Amazon.com's daily stock price. Then calculate continuous returns. Finally, calculate the annual standard deviation of the continuous returns.

FIGURE 15.1 Excel Model of Binomial Option Pricing - Estimating Volatility.

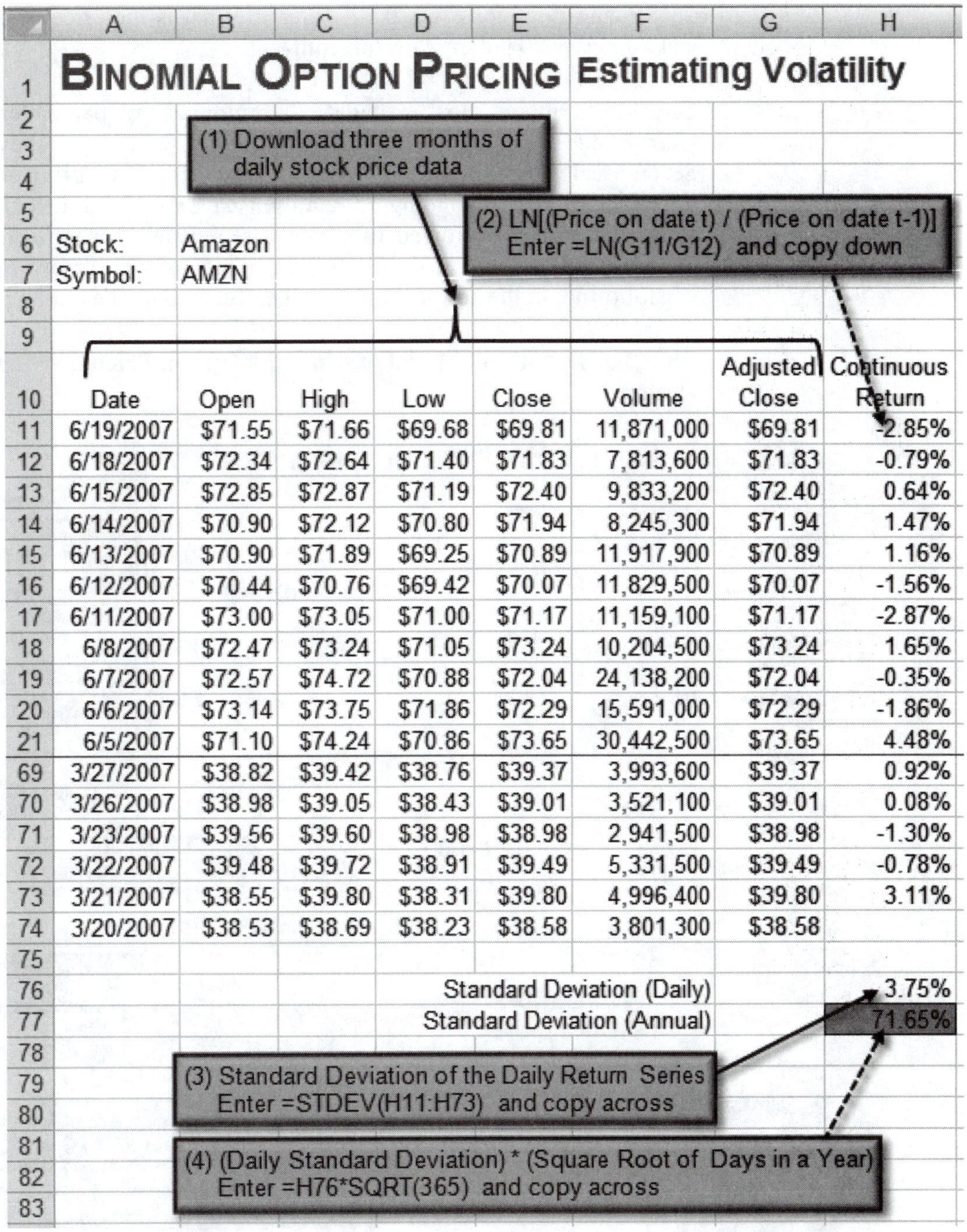

	A	B	C	D	E	F	G	H
1	**BINOMIAL OPTION PRICING Estimating Volatility**							
2								
3			(1) Download three months of daily stock price data					
4								
5						(2) LN[(Price on date t) / (Price on date t-1)] Enter =LN(G11/G12) and copy down		
6	Stock:	Amazon						
7	Symbol:	AMZN						
8								
9								
10	Date	Open	High	Low	Close	Volume	Adjusted Close	Continuous Return
11	6/19/2007	$71.55	$71.66	$69.68	$69.81	11,871,000	$69.81	-2.85%
12	6/18/2007	$72.34	$72.64	$71.40	$71.83	7,813,600	$71.83	-0.79%
13	6/15/2007	$72.85	$72.87	$71.19	$72.40	9,833,200	$72.40	0.64%
14	6/14/2007	$70.90	$72.12	$70.80	$71.94	8,245,300	$71.94	1.47%
15	6/13/2007	$70.90	$71.89	$69.25	$70.89	11,917,900	$70.89	1.16%
16	6/12/2007	$70.44	$70.76	$69.42	$70.07	11,829,500	$70.07	-1.56%
17	6/11/2007	$73.00	$73.05	$71.00	$71.17	11,159,100	$71.17	-2.87%
18	6/8/2007	$72.47	$73.24	$71.05	$73.24	10,204,500	$73.24	1.65%
19	6/7/2007	$72.57	$74.72	$70.88	$72.04	24,138,200	$72.04	-0.35%
20	6/6/2007	$73.14	$73.75	$71.86	$72.29	15,591,000	$72.29	-1.86%
21	6/5/2007	$71.10	$74.24	$70.86	$73.65	30,442,500	$73.65	4.48%
69	3/27/2007	$38.82	$39.42	$38.76	$39.37	3,993,600	$39.37	0.92%
70	3/26/2007	$38.98	$39.05	$38.43	$39.01	3,521,100	$39.01	0.08%
71	3/23/2007	$39.56	$39.60	$38.98	$38.98	2,941,500	$38.98	-1.30%
72	3/22/2007	$39.48	$39.72	$38.91	$39.49	5,331,500	$39.49	-0.78%
73	3/21/2007	$38.55	$39.80	$38.31	$39.80	4,996,400	$39.80	3.11%
74	3/20/2007	$38.53	$38.69	$38.23	$38.58	3,801,300	$38.58	
75								
76						Standard Deviation (Daily)		3.75%
77						Standard Deviation (Annual)		71.65%
78								
79			(3) Standard Deviation of the Daily Return Series Enter =STDEV(H11:H73) and copy across					
80								
81			(4) (Daily Standard Deviation) * (Square Root of Days in a Year) Enter =H76*SQRT(365) and copy across					
82								
83								

We find that Amazon.com's annual standard deviation is 71.65%.

15.2 Single Period

Problem. At the close of trading on June 20, 2007, the stock price of Amazon.com was $69.81, the standard deviation of daily returns is 71.65%, the yield on a six-month U.S. Treasury Bill was 4.95%, the exercise price of a January 70 call on Amazon.com was $70.00, the exercise price of a January 70 put on Amazon.com was $70.00, and the time to maturity for both January 18, 2008 maturity options was 0.5777 years. What is the price of a January 70 call and a January 70 put on Amazon.com?

Solution Strategy. First, calculate the binomial tree parameters: time / period, riskfree rate / period, up movement / period, and down movement / period. Second, calculate the date 1, maturity date items: stock up price, stock down price, and the corresponding call and put payoffs. Third, calculate the shares of stock and money borrowed to create a replicating portfolio that replicates the option payoff at maturity. Finally, calculate the price now of the replicating portfolio and, in the absence of arbitrage, this will be the option price now.

FIGURE 15.2 Excel Model of Binomial Option Pricing - Single Period - Call Option.

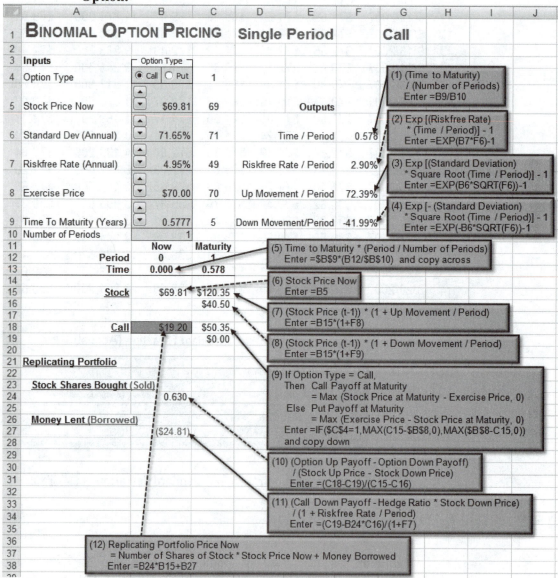

We see that the Binomial Option Pricing model predicts a one-period European call price of $19.20. Now let's check the put.

FIGURE 15.3 Excel Model of Binomial Option Pricing - Single Period - Put

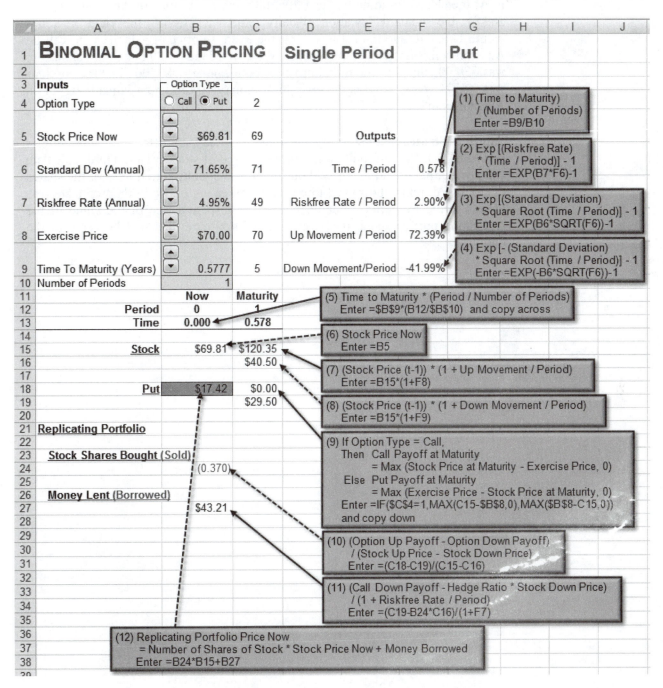

We see that the Binomial Option Pricing model predicts a one-period European put price of $17.42.

15.3 Multi-Period

Problem. Same as before, except we will use an eight-period model to evaluate it. At the close of trading on June 20, 2007, the stock price of Amazon.com was $69.81, the standard deviation of daily returns is 71.65%, the yield on a six-month U.S. Treasury Bill was 4.95%, the exercise price of a January 70 call on Amazon.com was $70.00, the exercise price of a January 70 put on Amazon.com was $70.00, and the time to maturity for both January 18, 2008 maturity options was 0.5777 years. What is the price of a January 70 call and a January 70 put on Amazon.com?

Solution Strategy. First, copy the binomial tree parameters from the single-period model. Second, build a multi-period tree of stock prices. Third, calculate call and put payoffs at maturity. Fourth, build the multi-period trees of the shares of stock and money borrowed to create a replicating portfolio that replicates the option period by period. Finally, build a multi-period tree of the value of the replicating portfolio and, in the absence of arbitrage, this will be value of the option.

FIGURE 15.4 Binomial Option Pricing - Multi-Period - Call.

	A	B	C	D	E	F	G	H	I	J
1	**BINOMIAL OPTION PRICING**			**Multi-Period**			**Call**			
2										
3	**Inputs**	Option Type								
4	Option Type	⦿ Call ○ Put	1				(1) Copy the Outputs column from the previous sheet			
5	Stock Price Now	$69.81	69		**Outputs**		Copy the range F6:F9 from the previous sheet			
6	Standard Dev (Annual)	71.65%	71	Time / Period		0.072	to the range F6:F9 on this sheet			
7	Riskfree Rate (Annual)	4.95%	49	Riskfree Rate / Period		0.36%				
8	Exercise Price	$70.00	70	Up Movement / Period		21.23%	(2) Time to Maturity			
9	Time To Maturity (Years)	0.5777	5	Down Movement/Period		-17.51%	* (Period / Number of Periods) Enter =$B$9*(B12/$B$10) and copy across			
10	Number of Periods	8								
11		**Now**								**Maturity**
12	Period	0	1	2	3	4	5	6	7	8
13	Time	0.000	0.072	0.144	0.217	0.289	0.361	0.433	0.505	0.578
14										
15	Stock	$69.81	$84.63	$102.60	$124.39	$150.80	$182.82	$221.63	$268.69	$325.74
16			$57.58	$69.81	$84.63	$102.60	$124.39	$150.80	$182.82	$221.63
17				$47.50	$57.58	$69.81	$84.63	$102.60	$124.39	$150.80
18	(3) Stock Price Now Enter =B5				$39.18	$47.50	$57.58	$69.81	$84.63	$102.60
19						$32.32	$39.18	$47.50	$57.58	$69.81
20							$26.66	$32.32	$39.18	$47.50
21								$21.99	$26.66	$32.32
22	(4) If Cell to the Left = Blank,								$18.14	$21.99
23	Then If Cell to the Left & Up One = Blank, Then Blank									$14.96
24	Else Down Price = (Stock Price to the Left & Up One) * (1+ Down Movement / Period)									
25	Else Up Price = (Stock Price to the Left) * (1 + Up Movement / Period)									
26	Enter =IF(B15="",IF(B14="","",B14*(1+$F$9)),B15*(1+$F$8))									
27	and copy to the range C15:J23									
28										
29				(5) If Option Type = Call,						
30				Then Call Payoff at Maturity = Max (Stock Price at Maturity - Exercise Price, 0)						
31				Else Put Payoff at Maturity = Max (Exercise Price - Stock Price at Maturity, 0)						
32				Enter =IF($C$4=1,MAX(J15-$B$8,0),MAX($B$8-J15,0))						
33				and copy to the range J35:J42						
34	Call	$15.27	$24.38	$37.81	$56.67	$81.81	$113.56	$152.13	$198.94	$255.74
35			$7.57	$13.06	$21.91	$35.52	$55.16	$81.30	$113.07	$151.63
36				$2.92	$5.56	$10.40	$18.94	$33.16	$54.64	$80.80
37					$0.67	$1.45	$3.17	$6.89	$14.98	$32.60
38						$0.00	$0.00	$0.00	$0.00	$0.00
39							$0.00	$0.00	$0.00	$0.00
40								$0.00	$0.00	$0.00
41	(8) If Cell to the Right & Down One = Blank, Then Blank								$0.00	$0.00
42	Else Set Option Price = Price of the Corresponding Replicating Portfolio									$0.00
43	= Number of Shares of Stock * Stock Price + Money Borrowed									
44	Enter =IF(C35="","",B50*B15+B61) and copy to the range B34:I41									
45	Do NOT copy to column J, which contains the option payoffs at maturity									

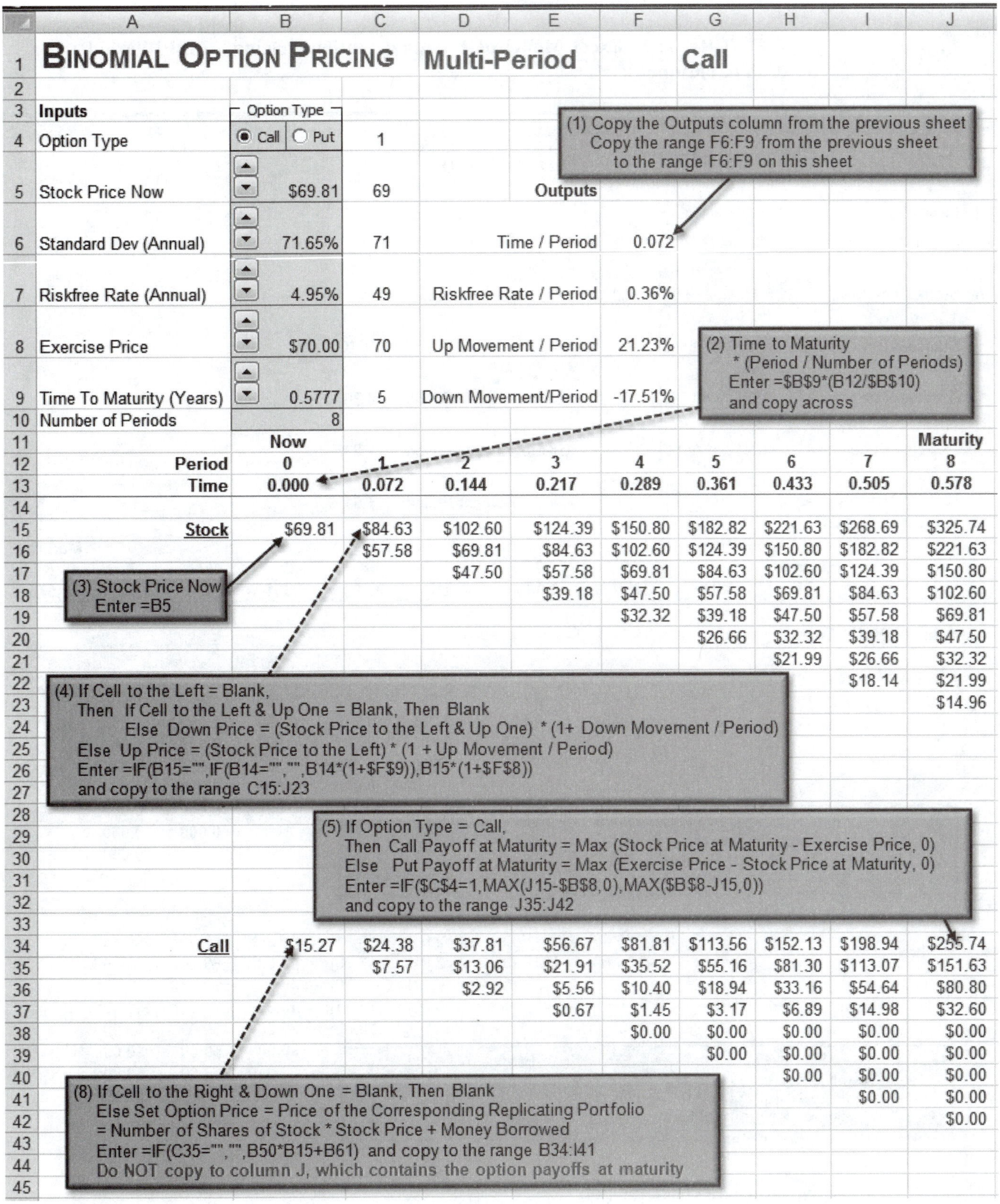

We see that the Binomial Option Pricing model predicts an eight-period European call price of $15.27.

FIGURE 15.5 Excel Model of Binomial Option Pricing - Multi-Period - Call (Continued).

	A	B	C	D	E	F	G	H	I	J
1	**BINOMIAL OPTION PRICING**			**Multi-Period**			**Call**			
2										
3	**Inputs**	Option Type								
4	Option Type	● Call ○ Put	1							
5	Stock Price Now	$69.81	69		Outputs					
6	Standard Dev (Annual)	71.65%	71	Time / Period		0.072				
7	Riskfree Rate (Annual)	4.95%	49	Riskfree Rate / Period		0.36%				
8	Exercise Price	$70.00	70	Up Movement / Period		21.23%				
9	Time To Maturity (Years)	0.5777	5	Down Movement/Period		-17.51%				
10	Number of Periods	8								
11		**Now**								**Maturity**
12	Period	**0**	1	2	3	4	5	6	7	8
13	Time	0.000	0.072	0.144	0.217	0.289	0.361	0.433	0.505	0.578
46										
47	**Replicating Portfolio**									
48										
49	**Stock Shares Bought (Sold)**									
50		0.622	0.755	0.874	0.960	0.999	1.000	1.000	1.000	
51			0.454	0.604	0.766	0.911	0.999	1.000	1.000	
52				0.266	0.401	0.583	0.801	0.997	1.000	
53					0.096	0.172	0.309	0.554	0.994	
54						0.000	0.000	0.000	0.000	
55							0.000	0.000	0.000	
56								0.000	0.000	
57									0.000	
58										
59										
60	**Money Lent (Borrowed)**									
61		($28.14)	($39.49)	($51.90)	($62.80)	($68.91)	($69.25)	($69.50)	($69.75)	
62			($18.60)	($29.13)	($42.91)	($57.98)	($69.08)	($69.50)	($69.75)	
63				($9.71)	($17.53)	($30.30)	($48.86)	($69.18)	($69.75)	
64					($3.09)	($6.71)	($14.61)	($31.79)	($69.16)	
65						$0.00	$0.00	$0.00	$0.00	
66							$0.00	$0.00	$0.00	
67								$0.00	$0.00	
68									$0.00	
69										
70										

(6) If Corresponding Option Down Price = Blank, Then Blank
   Else Hedge Ratio = (Option Up Price - Option Down Price)
   / (Stock Up Price - Stock Down Price)
   Enter =IF(C35="","",(C34-C35)/(C15-C16)) and copy to the range B50:I57

(7) If Corresponding Option Down Price = Blank, Then Blank
   Else (Option Down Price - Hedge Ratio * Stock Down Price)
   / (1 + Riskfree Rate / Period)
   Enter =IF(C35="","",(C35-B50*C16)/(1+$F$7)) and copy in range B61:I68

Now let's check the put.

FIGURE 15.6 Binomial Option Pricing - Multi-Period - Put.

	A	B	C	D	E	F	G	H	I	J
1	**BINOMIAL OPTION PRICING**			**Multi-Period**			**Put**			
2										
3	Inputs	Option Type								
4	Option Type	○ Call ● Put	2							
5	Stock Price Now	$69.81	69		**Outputs**					
6	Standard Dev (Annual)	71.65%	71		Time / Period	0.072				
7	Riskfree Rate (Annual)	4.95%	49		Riskfree Rate / Period	0.36%				
8	Exercise Price	$70.00	70		Up Movement / Period	21.23%				
9	Time To Maturity (Years)	0.5777	5		Down Movement/Period	-17.51%				
10	Number of Periods	8								
11		**Now**								**Maturity**
12	Period	0	1	2	3	4	5	6	7	8
13	Time	0.000	0.072	0.144	0.217	0.289	0.361	0.433	0.505	0.578
14										
15	**Stock**	$69.81	$84.63	$102.60	$124.39	$150.80	$182.82	$221.63	$268.69	$325.74
16			$57.58	$69.81	$84.63	$102.60	$124.39	$150.80	$182.82	$221.63
17				$47.50	$57.58	$69.81	$84.63	$102.60	$124.39	$150.80
18					$39.18	$47.50	$57.58	$69.81	$84.63	$102.60
19						$32.32	$39.18	$47.50	$57.58	$69.81
20							$26.66	$32.32	$39.18	$47.50
21								$21.99	$26.66	$32.32
22									$18.14	$21.99
23										$14.96
34	**Put**	$13.49	$8.02	$3.72	$1.04	$0.02	$0.00	$0.00	$0.00	$0.00
35			$18.25	$11.76	$6.04	$1.92	$0.03	$0.00	$0.00	$0.00
36				$23.93	$16.74	$9.60	$3.56	$0.05	$0.00	$0.00
37					$30.25	$22.96	$14.84	$6.58	$0.10	$0.00
38						$36.69	$30.07	$22.00	$12.17	$0.19
39							$42.60	$37.18	$30.57	$22.50
40								$47.51	$43.09	$37.68
41									$51.61	$48.01
42										$55.04

(1) Copy the Outputs column from the previous sheet Copy the range F6:F9 from the previous sheet to the range F6:F9 on this sheet

(2) Time to Maturity * (Period / Number of Periods) Enter =$B$9*(B12/$B$10) and copy across

(3) Stock Price Now Enter =B5

(4) If Cell to the Left = Blank, Then If Cell to the Left & Up One = Blank, Then Blank Else Down Price = (Stock Price to the Left & Up One) * (1+ Down Movement / Period) Else Up Price = (Stock Price to the Left) * (1 + Up Movement / Period) Enter =IF(B15="",IF(B14="","",B14*(1+$F$9)),B15*(1+$F$8)) and copy to the range C15:J23

(5) If Option Type = Call, Then Call Payoff at Maturity = Max (Stock Price at Maturity - Exercise Price, 0) Else Put Payoff at Maturity = Max (Exercise Price - Stock Price at Maturity, 0) Enter =IF($C$4=1,MAX(J15-$B$8,0),MAX($B$8-J15,0)) and copy to the range J35:J42

(8) If Cell to the Right & Down One = Blank, Then Blank Else Set Option Price = Price of the Corresponding Replicating Portfolio = Number of Shares of Stock * Stock Price + Money Borrowed Enter =IF(C35="","",B50*B15+B61) and copy to the range B34:I41 Do NOT copy to column J, which contains the option payoffs at maturity

We see that the Binomial Option Pricing model predicts an eight-period European put price of $13.49.

FIGURE 15.7 Binomial Option Pricing - Multi-Period - Put (Continued).

	A	B	C	D	E	F	G	H	I	J
1	**BINOMIAL OPTION PRICING**			**Multi-Period**			**Put**			
2										
3	**Inputs**	Option Type								
4	Option Type	○ Call ● Put	2							
5	Stock Price Now	$69.81	69		Outputs					
6	Standard Dev (Annual)	71.65%	71		Time / Period	0.072				
7	Riskfree Rate (Annual)	4.95%	49	Riskfree Rate / Period		0.36%				
8	Exercise Price	$70.00	70	Up Movement / Period		21.23%				
9	Time To Maturity (Years)	0.5777	5	Down Movement/Period		-17.51%				
10	Number of Periods	8								
11		**Now**								**Maturity**
12	Period	0	1	2	3	4	5	6	7	8
13	Time	0.000	0.072	0.144	0.217	0.289	0.361	0.433	0.505	0.578
46										
47	**Replicating Portfolio**									
48										
49	**Stock Shares Bought (Sold)**									
50		(0.378)	(0.245)	(0.126)	(0.040)	(0.001)	0.000	0.000	0.000	
51			(0.546)	(0.396)	(0.234)	(0.089)	(0.001)	0.000	0.000	
52				(0.734)	(0.599)	(0.417)	(0.199)	(0.003)	0.000	
53					(0.904)	(0.828)	(0.691)	(0.446)	(0.006)	
54						(1.000)	(1.000)	(1.000)	(1.000)	
55							(1.000)	(1.000)	(1.000)	
56								(1.000)	(1.000)	
57									(1.000)	

(6) If Corresponding Option Down Price = Blank, Then Blank
 Else Hedge Ratio = (Option Up Price - Option Down Price)
  / (Stock Up Price - Stock Down Price)
 Enter =IF(C35="","",(C34-C35)/(C15-C16)) and copy to the range B50:I57

	A	B	C	D	E	F	G	H	I	J
60	**Money Lent (Borrowed)**									
61		$39.89	$28.78	$16.61	$5.96	$0.09	$0.00	$0.00	$0.00	
62			$49.67	$39.38	$25.85	$11.03	$0.17	$0.00	$0.00	
63				$58.80	$51.23	$38.71	$20.39	$0.32	$0.00	
64					$65.67	$62.29	$54.64	$37.72	$0.59	
65						$69.01	$69.25	$69.50	$69.75	
66							$69.25	$69.50	$69.75	
67								$69.50	$69.75	
68									$69.75	

(7) If Corresponding Option Down Price = Blank, Then Blank
 Else (Option Down Price - Hedge Ratio * Stock Down Price)
 / (1 + Riskfree Rate / Period)
 Enter =IF(C35="","",(C35-B50*C16)/(1+$F$7)) and copy in range B61:I68

As in the single period case, replicating a Call option requires **Buying** Shares of Stock and **Borrowing** Money, whereas a Put option requires **Selling** Shares of Stock and **Lending** Money. Notice that the quantity of Money Borrowed or Lent and the quantity of Shares Bought or Sold changes over time and differs for up nodes vs. down nodes. This process of changing the replicating portfolio every period based on the realized up or down movement in the underlying stock price is called dynamic replication.

Price accuracy can be increased by subdividing the option's time to maturity into more periods (15, 30, etc.). Typically, from 50 to 100 periods are required in order to achieve price accuracy to the penny.

15.4 Risk Neutral

The previous Excel model, **Binomial Option Pricing Multi-Period**, determined the price of an option by constructing a replicating portfolio, which combines a stock and a bond to replicate the payoffs of the option. An alternative way to price an option is the Risk Neutral method. Both techniques give you the same answer. The main advantage of the Risk Neutral method is that it is faster and easier to implement. The Replicating Portfolio method required the construction of four trees (stock prices, shares of stock **bought (sold)**, money **lent (borrowed)**, and option prices). The Risk Neutral method will only require two trees (stock prices and option prices).

Problem. Same as before, except we will use the risk neutral method to evaluate it. At the close of trading on June 20, 2007, the stock price of Amazon.com was $69.81, the standard deviation of daily returns is 71.65%, the yield on a six-month U.S. Treasury Bill was 4.95%, the exercise price of a January 70 call on Amazon.com was $70.00, the exercise price of a January 70 put on Amazon.com was $70.00, and the time to maturity for both January 18, 2008 maturity options was 0.5777 years. What is the price of a January 70 call and a January 70 put on Amazon.com?

Solution Strategy. First, copy the binomial tree parameters, stock price tree, and option payoffs at maturity from the multi-period model. Second, calculate the risk neutral probability. Finally, build a option value tree using the risk neutral probability.

FIGURE 15.8 Binomial Option Pricing – Risk Neutral - Call.

	A	B	C	D	E	F	G	H	I	J
1	**BINOMIAL OPTION PRICING**			**Risk Neutral**			**Call**			
2										
3	Inputs	Option Type								
4	Option Type	⦿ Call ○ Put	1			(1) Copy the Outputs column from the previous sheet				
5	Stock Price Now	$69.81	69		Outputs	Copy the range F6:F9 from the previous sheet				
6	Standard Dev (Annual)	71.65%	71	Time / Period		0.072	to the range F6:F9 on this sheet			
7	Riskfree Rate (Annual)	4.95%	49	Riskfree Rate / Period		0.36%	(2) (Riskfree Rate / Period			
8	Exercise Price	$70.00	70	Up Movement / Period		21.23%	- Down Movement / Period)			
9	Time To Maturity (Years)	0.5777	5	Down Movement/Period		-17.51%	/ (Up Movement / Period - Down Movement / Period)			
10	Number of Periods	8		Risk Neutral Probability		46.13%	Enter =(F7-F9)/(F8-F9)			
11		**Now**								**Maturity**
12	**Period**	0	1	2	3	4	5	6	7	8
13	**Time**	0.000	0.072	0.144	0.217	0.289	0.361	0.433	0.505	0.578
14										
15	**Stock**	$69.81	$84.63	$102.60	$124.39	$150.80	$182.82	$221.63	$268.69	$325.74
16			$57.58	$69.81	$84.63	$102.60	$124.39	$150.80	$182.82	$221.63
17				$47.50	$57.58	$69.81	$84.63	$102.60	$124.39	$150.80
18	(3) Copy the Stock Price Tree from the previous sheet				$39.18	$47.50	$57.58	$69.81	$84.63	$102.60
19	Copy the range B15:J23 from the previous sheet					$32.32	$39.18	$47.50	$57.58	$69.81
20	to the range B15:J23 on this sheet						$26.66	$32.32	$39.18	$47.50
21								$21.99	$26.66	$32.32
22									$18.14	$21.99
23										$14.96
24										
25										
26										
27										
28										
29										
30						(4) Copy the Payoffs at Maturity from the previous sheet				
31						Copy the range J34:J42 from the previous sheet				
32						to the range J34:J42 on this sheet				
33										
34	**Call**	$15.27	$24.38	$37.81	$56.67	$81.81	$113.56	$152.13	$198.94	$255.74
35			$7.57	$13.06	$21.91	$35.52	$55.16	$81.30	$113.07	$151.63
36				$2.92	$5.56	$10.40	$18.94	$33.16	$54.64	$80.80
37					$0.67	$1.45	$3.17	$6.89	$14.98	$32.60
38						$0.00	$0.00	$0.00	$0.00	$0.00
39							$0.00	$0.00	$0.00	$0.00
40								$0.00	$0.00	$0.00
41									$0.00	$0.00
42										$0.00
43	(5) If Cell to the Right & Down One = Blank, Then Blank									
44	Else Expected Value of Option Price Next Period (using the Risk Neutral Probability)									
45	Discounted at the Riskfree Rate									
46	= [(Risk Neutral Probability) * (Stock Up Price) + (1 - Risk Neutral Probability) * (Stock Down Price)]									
47	/ (1+ Riskfree Rate / Period)									
48	Enter =IF(C35="","",($F$10*C34+(1-$F$10)*C35)/(1+$F$7)) and copy to the range B34:I41									
49	Do NOT copy to column J, which contains the option payoffs at maturity									

We see that the Risk Neutral method predicts an eight-period European call price of $15.27. This is identical to previous section's Replicating Portfolio Price. Now let's check the put.

FIGURE 15.9 Binomial Option Pricing – Risk Neutral - Put.

	A	B	C	D	E	F	G	H	I	J
1	**BINOMIAL OPTION PRICING**				**Risk Neutral**		**Put**			
2										
3	**Inputs**	Option Type				(1) Copy the Outputs column from the previous sheet Copy the range F6:F9 from the previous sheet to the range F6:F9 on this sheet				
4	Option Type	○ Call ● Put	2							
5	Stock Price Now	$69.81	69		Outputs					
6	Standard Dev (Annual)	71.65%	71	Time / Period	0.072					
7	Riskfree Rate (Annual)	4.95%	49	Riskfree Rate / Period	0.36%		(2) (Riskfree Rate / Period - Down Movement / Period) / (Up Movement / Period - Down Movement / Period) Enter =(F7-F9)/(F8-F9)			
8	Exercise Price	$70.00	70	Up Movement / Period	21.23%					
9	Time To Maturity (Years)	0.5777	5	Down Movement/Period	-17.51%					
10	Number of Periods	8		Risk Neutral Probability	46.13%					
11		**Now**								**Maturity**
12	**Period**	0	1	2	3	4	5	6	7	8
13	**Time**	0.000	0.072	0.144	0.217	0.289	0.361	0.433	0.505	0.578
14										
15	**Stock**	$69.81	$84.63	$102.60	$124.39	$150.80	$182.82	$221.63	$268.69	$325.74
16			$57.58	$69.81	$84.63	$102.60	$124.39	$150.80	$182.82	$221.63
17				$47.50	$57.58	$69.81	$84.63	$102.60	$124.39	$150.80
18	(3) Copy the Stock Price Tree from the previous sheet Copy the range B15:J23 from the previous sheet to the range B15:J23 on this sheet				$39.18	$47.50	$57.58	$69.81	$84.63	$102.60
19						$32.32	$39.18	$47.50	$57.58	$69.81
20							$26.66	$32.32	$39.18	$47.50
21								$21.99	$26.66	$32.32
22									$18.14	$21.99
23										$14.96
24										
25										
26										
27										
28										
29										
30						(4) Copy the Payoffs at Maturity from the previous sheet Copy the range J34:J42 from the previous sheet to the range J34:J42 on this sheet				
31										
32										
33										
34	**Put**	$13.49	$8.02	$3.72	$1.04	$0.02	$0.00	$0.00	$0.00	$0.00
35			$18.25	$11.76	$6.04	$1.92	$0.03	$0.00	$0.00	$0.00
36				$23.93	$16.74	$9.60	$3.56	$0.05	$0.00	$0.00
37					$30.25	$22.96	$14.84	$6.58	$0.10	$0.00
38						$36.69	$30.07	$22.00	$12.17	$0.19
39							$42.60	$37.18	$30.57	$22.50
40								$47.51	$43.09	$37.68
41									$51.61	$48.01
42										$55.04
43	(5) If Cell to the Right & Down One = Blank, Then Blank									
44	Else Expected Value of Option Price Next Period (using the Risk Neutral Probability)									
45	Discounted at the Riskfree Rate									
46	= [(Risk Neutral Probability) * (Stock Up Price) + (1 - Risk Neutral Probability) * (Stock Down Price)] / (1+ Riskfree Rate / Period)									
47	Enter =IF(C35="","",($F$10*C34+(1-$F$10)*C35)/(1+$F$7)) and copy to the range B34:I41									
48	Do NOT copy to column J, which contains the option payoffs at maturity									

We see that the Risk Neutral method predicts an eight-period European put price of $13.49. This is identical to previous section's Replicating Portfolio Price. Again, we get the same answer either way. The advantage of the Risk Neutral method is that we only have to construct two trees, rather than four trees.

15.5 American With Discrete Dividends

Problem. Same as before, except we will value American options where the underlying stock pays dividends. At the close of trading on June 20, 2007, the stock price of Amazon.com was $69.81, the standard deviation of daily returns is 71.65%, the yield on a six-month U.S. Treasury Bill was 4.95%, the exercise price of an American January 70 call on Amazon.com was $70.00, the exercise price of an American January 70 put on Amazon.com was $70.00, and the time to maturity for both January 18, 2008 maturity options was 0.5777 years. Assume that Amazon.com pays certain, riskfree $4.00 dividends on the periods show below. What is the price of an American January 70 call and an American January 70 put on Amazon.com?

Solution Strategy. First, copy the binomial tree parameters, the risk neutral probability, stock price tree, and option payoffs at maturity from the risk neutral model. Second, calculate the total stock price as the sum of the risky stock price plus the discounted value of future dividends. Finally, build a option value tree using the risk neutral probability and accounting for optimal early exercise.

FIGURE 15.10 Excel Model of Binomial Option Pricing – American With Discrete Dividends – Call.

	A	B	C	D	E	F	G	H	I	J
1	**BINOMIAL OPTION PRICING**			**American With Discrete Dividends**						**Call**
2										
3	**Inputs**	Option Type				Early Exercise				
4	Option Type	⦿ Call ⚪ Put	1		Early Exercise	⚪ European ⦿ American	2			
5	Stock Price Now	$69.81	69		**Outputs**					
6	Standard Dev (Annual)	71.65%	71		Time / Period	0.072				
7	Riskfree Rate (Annual)	4.95%	49		Riskfree Rate / Period	0.36%				
8	Exercise Price	$70.00	70		Up Movement / Period	21.23%				
9	Time To Maturity (Years)	0.5777	5		Down Movement/Period	-17.51%				
10	Number of Periods	8			Risk Neutral Probability	46.13%				
11		**Now**								**Maturity**
12	**Period**	**0**	**1**	**2**	**3**	**4**	**5**	**6**	**7**	**8**
13	**Time**	**0.000**	**0.072**	**0.144**	**0.217**	**0.289**	**0.361**	**0.433**	**0.505**	**0.578**
14										
15	**Risky Part of the Stock**	$69.81	$84.63	$102.60	$124.39	$150.80	$182.82	$221.63	$268.69	$325.74
16			$57.58	$69.81	$84.63	$102.60	$124.39	$150.80	$182.82	$221.63
17				$47.50	$57.58	$69.81	$84.63	$102.60	$124.39	$150.80
18					$39.18	$47.50	$57.58	$69.81	$84.63	$102.60
19						$32.32	$39.18	$47.50	$57.58	$69.81
20							$26.66	$32.32	$39.18	$47.50
21								$21.99	$26.66	$32.32
22									$18.14	$21.99
23										$14.96
24										
25	**Riskfree Dividends**		$0.00	$0.00	$0.00	$4.00	$0.00	$0.00	$4.00	$0.00
26										
27	**Cum. Pres Value Factor**	100.00%	95.28%	90.79%	86.51%	82.43%	78.54%	74.84%	71.31%	67.94%
28										
29	**Total Stock Price**	$75.96	$91.09	$109.38	$131.50	$154.26	$186.45	$225.44	$268.69	$325.74
30			$64.04	$76.58	$91.74	$106.06	$128.02	$154.61	$182.82	$221.63
31				$54.27	$64.69	$73.27	$88.26	$106.41	$124.39	$150.80
32					$46.29	$50.96	$61.22	$73.62	$84.63	$102.60
33						$35.78	$42.81	$51.31	$57.58	$69.81
34							$30.29	$36.13	$39.18	$47.50
35								$25.80	$26.66	$32.32
36									$18.14	$21.99
37										$14.96

Annotation boxes in figure:

(1) Copy the Outputs column (including the Risk Neutral Probability) from the previous sheet Copy the range F6:F10 from the previous sheet to the range F6:F10 on this sheet

(2) Copy the Stock Price Tree from the previous sheet Copy the range B15:J23 from the previous sheet to the range B15:J23 on this sheet

(3) 1 / ((1 + (Riskfree Rate / Period)) ^ Period) Enter =1/((1+$B$7)^C12) and copy across

(4) If corresponding cell on Risky Part of Stock tree is blank, Then blank, Else Risky Part of Stock + SUMPRODUCT(Riskfree Dividends Range, Cum. Pres Value Factor Range) / (Cum. Pres Value Factor(t)) Enter =IF(B15="","",B15+SUMPRODUCT(C$25:$J$25,C$27:$J$27)/B$27) and copy to the range B29:I36 Do NOT copy to column J, which contains a different formula

(5) Risky Part of the Stock Tree Enter =J15 and copy down

FIGURE 15.11 Excel Model of Binomial Option Pricing – American With Discrete Dividends - Call.

	A	B	C	D	E	F	G	H	I	J
1	**BINOMIAL OPTION PRICING**			**American With Discrete Dividends**						**Call**
2										
3	**Inputs**	Option Type				Early Exercise				
4	Option Type	◉ Call ○ Put	1	Early Exercise		○ European ◉ American		2		
5	Stock Price Now	$69.81	69	**Outputs**						
6	Standard Dev (Annual)	71.65%	71	Time / Period		0.072				
7	Riskfree Rate (Annual)	4.95%	49	Riskfree Rate / Period		0.36%				
8	Exercise Price	$70.00	70	Up Movement / Period		21.23%				
9	Time To Maturity (Years)	0.5777	5	Down Movement/Period		-17.51%				
10	Number of Periods	8		Risk Neutral Probability		46.13%				
11		**Now**								**Maturity**
12	**Period**	0	1	2	3	4	5	6	7	8
13	**Time**	0.000	0.072	0.144	0.217	0.289	0.361	0.433	0.505	0.578
44										
45						(6) Copy the Payoffs at Maturity from the previous sheet				
46						Copy the range J34:J42 from the previous sheet				
47						to the range J48:J56 on this sheet				
48	**American Call**	$16.35	$26.20	$40.79	$61.50	$85.08	$116.86	$155.44	$198.94	$255.74
49			$8.02	$13.88	$23.34	$37.83	$58.43	$84.61	$113.07	$151.63
50				$3.06	$5.88	$11.09	$20.43	$36.41	$54.64	$80.80
51					$0.67	$1.45	$3.17	$6.89	$14.98	$32.60
52						$0.00	$0.00	$0.00	$0.00	$0.00
53						$0.00	$0.00	$0.00	$0.00	$0.00
54							$0.00	$0.00	$0.00	$0.00
55								$0.00	$0.00	$0.00
56									$0.00	$0.00

(7) If Cell to the Right & Down One = Blank, Then Blank
    Else Max{ Not Exercised Value, Exercised Value}
where: Not Exercised Value = [(Risk Neutral Probability) * (Stock Up Price)
               + (1 - Risk Neutral Probability) * (Stock Down Price)]
               / (1+ Riskfree Rate / Period),
    Exercised Value = If Early Exercise = European, Then 0,
           Else If (Option Type = Call, 1, -1)
           * (Total Stock Price - Exercise Price) }
    Enter =IF(C49="","",MAX(($F$10*C48+(1-$F$10)*C49)/(1+$F$7),
               IF($H$4=1,0,IF($C$4=1,1,-1)*(B29-$B$8))))

Optionally, use Conditional Formatting to highlight Early Exercise cells:
    click on Home | Styles | Conditional Formatting | New Rule
    click on "use a formula to determine which cells to format"
    enter the rule: =AND($H$4=2,B48=IF($C$4=1,1,-1)*(B29-$B$8))
    click on the Format button, click on the Fill tab,
    click on the color of your choice, click on OK, click on OK

Then copy to the range B48:I55
Do NOT copy to column J, which contains the option payoffs at maturity

The purple-shading highlights the periods and call prices where it is optimal to exercise the American call early. Notice that it is optimal to exercise an

American call early just before a dividend is paid, which will reduce the value of the underlying stock and thus reduce the value of an unexercised call option. We see that the model predicts an eight-period American call price of $16.35.

FIGURE 15.12 American With Discrete Dividends - Put.

	A	B	C	D	E	F	G	H	I	J
1	**BINOMIAL OPTION PRICING**			**American With Discrete Dividends**						**Put**
2										
3	**Inputs**	⌐ Option Type ¬				⌐ Early Exercise ¬				
4	Option Type	○ Call ◉ Put	2		Early Exercise	○ European ◉ American	2			
5	Stock Price Now	$69.81	69		**Outputs**					
6	Standard Dev (Annual)	71.65%	71		Time / Period	0.072				
7	Riskfree Rate (Annual)	4.95%	49		Riskfree Rate / Period	0.36%				
8	Exercise Price	$70.00	70		Up Movement / Period	21.23%				
9	Time To Maturity (Years)	0.5777	5		Down Movement/Period	-17.51%				
10	Number of Periods	8			Risk Neutral Probability	46.13%				
11		**Now**								**Maturity**
12	Period	0	1	2	3	4	5	6	7	8
13	Time	0.000	0.072	0.144	0.217	0.289	0.361	0.433	0.505	0.578
44										
45					(6) Copy the Payoffs at Maturity from the previous sheet					
46					Copy the range J34:J42 from the previous sheet					
47					to the range J48:J56 on this sheet					
48	**American Put**	$13.63	$8.12	$3.78	$1.06	$0.02	$0.00	$0.00	$0.00	$0.00
49			$18.43	$11.90	$6.13	$1.96	$0.03	$0.00	$0.00	$0.00
50				$24.14	$16.92	$9.74	$3.63	$0.05	$0.00	$0.00
51					$30.48	$23.19	$15.03	$6.71	$0.10	$0.00
52						$36.94	$30.32	$22.25	$12.42	$0.19
53						42.84	$37.43	$30.82	$22.50	
54							$47.76	$43.34	$37.68	
55								$51.86	$48.01	
56									$55.04	

(7) If Cell to the Right & Down One = Blank, Then Blank
    Else Max{ Not Exercised Value, Exercised Value}
where: Not Exercised Value = [(Risk Neutral Probability) * (Stock Up Price)
                + (1 - Risk Neutral Probability) * (Stock Down Price)]
                / (1+ Riskfree Rate / Period),
        Exercised Value = If Early Exercise = European, Then 0,
                Else If (Option Type = Call, 1, -1)
                * (Total Stock Price - Exercise Price) }
Enter =IF(C49="","",MAX(($F$10*C48+(1-$F$10)*C49)/(1+$F$7),
                IF($H$4=1,0,IF($C$4=1,1,-1)*(B29-$B$8))))

Optionally, use Conditional Formatting to highlight Early Exercise cells:
        click on Home | Styles | Conditional Formatting | New Rule
        click on "use a formula to determine which cells to format"
        enter the rule: =AND($H$4=2,B48=IF($C$4=1,1,-1)*(B29-$B$8))
        click on the Format button, click on the Fill tab,
        click on the color of your choice, click on OK, click on OK

Then copy to the range B48:I55
Do NOT copy to column J, which contains the option payoffs at maturity

The purple-shading highlights the periods and call prices where it is optimal to exercise the American put early. Notice that it is optimal to exercise an American put early just when a dividend is paid, which will reduce the value of the underlying stock and thus increases the value of the put option. We see that the model predicts an eight-period American put price of $13.63.

15.6 Full-Scale

Problem. Same as before, except we will use a fifty-period model to evaluate it in order to increase accuracy. At the close of trading on June 20, 2007, the stock price of Amazon.com was $69.81, the standard deviation of daily returns is 71.65%, the yield on a six-month U.S. Treasury Bill was 4.95%, the exercise price of an American January 70 call on Amazon.com was $70.00, the exercise price of an American January 70 put on Amazon.com was $70.00, and the time to maturity for both January 18, 2008 maturity options was 0.5777 years. Assume that Amazon.com pays certain, riskfree $5.00 dividends on the periods show below. What is the price of an American January 70 call and an American January 70 put on Amazon.com?

Solution Strategy. First, copy the binomial tree parameters, the risk neutral probability, stock price tree, and option payoffs at maturity from the risk neutral model. Second, calculate the total stock price as the sum of the risky stock price plus the discounted value of future dividends. Finally, build a option value tree using the risk neutral probability and accounting for optimal early exercise.

FIGURE 15.13 Binomial Option Pricing - Full-Scale Estimation - Call.

	A	B	C	D	E	F	G	H
1	**BINOMIAL OPTION PRICING**			**Full-Scale**			**American Call**	
2								
3	**Inputs**	Option Type				Early Exercise		
4	Option Type	● Call ○ Put	1	Early Exercise		○ European ● American		2
5	Risky Part of Stock Now	$69.81	69	**Outputs**				
6	Standard Dev (Annual)	71.65%	71	Time / Period		0.012		
7	Riskfree Rate (Annual)	4.95%	49	Riskfree Rate / Period		0.06%		
8	Exercise Price	$70.00	70	Up Movement / Period		8.01%		
9	Time To Maturity (Years)	0.5777	5	Down Movement/Period		-7.41%		
10	Number of Periods	50		Risk Neutral Probability		48.45%		
11		**Now**						
12	**Period**	**0**	**1**	**2**	**3**	**4**	**5**	**6**
13	**Time**	**0.000**	**0.012**	**0.023**	**0.035**	**0.046**	**0.058**	**0.069**
14								
15	**Risky Part of the Stock**	$69.81	$75.40	$81.44	$87.96	$95.00	$102.60	$110.82
16			$64.64	$69.81	$75.40	$81.44	$87.96	$95.00
17				$59.84	$64.64	$69.81	$75.40	$81.44
18					$55.41	$59.84	$64.64	$69.81
19						$51.30	$55.41	$59.84
20							$47.50	$51.30
21								$43.98

(1) Risky Part of Stock Now
    Enter =B5

(2) Copy the Stock Price fomula from the previous sheet
    and expand it to a larger range
    Copy the cell C15 from the previous sheet
    to the range C15:AZ65 on this sheet

The up movement / period and down movement / period are calibrated to correspond to the stock's annual standard deviation. It is not necessary to calibrate them to the stock's expected return.[7]

---

[7] At full-scale (50 periods), the binomial option price is very insensitive to the expected return of the stock. For example, suppose that you calibrated this Amazon.com case to an annual expected return of 10%. Just add **.1*F6** to the formulas for the up and down movements / period. So the up movement / period in cell **F8** would become **=EXP(.1*F6+B6*SQRT(F6))-1** and the down movement / period in cell **F9** would become **=EXP(.1*F6-B6*SQRT(F6))-1**. This changes the option price by less than 1/100th of one penny! In the (Black Scholes) limit as the number of (sub)periods goes to infinity, the option price

FIGURE 15.14 Excel Model of Binomial Option Pricing - Full-Scale Estimation - Call Option (Continued).

	A	B	C	D	E	F	G	H
1	**BINOMIAL OPTION PRICING**			**Full-Scale**			**American Call**	
2								
3	**Inputs**	Option Type				Early Exercise		
4	Option Type	⦿ Call ○ Put	1		Early Exercise	○ European ⦿ American		2
5	Risky Part of Stock Now	$69.81	69		**Outputs**			
6	Standard Dev (Annual)	71.65%	71		Time / Period	0.012		
7	Riskfree Rate (Annual)	4.95%	49	Riskfree Rate / Period		0.06%		
8	Exercise Price	$70.00	70	Up Movement / Period		8.01%		
9	Time To Maturity (Years)	0.5777	5	Down Movement/Period		-7.41%		
10	Number of Periods	50		Risk Neutral Probability		48.45%		
11		**Now**						
12	**Period**	**0**	**1**	**2**	**3**	**4**	**5**	**6**
13	**Time**	**0.000**	**0.012**	**0.023**	**0.035**	**0.046**	**0.058**	**0.069**
62								
63	(3) (Cum. Pres Value Factor(t-1)) * EXP(- (Riskfree Rate / Period))							
64	Enter =B69*EXP(-$F$7)							
65	and copy across							
66								
67	**Riskfree Dividends**		$0.00	$0.00	$0.00	$0.00	$5.00	$0.00
68								
69	**Cum. Pres Value Factor**	100.000%	99.943%	99.886%	99.829%	99.771%	99.714%	99.657%
70								
71	**Total Stock Price**	$84.64	$90.24	$96.28	$102.81	$109.86	$112.47	$120.69
72			$79.47	$84.66	$90.25	$96.30	$97.83	$104.87
73				$74.69	$79.49	$84.67	$85.27	$91.31
74					$70.26	$74.71	$74.51	$79.69
75						$66.16	$65.28	$69.72
76	(4) If corresponding cell on Risky Part of Stock tree is blank,						$57.37	$61.18
77	Then blank,							$53.86
78	Else Risky Part of Stock							
79	+ SUMPRODUCT(Riskfree Dividends Range,							
80	Cum. Pres Value Factor Range)							
81	/ (Cum. Pres Value Factor(t))							
82	Enter =IF(B15="","",B15+SUMPRODUCT(C$67:$AZ$67,C$69:$AZ$69)/B$69)							
83	and copy to the range B71:AY120							
84	Do NOT copy to column AZ, which contains a different formula							

becomes totally insensitive to the expected return of the stock. Because of this insensitivity, the conventions for calculating the up movement / period and down movement / period ignore the expected return of the stock.

FIGURE 15.15 Excel Model of Binomial Option Pricing - Full-Scale Estimation - Call Option (Continued).

	AT	AU	AV	AW	AX	AY	AZ
11							**Maturity**
12	**44**	**45**	**46**	**47**	**48**	**49**	**50**
13	**0.508**	**0.520**	**0.531**	**0.543**	0.555	0.566	**0.578**
63					$1.73	$1.87	$2.02
64						$1.60	$1.73
65							$1.48
66							
67	$0.00	$0.00	$0.00	$0.00	$0.00	$0.00	$0.00
68							
69	97.514%	97.458%	97.403%	97.347%	97.291%	97.236%	97.180%
70							
71	$2,068.32	$2,233.91	$2,412.76	$2,605.92	$2,814.55	$3,039.88	$3,283.25
72	$1,773.06	$1,915.01	$2,068.32	$2,233.91	$2,412.76	$2,605.92	$2,814.55
73	$1,519.94	$1,641.63	$1,773.06	$1,915.01	$2,068.32	$2,233.91	$2,412.76
74	$1,302.96	$1,407.28	$1,519.94	$1,641.63	$1,773.06	$1,915.01	$2,068.32

(5) Risky Part of the Stock Tree
Enter =AZ15 and copy down

FIGURE 15.16 Excel Model of Binomial Option Pricing - Full-Scale Estimation - Call Option (Continued).

	AR	AS	AT	AU	AV	AW	AX	AY	AZ
11									**Maturity**
12	**42**	**43**	**44**	**45**	**46**	**47**	**48**	**49**	**50**
13	**0.485**	**0.497**	**0.508**	**0.520**	**0.531**	**0.543**	**0.555**	**0.566**	**0.578**
119							$1.73	$1.87	$2.02
120								$1.60	$1.73
121									$1.48
122									
123									
124									
125	$1,703.38	$1,845.29	$1,998.56	$2,164.11	$2,342.92	$2,536.04	$2,744.63	$2,969.92	$3,213.25
126	$1,450.26	$1,571.91	$1,703.30	$1,845.21	$1,998.48	$2,164.03	$2,342.84	$2,535.96	$2,744.55
127	$1,233.28	$1,337.56	$1,450.18	$1,571.83	$1,703.22	$1,845.13	$1,998.40	$2,163.95	$2,342.76
128	$1,047.28	$1,136.66	$1,233.20	$1,337.48	$1,450.10	$1,571.75	$1,703.14	$1,845.05	$1,998.32
129	$887.82	$964.44	$1,047.20	$1,136.58	$1,233.12	$1,337.40	$1,450.02	$1,571.67	$1,703.06

(6) If Option Type = Call,
Then Call Payoff at Maturity = Max (Stock Price at Maturity - Exercise Price, 0)
Else Put Payoff at Maturity = Max (Exercise Price - Stock Price at Maturity, 0)
Enter =IF($C$4=1,MAX(AZ71-$B$8,0),MAX($B$8-AZ71,0))
and copy to the range AZ126:AZ175

FIGURE 15.17 Excel Model of Binomial Option Pricing - Full-Scale Estimation - Call Option (Continued).

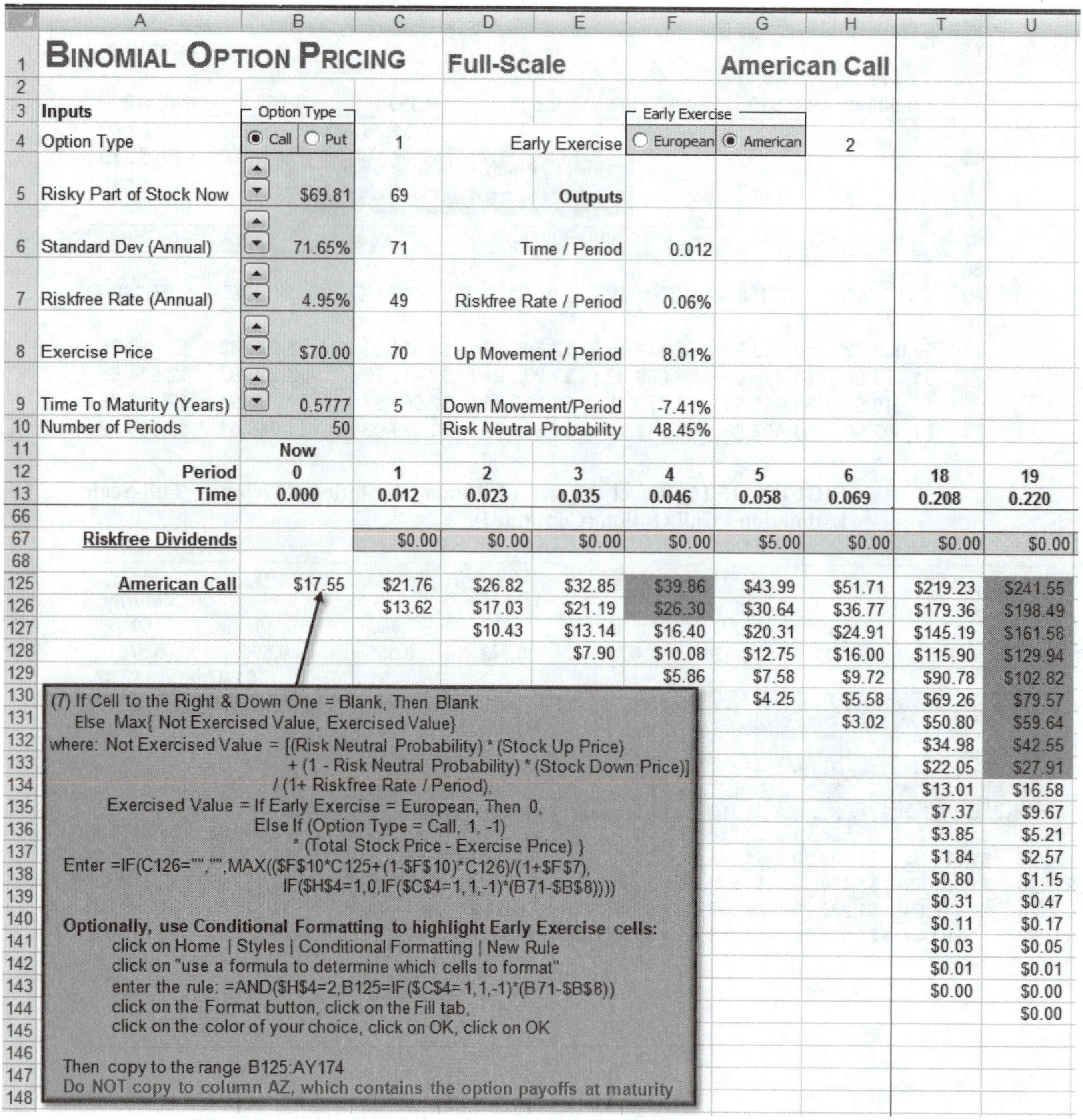

	A	B	C	D	E	F	G	H	T	U
1	**BINOMIAL OPTION PRICING**			**Full-Scale**			**American Call**			
2										
3	**Inputs**	⌐ Option Type ¬				⌐ Early Exercise				
4	Option Type	◉ Call ○ Put	1	Early Exercise		○ European ◉ American		2		
5	Risky Part of Stock Now	$69.81	69	**Outputs**						
6	Standard Dev (Annual)	71.65%	71	Time / Period		0.012				
7	Riskfree Rate (Annual)	4.95%	49	Riskfree Rate / Period		0.06%				
8	Exercise Price	$70.00	70	Up Movement / Period		8.01%				
9	Time To Maturity (Years)	0.5777	5	Down Movement/Period		-7.41%				
10	Number of Periods	50		Risk Neutral Probability		48.45%				
11		**Now**								
12	**Period**	**0**	**1**	**2**	**3**	**4**	**5**	**6**	**18**	**19**
13	**Time**	**0.000**	**0.012**	**0.023**	**0.035**	**0.046**	**0.058**	**0.069**	**0.208**	**0.220**
66										
67	**Riskfree Dividends**		$0.00	$0.00	$0.00	$0.00	$5.00	$0.00	$0.00	$0.00
68										
125	**American Call**	$17.55	$21.76	$26.82	$32.85	$39.86	$43.99	$51.71	$219.23	$241.55
126			$13.62	$17.03	$21.19	$26.30	$30.64	$36.77	$179.36	$198.49
127				$10.43	$13.14	$16.40	$20.31	$24.91	$145.19	$161.58
128					$7.90	$10.08	$12.75	$16.00	$115.90	$129.94
129						$5.86	$7.58	$9.72	$90.78	$102.82
130							$4.25	$5.58	$69.26	$79.57
131								$3.02	$50.80	$59.64
132									$34.98	$42.55
133									$22.05	$27.91
134									$13.01	$16.58
135									$7.37	$9.67
136									$3.85	$5.21
137									$1.84	$2.57
138									$0.80	$1.15
139									$0.31	$0.47
140									$0.11	$0.17
141									$0.03	$0.05
142									$0.01	$0.01
143									$0.00	$0.00
144										$0.00

Callout box (rows 130–148):

(7) If Cell to the Right & Down One = Blank, Then Blank
   Else Max{ Not Exercised Value, Exercised Value}
where: Not Exercised Value = [(Risk Neutral Probability) * (Stock Up Price)
         + (1 - Risk Neutral Probability) * (Stock Down Price)]
         / (1+ Riskfree Rate / Period),
   Exercised Value = If Early Exercise = European, Then 0,
         Else If (Option Type = Call, 1, -1)
         * (Total Stock Price - Exercise Price) }
Enter =IF(C126="","",MAX(($F$10*C125+(1-$F$10)*C126)/(1+$F$7),
         IF($H$4=1,0,IF($C$4=1, 1,-1)*(B71-$B$8))))

Optionally, use Conditional Formatting to highlight Early Exercise cells:
   click on Home | Styles | Conditional Formatting | New Rule
   click on "use a formula to determine which cells to format"
   enter the rule: =AND($H$4=2,B125=IF($C$4=1,1,-1)*(B71-$B$8))
   click on the Format button, click on the Fill tab,
   click on the color of your choice, click on OK, click on OK

Then copy to the range B125:AY174
Do NOT copy to column AZ, which contains the option payoffs at maturity

Again, optimal early exercise for an American call occurs just before a dividend is paid. We see that the Full-Scale model predicts an American call price of $17.55. Now let's check the put.

FIGURE 15.18 Excel Model of Binomial Option Pricing - Full-Scale Estimation - Put Option.

	A	B	C	D	E	F	G	H	AY	AZ
1	**BINOMIAL OPTION PRICING**			**Full-Scale**			**American Put**			
2										
3	Inputs	Option Type				Early Exercise				
4	Option Type	○ Call ◉ Put	2		Early Exercise	○ European ◉ American		2		
5	Risky Part of Stock Now	$69.81	69		Outputs					
6	Standard Dev (Annual)	71.65%	71		Time / Period	0.012				
7	Riskfree Rate (Annual)	4.95%	49	Riskfree Rate / Period		0.06%				
8	Exercise Price	$70.00	70	Up Movement / Period		8.01%				
9	Time To Maturity (Years)	0.5777	5	Down Movement/Period		-7.41%				
10	Number of Periods	50		Risk Neutral Probability		48.45%				
11		**Now**								**Maturity**
12	Period	0	1	2	3	4	5	6	49	50
13	Time	0.000	0.012	0.023	0.035	0.046	0.058	0.069	0.566	0.578
14										
15	**Risky Part of the Stock**	$69.81	$75.40	$81.44	$87.96	$95.00	$102.60	$110.82	$3,039.88	$3,283.25
16			$64.64	$69.81	$75.40	$81.44	$87.96	$95.00	$2,605.92	$2,814.55
17				$59.84	$64.64	$69.81	$75.40	$81.44	$2,233.91	$2,412.76
18					$55.41	$59.84	$64.64	$69.81	$1,915.01	$2,068.32
19						$51.30	$55.41	$59.84	$1,641.63	$1,773.06
20							$47.50	$51.30	$1,407.28	$1,519.94
21								$43.98	$1,206.38	$1,302.96
22									$1,034.16	$1,116.96
23									$886.53	$957.50
24									$759.97	$820.81
25									$651.48	$703.64
26									$558.48	$603.19
27									$478.75	$517.08
28									$410.41	$443.26
29									$351.82	$379.99

FIGURE 15.19 Excel Model of Binomial Option Pricing - Full-Scale Estimation - Put Option.

	A	B	C	D	E	F	G	H	AJ	AK
1	**BINOMIAL OPTION PRICING**			**Full-Scale**			**American Put**			
2										
3	**Inputs**	Option Type				Early Exercise				
4	Option Type	○ Call ● Put	2	Early Exercise		○ European ● American		2		
5	Risky Part of Stock Now	$69.81	69		**Outputs**					
6	Standard Dev (Annual)	71.65%	71	Time / Period		0.012				
7	Riskfree Rate (Annual)	4.95%	49	Riskfree Rate / Period		0.06%				
8	Exercise Price	$70.00	70	Up Movement / Period		8.01%				
9	Time To Maturity (Years)	0.5777	5	Down Movement/Period		-7.41%				
10	Number of Periods	50		Risk Neutral Probability		48.45%				
11		**Now**								
12	**Period**	**0**	**1**	**2**	**3**	**4**	**5**	**6**	**34**	**35**
13	**Time**	**0.000**	**0.012**	**0.023**	**0.035**	**0.046**	**0.058**	**0.069**	**0.393**	**0.404**
66										
67	**Riskfree Dividends**		$0.00	$0.00	$0.00	$0.00	$5.00	$0.00	$0.00	$5.00
68										
69	**Cum. Pres Value Factor**	100.000%	99.943%	99.886%	99.829%	99.771%	99.714%	99.657%	98.074%	98.018%
70										
71	**Total Stock Price**	$84.64	$90.24	$96.28	$102.81	$109.86	$112.47	$120.69	$962.50	$1,034.16
72			$79.47	$84.66	$90.25	$96.30	$97.83	$104.87	$825.81	$886.53
73				$74.69	$79.49	$84.67	$85.27	$91.31	$708.64	$759.97
74					$70.26	$74.71	$74.51	$79.69	$608.19	$651.48
75						$66.16	$65.28	$69.72	$522.08	$558.48
76							$57.37	$61.18	$448.26	$478.75
77								$53.86	$384.98	$410.41
78									$330.74	$351.82
79									$284.24	$301.60
80									$244.37	$258.54
81									$210.20	$221.63
82									$180.91	$189.99
83									$155.79	$162.87
84									$134.27	$139.62
85									$115.81	$119.69

FIGURE 15.20 Excel Model of Binomial Option Pricing - Full-Scale Estimation - Put Option (Continued).

	AI	AJ	AK	AL	AM	AN
11						
12	33	34	35	36	37	38
13	0.381	0.393	0.404	0.416	0.427	0.439
66						
67	$0.00	$0.00	$5.00	$0.00	$0.00	$0.00
68						
125	$0.00	$0.00	$0.00	$0.00	$0.00	$0.00
126	$0.00	$0.00	$0.00	$0.00	$0.00	$0.00
127	$0.00	$0.00	$0.00	$0.00	$0.00	$0.00
128	$0.00	$0.00	$0.00	$0.00	$0.00	$0.00
129	$0.00	$0.00	$0.00	$0.00	$0.00	$0.00
130	$0.00	$0.00	$0.00	$0.00	$0.00	$0.00
131	$0.00	$0.00	$0.00	$0.00	$0.00	$0.00
132	$0.00	$0.00	$0.00	$0.00	$0.00	$0.00
133	$0.00	$0.00	$0.00	$0.00	$0.00	$0.00
134	$0.00	$0.00	$0.00	$0.00	$0.00	$0.00
135	$0.00	$0.00	$0.00	$0.00	$0.00	$0.00
136	$0.02	$0.00	$0.00	$0.00	$0.00	$0.00
137	$0.11	$0.04	$0.01	$0.00	$0.00	$0.00
138	$0.43	$0.18	$0.06	$0.02	$0.00	$0.00
139	$1.30	$0.67	$0.30	$0.11	$0.03	$0.00
140	$3.15	$1.90	$1.02	$0.48	$0.18	$0.05
141	$6.35	$4.33	$2.72	$1.54	$0.76	$0.30
142	$10.99	$8.26	$5.84	$3.83	$2.27	$1.18
143	$16.76	$13.57	$10.53	$7.74	$5.30	$3.30
144	$23.07	$19.77	$16.45	$13.17	$10.04	$7.18
145	$29.30	$26.19	$22.92	$19.55	$16.13	$12.74
146	$35.02	$32.26	$29.29	$26.12	$22.78	$19.32
147	$40.00	$37.64	$35.09	$32.30	$29.28	$26.06
148	$44.27	$42.26	$40.08	$37.68	$35.09	$32.30
149	$47.93	$46.21	$44.35	$42.30	$40.08	$37.68
150	$51.07	$49.60	$48.01	$46.25	$44.35	$42.30
151	$53.76	$52.51	$51.15	$49.64	$48.01	$46.25
152	$56.07	$55.00	$53.84	$52.55	$51.15	$49.64
153	$58.05	$57.13	$56.15	$55.04	$53.84	$52.55
154	$59.74	$58.97	$58.13	$57.17	$56.15	$55.04
155	$61.19	$60.54	$59.82	$59.01	$58.13	$57.17
156	$62.44	$61.88	$61.27	$60.58	$59.82	$59.01
157	$63.51	$63.03	$62.52	$61.92	$61.27	$60.58
158	$64.42	$64.02	$63.59	$63.07	$62.52	$61.92
159		$64.87	$64.50	$64.06	$63.59	$63.07
160			$65.29	$64.91	$64.50	$64.06
161				$65.64	$65.29	$64.91
162					$65.96	$65.64
163						$66.26

Optimal early exercise for an American put often occurs on the date that the dividend is paid. More generally, it is optimal to exercise an American put option when the underlying stock price is very low for a given amount of time to maturity.

FIGURE 15.21 Excel Model of Binomial Option Pricing - Full-Scale Estimation - Put Option (Continued).

	A	B	C	D	E	F	G	H	AJ	AK
1	**BINOMIAL OPTION PRICING**			**Full-Scale**			**American Put**			
2										
3	**Inputs**	Option Type				Early Exercise				
4	Option Type	○ Call ● Put	2		Early Exercise	○ European ● American		2		
5	Risky Part of Stock Now	$69.81	69		Outputs					
6	Standard Dev (Annual)	71.65%	71		Time / Period	0.012				
7	Riskfree Rate (Annual)	4.95%	49	Riskfree Rate / Period	0.06%					
8	Exercise Price	$70.00	70	Up Movement / Period	8.01%					
9	Time To Maturity (Years)	0.5777	5	Down Movement/Period	-7.41%					
10	Number of Periods	50		Risk Neutral Probability	48.45%					
11		**Now**								
12	**Period**	**0**	**1**	**2**	**3**	**4**	**5**	**6**	**34**	**35**
13	**Time**	**0.000**	**0.012**	**0.023**	**0.035**	**0.046**	**0.058**	**0.069**	**0.393**	**0.404**
66										
67	**Riskfree Dividends**		$0.00	$0.00	$0.00	$0.00	$5.00	$0.00	$0.00	$5.00
68										
125	**American Put**	$14.02	$11.92	$9.96	$8.18	$6.58	$5.17	$3.97	$0.00	$0.00
126			$16.02	$13.77	$11.66	$9.69	$7.90	$6.31	$0.00	$0.00
127				$18.14	$15.78	$13.52	$11.38	$9.41	$0.00	$0.00
128					$20.38	$17.92	$15.53	$13.25	$0.00	$0.00
129						$22.72	$20.19	$17.70	$0.00	$0.00
130							$25.12	$22.55	$0.00	$0.00
131								$27.56	$0.00	$0.00
132									$0.00	$0.00
133									$0.00	$0.00
134									$0.00	$0.00

We see that the Full-Scale model predicts an American put price of $14.02.

Problems

1. Download three months of daily stock price for any stock that has listed options on it. What is the annual standard deviation of your stock based on continuous returns?

2. Lookup the current stock price of your stock, use the standard deviation of daily returns you computed, lookup the yield on a six-month U.S. Treasury Bill, lookup the exercise price of a call on your stock that matures in

approximately six months, lookup the exercise price of a put on your stock that matures in approximately six months, and compute the time to maturity for both options in fractions of a year. For the call and put that you identified on your stock, determine the replicating portfolio and the price of the call and put using a single-period, replicating portfolio model.

3. For the same inputs as problem 2, determine the replicating portfolio and the price of the call and put using an eight-period, replicating portfolio model.

4. For the same inputs as problem 3, determine the price of the call and put using an eight-period, risk neutral model.

5. Use the same inputs as problem 4. Further, forecast the dividends that you stock pays or make an assumption about the dividends that your stock pays. What is the price of an American call and an American put using an eight-period, risk neutral model of American options with discrete dividends?

6. For the same inputs as problem 5, determine the price of an American call and an American put using a fifty-period, risk neutral model of American options with discrete dividends?

5. Extend the Binomial Option Pricing model to analyze Digital Options. The only thing which needs to be changed is the option's payoff at maturity.
   (a.) For a Digital Call, the Payoff At Maturity
                       = $1.00 When Stock Price At Mat > Exercise Price
                   Or $0.00 Otherwise.
   (b.) For a Digital Put, the Payoff At Maturity
                       = $1.00 When Stock Price At Mat < Exercise Price
                   Or $0.00 Otherwise.

6. Extend the **Binomial Option Pricing – Full-Scale Estimation** model to determine how fast the binomial option price converges to the price in the **Black Scholes Option Pricing – Basics** model. Reduce the Full-Scale model to a 10 period model and to a 20 period model. Increase the 50 period model to a 100 period model. Then for the same inputs, compare call and put prices of the 10 period, 20 period, 50 period, 100 period, and Black-Scholes models.

7. Extend the **Binomial Option Pricing – Full-Scale Estimation** model to determine how fast the binomial option price with averaging of adjacent odd and even numbers of periods converges to the price in the **Black Scholes Option Pricing – Basics** model. As you increase the number of periods in the binomial model, it oscillates between overshooting and undershooting the true price. A simple technique to increase price efficiency is to average adjacent odd and even numbers of periods. For example, average the 10 period call price and the 11 period call price. Reduce the Full-Scale model to a 10 period, 11 period, 20 period, and 21 period model. Increase the 50 period model to a 51 period, 100 period, and 101 period model. Then for the same inputs, compare call and put prices of the average of the 10 and 11 period models, 20 and 21 period models, 50 and 51 period models, 100 and 101 period models, and Black-Scholes model.

Chapter 16 Black Scholes Option Pricing

16.1 Basics

Problem. At the close of trading on June 20, 2007, the stock price of Amazon.com was $69.81, the standard deviation of daily returns was 71.65%, the yield on a six-month U.S. Treasury Bill was 4.95%, the exercise price of a January 70 call on Amazon.com was $70.00, the exercise price of a January 70 put on Amazon.com was $70.00, and the time to maturity for both January 18, 2008 maturity options was 0.5777 years. What is the price of a January 70 call and a January 70 put on Amazon.com?

FIGURE 16.1 Excel Model for Black Scholes Option Pricing - Basics.

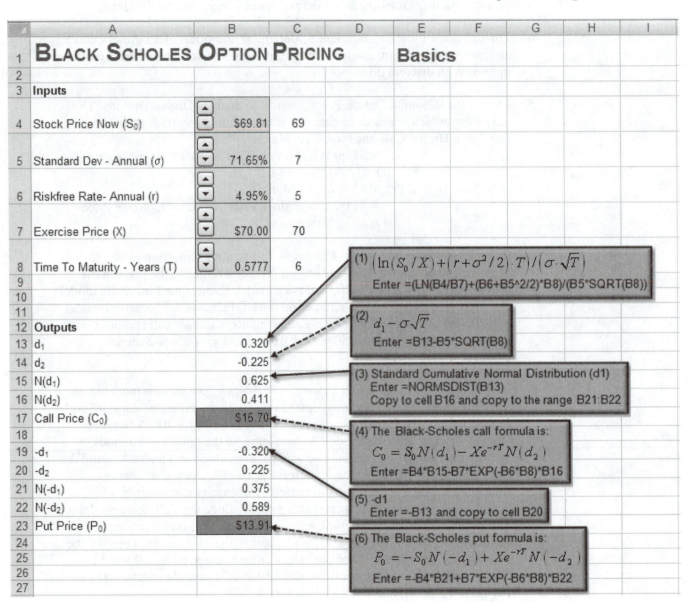

The Black-Scholes model predicts a call price of $15.70. This is seven cents different that what the Binominal Option Pricing - Full-Scale Estimation model predicts for a European call with identical inputs (including no dividends). The Black-Scholes model predicts a put price of $13.91. This is six cents different that what the Binominal Option Pricing - Full-Scale Estimation model predicts for a European put with identical inputs (including no dividends).. The advantage of the Black Scholes model and its natural analytic extensions is they are quick and easy to calculate. The disadvantage is that they are limited to a narrow range of derivatives (such as European options only, etc.).

16.2 Continuous Dividend

Problem. Suppose that Amazon.com paid dividends in tiny amounts on a continuous basis throughout the year at a 1.0% / year rate. What would be the new price of the call and put?

Solution Strategy. Modify the basic Black Scholes formulas from above to include the continuous dividend.

FIGURE 16.2 Black Scholes Option Pricing – Continuous Dividend

	A	B	C	D	E	F	G	H	I	J
30	**BLACK SCHOLES OPTION PRICING**				**Continuous Dividend**					
31										
32	Inputs	Option Type								
33	Option Type	⦿ Call ◯ Put	1							
34	Stock Price Now (S₀)	$69.81	69							
35	Standard Dev - Annual (σ)	71.65%	7							
36	Riskfree Rate- Annual (r)	4.95%	5							
37	Exercise Price (X)	$70.00	70							
38	Time To Maturity - Years (T)	0.5777	6							
39	Dividend Yield (d)	1.00%	1							
40										
41										
42	Outputs									
43	d_1	0.309								
44	d_2	-0.235								
45	$N(d_1)$	0.621								
46	$N(d_2)$	0.407								
47	Call Price (C₀)	$15.45								
48										
49	$-d_1$	-0.309								
50	$-d_2$	0.235								
51	$N(-d_1)$	0.379								
52	$N(-d_2)$	0.593								
53	Put Price (P₀)	$14.07								
54										
55										

Dynamic Chart of Black Scholes Option Pricing

(7) Copy the basic Black-Scholes formulas from above
Copy the range B13:B23 to the cell B43

(8) Add dividend yield (*d*) to the *d1* formula:

$$\left(\ln\left(S_0 / X \right) + \left(r - d + \sigma^2 / 2 \right) \cdot T \right) / \left(\sigma \cdot \sqrt{T} \right)$$

Enter =(LN(B34/B37)+(B36-B39+B35^2/2)*B38)/(B35*SQRT(B38))

(9) Add dividend yield (*d*) to the call formula:

$$C_0 = S_0 e^{-dT} N\left(d_1 \right) - X e^{-rT} N\left(d_2 \right)$$

Enter =B34*EXP(-B39*B38)*B45-B37*EXP(-B36*B38)*B46

(10) Add dividend yield (*d*) to the put formula:

$$P_0 = -S_0 e^{-dT} N\left(-d_1 \right) + X e^{-rT} N\left(-d_2 \right)$$

Enter =-B34*EXP(-B39*B38)*B51+B37*EXP(-B36*B38)*B52

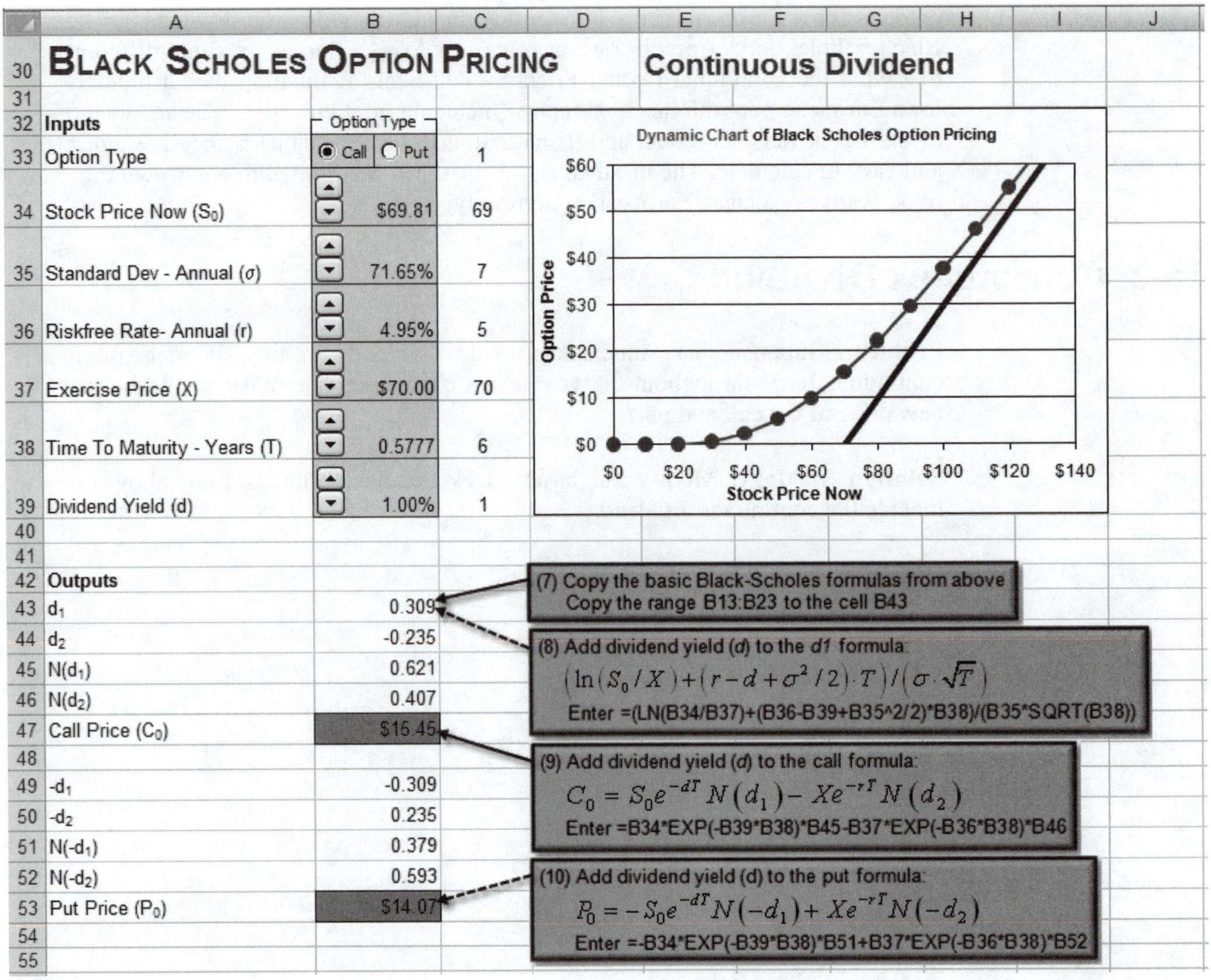

We see that the continuous dividend model predicts a call price of $15.45. This is a drop of 25 cents from the no dividend version. The continuous dividend model predicts a put price of $14.07. This is a rise of 16 cents from the no dividend version. To create a dynamic chart, we have a few more steps.

FIGURE 16.3 Excel Model for Black Scholes – Cont. Div. – Dynamic Chart

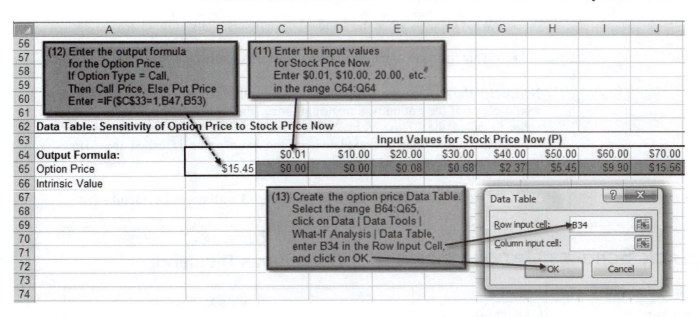

Excel 2003 Equivalent

To call up a Data Table in Excel 2003. click on **Data | Table**

FIGURE 16.4 Excel Model for Black Scholes – Cont. Div. – Dynamic Chart

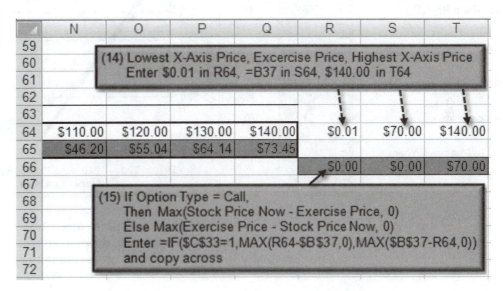

The spin buttons allows you to change Black-Scholes inputs and instantly see the impact on a graph of the option price and intrinsic value. This allows you to perform instant experiments on the Black-Scholes option pricing model. Here is a list of experiments that you might want to perform:

- What happens when the standard deviation is increased?

- What happens when the time to maturity is increased?

- What happens when the exercise price is increased?

- What happens when the riskfree rate is increased?

- What happens when the dividend yield is increased?

- What happens when the standard deviation is really close to zero?

- What happens when the time to maturity is really close to zero?

Notice that the Black-Scholes option price is usually greater than the payoff you would obtain if the option was maturing today (the "intrinsic value"). This extra value is called the "Time Value" of the option. Given your result in the last experiment above, can you explain *why* the extra value is called the "Time Value"? Now let's look at the put option.

FIGURE 16.5 Excel Model for Black Scholes - Continuous Dividend - Put

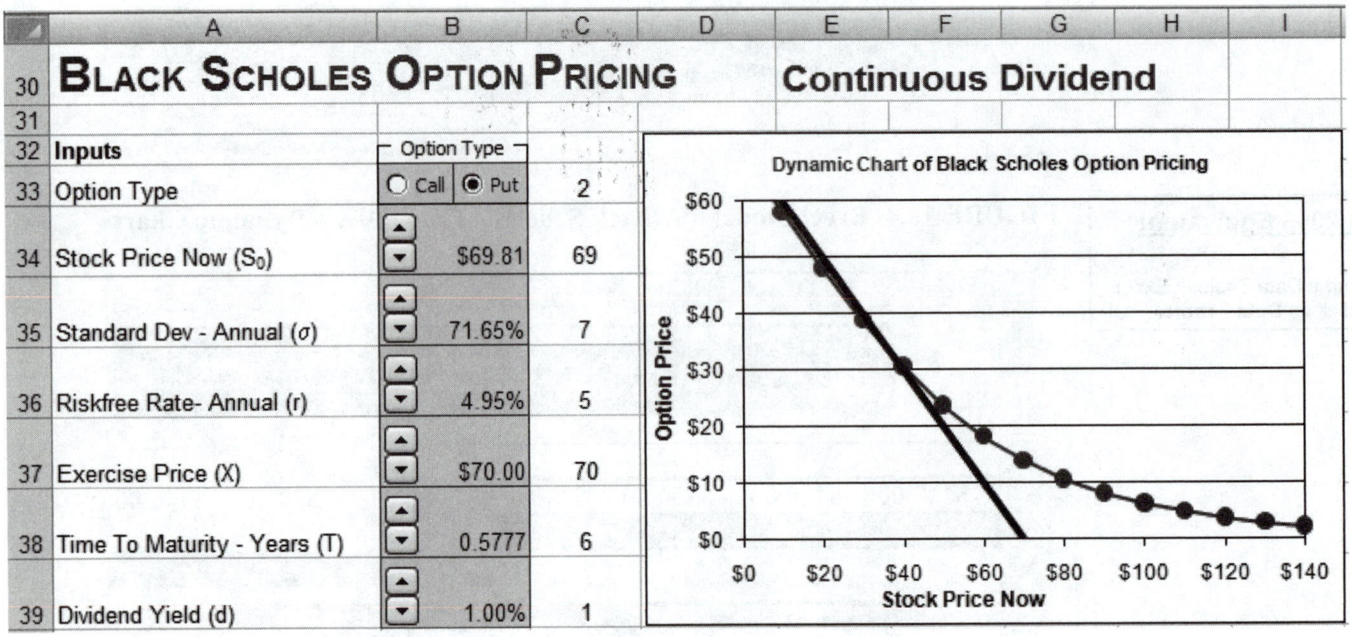

Notice that the put option value sometime drops below the intrinsic value. To understand why, reduce the riskfree rate down to zero and see what happens. You can perform many similar experiments on the put option.

16.3 Greeks

Problem. What is the sensitivity of the call price to changes in the stock price, time, standard deviation, and the riskfree rate? What is the sensitivity of the sensitivity of the call price to changes in the stock price? And same questions with respect to the put price? How does each sensitivity change by stock price now and how does each sensitivity change by time to maturity?

Solution Strategy. These sensitivities are the so-called "Greeks," because each sensitivity is called by a greek letter, such as Delta, Gamma, etc. Each sensitivity has a specific formula and it just a matter of entering each formula in turn. Then create a data table to see how each greek changes by stock price now and another data table to see how each greek changes by time to maturity.

FIGURE 16.6 Excel Model for Black Scholes Option Pricing - Greeks.

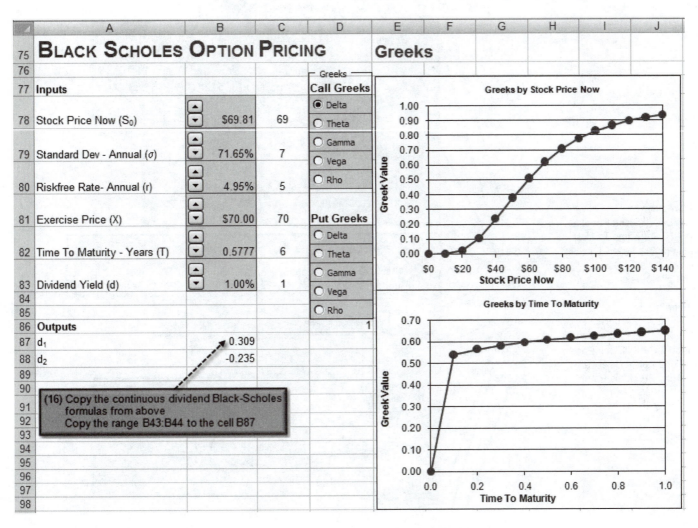

FIGURE 16.7 Excel Model for Black Scholes Option Pricing - Greeks.

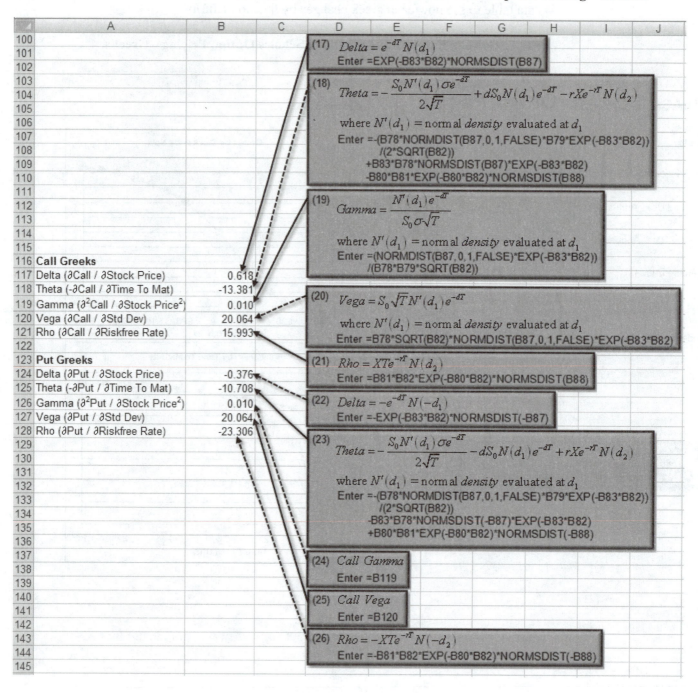

FIGURE 16.8 Excel Model for Black Scholes Option Pricing - Greeks.

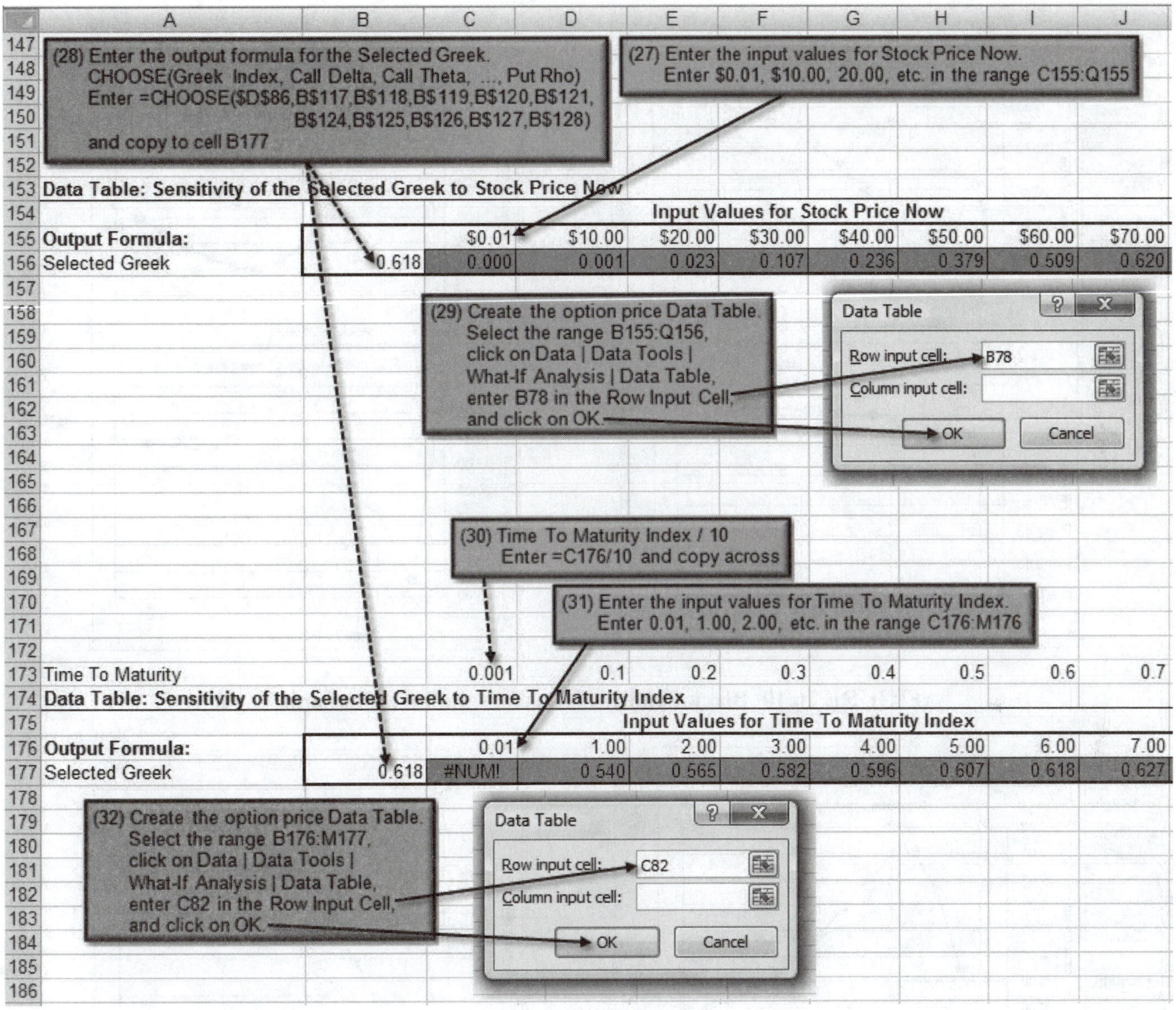

	A	B	C	D	E	F	G	H	I	J
147	(28) Enter the output formula for the Selected Greek.					(27) Enter the input values for Stock Price Now.				
148	CHOOSE(Greek Index, Call Delta, Call Theta, ..., Put Rho)					Enter $0.01, $10.00, 20.00, etc. in the range C155:Q155				
149	Enter =CHOOSE($D$86,B$117,B$118,B$119,B$120,B$121,									
150	B$124,B$125,B$126,B$127,B$128)									
151	and copy to cell B177									
152										
153	Data Table: Sensitivity of the Selected Greek to Stock Price Now									
154					Input Values for Stock Price Now					
155	Output Formula:		$0.01	$10.00	$20.00	$30.00	$40.00	$50.00	$60.00	$70.00
156	Selected Greek	0.618	0.000	0.001	0.023	0.107	0.236	0.379	0.509	0.620
157										
158			(29) Create the option price Data Table.							
159			Select the range B155:Q156,					Data Table		
160			click on Data	Data Tools							
161			What-If Analysis	Data Table,				Row input cell: B78		
162			enter B78 in the Row Input Cell,					Column input cell:		
163			and click on OK.							
164									OK Cancel		
165										
166										
167			(30) Time To Maturity Index / 10							
168			Enter =C176/10 and copy across							
169										
170				(31) Enter the input values for Time To Maturity Index.						
171				Enter 0.01, 1.00, 2.00, etc. in the range C176:M176						
172										
173	Time To Maturity		0.001	0.1	0.2	0.3	0.4	0.5	0.6	0.7
174	Data Table: Sensitivity of the Selected Greek to Time To Maturity Index									
175					Input Values for Time To Maturity Index					
176	Output Formula:		0.01	1.00	2.00	3.00	4.00	5.00	6.00	7.00
177	Selected Greek	0.618	#NUM!	0.540	0.565	0.582	0.596	0.607	0.618	0.627
178										
179		(32) Create the option price Data Table.				Data Table				
180		Select the range B176:M177,								
181		click on Data	Data Tools				Row input cell: C82				
182		What-If Analysis	Data Table,								
183		enter C82 in the Row Input Cell,				Column input cell:				
184		and click on OK.								
185						OK Cancel				
186										

Excel 2003 Equivalent	It is interesting to see how each greek changes by stock price now and by time to maturity. The graphs below show each greek by stock price now and by time to maturity.
To call up a Data Table in Excel 2003. click on **Data	Table**	

FIGURE 16.9 Black Scholes – Greeks – Call Delta and Theta.

FIGURE 16.10 Black Scholes – Greeks – Call Gamma and Vega.

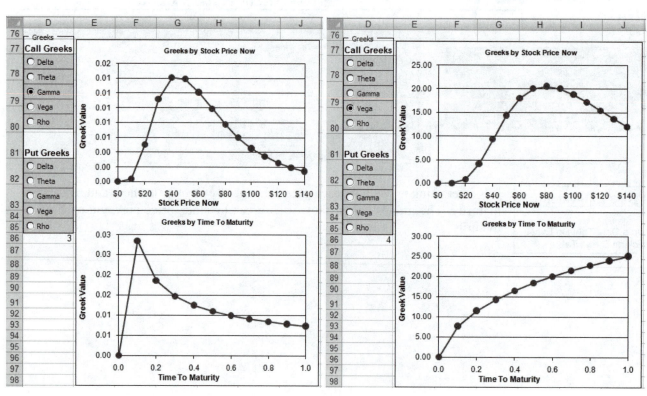

FIGURE 16.11 Black Scholes – Grees – Call Rho and Put Delta.

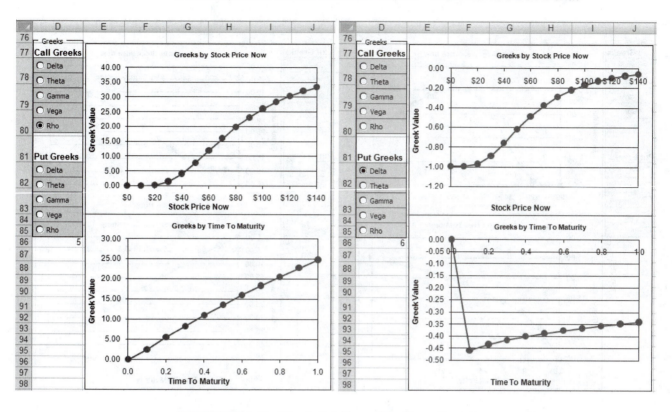

FIGURE 16.12 Black Scholes – Greeks – Put Theta and Gamma.

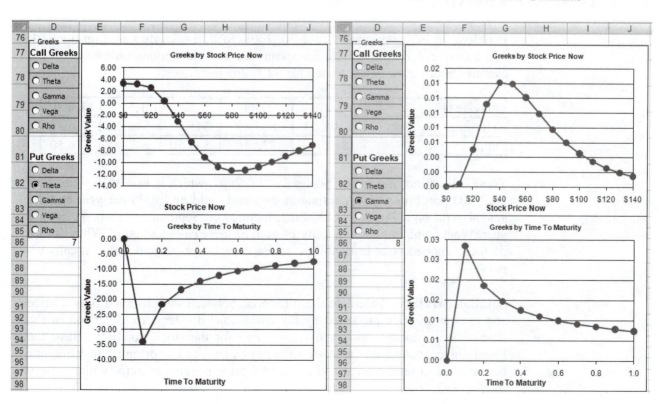

FIGURE 16.13 Black Scholes – Greeks – Put Vega and Rho.

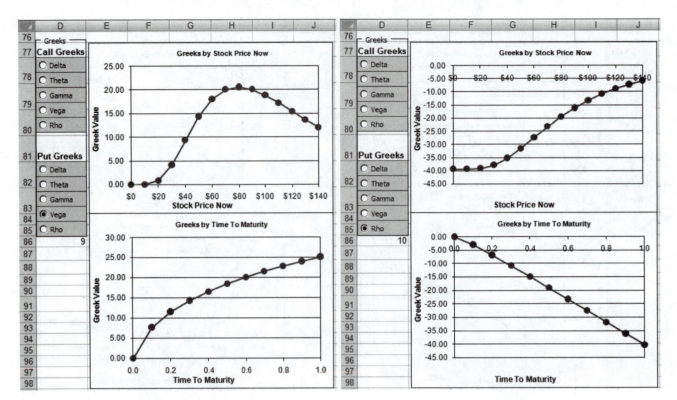

16.4 Implied Volatility

Problem. In the afternoon of June 20, 2007, SPX, a security based on the S&P 500 index, traded at 1,512.84. European call and put options on SPX with the exercise prices show below traded for the following prices:

Exercise price	1,450	1,500	1,520	1,540	1,600
Call price	$105.60	$63.40	$45.50	$40.00	$14.50
Put price	$17.70	$32.40	$39.50	$42.00	$76.50

These call options mature on September 17, 2007, which is in 0.2416 years. The S&P 500 portfolio pays a continuous dividend yield of 1.62% per year and the annual yield on a Treasury Bill which matures on September 13th is 4.62% per year. What is the implied volatility of each of these calls and puts? What pattern do these implied volatilities follow across exercise prices and between calls vs. puts?

Solution Strategy. Calculate the difference between the observed option price and the option price predicted by the continuous dividend yield version of the Black-Scholes model using a dummy value for the stock volatility. Have the Excel Solver tool adjust the stock volatility by trial and error until the difference between the observed price and the model price is equal to zero (within a very small error tolerance).

FIGURE 16.14 Excel Model of Black Scholes - Implied Volatility.

	A	B	C	D	E	F	G	H	I	J	K
188	**BLACK SCHOLES OPTION PRICING**					**Implied Volatility**					
189											
190			(33) Copy the continuous dividend Black-Scholes formulas from above								
			Copy the range B43:B53 to the range B202:K212								
191	**Inputs**										
192	Option Type: 1=Call, 2=Put	1	1	1	1	1	2	2	2	2	2
193	Stock Price Now (S_0)	$1,513	$1,513	$1,513	$1,513	$1,513	$1,513	$1,513	$1,513	$1,513	$1,513
194	Standard Dev - Annual (σ)	21.66%	17.31%	14.77%	16.01%	13.81%	15.66%	14.73%	14.02%	11.25%	6.31%
195	Riskfree Rate- Annual (r)	4.62%	4.62%	4.62%	4.62%	4.62%	4.62%	4.62%	4.62%	4.62%	4.62%
196	Exercise Price (X)	$1,450	$1,500	$1,520	$1,540	$1,600	$1,450	$1,500	$1,520	$1,540	$1,600
197	Time To Maturity - Years (T)	0.2416	0.2416	0.2416	0.2416	0.2416	0.2416	0.2416	0.2416	0.2416	0.2416
198	Dividend Yield (d)	1.62%	1.62%	1.62%	1.62%	1.62%	1.62%	1.62%	1.62%	1.62%	1.62%
199	Observed Option Price	$105.60	$63.40	$45.50	$40.00	$14.50	$17.70	$32.40	$39.50	$42.00	$76.50
200											
201	**Outputs**										
202	d_1	0.520	0.228	0.071	-0.095	-0.685	0.684	0.254	0.071	-0.163	-1.556
203	d_2	0.413	0.143	-0.001	-0.173	-0.753	0.607	0.182	0.002	-0.218	-1.587
204	$N(d_1)$	0.698	0.590	0.528	0.462	0.247	0.753	0.600	0.528	0.435	0.060
205	$N(d_2)$	0.660	0.557	0.499	0.431	0.226	0.728	0.572	0.501	0.414	0.056
206	Model Call Price (C_0)	$105.60	$63.40	$45.50	$40.00	$14.50	$90.73	$55.98	$43.30	$26.02	$1.19
207											
208	$-d_1$	-0.520	-0.228	-0.071	0.095	0.685	-0.684	-0.254	-0.071	0.163	1.556
209	$-d_2$	-0.413	-0.143	0.001	0.173	0.753	-0.607	-0.182	-0.002	0.218	1.587
210	$N(-d_1)$	0.302	0.410	0.472	0.538	0.753	0.247	0.400	0.472	0.565	0.940
211	$N(-d_2)$	0.340	0.443	0.501	0.569	0.774	0.272	0.428	0.499	0.586	0.944
212	Model Put Price (P_0)	$32.57	$39.82	$41.70	$55.98	$89.81	$17.70	$32.40	$39.50	$42.00	$76.50
213											
214	**Solver**										
215	Difference (observed - model)	4E-07	7.2E-08	4E-08	9.5E-07	2.2E-07	9.6E-07	4.8E-07	-3.2E-07	7.2E-08	8.0E-07

(34) If Option Type = Call,
Then Observed Option Price - Model Call Price
Else Observed Option Price - Model Put Price
Enter =IF(B192=1,B199-B206,B199-B212)

(35) Use Solver to determine the
Implied Volatility.
* Click on **Data | Analysis | Solver**
* enter B215 in Set Target Cell,
* click on the **Value Of** button
* enter 0 in the adjacent box,
* enter B194 in By Changing Cells,
* and click on **Solve**
When Solver finds a solution,
* click on the **Keep Solver Solution**
button
* and click on OK.
Repeat using Solver to determine
the implied volatility for column C.

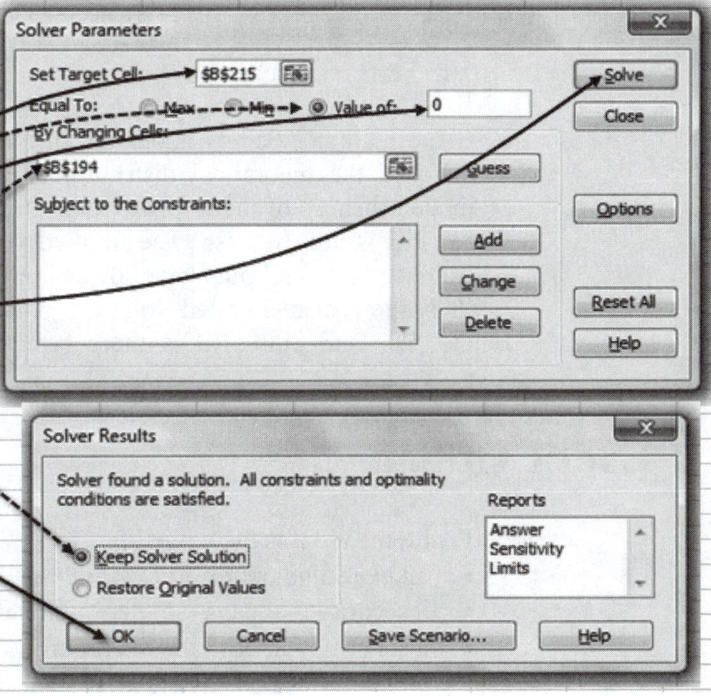

Solver Parameters

Set Target Cell: $B$215

Equal To: Max / Min / Value of: 0

By Changing Cells: $B$194

Subject to the Constraints:

Solve / Close / Guess / Options / Add / Change / Delete / Reset All / Help

Solver Results

Solver found a solution. All constraints and optimality conditions are satisfied.

Reports: Answer / Sensitivity / Limits

Keep Solver Solution
Restore Original Values

OK / Cancel / Save Scenario... / Help

If you don't see **Solver** on the **Data** Tab in the **Analysis** Group, then you need to install the Solver. To install the Solver, click on the **Office** button, click on the Excel Options button at the bottom of the drop-down window, click on **Add-Ins**, highlight **Solver** in the list of Inactive Applications, click on **Go**, check **Solver**, and click on **OK**.

FIGURE 16.15 Graph of the "Scowl" Pattern of Implied Volatilities.

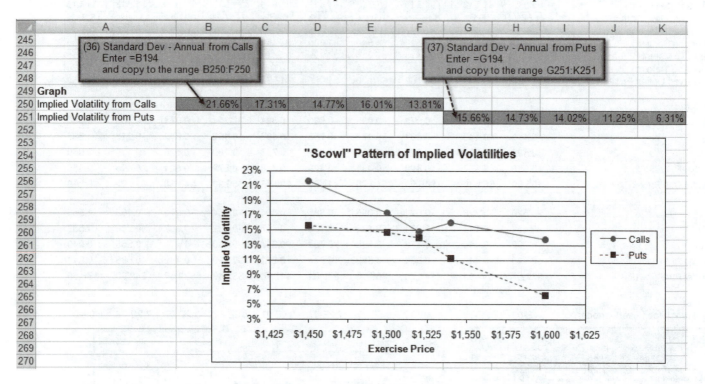

If the market's beliefs about the distribution of returns of the S&P 500 Index matched the theoretical distribution of returns assumed by the Black-Scholes model, then all of the implied volatilities would be the same. From the graph we see this is not the case. The implied volatility pattern declines sharply with the exercise price and puts have lower implied volatilities than calls. In the '70s and '80s, the typical implied volatility pattern was a U-shaped, "Smile" pattern. In the '90s and 2000s, it is more typical to see a downward-sloping, "Scowl" pattern.

16.5 Exotic Options

Problem. What is the value of:
- an exchange option (the right to exchange one asset for another asset)?
- a security that pays the minimum value of two assets?
- a security that pays the maximum value of two assets?
- a chooser option (where after a specified time, the holder can choose whether the option is a call or a put)?
- a cash-or-nothing call (which pays a fixed cash amount when the asset price is greater than the strike price or nothing otherwise)?

- a cash-or-nothing put (which pays a fixed cash amount when the asset price is less than the strike price or nothing otherwise)?
- an asset-or-nothing call (which pays the asset price when the asset price is greater than the strike price or nothing otherwise)?
- an asset-or-nothing put (which pays the asset price when the asset price is less than the strike price or nothing otherwise)?
- a gap call (which pays the asset price minus the strike price when the asset price is greater than a trigger price and nothing otherwise)?
- a gap put (which pays the strike price minus the asset price when the asset price is less than the trigger price and nothing otherwise)?
- a supershare (which pays the asset price when the asset price is between an upper and lower bound and nothing otherwise)?

Solution Strategy. Each exotic option has a specific formula and it just a matter of entering each formula in turn. Then create a data table to see how each exotic option changes by the stock price now.

FIGURE 16.16 Excel Model of Black Scholes – Exotic Options.

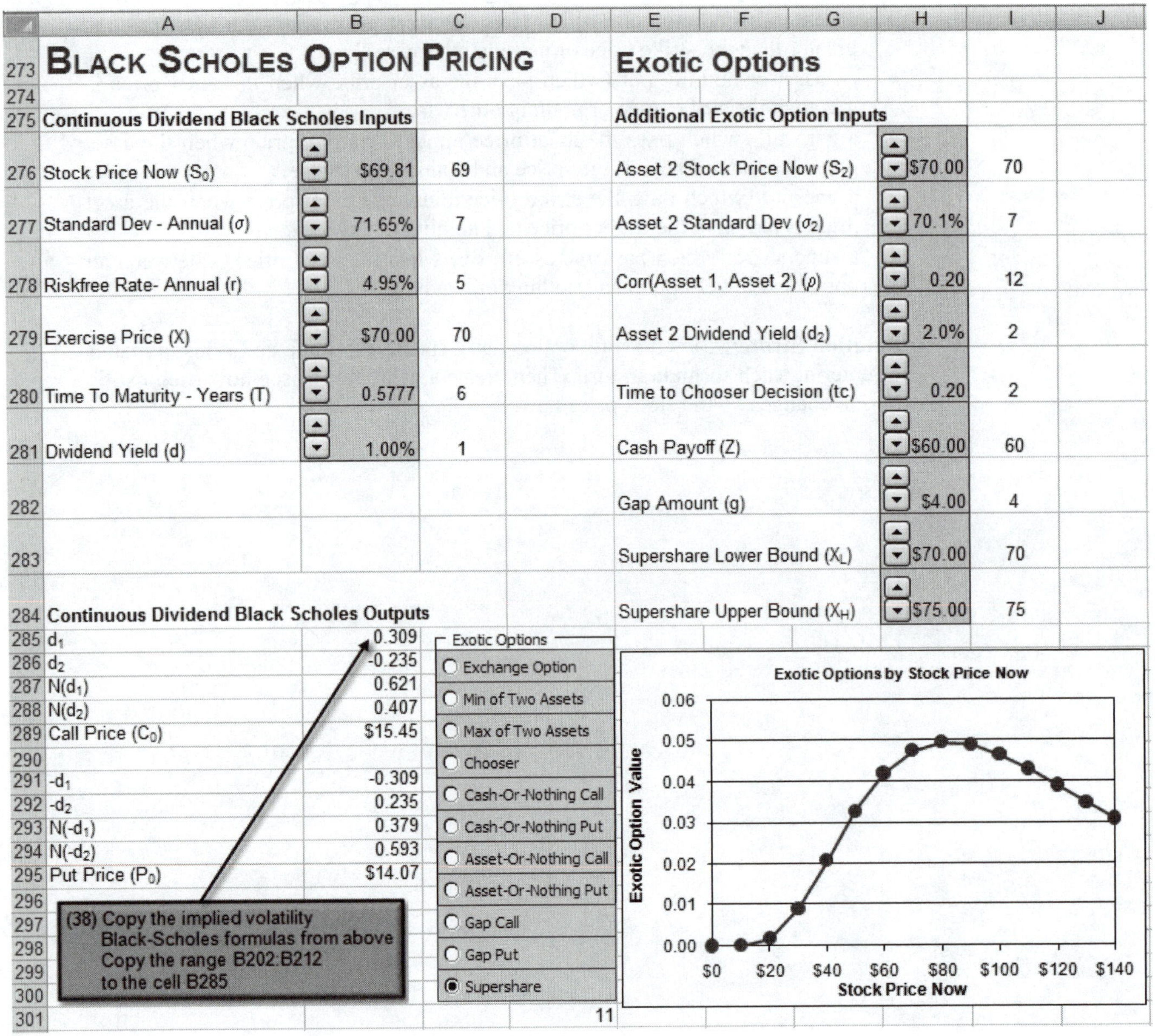

	A	B	C	D	E	F	G	H	I	J
273	**BLACK SCHOLES OPTION PRICING**				**Exotic Options**					
274										
275	**Continuous Dividend Black Scholes Inputs**				**Additional Exotic Option Inputs**					
276	Stock Price Now (S_0)	$69.81	69		Asset 2 Stock Price Now (S_2)			$70.00	70	
277	Standard Dev - Annual (σ)	71.65%	7		Asset 2 Standard Dev (σ_2)			70.1%	7	
278	Riskfree Rate- Annual (r)	4.95%	5		Corr(Asset 1, Asset 2) (ρ)			0.20	12	
279	Exercise Price (X)	$70.00	70		Asset 2 Dividend Yield (d_2)			2.0%	2	
280	Time To Maturity - Years (T)	0.5777	6		Time to Chooser Decision (tc)			0.20	2	
281	Dividend Yield (d)	1.00%	1		Cash Payoff (Z)			$60.00	60	
282					Gap Amount (g)			$4.00	4	
283					Supershare Lower Bound (X_L)			$70.00	70	
284	**Continuous Dividend Black Scholes Outputs**				Supershare Upper Bound (X_H)			$75.00	75	
285	d_1	0.309								
286	d_2	-0.235								
287	$N(d_1)$	0.621								
288	$N(d_2)$	0.407								
289	Call Price (C_0)	$15.45								
290										
291	$-d_1$	-0.309								
292	$-d_2$	0.235								
293	$N(-d_1)$	0.379								
294	$N(-d_2)$	0.593								
295	Put Price (P_0)	$14.07								

Exotic Options:
- ○ Exchange Option
- ○ Min of Two Assets
- ○ Max of Two Assets
- ○ Chooser
- ○ Cash-Or-Nothing Call
- ○ Cash-Or-Nothing Put
- ○ Asset-Or-Nothing Call
- ○ Asset-Or-Nothing Put
- ○ Gap Call
- ○ Gap Put
- ● Supershare

(38) Copy the implied volatility Black-Scholes formulas from above Copy the range B202:B212 to the cell B285

Exotic Options by Stock Price Now

11

FIGURE 16.17 Excel Model of Black Scholes – Exotic Options.

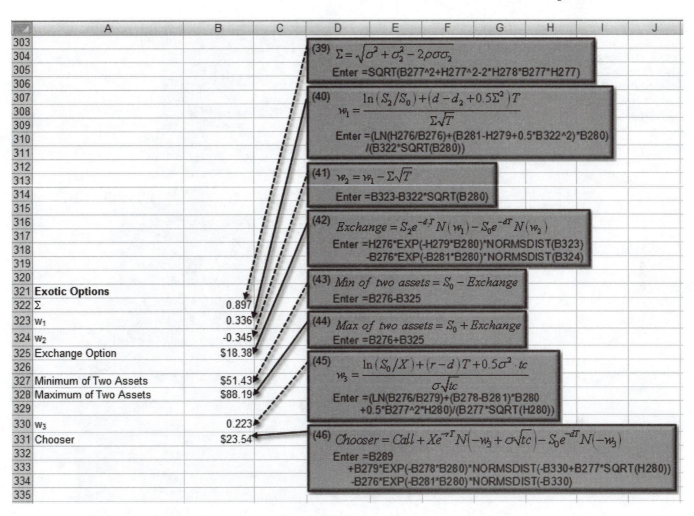

FIGURE 16.18 Excel Model of Black Scholes – Exotic Options.

	A	B	C	D	E	F	G	H	I
337									
338	Binary Options(Digital Options):								
339	Cash-or-Nothing Call	$23.73							
340	Cash-or-Nothing Put	$34.58							
341	Asset-or-Nothing Call	$28.25							
342	Asset-or-Nothing Put	$41.16							
343	Gap Call	$13.87							
344	Gap Put	$16.37							
345	w_L	0.309							
346	w_H	0.183							
347	Supershare	$0.05							
348									
349									
350									
351									
352									
353									
354									
355									
356									
357									
358									
359									
360									
361									
362									
363									
364									
365									
366									
367									
368									
369									
370									
371									
372									
373									
374									

(47) $Cash\text{-}Or\text{-}Nothing\ Call = Ze^{-rT}N(d_2)$
Enter =H281*EXP(-B278*B280)*B288

(48) $Cash\text{-}Or\text{-}Nothing\ Put = Ze^{-rT}N(-d_2)$
Enter =H281*EXP(-B278*B280)*B294

(49) $Asset\text{-}Or\text{-}Nothing\ Call = e^{-dT}S_0N(d_1)$
Enter =EXP(-B281*B280)*B276*B288

(50) $Asset\text{-}Or\text{-}Nothing\ Put = e^{-dT}S_0N(-d_2)$
Enter =EXP(-B281*B280)*B276*B294

(51) $Gap\ Call = e^{-dT}S_0N(d_1)-(X+g)e^{-rT}N(d_2)$
Enter =EXP(-B281*B280)*B276*B287
        -(B279+H282)*EXP(-B278*B280)*B288

(52) $Gap\ Put = (X+g)e^{-rT}N(-d_2)-e^{-dT}S_0N(-d_1)$
Enter =(B279+H282)*EXP(-B278*B280)*B294
        -EXP(-B281*B280)*B276*B293

(53)
$$w_L = \frac{\ln(S_0/X_L)+(r-d+0.5\sigma^2)T}{\sigma\sqrt{T}}$$
Enter =(LN(B276/H283)+(B278-B281+0.5*B277^2)*B280)
        /(B277*SQRT(B280))

(54)
$$w_H = \frac{\ln(S_0/X_H)+(r-d+0.5\sigma^2)T}{\sigma\sqrt{T}}$$
Enter =(LN(B276/H284)+(B278-B281+0.5*B277^2)*B280)
        /(B277*SQRT(B280))

(55)
$$Supershare = \frac{S_0e^{-d_1T}}{X_L}\left[N(w_L)-N(w_H)\right]$$
Enter =(B276*EXP(-B278*B280)/H283)
        *(NORMSDIST(B345)-NORMSDIST(B346))

FIGURE 16.19 Excel Model of Black Scholes – Exotic Options.

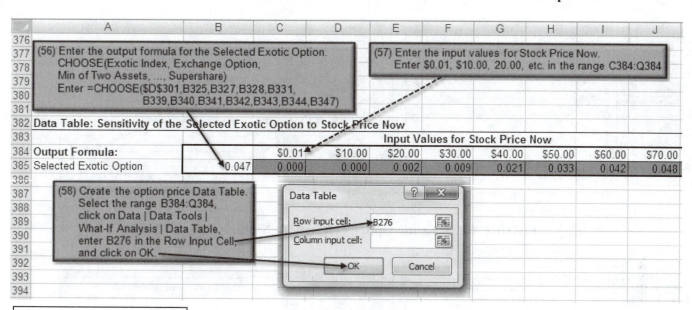

Excel 2003 Equivalent

To call up a Data Table in Excel 2003. click on **Data | Table**

It is interesting to see how each exotic option changes by the stock price now. The graphs below show each exotic option by stock price now.

FIGURE 16.20 Exotic Options – Exchange Option and Min of Two Assets.

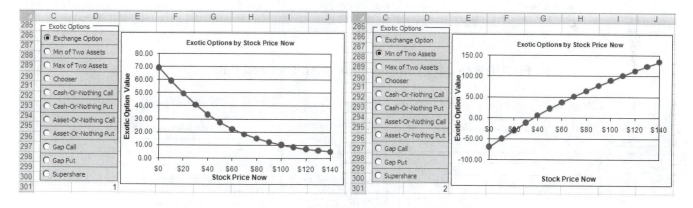

FIGURE 16.21 Exotic Options –Max of Two Assets and Chooser.

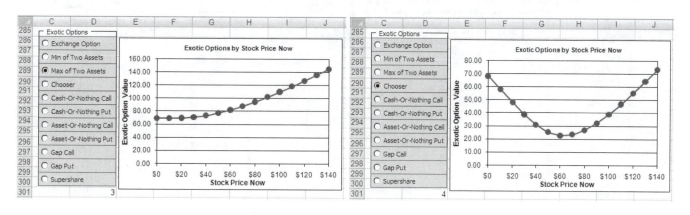

FIGURE 16.22 Exotic Options –Cash-Or-Nothing Call and Put.

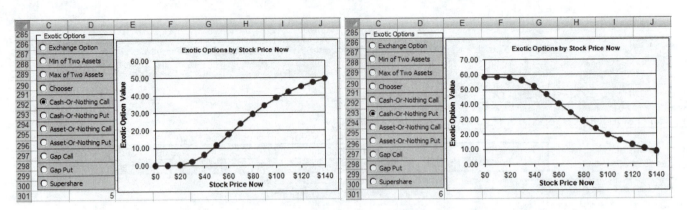

FIGURE 16.23 Exotic Options –Asset-Or-Nothing Call and Put.

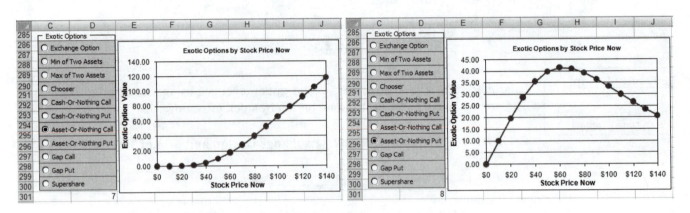

FIGURE 16.24 Exotic Options –Gap Call and Put.

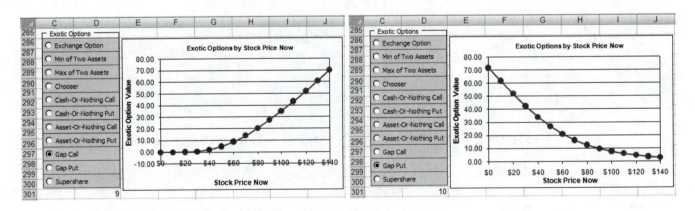

FIGURE 16.25 Exotic Options –Supershare.

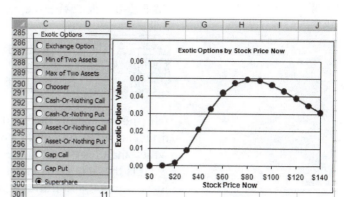

Problems

1. Download three months of daily stock price for any stock that has listed options on it and compute the standard deviation of daily returns. Lookup the current stock price of your stock, use the standard deviation of daily returns you just computed, lookup the yield on a six-month U.S. Treasury Bill, lookup the exercise price of a call on your stock that matures in approximately six months, lookup the exercise price of a put on your stock that matures in approximately six months, and compute the time to maturity for both options in fractions of a year. For the call and put that you identified on your stock, determine the price of the call and put using the Black-Scholes basics model.

2. Use the same inputs as problem 1. Forecast the continuous dividend that your stock pays or make an assumption about the continuous dividend that your stock pays. Determine the price of the call and put using the Black-Scholes continuous dividend model.

3. Perform instant experiments on whether changing various inputs causes an increase or decrease in the Call Price and in the Put Price and by how much.

    (a.) What happens when the standard deviation is increased?
    (b.) What happens when the time to maturity is increased?
    (c.) What happens when the exercise price is increased?
    (d.) What happens when the riskfree rate is increased?
    (e.) What happens when the dividend yield is increased?
    (f.) What happens when the standard deviation is really close to zero?
    (g.) What happens when the time to maturity is really close to zero?

4. What is the sensitivity of the call price to changes in the stock price, time, standard deviation, and the riskfree rate? What is the sensitivity of the sensitivity of the call price to changes in the stock price? And same questions with respect to the put price? How does each sensitivity change by stock price now and how does each sensitivity change by time to maturity?

5. The S&P 500 index closes at 2000. European call and put options on the S&P 500 index with the exercise prices show below trade for the following prices:

Exercise price	1,950	1,975	2,000	2,025	2,050
Call price	$88	$66	$47	$33	$21
Put price	$25	$26	$32	$44	$58

All options mature in 88 days. The S&P 500 portfolio pays a continuous dividend yield of 1.56% per year and the annual yield on a Treasury Bill which matures on the same day as the options is 4.63% per year. Determine what is the implied volatility of each of these calls and puts. What pattern do these implied volatilities follow across exercise prices and between calls vs. puts?

6. What is the value of:
   - an exchange option (the right to exchange one asset for another asset)?
   - a security that pays the minimum value of two assets?
   - a security that pays the maximum value of two assets?
   - a chooser option (where after a specified time, the holder can choose whether the option is a call or a put)?
   - a cash-or-nothing call (which pays a fixed cash amount when the asset price is greater than the strike price or nothing otherwise)?
   - a cash-or-nothing put (which pays a fixed cash amount when the asset price is less than the strike price or nothing otherwise)?
   - an asset-or-nothing call (which pays the asset price when the asset price is greater than the strike price or nothing otherwise)?
   - an asset-or-nothing put (which pays the asset price when the asset price is less than the strike price or nothing otherwise)?
   - a gap call (which pays the asset price minus the strike price when the asset price is greater than a trigger price and nothing otherwise)?
   - a gap put (which pays the strike price minus the asset price when the asset price is less than the trigger price and nothing otherwise)?
   - a supershare (which pays the asset price when the asset price is between an upper and lower bound and nothing otherwise)?

Chapter 17 Spot-Futures Parity (Cost of Carry)

17.1 Basics

Problem. Suppose we recorded the monthly spot price of the S&P 500 index and corresponding futures price over a seven month period for a stock index futures contract maturing in month 7. Here are the prices in index points:

Month	1	2	3	4	5	6	7
Spot price	1117.36	1126.37	1136.73	1146.86	1155.14	1165.69	1178.23
Futures price	1144.38	1149.94	1155.05	1162.00	1167.24	1170.23	1178.23

Suppose that the riskfree rate is 0.42% per month. Analyze what happened over time to the basis and to the price difference between the model futures price implied by Spot-Futures Parity versus the actual futures price.

Solution Strategy. First calculate the basis. Then substitute the spot price into the Spot-Futures Parity to determine the model futures price. Then calculate the price difference between the model futures price and the actual futures price.

FIGURE 17.1 Excel Model of Spot-Future Parity (Cost of Carry) - Basics.

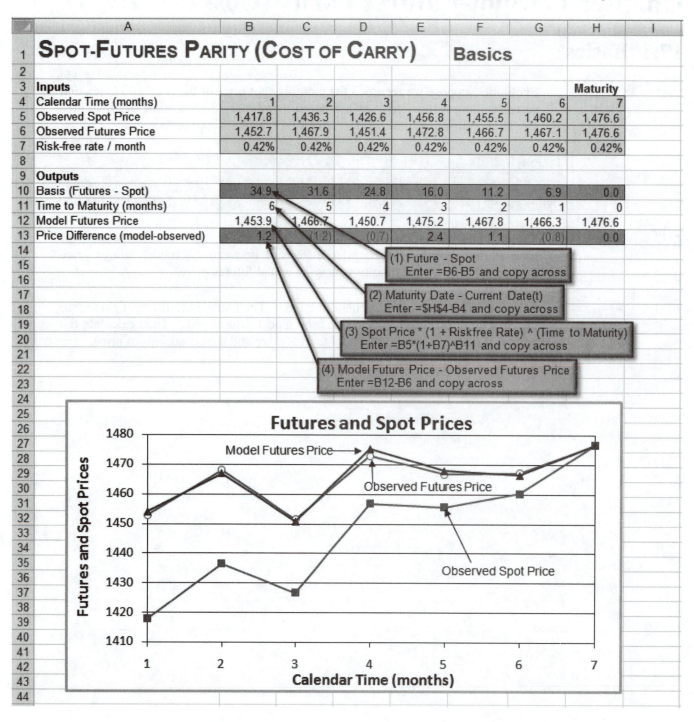

	A	B	C	D	E	F	G	H	I
1	**SPOT-FUTURES PARITY (COST OF CARRY)**					**Basics**			
2									
3	**Inputs**							**Maturity**	
4	Calendar Time (months)	1	2	3	4	5	6	7	
5	Observed Spot Price	1,417.8	1,436.3	1,426.6	1,456.8	1,455.5	1,460.2	1,476.6	
6	Observed Futures Price	1,452.7	1,467.9	1,451.4	1,472.8	1,466.7	1,467.1	1,476.6	
7	Risk-free rate / month	0.42%	0.42%	0.42%	0.42%	0.42%	0.42%	0.42%	
8									
9	**Outputs**								
10	Basis (Futures - Spot)	34.9	31.6	24.8	16.0	11.2	6.9	0.0	
11	Time to Maturity (months)	6	5	4	3	2	1	0	
12	Model Futures Price	1,453.9	1,466.7	1,450.7	1,475.2	1,467.8	1,466.3	1,476.6	
13	Price Difference (model-observed)	1.2	(1.2)	(0.7)	2.4	1.1	(0.8)	0.0	

(1) Future - Spot
  Enter =B6-B5 and copy across

(2) Maturity Date - Current Date(t)
  Enter =$H$4-B4 and copy across

(3) Spot Price * (1 + Riskfree Rate) ^ (Time to Maturity)
  Enter =B5*(1+B7)^B11 and copy across

(4) Model Future Price - Observed Futures Price
  Enter =B12-B6 and copy across

Futures and Spot Prices

(Chart: Futures and Spot Prices, with y-axis "Futures and Spot Prices" ranging 1410 to 1480, x-axis "Calendar Time (months)" from 1 to 7. Series: Model Futures Price, Observed Futures Price, Observed Spot Price.)

Notice that the basis is a substantial positive value and steadily declines over time before finally reaching zero when the futures contract matures. By contrast, the price difference is very small value and fluctuates between positive and negative values before going to zero when the futures contract matures.

17.2 Index Arbitrage

Given that there is a (nonzero) price difference between the two markets, is it possible to make an arbitrage profit? Suppose that the round trip transaction cost for doing an index arbitrage trade is 1.60 index points. Analyze the monthly data to determine if was possible to have made an arbitrage profit.

FIGURE 17.2 Excel Model of Spot-Future Parity (Cost of Carry) - Index Arbitrage.

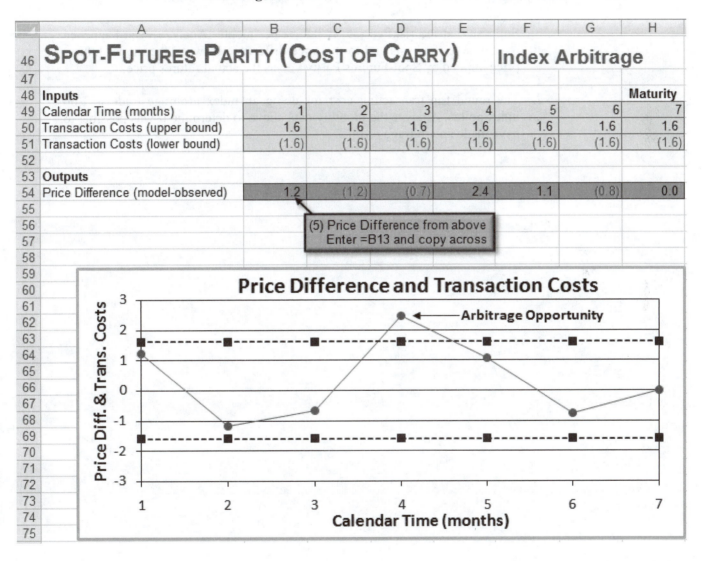

	A	B	C	D	E	F	G	H
46	**SPOT-FUTURES PARITY (COST OF CARRY)**					**Index Arbitrage**		
47								
48	**Inputs**							**Maturity**
49	Calendar Time (months)	1	2	3	4	5	6	7
50	Transaction Costs (upper bound)	1.6	1.6	1.6	1.6	1.6	1.6	1.6
51	Transaction Costs (lower bound)	(1.6)	(1.6)	(1.6)	(1.6)	(1.6)	(1.6)	(1.6)
52								
53	**Outputs**							
54	Price Difference (model-observed)	1.2	(1.2)	(0.7)	2.4	1.1	(0.8)	0.0

(5) Price Difference from above
Enter =B13 and copy across

Most of the time the price difference was inside the transaction cost boundaries, so there wasn't an arbitrage opportunity. However in month 4, the price difference went outside the boundaries by rising above the upper bound. Thus, an arbitrage profit could made in month 4 by selling in the index portfolio in the spot market, using the proceeds to lend money at the riskfree rate, and going long in the futures market.

Problems

1. Suppose we recorded the monthly spot price of the S&P 500 index and corresponding futures price over a seven month period for a stock index futures contract maturing in month 7. Here are the prices in index points:

Month	1	2	3	4	5	6	7
Spot price	1539.21	1552.95	1587.44	1603.48	1659.12	1653.47	1693.59
Futures price	1590.33	1593.68	1619.93	1630.37	1679.38	1661.81	1693.59

Suppose that the riskfree rate is 0.53% per month. Analyze what happened over time to the basis and to the price difference between the model futures price implied by Spot-Futures Parity versus the actual futures price.

2. The round trip transaction cost for doing an index arbitrage trade is 1.60 index points. Analyze the monthly data above to determine if was possible to have made an arbitrage profit.

PART 4 EXCEL SKILLS

Chapter 18 Useful Excel Tricks

18.1 Quickly Delete The Instruction Boxes and Arrows

Task. Quickly get rid of all of the instruction boxes and arrows after you are done building the Excel model/estimation.

How To. All of the instruction boxes and arrows are *objects* and there is an easy way to select all of them at once. Click on **Home | Editing | Find & Select**

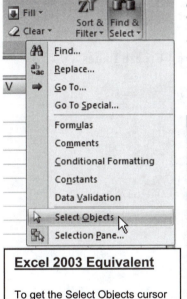

down-arrow | **Select Objects.** This causes the cursor to become a pointer. Then point to a **location above and to the left** of the instruction boxes and arrows, continue to hold down the left mouse button while you drag the pointer to a **location below and to the right** of the instruction boxes and arrows, and then let go of the left mouse button. This selects *all* of the instruction boxes and arrows (see example below). Then just press the **Delete** key and they are all gone!

Excel 2003 Equivalent

To get the Select Objects cursor in Excel 2003, click on the **Drawing** icon on the Standard toolbar and then click on the **Select Objects** icon (which looks like pointer) on the Drawing toolbar in the lower-left corner of the screen.

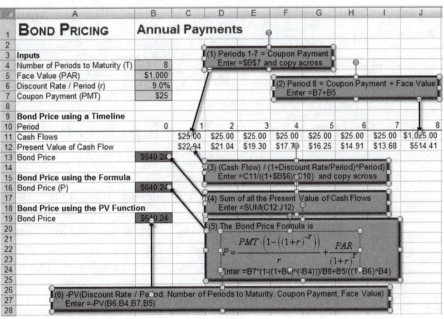

18.2 Freeze Panes

Task. Freeze column titles at the top of the columns and/or freeze row titles on the left side of the rows. This is especially useful for large spreadsheets.

How To. In the example below, suppose you want to freeze the column titles from row 8 and above (freezing Barrick over column B, Hanson over column C, etc.) and you want to freeze the row titles in column A. Select cell **B9** (as shown), because cell **B9** this is just below row 8 that want to freeze and just to the right of column A that you want to freeze.

	A	B	C	D	E	F	G	H
1	ASSET PRICING		Static CAPM Using Fama-MacBeth Method					
2								
3	Inputs							
4	Market Portfolio Benchmark	○ SPDR ETF ◉ CRSP VWMR ○ DJ World Stock			2			
5	Asset Type	○ Stock ◉ US Port ○ Country Port			2			
6								
7		Stock	Stock	Stock	Stock	Stock	Stock	US Portfolio
8		Barrick	Hanson	IBM	Nokia	Telefonos	YPF	Small-Growth
9	Monthly Returns							
10	Dec 2006	-3.50%	-0.24%	2.06%	8.76%	8.63%	0.50%	-0.59%
11	Nov 2006	-2.37%	4.88%	5.69%	0.51%	9.01%	-0.95%	2.58%
12	Oct 2006	1.79%	3.78%	-0.12%	1.70%	-1.08%	3.49%	5.87%
13	Sep 2006	0.92%	-3.49%	12.69%	0.93%	3.14%	7.02%	1.09%
14	Aug 2006	-8.23%	14.36%	1.20%	-5.68%	6.76%	-3.83%	3.22%

Then click on **View | Window | Freeze Panes down-arrow | Freeze Panes**.

Excel 2003 Equivalent

To Freeze Paines in Excel 2003, click on **Window | Freeze Panes**.

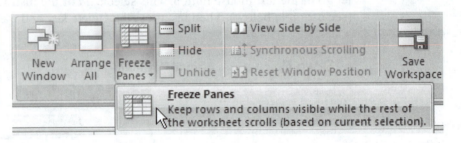

18.3 Spin Buttons and the Developer Tab

Task. Add a spin button to make an input interactive.

How To. Spin buttons and other so-called "form controls" are located on the Developer tab. If you don't see a Developer tab, then you need to take a simple step to make it visible. Click on the **Office** button, click on the **Excel Options** button at the bottom of the drop-down window, in the section **Top options for working with Excel** check the **Show Developer tab in the Ribbon** checkbox ☑ Show Developer tab in the Ribbon ⓘ , and click **OK**.

Excel 2003 Equivalent

To insert a Spin Button in Excel 2003, click on **View | Toolbars | Forms**. Then click on the **Spinner** icon on the Forms Toolbar.

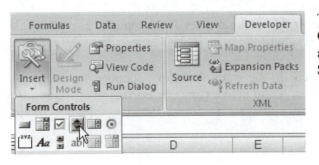

Then click on **Developer | Controls | Insert down-arrow | Form Controls | Spin Button**.

Then point the cursor crosshairs to the upper-left corner of where you want the spin button to be, click and drag to the lower-right corner, and release. You get a

spin button . Now place the cursor over the top of the spin button, right-click, and select **Format Control** from the pop-up menu. On the **Control** tab of the **Format Control** dialog box, enter **C4** in the **Cell Link** entry box, and click **OK**.

Now when you spin button, the value in cell **C4** will increase or decrease by 1. For convenience, I scale the spin button output to appropriate scale of the input. For example, in the spreadsheet below the spin button in cell **B6** is linked to the cell **C6** and creates the integer value **5**. The formula in cell B6 is **=C6/100** and this create the value **5.0%** for the riskfree rate.

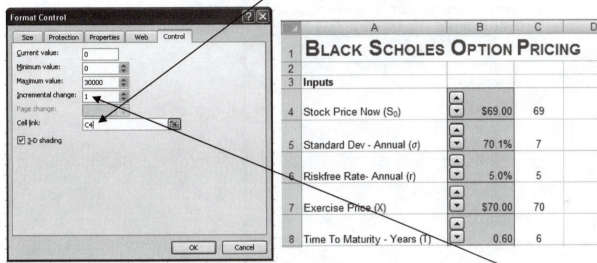

Unfortunately, Spin Buttons are only allowed to have **Incremental Changes** that are integers (1, 2, 3, etc.). It would be convenient if they could have **Incremental Changes** of any value, such as .01 or -.0043.

18.4 Option Buttons and Group Boxes

Task. Add option buttons to allow input choices.

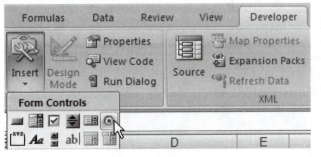

Excel 2003 Equivalent

To insert a Option Button in Excel 2003, click on **View | Toolbars | Forms**. Then click on the **Option Button** icon on the Forms Toolbar.

How To. Option buttons and other so-called "form controls" are located on the Developer tab . If you don't see a Developer tab, then you need to take a simple step to make it visible (see the section above).

Then click on **Developer | Controls | Insert down-arrow | Form Controls | Option Button**.

Then point the cursor crosshairs to the upper-left corner of where you want the option button to be, click and drag to the lower-right corner, and release. You get

a option button 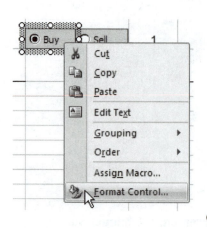. Repeat this process to get more option buttons.

Now place the cursor over the top of the first option button, right-click, then click over the blank text area, click a second time over the blank text area, delete any unwanted text (e.g., "Option Button1"), enter a text description of the choice

(e.g., "Buy"), and then click outside the option button to finish.

Repeat this process for the other option buttons (e.g., "Sell").

Now place the cursor over the top of the first option button, right-click, and select **Format Control** from the pop-up menu. On the **Control** tab of the **Format Control** dialog box, enter **C5** in the **Cell Link** entry box, and click

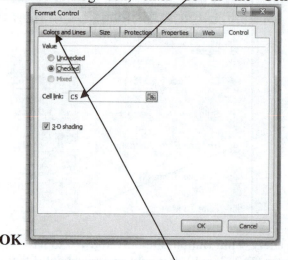

OK.

Now when the first option button is clicked, then the cell **C5** will show a **1**, and when the second option button is clicked, then the cell **C5** will show a **2**. Optionally, you click on the **Colors and Lines** tab of **Format Control** dialog box and specify the option button's fill color, line color, etc.

If you just want to have *one set* of option buttons on a spreadsheet, then you are done. However, if you want to have two or more sets of option buttons (the example below has four sets of option buttons), then you need to use **Group Boxes** to indicate which option buttons belong to which set.

	A	B	C	D	E
1	**O**PTION **T**RADING **S**TRATEGIES **T**wo **A**ssets				
2					
3	**Inputs**	**Buying a Bullish Spread**			
4		Trade Direction		Asset Type	
5	First Asset (Lowest Exercise Price)	1st Trade Direction ⦿ Buy ○ Sell	1	1st Asset Type ⦿ Call ○ Put ○ Stock	1
6	Second Asset (Highest Exercise Price)	2nd Trade Direction ○ Buy ⦿ Sell	2	2nd Asset Type ⦿ Call ○ Put ○ Stock	1

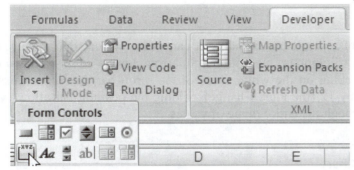

Click on **Developer | Controls | Insert down-arrow | Form Controls | Group Box**.

Then point the cursor crosshairs above and left of the first option button, click and drag to below and right of the second option button (or last option button in the set), and release. A Group Box is created which surrounds the option buttons. Click on the title of the Group Box, delete any unwanted text (e.g., "Group Box 1"), enter a text description (e.g., "1st Trade Direction"). Now when you click on the Buy or Sell option button in cell **B5** of the example above, then the linked cell **C5** changes to 1 or 2. Repeat the process of creating option buttons and surrounding them by group boxes to create all of the sets of option buttons that you want.

Excel 2003 Equivalent

To insert a Group Box in Excel 2003, click on **View | Toolbars | Forms**. Then click on the **Group Box** icon on the Forms Toolbar.

18.5 Scroll Bar

Excel 2003 Equivalent

To insert a Scroll Bar in Excel 2003, click on **View | Toolbars | Forms**. Then click on the **Scroll Bar** icon on the Forms Toolbar.

Task. Add a scroll bar call option to make big or small changes to an input.

How To. Option buttons and other so-called "form controls" are located on the Developer tab ⟨ Developer ⟩. If you don't see a Developer tab, then you need to take a simple step to make it visible (see two sections above).

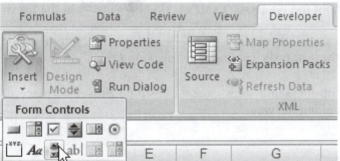

Then click on **Developer | Controls | Insert down-arrow | Form Controls | Scroll Bar**.

Then point the cursor crosshairs to the upper-left corner of where you want the option button to be, click and drag to the lower-right corner, and release. You get a scroll bar ◄_____►.

Now place the cursor over the top of the scroll bar, right-click, and select **Format Control** from the pop-up menu. On the **Control** tab of the **Format Control** dialog box, enter **I7** in the **Cell Link** entry box, and click **OK**. Optionally, you can specify the **Page Change** amount, which is the change in the cell link when you click on the white space of the scroll bar. In this example, a ~~Page Change of 12~~ months jumps a year ahead.

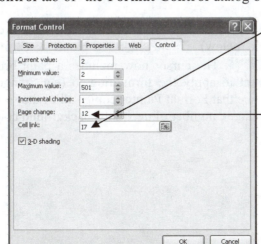

The advantage of a scroll bar is that you can make big or small changes (see example below). Clicking on the left or right arrow, lowers or raises the value in cell **I7** by 1. Clicking on the white space of the scroll bar, lowers or raises the value in cell **I7** by 12 (the Page Change). Sliding the position bar allows you to rapidly scroll through the entire range of values.

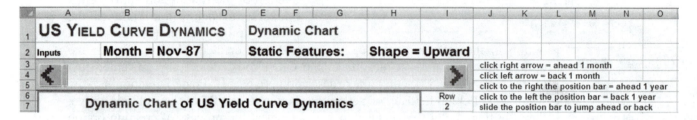

18.6 Install Solver or the Analysis ToolPak

Task. Install Solver or the Analysis ToolPak.

How To. Excel provides several special tools, such as Solver and the Analysis ToolPak, which need to be separately installed. Solver is a sophisticated, yet easy to use optimizer. The Analysis ToolPak contains advanced statistical programs and advanced functions.

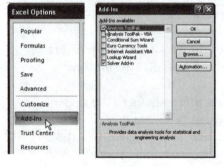

To install the Analysis ToolPak, click on the **Office** button , click on the **Excel Options** button at the bottom of the drop-down window, click on **Add-Ins**, highlight the **Analysis ToolPak** `Analysis ToolPak` in the list of Inactive Applications, click on **Go** `Go...` near the bottom of the dialog box, check the **Analysis ToolPak**, and click on **OK**.

To install Solver, do the same steps except substitute **Solver** in place of **Analysis ToolPak** along the way.

18.7 Format Painter

Task. Apply formatting from one cell to other cells.

How To. Select the cell(s) whose format you want to copy (e.g., select **D5:E5** in the example below). Then click on **Home | Clipboard | Format Painter** `Format Painter`. The cursor now includes a paint brush. Then select the range that you want to apply the formatting to (e.g., range **D6:E17** in the example below). Notice that Format Painter copies all of the formatting, including number type (percentage), number of decimals, background color, and border color.

Before

	A	B	C	D	E
1	**THE YIELD CURVE**	**Obtaining and Using It**			
2		Maturity	Time To	Yield To	Forward
3	**Yield Curve Inputs**	Date	Maturity	Maturity	Rates
4	Today's Date	5/22/2007			
5	One Month Treasury Bill	6/22/2007	0.08	4.90%	4.90%
6	Three Month Treasury Bill	8/22/2007	0.25	0.0477	0.0471
7	Six Month Treasury Bill	11/22/2007	0.50	0.0481	0.0485
8	One Year Treasury Strip	5/15/2008	0.98	0.0489	0.0497
9	Two Year Treasury Strip	8/15/2009	2.23	0.0482	0.0477
10	Three Year Treasury Strip	8/15/2010	3.23	0.0474	0.0456
11	Four Year Treasury Strip	8/15/2011	4.23	0.0472	0.0466
12	Five Year Treasury Strip	8/15/2012	5.23	0.0471	0.0467
13	Ten Year Treasury Strip	8/15/2017	10.23	0.0493	0.0516
14	Fifteen Year Treasury Bond	8/15/2022	15.23	0.0514	0.0557
15	Twenty Year Treasury Bond	8/15/2027	20.23	0.0511	0.0502
16	Twenty Five Year Treasury Bond	8/15/2032	25.23	0.0497	0.0441
17	Thirty Year Treasury Bond	2/15/2037	29.73	0.0495	0.0484

After

	A	B	C	D	E
1	**THE YIELD CURVE**	**Obtaining and Using It**			
2		Maturity	Time To	Yield To	Forward
3	**Yield Curve Inputs**	Date	Maturity	Maturity	Rates
4	Today's Date	5/22/2007			
5	One Month Treasury Bill	6/22/2007	0.08	4.90%	4.90%
6	Three Month Treasury Bill	8/22/2007	0.25	4.77%	4.71%
7	Six Month Treasury Bill	11/22/2007	0.50	4.81%	4.85%
8	One Year Treasury Strip	5/15/2008	0.98	4.89%	4.97%
9	Two Year Treasury Strip	8/15/2009	2.23	4.82%	4.77%
10	Three Year Treasury Strip	8/15/2010	3.23	4.74%	4.56%
11	Four Year Treasury Strip	8/15/2011	4.23	4.72%	4.66%
12	Five Year Treasury Strip	8/15/2012	5.23	4.71%	4.67%
13	Ten Year Treasury Strip	8/15/2017	10.23	4.93%	5.16%
14	Fifteen Year Treasury Bond	8/15/2022	15.23	5.14%	5.57%
15	Twenty Year Treasury Bond	8/15/2027	20.23	5.11%	5.02%
16	Twenty Five Year Treasury Bond	8/15/2032	25.23	4.97%	4.41%
17	Thirty Year Treasury Bond	2/15/2037	29.73	4.95%	4.84%

18.8 Conditional Formatting

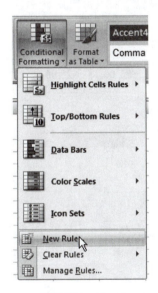

Task. Conditionally format a cell. This allows the displayed format to change based upon the results of a formula calculation.

How To. Suppose you want to use special formatting to highlight the best portfolio in constrained portfolio optimization (see example below). Select cell **M166**. Click on **Home | Styles | Conditional Formatting down-arrow | New Rule**. Then click on Use a formula to determine which cells to format ▶ Use a formula to determine which cells to format . In the text entry box, enter **=M166=1**. This checks whether the value of cell M166 is equal to one. Formulas for conditional fomatting must begin with an equal sign, so oddly you end up with two equal signs in the formula. Then click on the **Format** button. In the **Format Cells** dialog box, click on the **Fill** tab, select the **color** you like, click **OK**, and then click **OK** again. Finally, copy this new conditional format down the column using Format Painter. Click on **Home | Clipboard | Format Painter** ✔ Format Painter . The cursor now includes a paint brush. Then select the range **M167:M181**. In this example, the cell **M173** turns orange because it is the highest ranking (#1) portfolio. If you changed one of the problem inputs, then a different portfolio might be ranked #1 and the cell corresponding to the new #1 would be highlighted in orange.

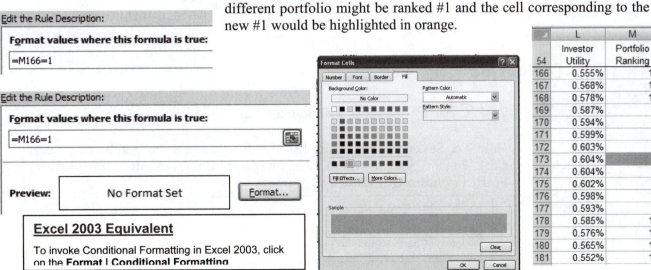

	L	M
	Investor	Portfolio
54	Utility	Ranking
166	0.555%	15
167	0.568%	13
168	0.578%	11
169	0.587%	9
170	0.594%	7
171	0.599%	5
172	0.603%	3
173	0.604%	1
174	0.604%	2
175	0.602%	4
176	0.598%	6
177	0.593%	8
178	0.585%	10
179	0.576%	12
180	0.565%	14
181	0.552%	16

Edit the Rule Description:

Format values where this formula is true:

=M166=1

Edit the Rule Description:

Format values where this formula is true:

=M166=1

Preview: No Format Set   Format...

Excel 2003 Equivalent

To invoke Conditional Formatting in Excel 2003, click on the **Format | Conditional Formatting**

18.9 Fill Handle

Task. Fill in row 10 with integers from 0 to 8 to create the timeline (see example below). This fill technique works for wide range of patterns.

How To. Enter **0** in cell **B10** and **1** in cell **C10**. Select the range **B10:C10**, then hover the cursor over the fill handle ▬ (the square in the lower-right corner) of cell **C10** and the cursor turns to a plus symbol ✛. Click, drag the plus symbol to cell **J10**, and release. The range fills up with the rest the pattern from 2 to 8.

Before

	A	B	C	D	E	F	G	H	I	J
1	**BOND PRICING**	**Annual Payments**								
2										
3	Inputs									
4	Number of Periods to Maturity (T)	8								
5	Face Value (PAR)	$1,000								
6	Discount Rate / Period (r)	9.0%								
7	Coupon Payment (PMT)	$25								
8										
9	**Bond Price using a Timeline**									
10	Period	0	1							
11	Cash Flows		$25.00	$25.00	$25.00	$25.00	$25.00	$25.00	$25.00	$1,025.00
12	Present Value of Cash Flow		$22.94	$25.00	$25.00	$25.00	$25.00	$25.00	$25.00	$1,025.00
13	Bond Price	########								

After

	A	B	C	D	E	F	G	H	I	J
1	**BOND PRICING**	**Annual Payments**								
2										
3	Inputs									
4	Number of Periods to Maturity (T)	8								
5	Face Value (PAR)	$1,000								
6	Discount Rate / Period (r)	9.0%								
7	Coupon Payment (PMT)	$25								
8										
9	**Bond Price using a Timeline**									
10	Period	0	1	2	3	4	5	6	7	8
11	Cash Flows		$25.00	$25.00	$25.00	$25.00	$25.00	$25.00	$25.00	$1,025.00
12	Present Value of Cash Flow		$22.94	$21.04	$19.30	$17.71	$16.25	$14.91	$13.68	$514.41
13	Bond Price	$640.24								

18.10 2-D Scatter Chart

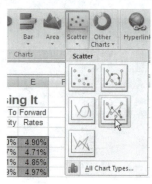

Task. Create a two-dimensional Scatter Chart.

How To. Select the range that has the data you wish to graph (e.g., select **C5:E17** in the example below). Click on **Insert | Charts | Scatter down-arrow | Scatter with Straight Lines and Markers**.

> **Excel 2003 Equivalent**
>
> To insert a 2-D Scatter Chart in Excel 2003, click on the **Insert | Chart | XY (Scatter) | Scatter with data points connected by lines**

	A	B	C	D	E
1	**THE YIELD CURVE**	**Obtaining and Using It**			
2		Maturity	Time To	Yield To	Forward
3	**Yield Curve Inputs**	Date	Maturity	Maturity	Rates
4	Today's Date	5/22/2007			
5	One Month Treasury Bill	6/22/2007	0.08	4.90%	4.90%
6	Three Month Treasury Bill	8/22/2007	0.25	4.77%	4.71%
7	Six Month Treasury Bill	11/22/2007	0.50	4.81%	4.85%
8	One Year Treasury Strip	5/15/2008	0.98	4.89%	4.97%
9	Two Year Treasury Strip	8/15/2009	2.23	4.82%	4.77%
10	Three Year Treasury Strip	8/15/2010	3.23	4.74%	4.56%
11	Four Year Treasury Strip	8/15/2011	4.23	4.72%	4.66%
12	Five Year Treasury Strip	8/15/2012	5.23	4.71%	4.67%
13	Ten Year Treasury Strip	8/15/2017	10.23	4.93%	5.16%
14	Fifteen Year Treasury Bond	8/15/2022	15.23	5.14%	5.57%
15	Twenty Year Treasury Bond	8/15/2027	20.23	5.11%	5.02%
16	Twenty Five Year Treasury Bond	8/15/2032	25.23	4.97%	4.41%
17	Thirty Year Treasury Bond	2/15/2037	29.73	4.95%	4.84%

A rough version of the 2-D Scatter Chart appears.

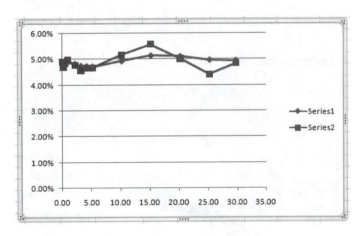

As long as the Chart is selected, three new tabs appear that provide lots of chart options for Design, Layout, and Formatting.

Chart Tools

Design   Layout   Format

Alternatively, you can right-click on parts of the chart to get pop-up menus with formatting choices. Here is what a fully-formatted 2-D Scatter Chart looks like.

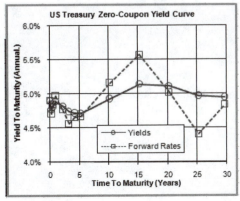

18.11 3-D Surface Chart

Task. Create a three-dimensional Surface Chart.

How To. Select the range that has the data you wish to graph (e.g., select **C94:G98** in the example below). Click on **Insert | Charts | Other Charts down-arrow | Surface | 3-D Surface.**

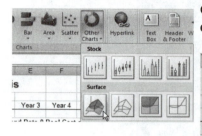

Excel 2003 Equivalent

To insert a 3-D Surface Chart in Excel 2003, click on the **Insert | Chart | Surface | 3-D Surface**.

	A	B	C	D	E	F	G
1	PROJECT NPV	Sensitivity Analysis					
2	(in thousands of $)						
3			Year 0	Year 1	Year 2	Year 3	Year 4	Year 5
90							
91	Data Table: Sensitivity of the Net Present Value to Unit Sales and Date 0 Real Cost of Capital						
92			Input Values for Unit Sales Scale Factor				
93	Out Formula: Net Present Value	$3,180	80%	90%	100%	110%	120%
94		9.0%	($1,324)	$1,667	$4,658	$7,649	$10,640
95	Input Values for	11.0%	($2,336)	$422	$3,180	$5,938	$8,696
96	Date 0 Real Cost of Capital	13.0%	($3,246)	($698)	$1,851	$4,399	$6,947
97		15.0%	($4,065)	($1,706)	$652	$3,010	$5,369
98		17.0%	($4,804)	($2,617)	($431)	$1,755	$3,941

A rough version of the 3-D Surface Chart appears.

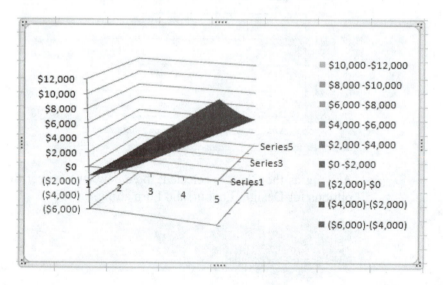

As long as the Chart is selected, three new tabs appear that provide lots of chart options for Design, Layout, and Formatting.

Alternatively, you can right-click on parts of the chart to get pop-up menus with formatting choices.

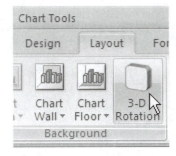

It is often useful to rotate a 3-D chart. To do this, click on **Layout | Background | 3-D Rotation**. 3-D Rotation provides the ability to rotate the surface in the X-axis direction, Y-axis direction, or Z-axis direction.

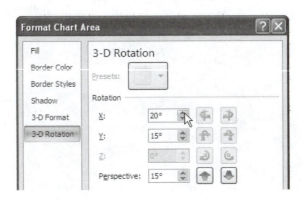

Here is what a fully-formatted 3-D Surface Chart looks like.

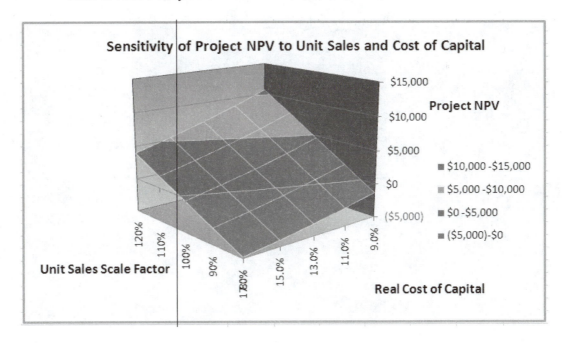

READ THIS LICENSE CAREFULLY BEFORE OPENING THIS PACKAGE. BY OPENING THIS PACKAGE, YOU ARE AGREEING TO THE TERMS AND CONDITIONS OF THIS LICENSE. IF YOU DO NOT AGREE, DO NOT OPEN THE PACKAGE. PROMPTLY RETURN THE UNOPENED PACKAGE AND ALL ACCOMPANYING ITEMS TO THE PLACE YOU OBTAINED THEM FOR A FULL REFUND OF ANY SUMS YOU HAVE PAID FOR THE SOFTWARE. *THESE TERMS APPLY TO ALL LICENSED SOFTWARE ON THE DISK EXCEPT THAT THE TERMS FOR USE OF ANY SHAREWARE OR FREEWARE ON THE DISKETTES ARE AS SET FORTH IN THE ELECTRONIC LICENSE LOCATED ON THE CD-ROM:*

1.   GRANT OF LICENSE and OWNERSHIP: The enclosed computer programs and data ("Software") are licensed, not sold, to you by Pearson Education, Inc. publishing as Prentice-Hall, Inc. ("We" or the "Company") and in consideration of your purchase or adoption of the accompanying Company textbooks and/or other materials, and your agreement to these terms. We reserve any rights not granted to you. You own only the disk(s) but we and/or our licensors own the Software itself. This license allows you to use and display your copy of the Software on a single computer (i.e., with a single CPU) at a single location for <u>academic</u> use only, so long as you comply with the terms of this Agreement. You may make one copy for back up, or transfer your copy to another CPU, provided that the Software is usable on only one computer.

2.   RESTRICTIONS: You may <u>not</u> transfer or distribute the Software or documentation to anyone else. Except for backup, you may <u>not</u> copy the documentation or the Software. You may <u>not</u> network the Software or otherwise use it on more than one computer or computer terminal at the same time. You may <u>not</u> reverse engineer, disassemble, decompile, modify, adapt, translate, or create derivative works based on the Software or the Documentation. You may be held legally responsible for any copying or copyright infringement that is caused by your failure to abide by the terms of these restrictions.

3.   TERMINATION: This license is effective until terminated. This license will terminate automatically without notice from the Company if you fail to comply with any provisions or limitations of this license. Upon termination, you shall destroy the Documentation and all copies of the Software. All provisions of this Agreement as to limitation and disclaimer of warranties, limitation of liability, remedies or damages, and our ownership rights shall survive termination.

4.   LIMITED WARRANTY AND DISCLAIMER OF WARRANTY: Company warrants that for a period of 60 days from the date you purchase this SOFTWARE (or purchase or adopt the accompanying textbook), the Software, when properly installed and used in accordance with the Documentation, will operate in substantial conformity with the description of the Software set forth in the Documentation, and that for a period of 30 days the disk(s) on which the Software is delivered shall be free from defects in materials and workmanship under normal use. The Company does <u>not</u> warrant that the Software will meet your requirements or that the operation of the Software will be uninterrupted or error-free. Your only remedy and the Company's only obligation under these limited warranties is, at the Company's option, return of the disk for a refund of any amounts paid for it by you or replacement of the disk. THIS LIMITED WARRANTY IS THE ONLY WARRANTY PROVIDED BY THE COMPANY AND ITS LICENSORS, AND THE COMPANY AND ITS LICENSORS DISCLAIM ALL OTHER WARRANTIES, EXPRESS OR IMPLIED, INCLUDING WITHOUT LIMITATION, THE IMPLIED WARRANTIES OF MERCHANTABILITY AND FITNESS FOR A PARTICULAR PURPOSE. THE COMPANY DOES NOT WARRANT, GUARANTEE OR MAKE ANY REPRESENTATION REGARDING THE ACCURACY, RELIABILITY, CURRENTNESS, USE, OR RESULTS OF USE, OF THE SOFTWARE.

5.   LIMITATION OF REMEDIES AND DAMAGES: IN NO EVENT, SHALL THE COMPANY OR ITS EMPLOYEES, AGENTS, LICENSORS, OR CONTRACTORS BE LIABLE FOR ANY INCIDENTAL, INDIRECT, SPECIAL, OR CONSEQUENTIAL DAMAGES ARISING OUT OF OR IN CONNECTION WITH THIS LICENSE OR THE SOFTWARE, INCLUDING FOR LOSS OF USE, LOSS OF DATA, LOSS OF INCOME OR PROFIT, OR OTHER LOSSES, SUSTAINED AS A RESULT OF INJURY TO ANY PERSON, OR LOSS OF OR DAMAGE TO PROPERTY, OR CLAIMS OF THIRD PARTIES, EVEN IF THE COMPANY OR AN AUTHORIZED REPRESENTATIVE OF THE COMPANY HAS BEEN ADVISED OF THE POSSIBILITY OF SUCH DAMAGES. IN NO EVENT SHALL THE LIABILITY OF THE COMPANY FOR DAMAGES WITH RESPECT TO THE SOFTWARE EXCEED THE AMOUNTS ACTUALLY PAID BY YOU, IF ANY, FOR THE SOFTWARE OR THE ACCOMPANYING TEXTBOOK. BECAUSE SOME JURISDICTIONS DO NOT ALLOW THE LIMITATION OF LIABILITY IN CERTAIN CIRCUMSTANCES, THE ABOVE LIMITATIONS MAY NOT ALWAYS APPLY TO YOU.

6.   GENERAL: THIS AGREEMENT SHALL BE CONSTRUED IN ACCORDANCE WITH THE LAWS OF THE UNITED STATES OF AMERICA AND THE STATE OF NEW YORK, APPLICABLE TO CONTRACTS MADE IN NEW YORK, AND SHALL BENEFIT THE COMPANY, ITS AFFILIATES AND ASSIGNEES. HIS AGREEMENT IS THE COMPLETE AND EXCLUSIVE STATEMENT OF THE AGREEMENT BETWEEN YOU AND THE COMPANY AND SUPERSEDES ALL PROPOSALS OR PRIOR AGREEMENTS, ORAL, OR WRITTEN, AND ANY OTHER COMMUNICATIONS BETWEEN YOU AND THE COMPANY OR ANY REPRESENTATIVE OF THE COMPANY RELATING TO THE SUBJECT MATTER OF THIS AGREEMENT. If you are a U.S. Government user, this Software is licensed with "restricted rights" as set forth in subparagraphs (a)-(d) of the Commercial Computer-Restricted Rights clause at FAR 52.227-19 or in subparagraphs (c)(1)(ii) of the Rights in Technical Data and Computer Software clause at DFARS 252.227-7013, and similar clauses, as applicable.

Should you have any questions concerning this agreement or if you wish to contact the Company for any reason, please contact in writing: Director of New Media, Higher Education Division, Prentice Hall, Inc., Upper Saddle River, NJ 07458